The Multinational Corporation in the 1980s

The Multinational Corporation in the 1980s

edited by Charles P. Kindleberger
and David B. Audretsch

The MIT Press
Cambridge, Massachusetts
London, England

The Middlebury College Conference on Economic Issues is made possible through the generosity of the Christian A. Johnson Endeavor Foundation.

This book was set in Times Roman by The MIT Press Computergraphics Department and printed and bound by The Murray Printing Co. in the United States of America.

Library of Congress Cataloging in Publication Data

Main entry under title:

The Multinational Corporation in the 1980s.

"Papers presented at the Fourth Annual Middlebury College Conference on Economic Issues, held on April 15–17, 1982"—Foreword.
  Includes bibliographies and index.
  1. International business enterprises—Congresses.
2. Investments, Foreign—Congresses. I. Kindleberger,
Charles Poor, 1910–. II. Audretsch, David B.
III. Middlebury College Conference on Economic Issues (4th : 1982)
HD2755.5.M817 1983   338.8′8   82-22951
ISBN 0–262–11086–5

Contents

Foreword

This volume contains the papers presented at the Fourth Annual Middlebury College Conference on Economic Issues, held on April 15–17, 1982. Funded by the Christian A. Johnson Distinguished Professorship in Economics, this conference assembled outstanding scholars to discuss and present current research on the theory and selected case studies of the multinational corporation. Seven of the authors were invited to participate in the conference. The remainder were competitively selected from submissions in response to a call for papers. The papers were presented by the authors to a group of scholars, Middlebury economics students, and interested observers. Following a critique by a discussant, each paper was subject to debate by all participants, which frequently proved to be lively and stimulating.

To a certain extent this conference was an extension of the 1969 Symposium on the International Corporation held at the Sloan School of Management at the Massachusetts Institute of Technology. Two of the participants, Robert Z. Aliber and Morris A. Adelman, presented papers at both gatherings, providing continuity and contrast on the state of the art between 1969 and 1982. A reading of their papers, along with others, suggests how prescient the earlier symposium was.

This volume is a sequel to its predecessor in providing empirical work and expanding the theory and adapting it to current conditions. For example, Stephen P. Magee and Leslie Young extend international trade theory to include political groups in the explanation of allocation and distributional issues. Bruce Kogut discusses new theories of the multinational enterprise, focusing particularly on internalization. Paul R. Krugman applies aspects of the imperfect competition model to international trade theory, yielding insights congruent with the field of industrial organization, a trend that emerged throughout the conference.

Because all papers were written for presentation to advanced undergraduate economics majors, this book will have particular appeal to teachers of both graduate and undergraduate students as well as to policymakers.

Contributors

Morris A. Adelman, Massachusetts Institute of Technology
Robert Z. Aliber, University of Chicago
Adhip Chaudhuri, Georgetown University
David J. Fowler, McGill University
K. Celeste Gaspari, University of Vermont
Myron J. Gordon, University of Toronto
Eric W. Kierans, McGill University
Bruce Kogut, Massachusetts Institute of Technology
Paul R. Krugman, Massachusetts Institute of Technology
Stephen P. Magee, University of Texas at Austin
Rachel McCulloch, University of Wisconsin
David McClain, Boston University
Richard S. Newfarmer, Overseas Development Council and University of Notre Dame
Joseph S. Nye, Jr., Harvard University
Robert F. Owen, University of Wisconsin
Howard Curtis Reed, University of Texas at Austin
Daniel M. Shapiro, Concordia University
Leslie Young, University of Texas at Austin

The Multinational Corporation in the 1980s

The Multinational Corporation in the 1980s

Joseph S. Nye, Jr.

I

A decade ago there was growing interest in the role of multinational corporations in world politics. The very term implied a political visibility not associated with the words "direct investment" that were used in the prior decade. The private foreign policy of ITT in Chile made daily headlines, as did the extensive hearings on multinationals by the Senate Foreign Relations Committee. Internationally, the role of multinationals was debated in the International Labor Organization, the Organization for Economic Cooperation and Development, the European Community, and the United Nations. The UN set up a "Group of Eminent Persons" to hold hearings on the role of multinationals, and subsequently established a Center on Transnational Corporations. While direct foreign investment had long antecedents, it was in the 1970s that the multinational corporation came of age politically.

Some scholars engaged in exuberant projections that a few hundred giant corporations would rule the world economy by the end of the decade. Enthusiasts saw the multinational corporation as the vehicle by which humankind was transcending the nation-state and creating a broader welfare-oriented world order. Pessimists shared these projections, but saw the effects as leading to increased dependence, threatened status, and lost autonomy. The decline of the nation-state would not be a sign of health but a sign of disaster for democratic values.

In contrast to the 1970s exuberance about multinational corporations, the discourse in the 1980s thus far seems more restrained. Certainly the tone of the discussion has changed. As Raymond Vernon has written, "the tumult of the 1970s over the multinational issue has lost some of its stridence. The incidence of nationalizations in developing countries has declined dramatically. Kolko, Williams, Barnet, and Muller seem somehow out of date, while the various scholars of *dependista* theory seem a bit jaded. The UN Center on Transnational Corporations has developed a businesslike air, more akin to the professionalism of the Securities and Exchange Commission than to the prosecuting fervor of the Church Committee."[1] To some extent, this diminished political profile reflects changes in bargaining power and learning by companies and governments, but it is also a comment on the exaggerated rhetoric and projections of the 1970s. As I wrote at the time, "at the extremes, neither the optimistic nor pessimistic view of the future seems likely to come to pass. Indeed, it is unlikely that there are any prognoses that represent reality as it will be at the end of the century."[2] If nothing else, the 1980s may show a better balance between the roles and the analyses of multinational corporations as scholars better understand the phenomena.

But there is also a more pessimistic view, which foresees the 1980s as a decade of decline for the multinationals. In this view, both the nature of world politics and the US power position in the world are changing, and the role of the multinationals will change accordingly.

The "New Orthodoxy" in foreign policy analysis sees the 1970s as a period concerned with welfare and economic interdependence, but the 1980s will be a period concerned with military force and political conflict.[3] The "New Orthodoxy" equates US inability to control events in today's world with a decline in US military power. It asserts that an increase in military power will allow the United States to again play the role to which its latent power entitles it. The implications of these trends for the multinational corporation are double-edged. On the one hand, an increased role of military force rather than economic welfare stresses power resources in which the corporation is weak. But on the other hand, to the extent that the corporation has depended upon the order created by a Pax Americana, its environment will be enhanced.

Some analysts would accept this relationship of the multinational corporation to a Pax Americana, but because they project a decline in American power, they see a bleak future for the corporation in the 1980s. A decade ago, Robert Gilpin wrote that "a diminution of the Pax Americana and the rise of powers hostile to the global activities of multinational corporations would bring their reign over international economic relations to an end."[4] More recently, Stephen Krasner has argued that "the resources available to the United States are no longer as relatively large as they were in the period after the Second World War. Domestic support for the unrestricted movement of capital and goods is waning. Disaffection in other countries, particularly the Third World, is growing. As the slack provided by America's hegemonic position dissipates, the costs of domestic political fragmentation will become more severe. Corporations cannot operate efficiently without a stable environment, but the state may not be able to provide one."[5]

To evaluate these political prognoses for the multinational corporation, we need to examine three questions: To what extent will US power decline in the 1980s? To what extent is world politics changing from an emphasis on economic interdependence to an emphasis on military force? To what extent does the fate of the multinational corporation depend directly or indirectly upon American power? I shall examine each in turn.

II

The 1970s was a strange decade in American foreign policy, beginning with public concern over the excess and arrogance of American power and ending with worry about its paucity and humiliation. Some observers see the decline of American power in the 1970s as a result of poor policy which will be righted by the Reagan administration in the 1980s. Others, however, see the 1970s as part of a long-term decline in the American hegemony that has characterized world politics since the end of World War II.

What are the facts about American power? Some simple measures are relatively clear. At the beginning of 1950, before the Korean War, the United States accounted for roughly a third of the total world defense expenditures and of total gross world product. Today, the United States accounts for a little less than a quarter of the world total on each measure.[6] In 1953, the United States accounted for 30% of world trade. Today, our share of world trade is 13%. In 1971, the United States was the home of 56% of the top 500 corporations in the world. Today the United States is the home of 42% of such corporations. Moreover, our dependence upon the outside world has increased. Total trade was only 5% of our GNP in 1968. Today it is more than 10%. On the other hand, these trends must be kept in perspective. The United States remains the world's largest economy; nearly twice as large as the second-place Soviet economy. And while Soviet military spending exceeds that of the United States, the United States remains part of the North

Atlantic Treaty Organization (NATO) whose overall military expenditures slightly exceed those of the Soviets' Warsaw Pact.

Simple measures can be misleading because power is a complex relational concept. Our power depends on the action of others as well as what we try to get them to do. Even if the trends indicated by these simple measures are roughly correct, we must look more closely at the causes of the change in American power if we are to make judgments about the future.

Looking over the past decade, it is possible to discern at least six major causes of the change in the American power position in the world. Four of these causes could be called "short-term" in the sense that they may be reversible within the next decade. Two of the causes should be called "long-term" in the sense that they are probably irreversible. The short-term causes are the Vietnam syndrome, Soviet military growth, energy vulnerability, and declining economic productivity.

One of the most obvious causes of the decline of American power in the 1970s was our own self-limiting attitudes toward foreign affairs. Because these attitudes focused on American involvement in Vietnam in the 1960s and 1970s, they have sometimes been characterized as the "Vietnam syndrome." But American foreign policy has long been characterized by cycles of inward- and outward-turning attitudes and by alternations between moralism and realism. Thus, it was not surprising that moralistic reaction against American involvement and failure in Vietnam would lead to self-limitation on the uses of American power in other areas as well. In any event, by the end of the 1970s, the United States was investing less in real terms in great power status—mainly national defense and foreign aid—than it did at the beginning of the 1960s.

What is interesting, however, is that the Vietnam syndrome did not persist as long as prophesied by those who warned against neo-isolationism in the 1970s. One need only compare the foreign policy attitudes expressed in the presidential campaigns of 1976 and 1980 to see how strikingly American public opinion changed in the latter half of the 1970s. As the polls show, the swing back toward international assertion began well before the fall of the Shah or the Soviet invasion of Afghanistan.[7]

It is not entirely clear why the period of self-limiting attitudes proved to be so short—less than a decade if one dates the onset of retrenchment in the mid-1960s. Perhaps in an age when most Americans received their news from television rather than newspapers, political generations have shortened and attitudes have become more volatile. But the shortness of the inward-turning period also reflected the reality of the outside world. Increased dependence on exports and imports, the increased effect of international events on the value of the dollar, and vulnerability to embargoes of imported oil all indicated to the American public that neo-isolationism was not a real option. Moreover, the behavior of the Soviet Union also reminded Americans that there is military interdependence as well. And this was the second short-term cause of the changing American power position.

Over the course of the past two decades, the military dimensions of the US-Soviet balance shifted. The CIA estimates that the Soviet Union consistently added at least 3% a year to its total defense efforts, while United States real defense spending in 1980 was the same as it had been in the 1960s. Indeed, the CIA estimates that Soviet defense spending exceeds American defense spending by some 30–50%. There are methodological difficulties in calculating exact comparisons of defense spending in different social and economic systems, and defense spending is a crude measure of inputs rather than military outputs. Moreover, such figures fail to reflect the fact that the Soviet Union also feels threatened by China and that, when alliances are compared, NATO and Warsaw Pact spending is similar. Nonetheless, as a Carnegie Panel concluded, "We can say with some confidence that Soviet increases in defense expenditures, especially in the area of investment, have led and will continue to lead to improved military capability relative to the United States."[8] Certainly, the American strategic superiority of the 1960s had vanished by the early 1970s, and the effects of Soviet defense growth raised concern among some of our allies in Europe and the Middle East.

A third cause of diminished American power was our increased dependence upon imported oil. In 1970, the United States was the world's largest oil producer (today the Soviet Union is). Although we imported nearly a quarter of our oil, our surplus capacity had allowed us easily to weather an Arab oil embargo in 1967. By the end of the decade, we were importing nearly half our needs, and home production was declining. Our response to the 1973 Arab oil embargo was inept. While President Nixon called for energy independence by 1980, the price controls he imposed led to a 25% increase in our oil imports between the shock of 1973 and the second shock of 1979. Moreover, we failed to fill our strategic petroleum reserve—it contained only 13 days' supply in 1979—and we allowed our political-military posture in the Persian Gulf to weaken during the course of the decade.[9]

By 1980, two-fifths of the total oil consumed in the free world economy came from the Persian Gulf, a fragile area that saw three political interruptions of oil in eight years. The sudden loss of Persian Gulf oil could stagger the world's economy and the Western Alliance. The smaller cutoffs that had already occurred had dealt heavy blows to western economic strength: lowering growth, exacerbating inflation, and contributing to the decline in productivity. And the different energy vulnerabilities among the Western nations presented better opportunities than did direct military threats for the Soviets or others to disrupt Western alliances.

A fourth cause of the decline of American power in the past decade was the lowered performance of the American economy, particularly the decline of productivity. Part of the economic problems of the 1970s can be attributed to the energy shock of 1973. Not only did the energy shock contribute to inflation, but it also created a downturn for almost all the major Western economies in the mid-1970s. As the *Economist* of London has noted, "the most striking feature of the 1970s was not the steady relative decline of America (though that is plain to see), but the poor performance of all the big capitalist economies in the 1970s compared to the 1960s. Real growth fell and inflation and unemployment rose everywhere."[10] Annual average economic growth in the United States was 4.1% in 1960 to 1973 and only 2.7% in 1973 to 1980. Yet, other industrial countries' growth rates declined even more steeply. While Japan, for example, did better than the United States in the 1970s, it had outgrown us even more impressively in the 1960s. Although the American economy continued its relative decline in the 1970s, it was at a slower pace than during the 1960s. Thus one must be careful not to overstate the decline in relative performance of the American economy in the past decade.

What is particularly worrisome, however, is the decline of productivity or output per man-hour, which had previously grown at about 3% per year in the United States in the postwar period as a result of increased capital investment, increased efficiency in the use of labor, and improved knowledge and technology. By the end of the decade, annual productivity had ceased growing. Economists differ on the causes and cures for diminished productivity growth. One-time demographic changes somewhat reduced the overall efficiency of the labor force, and the rise in energy prices led to a substitution of capital for energy instead of for labor. Overall, this was a healthy response to improving energy productivity but may have diminished labor productivity. On the other hand, there was a slowdown in the growth of capital stock from 4.1% per year in the period from 1960 to 1973 to 3.6% per year in the period from 1973 to 1979. Moreover, while the United States invested 2.9% of its gross national product in basic research and development in the 1960s, it only invested 2.3% in the 1970s. At the end of the decade, it was unclear whether the loss of productivity was temporary and largely self-correcting or whether it was a response to more deeply rooted economic problems. What is clear is that it contributed to a loss of dynamism in American economic growth, the loss of a buffer that helps in coping with inflationary pressures, reduced capability to compete with countries such as Germany and Japan whose productivity rates stayed higher, and fewer resources available to be invested in foreign affairs.

Contrary to theories of a linear decline of American power, these four short-term or decade-long causes of decline in the 1970s may be reversed in the 1980s. First, the problem of self-limiting attitudes has been largely overcome. Indeed, public opinion polls indicated that it had been partly overcome even before the new administration assumed office. The big change in foreign policy attitudes occurred around 1978–1979 and is ratified rather than caused by the outcome of the 1980 election. "The post-war low point for internationalism came in 1974. The moral self-doubt that characterized the Ford/Carter period had now been replaced by a powerful assertion of national pride and a desire to get tough."[11]

On the other hand, we have not simply returned to the world of the 1950s in attitudes. There have been "lessons from Vietnam." Mark Twain noted that a cat that had sat on a hot stove would not sit on a hot stove again, nor would it sit on a cold one. The false lesson of Vietnam was to turn away from all foreign involvement. On the other hand, some Third World conflicts and civil wars remain hot stoves, and popular responses to early administration hints of military involvement in Central America indicated that the American public may have learned to draw such distinctions.

While the Carter and Reagan administrations may have erred in opposite directions in trying to strike a balance between the poles of military power and political idealism that characterize American approaches to foreign policy, the self-limiting attitudes that contributed to the decline of American power in the 1970s are unlikely to be a problem in the 1980s unless the Administration intervenes unilaterally in some area perceived as marginal to our interests.

Second, the new popular attitudes also stimulated efforts to redress the perceived changes in the military balance. Reagan's original economic projections assumed a real economic growth rate of 4.4% from 1982 through 1986, which would mean that his budget would raise the military share from 5.7% to 7.1% of the gross national product. This assumed a high rate of productivity. With the economy not performing as well as projected, the prospects are that the defense budget will rise to 8% of gross national product unless political concern over large deficits leads to some scaleback in projected defense spending. In any case, however, the United States is reversing the downward trend in the defense share of the national product that occurred in the 1970s, albeit to a level still below that of the 1950s and 1960s.

Military strategists disagree about the timing and composition of some aspects of the Reagan defense program. There are fears that the B-1 bomber and the massive naval program, including the resurrection of battleships, will suffer cost overruns that will eat into funds for readiness, operations, and maintenance. Some worry about the failure to find an invulnerable basing mode for the MX missile. Others feel that the development of air- and sea-launched cruise missiles and the development of the invulnerable and highly accurate Trident II submarine system mean that we will have sufficient redundancy in our forces to reduce concern about land-based missiles. Despite these differences about some aspects of the Reagan strategic program, and while such measures take time to implement, there is good reason to believe that the perceived changes in the military balance, which created anxiety among allies in the 1970s, may well be remedied during the 1980s.

In the energy area as well, the trends are in a stronger direction. Painful though it was, the United States learned useful lessons from the interruption of Iranian supply in 1979. At that point, President

Carter began the gradual decontrol of domestic oil prices that was accelerated by the new administration soon after taking office. The effect of realistic pricing has been impressive. Oil imports are one-third below their 1978 high, and this is not merely a result of declining economic conditions.

Overall energy use in the American economy decreased by 8% and 7% over the last two years despite a modest positive rate of economic growth. There is reason to believe there will be further efficiency gains from the drastic price increases of the late 1970s. In addition, the Reagan administration has taken advantage of soft oil markets in the past year to rapidly increase the rate of fill of the strategic petroleum reserve, more than doubling its contents to nearly 250 million barrels by the end of its first year in office. In addition, the administration has continued to improve the American military posture in the Persian Gulf area so that a deterrent and protective role, albeit over the horizon, can help to fill the military vacuum in the area left by the fall of the Shah of Iran.

There is always a danger that in a period of increasing budgetary stringency the administration will relax its impressive performance in filling the strategic petroleum reserve and will further cut back the development of alternative energy sources. This would be like reducing the insurance policy on a house because the family budget was tight, not because the threat of fire had diminished. And it would be doubly ironic in the context of increases in the military budget to protect against military insecurities and threats that may be no more probable than the threat of disruptions of oil in the Persian Gulf sometime in the decade of the 1980s.

Nonetheless, if current trends continue and if we are lucky, the United States will be better placed to respond to an interruption in Persian Gulf oil in the 1980s than it was in the 1970s.

It is more difficult to describe the direction of change in the fourth major cause—economic stagflation and declining productivity. Economists differ on how rapidly the underlying rate of inflation will change and the degree to which economic productivity will recover in the 1980s. To the extent that the decline of productivity in the 1970s reflected one-time demographic changes and energy price shocks, there are grounds for expecting some degree of recovery of productivity in the 1980s regardless of the outcome of the president's efforts to raise savings and investment in the economy. On the other hand, to the extent that military spending drains capital away from more productive investment, and to the extent that there are deeper and poorly understood causes, productivity growth may continue to lag. It is still too soon to judge the effectiveness of efforts to reverse the fourth of the short-term causes of the loss of American power in the 1970s, or even to be certain that this cause is short term!

Summarizing the short-term causes of the relative decline of American power in the 1970s, there are grounds to believe that the situation will improve in the 1980s in regard to at least three of the four causes. In that sense, to the extent that there is a connection between American power and multinationals, the environment in the 1980s should be no worse than the 1970s, and could even be better.

III

What is more problematic is the longer-term cause of declining American power — the changes in world politics that extend beyond a given decade like the 1970s or 1980s. These changes in world politics are not likely to be reversed: the diffusion of economic power among other industrial states, and the increased complexity of world politics that makes control more difficult. These long-term changes tend to belie hopes that increased conflict with the Soviet Union and increased emphasis on military instruments will restore the bipolar structure of world politics that enhanced the hegemonic position of the United States as leader of the Western alliance.

One important long-term change is economic growth among other countries, in particular, America's allies. Even if American economic performance turns upward in the 1980s, the United States is unlikely to regain the preponderant economic position that it enjoyed in the early postwar period when the American economy and dollar were so predominant. The third quarter of the twentieth century was a unique period. The United States emerged from World War II as by far the strongest power in a world destroyed. Our economy and military position had been enhanced by a war that had brought enormous suffering and destruction to the other prewar great powers.

The United States was like the boy who awakens one morning to find that everybody else has been laid low by the flu and that he is suddenly the dominant kid on the block. It is only natural that this situation would change as others regained their health. Indeed, it is to the credit of US foreign policy that we helped to accelerate this recovery. The key component of our postwar foreign policy has been the restoration of economic prosperity and political stability in both Europe and Japan and our close alliance with both.

Thus the fashionable European concerns of the 1960s over the "technology gap" and the "défi Américain" of US investment were bound to be self-curing to some extent. Conversely, without belittling the serious current problems of inflation and productivity, the diagnosis of American economic decline is exaggerated by the artificial base period. Looking at the relative decline of the US share of gross world product, the largest part of the share that the United States lost was not represented by gain for the Soviet Union, but by the recovery of Germany and Japan, our close allies. In fact, the Soviet share of gross world product was 12.5% of the total in 1970 and only 11.5% at the end of the decade.[12] In that sense, even with repair of our current economic problems, nostalgic hope of recovering our preponderant economic position of the 1950s is bound to be disappointed. The diffusion of economic growth was our deliberate foreign policy goal and a wise one. Moreover, it is a net gain when considered in the context of overall alliance systems, so long as we maintain those alliances.

The other long-term cause of our changed position in the world is the increase in the complexity of world politics, which has reduced the potential for any country to exercise control over the whole system. There are more states and more issues and less hierarchy in international politics. For example, there are three times as many states in the United Nations today than at the time of its founding in 1945. Moreover, our foreign policy agenda has grown more complex. Added to the classic issues of military security and international trade are such subjects as food, population, environmental destruction, the governance of space, climate modification, terrorism, and whole hosts of others.

There has also been a change in the role of military force in world politics. In general, force has become more costly for great powers, particularly democratic ones, to apply effectively in world politics. This is an issue that is frequently misunderstood. It was fashionable in the 1970s, in the aftermath of Vietnam, to argue that force had lost its effectiveness. This is clearly not the case, then or now. Force remains the most effective form of power in many situations, but it also may prove to be the most costly form of power for some countries. Indeed, in some circumstances, it is too costly to be applied. While the military balance of power remains the bedrock or necessary condition of a sound policy, military force is difficult to apply to many of the new interdependence issues on the foreign policy agenda.

The use of force is made more costly for major states by four conditions: risk of nuclear escalation; uncertain and negative effects on the achievement of other goals; resistance by socially mobilized or awakened nationalistic populations in otherwise weak states; and domestic concern in democracies about the morality of the use of force. Even states relatively unaffected by the fourth condition, such as the communist countries, feel some constraints from the first three. For example, the Soviet invasion of Afghanistan and the threat of invasion of Poland may prove effective, but they may also prove more costly in terms of the second and third conditions than was true in the past. On the other hand, given modern technologies, lesser states involved in regional rivalries and terrorist groups may find it easier to use force. The net effect of these changes in the role of force is to somewhat erode the international hierarchy that has traditionally been based upon military power.

This erosion of international hierarchy is sometimes portrayed as a decline of American power, as though the causes lay solely in our own internal processes. As we have seen, there has been some decline, but American power remains impressive. With nearly one-quarter of world military expenditures and world economic product, the United States is still the most powerful state in the world.

To understand what has changed in the world, one must distinguish power over others from power over outcomes. What we are experiencing is not just an erosion of power resources that can be brought to bear against any single country (although there has been some), but an erosion of our power to control outcomes in the international system as a whole. The main reason is that this system itself has become more complex with the addition of more issues, more actors, and the erosion of hierarchy. The United States still has leverage over other countries, but far less leverage over the whole system. We are less well placed to extract unilaterally the positions which we prefer.

One must be careful, of course, not to overstate the degree of change in world politics. As Robert Keohane and I warned in *Power and Interdependence*, in a world of sovereign states, military force and balance of power will always remain a necessary condition for stability. But the New Orthodoxy which thinks that a resurgence in the role of force has restored the world of the 1950s is mistaken. To separate force and interdependence is to create a false dichotomy.[13] Interdependence is also an important source of power in the international system. States often try to manipulate dependency to achieve their goals. In addition, interdependence can be constraining. The multinationalization of business and banking creates a gap between power and the ability to mobilize it. Increased military spending will not be sufficient to solve these problems. In such a world, multilateral diplomacy in international institutions becomes more important because so much of the agenda is concerned with organizing collective actions. In short, the changes in world politics in the 1980s proclaimed by the New Orthodoxy are not likely to recreate American power or lay the basis for a new environment for the multinational corporation. On the contrary, diffusion of economic power and growing complexity will raise serious problems for creating international regimes to govern direct foreign investment.

IV

US power has declined in relative terms, but not as dramatically vis-à-vis any one country as is often supposed. On the other hand, the dispersion of economic power and the increased complexity of world politics make it more difficult to control the international system as a whole. The United States retains a deterrent and veto power, but finds it more difficult to compel or shape events than it did earlier in the postwar period. Hegemony, defined as a situation in which one state is able and willing to maintain the essential rules governing interstate relations, has been eroded to a large extent.

According to the theory of hegemonic stability, unless one nation has the capability and will to stabilize the international economic system, it will tend toward closure under the diverse pressures of domestic nationalist politics. Kindleberger argues that such leadership in maintaining an open economic system can be thought of as provision of a public good.[14] Such public goods are likely to be undersupplied unless there is a consumer who is large enough to be willing to invest in the public good even though he cannot appropriate all the benefits or exclude the free riders.

What does this mean for the multinational corporation in the 1980s? In the absence of US hegemony, will it succumb to diverse nationalisms? Not necessarily, for there are a number of important qualifications to the theory.

First, the relationship between the spread of multinationals and US power has never been quite as close as some formulations of military-security determinism imply. After all, American multinationals rose in the nineteenth century, when the United States was a net debtor; further, they were not directed to the area of US hegemony in the Caribbean, but toward Europe. In fact, US direct foreign investment was as large a percentage of GNP (7%) in 1914 as in the mid-1960s. Moreover, multinationals from smaller countries have been growing rapidly without any direct relationship to American power.[15]

In a simple, direct formulation, there is little correlation between the spread of multinationals and military power. But the theory can be reformulated to posit an important indirect role. Only if there is a preponderant power may there be a stabilizer for the open international economic system. Economic incentives may not be sufficient, but the incentives of an alliance leader may have kept the system open in an earlier period through tradeoffs between military and economic issues. The United States accepted trade imbalances and discrimination in the earlier period because it was an alliance leader. With diminished pre-ponderance in the alliance, according to this variant of the hegemony theory, the United States will not try to keep the system open. But this formulation of the theory must come to terms with the experience of the past decade.

A second qualification is based on the experience of the 1970s. The past decade was a period of declining American power *and* a period of enormous disruptive shocks to the international economy, including the breakdown of the postwar monetary regime; drastic increases in energy prices; inflation; and lowered growth. Predictions of coming trade and investment wars were rife in the first part of the decade, and conditions were present for closure. Obviously, there have been some protectionist measures, but not notably worse than in earlier decades. In the United States the threat of the Burke-Hartke Bill receded, and the Tokyo Round results were passed easily by the Senate. Trade volume continued to grow at about 5% annually, and trade in manufactures grew more than twice as fast as production (until the current recession). Similar patterns occurred in regard to direct foreign investment, with more countries involved. Banking systems became increasingly intertwined. This evidence raises questions about the theory of hegemonic stability.

One possibility, of course, is that there are lag effects and the erosion will not be fully felt until the 1980s. But two of the largest shocks occurred in 1971 (money) and 1973 (oil). Such long lags are hard to explain. Another possibility is that US power did not decline as much in the 1970s as was generally supposed. This may be true, but if my projection about the short-term causes of US decline in the 1970s being reversed are correct, that would make the prognosis for corporations even more sanguine in the 1980s.

Still another possibility is that the theory of hegemonic stability is flawed in the sense that economic openness does not have as much of the characteristics of a pure public good as the theory assumes. There may be enough divisibility and appropriability in international economic rules that bilateral bargaining may provide a significant component of second-best management.[16] Since corporations and nations are complementary institutions with different power resources—wealth for one, legitimacy and force for the other—there are ample incentives for bargaining, even in the absence of an effective interstate regime. In addition, other states which benefit from corporate activity may be playing more of a role in maintaining a degree of openess in the international system than the theory of hegemonic stability admits. In any event, we should be wary about concluding too much from the alleged decline of American power.

V. Conclusion

The political prospects for the multinational corporation in the 1980s appear to be less different from the 1970s than some theoretical formulations would lead one to believe. Obviously, a great depression and collapse of the open economic system would strongly and adversely affect multinationals. But such a collapse cannot be projected from the decline in American power that has occurred thus far or that seems likely in the 1980s. And there are enough qualifications about the theory of hegemonic stability to make one uncertain about such predictions even if American power were to decline more than was argued above.

On the other hand, the exaggerated 1970s projections about the power of multinational corporations vis-à-vis nation-states are also unlikely to be fulfilled. In 1974, I wrote that corporations played three political roles in world politics. The most dramatic were the "private foreign policies"—witness ITT in Chile—but these might be declining rather than increasing. The more important were the unintended roles as transnational instruments—witness the role of the oil companies in the 1970s—and as agenda-setters for governments—witness problems related to extraterritoriality.[17] Or as Raymond Vernon has put it, he might better have titled his 1971 volume, "Everyone at Bay." The central question is: "How do the sovereign states propose to deal with the fact that so many of their enterprises are conduits through which other sovereigns exert their influence?"[18]

One possibility is that states will respond by closure. But that is likely to be highly expensive for most states in terms of their welfare goals. Another possibility is that they will respond by establishing an international regime—a "GATT for Direct Investment"—or some equivalent.[19] But this may require more cooperation than the international system can generate in the 1980s. If we look at the institutional developments in this area in the past decade, such as the UN Center and the OECD Code, it is clear that they are useful, but gloss over rather than solve the basic problems.

The third and most likely possibility is that states and corporations will muddle through as they have in the past with a combination of bilateral agreements, weak multilateral measures, some sectoral closures, and a great deal of corporate flexibility and adaptation. Different industries and sectors and corporations may present different patterns. Grand generalizations will be foiled. The system may be second-best and messy, but that strikes me as a better guess than dramatic change to the clear alternatives of closure or of a strong new regime.

Notes

1. Raymond Vernon, "Sovereignty at Bay: Ten Years After," *International Organization* 35, no. 3 (Summer 1981), p. 527.

2. J. S. Nye, "Multinational Corporations in World Politics," *Foreign Affairs* 53, no. 1 (October 1974), p. 167.

3. Roger Hansen, "Power, Purpose, and Proportion: U.S. Foreign Policy in the 1980s," in R. Hansen et al. (eds.), *US Foreign Policy and the Third World: Agenda 1982* (New York: Praeger, 1982).

4. Robert Gilpin, "The Politics of Transnational Economic Relations," in Robert Keohane and J. S. Nye (eds.), *Transnational Relations and World Politics* (Cambridge, Mass.: Harvard University Press, 1971), p. 54.

5. Stephen Krasner, *Defending the National Interest* (Princeton University Press, 1978), p. 352.

6. See for example the calculations of Herbert Block, *The Planetary Product in 1980: A Creative Pause?* (Washington, D.C.: Department of State, 1982).

7. Bruce Russett and Donald DeLuca, "Don't Tread on Me: Public Opinion and Foreign Policy in the Eighties," *Political Science Quarterly* 96, no. 3 (Fall 1981), pp. 381–99.

8. Carnegie Panel on US Security and the Future of Arms Control, *Challenges for US National Security: Assessing the Balance*, part II (Washington, D.C.: Carnegie Endowment, 1981), p. 49.

9. David Deese and J. S. Nye (eds.), *Energy and Security: A Report of Harvard University's Energy and Security Research Project* (Cambridge, Mass.: Ballinger, December 1980).

10. *The Economist* (London), April 25, 1981.

11. Daniel Yankelovich and Larry Kaagan, "Assertive America," *Foreign Affairs* 59, no. 3, p. 710.

12. Herbert Block, *The Planetary Product*.

13. See the review of *Power and Interdependence* by Stanley Michalak, "Theoretical Perspectives for Understanding International Interdependence," *World Politics*, October 1979, p. 149.

14. Charles Kindleberger, *The World in Depression, 1929–39* (Berkeley: University of California Press, 1974), p. 207.

15. See Mira Wilkins, *The Emergence of Multinational Enterprise* (Cambridge, Mass.: Harvard Universtiy Press, 1970); also Tamir Agmon and Charles Kindleberger (eds.), *Multinationals From Small Countries* (Cambridge, Mass.: MIT Press, 1977).

16. See Robert O. Keohane, "The Theory of Hegemonic Stability and Changes in International Economic Regimes 1967–77," in Ole Holsti et al. (eds.), *Change in the International System* (Westview Press, 1980); also Kenneth Oye, Ph.D. thesis in progress, Harvard University.

17. J. S. Nye, "Multinational Corporations in World Politics," *Foreign Affairs* 53, no. 1 (October 1974), p. 167.

18. Raymond Vernon, "Sovereignty at Bay: Ten Years After," *International Organization* 35, no. 3 (Summer 1981), p. 527.

19. Charles Kindleberger and Paul Goldberg, "Toward a GATT for Investment: A Proposal for Supervision of the International Corporation," *Law and Policy in International Business*, 2 (Summer 1970).

I The Theory of Direct Foreign Investment

1 Multinationals, Tariffs, and Capital Flows with Endogenous Politicians

Stephen P. Magee and Leslie Young

The pure theory of international trade is long on demonstrations that tariffs can induce capital accumulation in capital-scarce economies. The same idea appears in the literature on tariff factories (see Kindleberger, 1963, chapter 12) and earlier in discussions of tariffs as engines of capital formation through redistribution effects toward savers (Johnson, 1908). The traditional literature examines the effects on international capital movements of exogenously given tariffs. In this paper we reverse the causation and examine the effects of international capital flows on the tariffs themselves. We do so in a model in which two factors of production, capital and labor, compete through lobbies and political parties in a democracy over the distribution of income. The economy is a developing one and is capital-scarce; thus the capital lobby provides resources to a procapital party in exchange for a tariff, while labor obtains an export subsidy from a prolabor party. All actors maximize: lobbies maximize factor incomes; parties maximize their probabilities of election; and all economic markets are competitive. We build on the "rent-seeking" model of trade restrictions pioneered by Krueger (1974). Subsequent work by Brock and Magee (1975, 1978, 1980) provided a partial equilibrium rent-seeking tariff model while an important paper by Findlay and Wellisz (1980) constructed a general equilibrium rent-seeking tariff model. The model used here is described in Magee and Brock (1980) and Young and Magee (1981). In a recent paper, Findlay and Wellisz (1981) examine the optimal inflow of foreign capital and the domestic conflict between opposing interests with and without tariffs. A useful survey of the political determinants of economic policy decisions in trade and direct investment models is provided in McCulloch (1979). While the issue being analyzed here is capital flow, all of the political modeling focuses on trade policy. A useful extension of our work would simultaneously involve trade policy and capital migration policy.

Consider a small developing economy in which capital and labor are engaged in the distributional squabble outlined above. Assume that the trade policies emerging from the political equilibrium result in a higher domestic price of the capital-intensive good than would be true with free trade. If foreign capital cannot be coerced to contribute to the capital lobby, it will enter since the domestic return exceeds the world return (we ignore risk here). However, if it must join local capital in contributing to the procapital party, it will enter only if the returns net of lobbying costs exceed the world return. We speculate that local capital in these situations prefer licensing over subsidiaries, local equity participation over full foreign ownership, and controlled vs. uncontrolled multinationals for political as well as economic reasons. Controls, even if implemented initially by the prolabor party, can be co-opted by the procapital party and used to force foreign capital to generate politically created scarcity rents. Olson (1965) has noted that lobbies, like cartels, are inherently unstable because of each member's incentive to cheat. The capital lobby that obtains a higher return to capital is providing a public good to all capital, regardless of which capital contributes. To summarize: Why are there extensive restrictions on multinationals in tariff-protected markets in developing countries?

In a rent-seeking economy with endogenous politicians, such restrictions provide appropriability mechanisms for the political activities of local capital. Multinationals can quickly erode politically created capital scarcities, and the local capital lobby obtains controls to prevent this. In what follows, we do not examine how these mechanisms develop; we merely assume that they exist and that they are effective.

What happens to an economy if the appropriability mechanisms work so that multinationals contribute the same proportion as local capital in supporting the procapitalist party in developing countries? The rest of this paper is devoted to answering this question. In effect, we provide a formal analysis of the Hymer (1970) case, later popularized by Barnet and Mueller (1974). In our framework, multinationals plus local capitalists provide resources to one party while labor provides help to the other. The framework here is symmetric, however, in that each factor attempts to exploit the other through political means. The results here are based on solutions generated by an admittedly specific model; they have not been tested empirically. But the model has several interesting implications:

1. policy independence;
2. increasing returns to capital;
3. geographical concentrations of capital;
4. unstable capital endowments;
5. symmetric factor exploitation;
6. capital cross flows;
7. synonomous interests of local and MNC capital.

These results have the following empirical implications:

1. Equilibrium tariffs and ex-post subsidies may be statistically independent of country endowments of capital per man.
2. The higher the capital/labor endowment, the higher the returns to capital.
3. Countries with low endowments of capital per man will have negative growth of capital (at least emanating from political considerations); those with high endowments should have positive growth. In effect prolabor governments will watch a continuous decline in their economy's capital stock (India?), while procapital governments will experience the reverse (Brazil?). Another implication is a geographical concentration of international capital in a few locations characterized by governments sympathetic to property rights and capitalists (e.g., developed countries).
4. The previous result suggests that endogenous political parties competing over trade policies plus capital mobility generate unstable capital endowments. That is, neither economic nor political forces in this model predict a stable factor endowment equilibrium.
5. More importantly, the model predicts that one factor will systematically exploit the other through its lobby and its political party. But the exploitation is symmetric in that either factor may dominate; it need not be the mobile factor only. If capital is sufficiently plentiful, it will grow without limit, increasing its return and reducing wages. If labor is more abundant, capital will leave (in response to low returns); throughout the period of capital emigration, wages rise and rentals fall.
6. For economies, in some endowment ranges, international capital will enter while domestic capital will leave. This requires that international capital "free rides" pays less than its pro rata share of the capital lobby costs. Countries in "middle" endowment ranges are more likely to exhibit capital cross-flows than those at the extremes.

7. Capitalists in closed economies in traditional models would oppose entry of foreign capital. Here, however, with politics endogenous, local capital as well as the procapitalist party will favor entry of foreign capital.

In section I we discuss the formal model, and in section II we report the simulation results. A summary of the results is provided at the beginning of section II.

I. The Model

This paper uses a model developed by Magee and Brock (1980) and Young and Magee (1981). The model explains the formation of commercial policies (a tariff and an export subsidy). The model adds the optimizing behavior of two lobbies and two political parties to the standard two-good, two factor small country model (Ronald Findlay has called this the "2×4 model").

An important consideration in the construction of these models is the game-theoretic equilibrium concept. For reasons detailed in Magee and Brock (1980), we assume that the economy is perfectly competitive; that voters choose between parties based solely on the policies they support and the economic resources that the parties possess; that the lobbies maximize their clientele incomes, taking into full account the general equilibrium behavior of the economy and the behavior of voters; and that the political parties each maximize their expected electoral success, taking into account the behavior of the lobbies, the voters and (only indirectly) the economy. We assume that each lobby takes as given the decision variable of the other lobby; we assume the same for the poltical parties. Thus, the equilibrium concept for both the lobbies and the parties is Cournot-Nash. Consider now the model.

A small economy produces two goods, X and Y, using linearly homogeneous production functions and two factors of production, K and L. Zero economic profits, perfect competition, and competitive factor markets guarantee that the following conditions hold:

$$X_k/Y_k = P^d, \tag{1}$$

$$X_l/Y_l = P^d, \tag{2}$$

where X_i and Y_i are partial derivatives with respect to input i and P^d is the domestic price of good Y in terms of good X (i.e., P_y/P_x). The two factors of production will be devoted to either the two economic activities (producing goods x and y) or to political activities

$$K = K_x + K_y + K_p, \tag{3}$$

$$L = L_x + L_y + L_p, \tag{4}$$

where K_p and L_p are the amounts of the economy's capital and labor that work for the political parties. As in the standard pure theory models, we take a long-term view so that full employment holds. The product markets need not be described, since international trade equilibrates deviations between domestic supply and demand.

Domestic prices and international prices can differ because of the two commercial policies and the weights attached to them because of political outcomes (i.e., the export subsidy s on good Y, the import tariff t on good X, and the probability of election, Π, of the procapital party). The domestic price is determined as follows:

$$
\begin{aligned}
P^d &= \left(\frac{P_y\, i}{P_x}\right)\frac{\Pi}{(1 + t)} + \left(\frac{P_y\, i}{P_x}\right)(1 + s)\,(1 - \Pi) \\
&\equiv P^i\left[\frac{\Pi}{(1 + t)} + (1 + s)\,(1 - \Pi)\right],
\end{aligned}
\tag{5}
$$

where

$P^d \equiv$ domestic price of Y in terms of X,

$P^i \equiv (P_y/P_x)^i \equiv$ international price of Y in terms of X,

$\Pi \equiv$ probability of election of the first (procapital) party,

$t \equiv$ tariff rate on imports of X,

$s \equiv$ export subsidy on Y.

Since we are dealing with a small economy, the international price P^i is exogenous. We assume that the economy is labor-abundant and exports good Y and imports good X with free trade. Thus, increases in t and Π both raise, ceteris paribus, the domestic price of X, the capital-intensive good, and hence raise the return to capital. By writing equation (5) in the form above, we are implicitly assuming that the political market clears more frequently than the economic market, so that the economy stays at the "expected value" of the relative goods prices rather than moving to either of the two extreme realizations following each election. If we think of the probability of success of the two parties in a broader context than just elections, i.e., as including bureaucratic decisions, court decisions and legislative outcomes which occur frequently, e.g., monthly, then the formalization in (5) is reasonable.

Consider next the political outcomes. The higher a distortionary policy supported by either party, the less success it will have with the voters, the bureaucrats, the legislature or the courts. However, the greater the level of economic resources possessed by a party, the greater will be its success. Since the procapital party sponsors t; the prolabor party sponsors s; the capitalist lobby gives all of its K_p to the procapital party; and the labor lobby gives all of its L_p to the other, we have the following result. The probability of success of the procapital party can be written as

$$\Pi = \Pi(K_p, \; L_p, \; s, \; t), \tag{6}$$
$$\quad\; + \quad - \quad + \; -$$

where

$\Pi \qquad \equiv$ probability of election of the procapital party 1 (the party supporting a tariff on imports of good X),

$1 - \Pi \equiv$ probability of election of the prolabor party, 2 (the party supporting an export subsidy on good Y),

$K_p \qquad \equiv$ capital supplied to party 1 by the capital lobby,

$L_p \qquad \equiv$ labor supplied to party 2 by the labor lobby,

$s \qquad \equiv$ the proportional ad valorem export subsidy on good Y supported by party 2,

$t \qquad \equiv$ the proportional ad valorem import tariff on good X supported by party 1.

Consider next the two lobbies. Each wishes to contribute resources to the political system so long as the increase in its gross income more than offsets the economic income lost from lobbying. Since we have normalized using good 1, both capital and labor will attempt to maximize its factor income in terms of good 1. Thus, the capital lobby will choose K_p to maximize $x_k(K - K_p)$ and the capital lobby will choose L_p to maximize $x_l(L - L_p)$. This leads to the following first-order conditions:

$$\left(\frac{\partial x_k}{\partial P^d}\right)\left(\frac{\partial P^d}{\partial K_p}\right)(K - K_p) = x_k, \tag{7}$$

$$\left(\frac{\partial x_l}{\partial P^d}\right)\left(\frac{\partial P^d}{\partial L_p}\right)(L - L_p) = x_l. \tag{8}$$

We assume that both lobbies fully overcome the Olson (1965) free rider problem as they tax their membership in raising K_p and L_p. The first terms in equations (7) and (8) are the Stolper-Samuelson effect relating product price changes to factor price changes while the second terms capture the effect of greater lobbying resources on Π and the effects of Π on P^d through the domestic price equation (5). Consider next the parties.

We cannot explain why the first party is procapital and the second is prolabor: these tendencies are assumed exogenous (they are given by historical accident or other political considerations). Furthermore, there may be many other issues more important than tariffs and export subsidies. In what follows, however, we consider only these two. The strategy of the first party is to choose t to maximize Π while the second will choose s to minimize Π. We assume a limited information Stackelberg equilibrium in which neither party incorporates the effects of its policy choice on the resource flows from the other lobby to the rival party. This yields the following first-order conditions for the two parties:

$$\frac{\partial \Pi}{\partial K_p}\frac{\partial K_p}{\partial t} + \frac{\partial \Pi}{\partial t} = 0,$$

$$\qquad + \quad + \qquad \quad -$$

$$\tag{9}$$

$$\frac{\partial \Pi}{\partial L_p}\frac{\partial L_p}{\partial s} + \frac{\partial \Pi}{\partial s} = 0.$$

$$\qquad - \quad + \qquad \quad +$$

Consider the economics behind the procapital party's choice. If it raises its tariff, there is increased alienation from voters and bureaucrats because of the social costs ($\partial\Pi/\partial t < 0$). However, the higher t generates more lobbying resources from the capital lobby ($\partial K_p/\partial t > 0$) and these resources can be spent on voters and on information to sway the system to a more procapital party position ($\partial\Pi/\partial K_p > 0$). So long as the "resource" effects dominate the alienation effect, the procapital party is quoting tariff rates which are below the equilibrium tariff.

Notice that when equations (1)–(10) hold, we have fully explained commercial policy, the level of lobbying activity, the level of economic activity, and the success rates of both political parties. There is some, though not complete, solace in that we have 10 unknowns (K_x, K_y, K_p, L_x, L_y, L_p, Π, s, t, and P^d) and 10 independent equations. We wish to emphasize that the model here focuses on the long term. By taking expected values of political outcomes and assuming employment, we ignore adjustment costs and paths of adjustment generated by short-term political outcomes. We also assume no barriers to "political entry" for the parties. This means that both parties set positive policy parameters and accept lobbying resources in equilibrium (see Young and Magee, 1981).

II. Simulation Results

We are interested in examining effects of international capital investments in which an MNC enters and joins the local capitalists in contributing to the procapital party. What happens to equilibrium tariff rates and returns to capital in this situation? We obtain six results.

1. The equilibrium policies are generally insensitive to changes in an economy's endowment of capital. For example, if the capital per labor endowment triples (from 0.28 to 0.84) the equilibrium tariff rate only increases from 36% to 41%.

2. In a closed economy, increases in the economy's capital stock would drive down the return to capital until an equilibrium capital stock were reached (at which the domestic returns equaled international returns). In the present model with endogenous tariffs and export subsidies, the returns to capital are positively (rather than negatively) related to the economy's endowment of capital. As capital accumulates, the procapital party's equilibrium tariff increases slightly; more importantly, its percentage of time in office increases. Both factors increase the domestic

price of the capital-intensive good and hence the return to capital (and lowers wages).

3. Result 2 generates a geographical concentration effect. Given the other economic parameters, there is a "watershed" value of an economy's capital stock at which the domestic capital returns equal the returns on world markets. If a country's capital endowment is below this value, domestic returns are lower than international returns and capital leaves the economy, causing its capital stock to decline to zero. If the capital endowment is above the watershed value, the capital stock expands indefinitely until revolution or factors outside our analysis intrude. The watershed value of the capital stock is an unstable equilibrium: at all other endowments a bang-bang result.

4. If the international capital fails to contribute to the procapital party, capital cross flows are possibly at endowment levels just below the watershed capital stock. There, international capital which entered would earn the gross return to capital while local capital supporting the procapital party would only earn the net return. Since the international return is between these two values, local capital leaves and international capital enters, generating capital cross flows.

5. Local capitalists will favor rather than oppose entry of foreign capital at all possible endowment levels so long as the international capital contributes to the lobbying effort. The net returns to local capital (i.e., returns after all lobbying costs have been subtracted) appear to always increase with entry of foreign capital. This result assumes, however, that the new foreign capital allocates the same proportion of its use to lobbying as does domestic capital.

6. Increases in the international price of labor-intensive goods raises wages and lowers rentals in this economy. However, it raises rentals in politicized (distorted) economies *relative to* nonpoliticized ones. This can result in a switch from capital outflows to capital inflows for the politicized (LDC?) regions.

The foregoing results have been obtained from simulation results of the model above. So far we have succeeded only with a Leontief production model; thus, equations (1) and (2) are replaced with a zero profit constraint. Good X is relatively capital intensive and is imported in the absence of distortions. The capital lobby contributes K_p to the first party which sponsors a tariff t on imports of good X. The labor lobby contributes L_p to party 2 in exchange for an export subsidy on labor-intensive goods. The international price of good Y is set at 0.64 while the capital/output ratio for good X is 1.0 and the ratio for good Y is $A = 0.20$. The labor/output ratios for both goods equal 1.0. The economy's labor endowment is fixed at 100 and the capital endowment is varied from 28 to 84. Both goods are produced and full employment holds. We assume a logit probability of election function for party 1 (see equation 6). The elasticities of the odds that a voter will vote for the procapital party equal 1.0 for K_p and s and equal -1.0 for L_p and t. For an elaboration of the model and the equations below, see Young and Magee (1981).

The results reported below are obviously specific to the functional forms assumed and may fail to hold in other contexts. We make no claim for their generality other than to note that they are representative of many other simulation results using different parameters for this same model. The generality of the results (or the lack thereof) could be established by empirical testing of the implications noted in the introduction.

The results in this section are based on the following setup.

$$r = \frac{1 - P^d}{1 - A}, \tag{1'}$$

$$w = \frac{P^d - A}{1 - A}, \tag{2'}$$

$$K = K_x + K_y + K_p, \tag{3'}$$

$$L = L_x + L_y + L_p, \tag{4'}$$

$$P^d = P^i \left[\frac{\Pi t_0}{T} + (1 - \Pi) s_0 \right], \tag{5'}$$

$$\Pi = \frac{1}{1 + L_p / K_p t_0 s_0}, \tag{6'}$$

$$\max \frac{(K - K_p)(K_p s_0 t_0 (1 - P t_0) + L_p (1 - P s_0)}{(K_p s_0 t_0 + L_p)(1 - A)}, \tag{7'}$$

$$\max \frac{(L - L_p)(K_p s_0 t_0 (P t_0 - A) + L(P t_0 - A)}{(K_p s_0 t_0 + L_p)(1 - A)}, \tag{8'}$$

$$\max \frac{(s_0 - t_0)(1 + Ks_0t_0/L_p)}{(1 - Pt_0)}, \tag{9'}$$

$$\min \frac{(t_0 - s_0)(1 + L/K_ps_0t_0)}{Ps_0 - A}, \tag{10'}$$

where

r $\equiv$ gross rentals,

w $\equiv$ gross wages,

$P^d \equiv$ domestic relative price of Y,

A $\equiv$ capital/output ratio in Y,

t $\equiv$ tariff rate on imports of X,

s $\equiv$ export subsidy on exports of Y,

t_0 $\equiv$ $1/(1 + t)$,

s_0 $\equiv$ $1 + s$.

We turn now to the results.

Policy Independence

What happens when a multinational corporation brings capital into the small economy described in the previous section? This result is simulated by an increase in the economy's endowment of capital in equation (3). Notice in table 1 that the amount of capital per man varies from 0.28 in case A to 0.84 in case D. An interesting result is the small effect which this movement in the economy's endowment has on either the tariff rate on imports of good X or the export subsidy on good Y. Notice the wide range in the economy's capital stock accompanied by the narrow range in tariff rates. If this result is general, it implies that government policies are virtually independent of an economy's factor endowment.

Increasing Returns to Capital

While the equilibrium policies chosen by the parties appear to be virtually independent of the economy's capital stock, the success ratio of

Table 1
Simulation results.

International Variables
  Relative Price of Good 2: $P = 0.64$
                           $A = 0.20$

Case	A	B	C	D
Capital/Labor Ratio	0.280	0.319	0.597	0.840

(1) Equilibrium Policies Are Virtually Independent of An Economy's Capital/Labor Ratio

Equilibrium Policies (%)				
Tariff on X	35.9	36.5	39.5	41.2
Export Subsidy on Y	10.9	9.7	4.1	1.1

(2) Increasing Returns to Capital: Capital Returns Are Positively Related to the Economy's Capital/Labor Ratio

Success of the Procapitalist Party	0.199	0.210	0.266	0.301
Domestic Price of Good 2	0.650	0.640	0.592	0.566
Return to Capital				
Gross	0.438	0.450	0.510	0.543
Net of Lobbying Costs	0.385	0.396	0.450	0.480
(Internat. Return = 0.450)				

(3) Polarization of Capital: Capital Exits from the Economy for K/L Values Below the Watershed Value of $(K/L)^* = 0.60$; Capital Enters for K/L Values Above 0.60

Capital Movements ← Capital Exits → | ← Capital Enters →
Net Returns to Capital ← $r_n < 0.450$ → ← $r_n > 0.450$ →

(4) Wage Rates Drop as the Capital/Labor Ratio Rises

Gross Wages	0.562	0.550	0.490	0.457

the procapitalist party is not. Notice in table 1 that the success ratio of the procapitalist party increases from 19.9% in case A to 30.1% in case D. Thus the major effect of the capital inflow is to increase the frequency with which the procapitalist party is elected by voters and to increase the frequency of success of the procapitalist party in the judiciary, the bureaucracy, and in the legislature in obtaining enforcement of the tariff rate on good X. The increased success of the procapitalist party in moving from case A to case D causes the domestic price of the labor-intensive good to fall from 0.650 to 0.566. Because of the magnification effect, the gross return to capital rises from 0.438 in case A to 0.543 in case D. The return to capital net of lobbying costs also increases, although it will always be below the gross return. Thus, because of the higher success rate of the procapital party with a larger endowment of capital in the economy, there is a positive relationship between capital returns and the amount of capital in the economy. This contrasts with closed-economy results (in which factor prices and product prices might be isolated from world market pressures by quotas). In that situation, an exogenous increase in the capital endowment would lower the return to capital. Our results are the reverse.

Similar arguments explain why this model predicts that wage rates fall as multinational or foreign capital enters the economy (see table 1). Wage rates drop from 0.562 to 0.457 as capital increases. The model here is discussed in the popular press (see Barnet and Mueller, 1974).

Geographical Concentration of Capital

The previous result generates a bang-bang result for country factor endowments. If international capital participates fully with local capital in contributing to the procapitalist party, both local and international capital earn an identical return which is less all lobbying costs (net of lobbying costs). Notice in table 1 that the net return to capital increases from 0.385 in case A to 0.480 in case D. Since capital on world markets earns a rental return equal to 0.450, both local and international capital tend to leave this economy if its endowment is below 0.597 and international capital will join local capital in entering the economy if the endowment exceeds 0.597. Thus, case C represents this "watershed" value of the economy's factor endowment. For capital values below C, the capital endowment implodes while it explodes above C.

The same result is shown in figure 1, wherein the return net of lobbying costs of capital is below the international return to the left of C while it is above the international return to the right of C. The interesting empirical implication of this result is that developing economies will segment into two groups. Those with low capital endowments would have slow or negative growth of their capital stocks while those with high endowments of capital would show increasing and rapid growth. This contrasts with the usual economic prediction that undercapitalized economies would engage in capital deepening while overcapitalized economies would show slow or even negative growth of their capital stocks.

Capital Cross Flows

Let us relax for a moment the assumption that internationally owned capital contributes to the local capital lobby. In this case, multinational corporation capital would earn the gross return to capital while domestic capital would still earn only the net return. Notice that in all endowments between cases B and C in table 1 and figure 1, international capital earns a return in the domestic economy above the international rate while domestic capital earns a return below the international rate. This generates cross flows in which international capital desires to enter the economy while domestic capital attempts to leave for higher returns abroad. We also speculate that local capitalists in many economies will use enforced licensing regulations, required sharing of equity with local capital holders and other schemes to induce international owners of capital (1) to share the politically created scarcity rents with them; (2) to contribute to their creation; and (3) to prevent their erosion via entry. Obviously, both domestic and international investors will attempt to free ride on the political investments already made to the domestic procapital party.

Synonymous Interests of Local and International Capital

The final result, which also contrasts with standard theory, is that local capitalists and international capital have synonymous interests with endogenous policy. All of the results in the model just developed assume that international capital pays the same "lobbying tax" to support the procapital party as is paid by local capital. Every time capital enters an economy and contributes to the local lobbying effort, this raises the success ratio of the procapital party and increases the relative price of the capital-intensive good. However, this is not an inevitable result. We can construct simple examples in which local capital might be worsened by capital inflows. Let the gross rental rate be 1.0 and let the local capital lobby use 20% of each machine for political purposes. Thus, the rental net of lobbying costs is 0.80. Assume that a multinational entered, contributed to the lobby, and that the increased success of the procapital party moved gross rentals up to 1.1. If however, the optimal capital lobby extraction increases up to 30%, then the net return to local capital falls to 0.77.

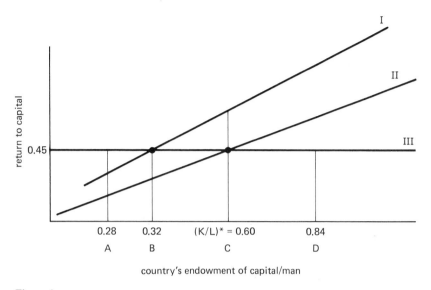

Figure 1
Domestic returns to capital. I, Gross return (free riders earn this). II, Return less net of lobbying costs (contributors to the lobby earn this). III, international return.

Capital Movements, Technology, and Prices

We can use these results to analyze the impacts of technology and terms of trade changes on movements of capital between free trade (non-rent-seeking) regions and politically distorted economies of the type analyzed here (hereafter referred to as "nondistorted" vs. "distorted" regions). Consider first technology. In general, technical changes increasing the capital-output ratio for good Y (this is parameter A) cause the factor intensities of the two goods to converge (the capital output ratio $= 1.0$ for good X). Low values of A are associated with high domestic returns relative to international returns (and high A's with low returns). Low values of A imply that returns in distorted regions are higher than are returns in nondistorted regions. *If technology moves factor intensities for goods further apart (A increases) capital will move from nondistorted to distorted regions.* This result is based on simulations underlying table 2. Notice that if $P = 0.8$, a distorted economy would have net capital returns everywhere higher than a nondistorted economy if the capital output ratio for good Y were 0.4 (this parameter is identical

Table 2
Equilibrium net domestic returns to capital in politically distorted economies relative to nondistorted international returns, as functions of world prices P and the relative factor intensities of production A.

Value of A						
0.7						L
0.6					L	L
0.5				L	L	M
0.4			L	L	L	H
0.3		L	L	L	M	H
0.2	L	L	L	M	M	H
0.1	L	L	M	L	H	H
Value of P	0.3	0.4	0.5	0.6	0.7	0.8

L ≡ domestic (distorted) returns less than international ones for wide ranges of domestic K/L endowments.

M ≡ domestic returns mixed (lower at low K/L and higher at high K/L) relative to international returns.

H ≡ domestic returns higher than international ones for wide ranges of domestic K/L endowments.

world-wide); it would have mixed returns (some above, some below, depending on factor endowments) if $A = 0.5$; and its net returns would be lower than foreign (nondistorted) returns if $A = 0.6$ or higher. As an aside, the simulations reported in section II apply to the "mixed" economy cases in table 2 (wherein countries with small capital endowments lose capital while those with large endowments acquire more).

Now hold technology and endowments constant and increase P, the price in nondistorted (world) markets of the labor-intensive good. It is reasonable to assume that developing countries are probably more politically distorted than advanced ones. If this is the case, *major improvements in the terms of trade of developing countries can move them from a situation with total capital flight to unending capital inflows* (i.e., from an L in table 2 to an H). And this is true despite the rent-seeking and politically created distortions. For example, at $P = 0.8$ and $A = 0.3$ in table 2, the returns to capital after all lobbying costs are higher in politically distorted economies than in nondistorted ones. Conversely, low prices for LDC exports generate a political as well as an economic curse: returns are lower than in nondistorted regions and the capital stock implodes (the only exception would be LDCs so capitalized that they produced only the capital-intensive good, but this is outside the scope of the present analysis).

The analysis in table 2 must be read with care. An increase in P raises the price of the labor-intensive good and this lowers rentals in our model (the usual result). But increases in P raise the return to capital in politically distorted areas *relative to* nondistorted areas (see Young and Magee, (1981).

References

Barnet, Richard J., and Ronald E. Mueller, 1974. *Global Reach.* New York: Simon and Schuster.

Brock, William A., and Stephen P. Magee, 1975. "The Economics of Pork-Barrel Politics," Center for Mathematical Studies in Business and Economics, Report 7511, University of Chicago, February.

————, 1978. "The Economics of Special-Interest Politics: The Case of the Tariff," *American Economic Review* 68 (May), pp. 246–250.

————, 1980. "Tariff Formation in a Democracy," in John Black and Brian Hindley (eds.), *Current Issues in Commercial Policy and Diplomacy.* New York: St. Martin's.

Findlay, Ronald, and Stan Wellisz, 1982. "Endogenous Tariffs, the Political Economy of Trade Restrictions and Welfare," in J. Bhagwati (ed.), *Import Competition and Response.* University of Chicago Press.

————, 1981. "Some Aspects of the Political Economy of Trade Restrictions." Draft, Columbia University, December.

Johnson, Alvin S., 1908. "Protection in the Formation of Capital," *Political Science Quarterly.*

Kindleberger, Charles P., 1963. *International Economics*, third edition. Homewood, Ill.: Irwin.

Magee, Stephen P., and William A. Brock, 1980. "A Model of Politics, Tariffs, and Rent Seeking in General Equilibrium," presented at the Sixth World Congress of Economists, Mexico City, August, and forthcoming in the Conference Volume, edited by Helen Hughes.

McCulloch, Rachel, 1979. "Trade and Direct Investment: Recent Policy Trends," in R. Dornbusch, and J. Frenkel (eds.), *International Economic Policy: Theory and Evidence.* Baltimore: Johns Hopkins University Press.

Olson, Mancur, 1965. *The Logic of Collective Action.* Cambridge, Mass.: Harvard University Press.

Young, Leslie, and Stephen Magee, 1981. "Politics and the Pure Theory of International Trade." University of Texas at Austin, April (mimeo, revised, July, 1982).

2 Foreign Direct Investment as a Sequential Process

Bruce Kogut

The primary advantage of the multinational firm, as differentiated from a national corporation, lies in its flexibility to transfer resources across borders through a globally maximizing network. Recent models of direct foreign investment have tended to downplay these advantages of a coordinated multinational system; rather, they have stressed the motivational behavior arising out of essentially national factors and market imperfections, e.g., proprietary knowledge, domestic industrial structure, and product differentiation. The neglect of the advantages of multinationality obscures, though, an important distinction between the original motivations to establish plants in foreign countries and the subsequent investment decisions. There is, in short, a fallacy of explanation of genesis in failing to distinguish between the initial investment decision and the subsequent incremental investment flows.

This paper argues that current foreign direct investment (FDI) must be understood as largely sequential flows stemming from the advantages of flexibility of a multinational system. The empirical foundation for this argument can be seen in the change over the past 30 years of the dominant channels of US FDI from new intercompany outflows to reinvested earnings. In 1970, the ratio of equity and intercompany account outflows to reinvested earnings was 1.39. By 1979, the ratio was 0.32. (The complete time series is given in table 1.) The predominant share of FDI flows are incremental investments in already established subsidiaries. In light of these trends, previous theories of FDI which stress the oligopolistic behavior of corporations in their home markets provide incomplete explanations for current FDI. What is required is a greater consideration of the systemic advantages inherent in a multinational network.

These trends carry implications also for the way data on FDI flows are categorized and used. Rather than collecting data according to entries and exits, information should be gathered concerning the conduit of flows as well as changes in the stock of FDI at the firm level. Data

Table 1
US Foreign Direct Investment (in millions of dollars).

Year	Total	Equity and intercompany account outflows	Reinvested earnings of incorporated affiliates	Ratio of equity outflows to reinvested earnings
1950	1,088	621	475	1.31
1955	1,766	823	962	0.86
1960	2,039	1,675	1,266	1.32
1965	4,994	3,468	1,542	2.25
1966	4,318	3,625	1,791	2.02
1967	4,768	3,050	1,757	1.74
1968	5,347	2,855	2,440	1.17
1969	6,186	3,130	2,830	1.11
1970	7,387	4,413	3,176	1.39
1971	7,280	4,441	3,176	1.40
1972	7,118	3,214	4,532	0.71
1973	11,435	3,195	8,158	0.39
1974	8,765	1,275	7,777	0.16
1975	13,971	6,196	8,048	0.77
1976	12,759	4,253	7,696	0.55
1977	13,039	5,612	7,286	0.77
1978	17,957	4,877	11,469	0.43
1979	24,844	5,904	18,414	0.32

Source: *Survey of Current Business*, US Department of Commerce, vol. 61, no. 2 (February 1981).

which reveals the industry and regional breakdown of both reinvested and new FDI flows would provide a critical platform by which the systemic advantages of the multinational corporation (MNC) can be appraised.

This is not to deny that the advantages of the MNC have been studied. The broader field of research on the MNC has been sensitive to these issues. Especially in the consideration of the political complexities posed by multinational corporations, the peculiar strengths attributed to the operation of a multinational network have been discussed.[1] Such issues as transfer pricing, tax arbitrage, bargaining or negotiating powers, and cost advantages have been analyzed in isolation or in group.[2] There has not been, however, a thorough integration of these issues and the theory of foreign direct investment in the literature, with the partial exception of Dunning (1979).

The purpose of this paper is to move toward such an integration. Section I reviews briefly the recent FDI literature and introduces a more generalized model in the hope of elucidating the importance of the multinationality factor in FDI flows. The cutting edges of this model is the view of the MNC as a collection of valuable options which permits the discretionary choice of altering real economic activities or financial flows from one country to the next. Section II discusses the valuation of systemic advantages. Finally, section III discusses the importance of this expanded theory from the point of view of host and home countries and comments upon trends likely to persist into the 1980s.

I

Particular aspects of the contribution of multinationality to the value of the firm and to explaining its behavior have been examined. Kindleberger (1969) considers the conflict between the host country and a multinational firm who are maximizing conflicting objective functions. Agmon and Lessard (1977) and Lessard (1979) note the incremental value of being able to arbitrage tax regimes. Hirsch (1976) cites in a revealing analysis the effects of joint production and trade in intermediate goods in the context of subsequent investment decisions. Vernon (1979) stresses the information- and profit-scanning functions of a multinational network. Davidson (1980) demonstrates the significance of experience effects upon FDI flows.

A growing body of research concerns the combination of location and trade theory with that of internalization. Magee (1977) argues that FDI is motivated by the difficulties of appropriating rents from the trade and licensing in proprietary knowledge. Buckley and Casson (1976) argue similarly that plant location is determined by, one, locational advantages and, two, market failure in the trade of proprietary knowledge, especially that of research and development.

Dunning (1977, 1979) has more recently expanded upon these ideas in developing what he calls the "eclectic theory" of FDI. The theory combines usefully the macroeconomics of standard trade theory with transportation theory. Thus, a country's endowment and geographical position create certain "locational" advantages. Dunning then proceeds to consider the factors which determine entry barriers and sustainable oligopolies. These factors, e.g., patented information, brand names,

location
advantaged   disadvantaged

	advantaged	disadvantaged
advantaged	export	FDI outward
disadvantaged	FDI inward	import

ownership

Figure 1
Trade and FDI outcome for a single industry in the home country.

technology, form what he calls "ownership" advantages. Ignoring the possibility of licensing, the various combinations of these advantages suggest a scheme such as shown in figure 1. In the upper right box, for example, the firm possesses a unique technology or some cost advantage. Its home domicile is, however, characterized by higher factor or transportation costs than foreign locations. As a result, it invests overseas. Thus investment occurs only when the home firm possesses a unique asset and the host country is relatively advantaged in location. Finally, the theory of internalization is introduced to explain why licensing is not a preferred mode to FDI.[3] Thus, trade and location theory is wedded to that of internalization in order to explain FDI flows as a response to market imperfections.

Nevertheless, the importance of a multinational network as an important contribution to the value of the firm and its economic opportunities and to the determination of the likely conduits of FDI have not been sufficiently analyzed. In the view of Buckley and Casson, for example, internationalization is the by-product of the search for minimum cost production sites and the internalization of markets. The absence of uniquely international factors is starkly apparent in Hirsch's model, which is considered in more detail in the next section. While Hirsch discusses economies of scale and joint production in marketing at a single location, there is no variable that represents the revenue impact of the ownership of a globally operated system. Dunning (1981) as well does not analyze the precise systemic opportunities generated by multinationality, though he does list several types of advantages.

But does the factor of multinationality add to our understanding of the determinants of FDI? One way to answer this question is to consider whether MNCs would still have cause to exist in the absence of the commonly listed market imperfections. Let us suppose, then, that the four of the five imperfections that Buckley and Casson list in the market for technology could be eliminated. These imperfections are (1) the absence of a forward markets to hedge the risk of development, (2) the impossibility to arrange contracts that would permit discriminatory pricing, (3) the presence of monoponistic purchasers, and (4) informational impactedness. (The fifth imperfection is that of government intervention, which—along with such events as changes in exchange rates—can create unique arbitrage opportunities for the MNC.) If in some idealized state, these imperfections were altered to the requirements of perfect markets, would there still be the MNC?

The answer would be affirmative, due to three characteristics which enable the MNC to exploit uniquely international distortions in markets or production: one, the ability to arbitrage institutional restrictions; two, the informational externalities captured by the firm in the conduct of international business; three, the cost saving gained by joint production in marketing and in manufacturing. These imperfections, which are carefully considered in the studies on the political dilemmas posed by multinationals and on multinational planning and control, are curiously understated in the mainstream economic literature.

This neglect is derived largely from not considering international projects as incremental at a global level. Although conceiving international investment within a dynamic theory of the firm, the internationalization literature fails to consider the value of the *operational* flexibility and externalities of a multinational system. Rather, the stress is placed upon the *structural* elements of plant location and the elimination of transactional costs.

There is, in short, a tendency to view FDI as a decision made at a discrete point of time. This is the fallacy of genesis to which I previously alluded. The decision to transfer resources internationally is only one aspect of FDI. Given the structural outcome of this decision, the other aspect is the series of sequential decisions which determine the volume and direction of these transferred resources.

Contrary to the structural approach, consideration of the operational value of a global system places stress upon the unique ability of multinationals to reduce the costs of operating in an uncertain world.[4] This is best illustrated by considering explicitly the three factors that were claimed above to be uniquely international attributes. The first is the ability of the MNC to arbitrage institutional restrictions, e.g., tax codes, antitrust provisions, financial limitations, and even national security prohibitions on trade. In effect, the operation of an international system has provided the multinational with a string of options written on contingent outcomes. The difference between the inclusion of taxes, financial incentives, etc., as part of a theory of location and this approach is that the consideration of institutional arbitrage as an option emphasizes the unique ability of the MNC to exploit the conditions of uncertainty and of institutional environments. The MNC can, in effect, exercise an option upon the occurrence of an event, e.g., its option to choose in which country to declare its profits. Boundaries do not represent only the costs of tariffs and transport; they also represent profit opportunities which can only be exploited by a multinational corporation.

The second factor concerns the capture of externalities in information, or what we call learning cost externalities. There is an information set required of international business that is separable from that required of domestic business. Corporations spend vast resources in their recruitment of internationally skilled personnel, in political analysis, in intercultural education programs, and in the development of monitoring and control mechanisms. They also invest in information scanning and processing in order locate markets and customers internationally. But most critically, there are important learning curves involved in these activities as well as "first mover advantages." Occidental Petroleum's knowledge and status as a long-standing supplier/customer of the Soviet Union is not easily duplicated.

Joint production economies can occur in both marketing and manufacturing on a global scale. Niehans (1977) has noted that economies of scale in marketing or servicing but constant or decreasing scale economies in manufacturing can serve to explain the growth of the MNC. Similarly, joint production economies due to the creation of a multinational network reduces the physical capital or labor costs of production and marketing of incremental investments. For example, the multinational network permits the export of otherwise nonexportable goods, since the fixed costs of establishing sales offices, hiring personnel, and locating plant sites are already sunk. The incremental cost saving can permit, as Hirsch suggests, an increase in the export of intermediate products or in the market entry of new products sharing production economies. In addition, the multinational network can serve to export additional final goods or to service the export of other firms' goods in times of slack capacity; the Japanese trading companies are an example of the latter facility. Unquestionably, the formation of a multinational network poses significant barriers to entry. The implications of these barriers are analyzed in greater detail in the conclusions.

II

The implications of considering the value of international factors can be illustrated in the formulation of a capital-budgeting procedure. In an instructive article, Hirsch (1976) suggests that the decision to service a market by exports or by foreign direct investment can be modeled by four cost variables discounted at some appropriate rate: production and tax transportation costs P, research and development costs K, marketing costs M, and control costs C. Demand is assumed as given. Marketing costs are argued to be higher for exports than host-manufactured goods, while control costs rise with the internalization of production. These assumptions are intuitively reasonable. Moreover, Hirsch argues that M and C are increasing functions of K. Implicitly, Magee argued the same in his claim that the opportunity loss of appropriability rises with information content at every stage of production. Hirsch's reasons rest in the costs of market exploration and organizational communication. Since neither argument is mutually exclusive, both can be subsumed in Hirsch's model.

Given this formulation of the model, Hirsch demonstrates convincingly that the failure of conventional trade theory is its consideration solely of the comparative costs of production. Expanding the model to include the production of several goods, Hirsch also shows that economies of joint production can change the investment decision when production for each good is maintained as an independent project. The model is also expanded to consider multistage production, whereby Hirsch shows that overseas investment production can increase the export of previously non-competitive intermediary goods.

While Hirsch discusses economies of joint production in marketing at a single location, there is no variable that represents the cost savings of the ownership of a globally operated system. As suggested earlier, these cost savings arise from considering a global network as a sunk cost and sequential investments as incremental. (There is also the factor that in a world of imperfectly diffused information, the scanning advantages of a multinational widens its set of investment opportunities.) The impact of these cost factors is to reduce the incremental values of C, K, and M and to expand the firm's investment opportunities.

We can illustrate the value of systemic advantages by considering explicitly how a capital budget formulation might account for these benefits, particularly those of the first factor. The first factor, that of arbitraging institutional and national barriers, contributes directly to the enhancement of the discounted revenue stream. Such a contribution is derived through, one, a possible reduction in the discount rate, and secondly, through the addition of a string of real but usually nontradeable options. The advantages accrued by international diversification in financial markets and the role of MNCs in providing diversification have been commented upon by several authors, in particular by Sonlik (1974), Lessard (1976), and Agmon and Lessard (1977). In a world of no barriers to portfolio flows and of purchasing power parity, the cost of capital at the margin is the same for all investors in a taxless world, regardless of nationality. Since changes in the exchange rates and nominal interest rates would reflect equally changes in prices, discounted cash flows before taxes are the same no matter what their currency denomination.[5] When capital markets are segmented by national barriers and policies, discount rates vary between countries. These variations reflect national differences in risk bearing and in time preferences. To the extent that barriers are imperfect, discount rates tend toward a world rate plus or minus the transactional costs of subventing these barriers. Considered in this light, the equilibrium discount rates can be viewed as prices for a single commodity adjusted for transportation costs, when all countries are equally distant from one another.

The argument for the advantages of the MNC in financial markets boils down to the following set of simple statements. Multinational firms are able to invest across national borders and thereby avoid the presumably more costly barriers to portfolio flows. Because of its access to more diversified international financial markets, the MNC can, holding everything else equivalent, invest in marginal projects otherwise rejected by host firms. Since the MNC adjusts its risk according to a world portfolio and the domestic firm according to a more home-weighted portfolio (due to capital market imperfections and barriers), the risk-adjusted cost of capital is relatively lower for the MNC. Secondly, if the foreign project represents a unique asset in terms of the available portfolio investments on the world market, the home investor is willing to pay the MNC a premium for contributing an otherwise unattainable asset to his or her portfolio. In conclusion, then, in a world of imperfect international capital flows, MNCs receive a premium relative to their purely domestic home competitors—if their foreign investments are unique and nontraded assets—and invest at a lower capital cost relative to the purely domestic host country competitors.[6]

An aspect that has received less attention in the literature regarding the evaluation of a multinational network is the value of holding a string of options defined by institutional barriers. These barriers can be typified by different currencies or more exactly by changes in relative exchange rates, taxes, sovereign risk, and legal prescriptions on equity ownership, form of remittance, etc. To illustrate the importance of these options, consider an MNC operating a series of plants in several countries which serve purely domestic markets. The future cash flows are uncertain. Upon realization of its cash flows, the MNC can through transfer pricing, financial packaging, and other methods alter to a nontrivial extent the structure and level of its obligations. The contingent events are the realization of taxable earnings in each of the various countries. The nature of the option is that the MNC can choose in which geographical jurisdiction to declare these profits so as to minimize the tax burden.

Consider, for a second example, the MNC with several export markets and a few manufacturing plants. By design, the plants operate on average at less than full capacity. In country X, it must renegotiate a set of extraction or labor contracts. In response to unacceptably (however subjectively defined) bargaining positions, the MNC can shift production to other plants to service its overseas markets, given that labor constraints are not binding. (This potential has secondary effects in terms of its bargaining strength, as discussed in section III.) Thus given the uncertainty over the outcomes of negotiations, the MNC has the real option of mitigating the costs of factor price increases or higher taxes in the short term, and the physical adjustment costs in the long term, through maintaining excess capacity in diverse national plants. A similar case is that of a real appreciating currency. The ability to shift exports from a country whose currency is appreciating to one where other plants are located is a valuable option—assuming that pricing is denominated in the currency of the importing country and factor payments are derived out of overseas revenues.

What is important to note is that all the above-described options are valuable because the future state of the world is uncertain.[7] Moreover, the more variable the environment, the more valuable are these options. From the point of view of the MNC, the variance of its cash flows and of factor prices in the context of national restrictions presents a set of valuable options relative to the opportunity set of a purely domestic firm. Since these options are exercisable only by the MNC and cannot be traded and purchased by individual investors in any meaningful sense, the value of the firm is enhanced by the incremental value of these options.[8]

The above discussion can be illustrated through the consideration of the elements that would enter into a capital-budgeting model. The value of the firm can be described as

$$NPV = \sum_{0}^{t} \frac{(\text{cash flows} + \text{learning} + \text{joint production} + \text{options})_t}{(1 + R)^t}.$$

The discount rate may be lower than that available on the world market and, as is more likely, lower than that available to host country firms when capital markets are segmented. (The appropriate discount rate for each term is likely to vary according to its systematic risk, but for simplicity, we assume one rate.) The first term represents simply the discounted cash flows from a series of independent projects that are owned by globally unintegrated firms. The next three terms capture the advantages arising out of the interdependence of the cash flows of projects undertaken by an MNC. We have indicated these advantages to be learning-cost and joint-production economies, and the possession of real nontradeable options.

How may these advantages be actually evaluated?[9] Once the initial investment is made, learning cost and joint production externalities are likely to be incorporated in the capital budget through an incremental analysis. A more complex analysis is to evaluate at the time of the initial investment the value of the option to expand into other products or into other markets. The option to arbitrage national barriers is similarly difficult to evaluate. Given the recent interest in evaluating financial options, it would appear that the analytical methods are already available to value real options numerically.[10] There are, however, serious obstacles to such an extension which are not always noted in the literature. In brief, a financial option can be valued because one assumes that there exists a shadow security whose price will follow a particular type of stochastic process. In the absence of such a shadow security, we have no reason to believe that the price of the real asset will also follow such a path since there is no means to arbitrage the real option against its shadow security. Nevertheless, the options literature provides the appropriate framework for understanding the reasoning behind the claim that the option to exercise certain rights, e.g., where to declare taxes, where to shift production, is a valuable hedge against contingent events.

The inclusion of these three elements in addition to the normal cash flows generated by project illustrates the opportunities that stem from a multinational system. As a result of these opportunities, we expect that growth in FDI is more likely to be in the form of reinvested earnings than in new entries. The consequences of this trend from the perspective of governments are discussed in the next section.

III

From the firms' point of view, the flexibility to transfer resources across borders is a positive contribution to its earning stream. As discussed in an abundant literature, the viewpoints of governments are often less sanguine. Rather than consider the larger issues of government and MNC relations, we concentrate on a few specific issues, e.g., monetary stabilization, regulation, and negotiation. Through these examples, we illustrate that the well-established issues of contention between governments and MNCs are comprehensible only within the context of the systemic flexibility of the MNCs.

How is a government likely to view these systemic advantages of MNCs when pursuing domestic monetary stabilization objectives? If an MNC speculates on currencies, its behavior tends to give markets greater liquidity and thereby accelerates the speed of adjustment. Even if the MNC is not a speculator, it forecasts and hedges its contractual and noncontractual exposure. Whether it speculates or is able merely to shift currencies more easily from one country to the next or to write more inexpensive contractual hedges, these activities clearly tend to negate the ability of governments to pursue objectives such as the stabilization of its currency countervailing to the market trend. Thus the presence of MNCs limits further the ability of governments to pursue independent objectives in an international economy.

If governments are more constrained in their ability to pursue monetary objectives due to the existence of MNCs, are they more constrained in pursuing other objectives? Consider a government which desires to regulate a foreign-owned industry. Under closed borders, enterprises are essentially hostage to the partisan coalitions of its environment. Since exit except in the form of selling its holdings is impossible, the regulated enterprise consents to government regulation, while it may itself seek to join a political coalition.[11] For the MNC whose foreign assets are primarily in the form of proprietary knowledge, regulation is unlikely to be successful. It is especially unsuccessful in its most extreme form—that of nationalization, for as long as the ongoing value of the subsidiary is dependent on a sequential stream of innovations, nationalization results merely in the elimination of industry. The effects of less extreme interventions, e.g., an increase in taxation, invoke most likely less extreme reactions. Nevertheless, the implications are the same. To the extent that multinational corporations contribute more to the economy than that of the new policies, their partial or total withdrawal are a real loss to the host country. Moreover, if multinational corporations are truly global, then the argument applies to home countries in which governments attempt to regulate, for example, outward flows of capital.

When FDI is primarily transmitted in the form of fixed capital with known and stable technologies, the bargaining position of the MNC and host government is reversed. This situation, which is known as the obsolescent bargain, has been extensively analyzed.[12] Mining is a classic example. The original investment requires a large fixed capital component. Presumably the MNC chooses to internalize this transaction in order to gain access to guaranteed supplies, to speculate on future prices when futures markets do not exist or do not trade claims on contracts many years out, or to acquire oligopolistic advantages. At the time of the investment, the host government's bargaining position is constrained by competition from other countries. The host government can, however, capture part, if not all, of the rents ex post to the investment through a process of renegotiation. If, for example, the value of its mineral resources is higher than expected, the host government has the option of capturing part of the consequent excess returns. To the extent that this gaming behavior is expected and that equity claims and other financial contracts are difficult to enforce, it is likely that MNCs will be reluctant to invest in mineral extraction without adequate guarantees or insurance.

What does the above analysis imply for the growth and the role of the MNC in the 1980s? There are three principal implications. First is that the entry of new firms in international markets is likely to slow, holding changes in investment opportunities constant. Evidence for this transition is suggested, as noted earlier, in the growth of reinvested earnings relative to new equity investment in total FDI flows. These figures have been given in table 1.

The benefits of institutional arbitrage, learning curve effects, and joint production economies create, then, substantial barriers to entry. The importance of these factors is underlined in light of the present proportion of intra-firm trade which accounted roughly for 48.4% of all US imports in 1977 (Helleiner, 1979). Discussions of antitrust implications have usually stressed the feedback of FDI on competition in the home market (Bergsten et al., 1978). Perhaps a more troubling aspect is the impact of these barriers on the entry of firms from LDCs or from developed countries which were slow to create international firms. While FDI between LDCs has been increasing, such investments appear to be characterized more by the capture by small firms of investment gaps ignored by the much larger MNCs. Thus, FDI by LDCs is likely to be explained by a theory of FDI by small firms than by entry openings unique to the skills of LDC enterprises.[13]

Another implication lies in the persisting role of research and development in explaining some, though perhaps a relatively decreasing amount, of flows of proprietary capital over international borders. For those end products that are oriented towards the home market, FDI is often in the form of overseas production of intermediary products. In this case, FDI is related to research and development only insofar as the end product embodies a large value of technological expenditure. The overseas production of intermediary goods can involve minimal research and development expenditures in terms of value added. Moreover, FDI is in this form partially trade enhancing.

What should be noted is that the production of technologically sophisticated products is of less importance—though still of indubitable significance—in future FDI flows. Instead, we can imagine the development of decentralized structures that permits the delegation of product selection and research and development to subsidiaries but leaves the strategic variables of financing, production, and tax arbitrage to the home office. There is some indication that this devolution is already perceptible in the food industry (Katz, 1981).

Related to the above implications is the tendency of the MNCs to develop and expand their trading divisions. In part, this evolution is derived from the hazards of the obsolescent bargain as well as from the erosion of market advantages as the original technological edge in some products evaporates. Vernon (1977) has termed this latter trend "senescence." The difference between these two trends is simply that the obsolescent bargain refers to loss of property rights, senescence to loss of market shares. The underlying cause of both trends is, however, similar, i.e., the loss of some technological advantage specific to the firm which maintains its bargaining or market position. In the first case, the MNC can limit its exposure by financing extraction in the form of debt with payoffs denominated in a specified quantity of the underlying mineral or product, or by long-term contracts, or by providing managerial services and downstream marketing and relinquishing its ownership or contractual obligations. In the second case, the MNC is also induced toward eliminating its productive activities and in effect leasing the services of its global network. In both cases, the possession of a multinational network provides a stream of benefits and investment opportunities independent of the products being traded. Examples of this development are the oil industry, Japanese trading companies, and the diversification of large firms into trading third-party products, such as in the case of Thyssen.

Consequently, the MNC of the 1980s is likely to be engaged less in equity investments in primary extraction industries, but relatively more in the provision of marketing and consulting services. Trade in intermediate products is also likely to increase, because the MNC can optimize production and marketing within an already existing global system. These trends, of course, are a continuation of a pattern that has been visible for several years.

IV. Conclusions

I have tried to detail the precise advantages arising from a multinational network and its implication for the identity of the agents and the type of investment flows in the future. By and large, policy implications have not been discussed. The reasons for this omission are simple. Having developed our model under the assumption of profit maximization, optimal policy recommendations which differ from a competitive profit-maximizing outcome can only be motivated if the national objective functions are specified. I have not attempted such a specification, although the dropping of the assumption of profit maximization would be an interesting exercise.

The question has been left open whether the profitability and growth of the MNC is a result of its market power or productive efficiency.[14] I have, however, implicitly suggested the importance of first-mover advantages that current MNCs possess relative to potential entrants. If we are concerned over the absence of bargaining power on behalf of many LDCs, then our analysis reinforces the recommendations for an international regulation of MNCs or the creation of countervailing institutions or enterprises to enhance the bargaining power of LDC countries. Such regional efforts as ASEAN's recent consideration of the formation of trading companies similar to those of the Japanese are illustrations of efforts to create potential countervailing enterprises. But hidden beneath such developments and recommendations is an irony often noted in the case of MNCs from developed countries. That is, though the rents from learning-curve and joint-production externalities accrue to the home MNC and hence potentially to the home countries, the creation of truly global enterprises poses challenges to the national sovereignty of governments through their maximization of global profits and through their arbitraging of institutional borders. In other words, is it reasonable to expect that an MNC originating in a developing country, which MNC maximizes its return from its global activities, should be more sensitive to the sovereignty and interests of its national government?

Consequently, the conflict of nation-states and international firms remains an issue in the 1980s. Countries face incentives not only to regulate the entry of firms, but also their exit. There has appeared the ironic evolution that LDCs have been concerned to establish strict rules of entry, whereas developed countries increasingly seek to control the exit of firms and the immediate loss of jobs and production. Whether the combined impact of these trends is to reduce the benefits of a global network remains to be seen; but, in any event, it represents the forefront of future discussions on the merits of FDI and the multinational corporation.

Notes

I would like to thank Stephen Kobrin of New York University and Richard D. Robinson of the Massachusetts Institute of Technology for their comments on an earlier draft. I am especially grateful to Donald Lessard of the Massachusetts Institute of Technology for his comments on the first and subsequent drafts.

1. See, for example, Kindleberger (1969), Vernon (1971, 1977), or Stopford and Wells (1972).

2. Such issues as transfer pricing, tax arbitrage, bargaining or negotiating power, and regulation are discussed by Lessard (1979), Bergsten et al. (1978), and Robinson (1976).

3. For a review of the internalization literature, see Rugman (1981). It should be noted that the concept of internalization is already adumbrated, like so many ideas in the literature on FDI, in Kindleberger (1969), pp. 19–22.

4. Undoubtedly, it can be claimed that the theory of internalization accounts precisely for these operational facets. (See, e.g., Buckley and Casson, 1976, p. 69.) But by placing stress upon the cost aspect of transactions, it fails to consider the profit opportunities generated by a global system.

5. This can be shown by considering whether to discount the overseas earnings by the home or foreign discount rate. If we assume purchasing power parity, changes of nominal interest rates are canceled by identical changes of nominal exchange rates.

6. In his contribution to this volume, Robert Aliber revives his earlier argument that FDI can be explained at the macroeconomic level, i.e., the arbitrage of international markets. Though such an approach appears weak in explaining such phenomena as cross-hauling, it has a tantalizing appeal in its attempts to link such anomalies as FDI waves to concepts as Tobin's q. There may be a macroeconomic story after all.

7. In the cases where uncertainty may appear as irrelevant, such as in tax arbitrage, governments are well-equipped to develop monitoring and enforcement services. It is the uncertainty of the realized profits that keeps the costs of these services relatively high to the benefits of reducing arbitrage behavior.

8. Some readers may be misled into inferring that the above argument suggests that total variance does matter after all to the investor. To the contrary, since these options are similar to monopoly or proprietary rents, the firms earn abnormally high rates of return but the stocks written on the firm, as long as they are traded in competitive capital markets, are priced in the expectation of a market rate of return adjusted for systematic risk.

9. See Lessard (1981) for a thorough discussion of the application of adjusted present value techniques for valuating international projects.

10. See the path-breaking article by Black and Scholes (1973) for the evaluation of financial options. Our concern with the shadow security is directed primarily at recent extensions of the Black-Scholes model into the evaluation of real assets. MacDonald and Segal (1981) are certainly aware of these difficulties, whereas Cooper and Broglie (1981) simply assume the existence of a shadow security without substantial comment.

11. See the interesting article by Magee in this volume which discusses the impact of political coalitions on FDI flows.

12. See the writings of Vernon (1971), Stopford and Wells (1972), and Bergsten et al., (1978).

13. We have not tried here to develop such a theory of FDI by small firms. Briefly, one relevant factor would seem to be trade in custom-designed products, i.e., small producers are more sensitive to the "voice" (in Hirschman's terminology) of smaller producers (Hirschman, 1971). Another factor is the trading by small firms of used capital equipment. Since used capital equipment is difficult to valuate, the seller may attempt to eliminate the costs of discounting incurred through the asymmetry in information by taking an equity position. Indeed, joint ventures between LDCs are relatively common. These factors, in addition to the ones discussed above, tend to explain some characteristics of FDI between LDCs, whose markets tend after all not to be dominated by large domestic enterprises as those in developed countries. For a discussion of FDI between LDCs, see Wells (1977).

14. A number of articles in this volume attempt to measure econometrically the relationship between the profitability of the MNC and barriers to entry. Though the factor of efficiency is not explicitly specified in these regressions, the results are nevertheless interesting in showing the significant correlation of these profits and barriers to entry.

References

Agmon, Tamir, and Donald Lessard, 1977. "Financial Factors and the International Expansion of Small-Country Firms," in T. Agmon and C. P. Kindleberger (eds.), *Multinationals from Small Countries*. Cambridge, Mass.: MIT Press.

Bergsten, C. Fred, Thomas Horst, and Theodore Moran, 1978. *American Multinationals and American Interests*, Washington, D.C.: Brookings.

Broyles, J. E., and I. A. Cooper, 1981. "Growth Opportunities and Real Investment Decisions," in F. G. L. Derkinderen and R. L. Crum (eds.), *Risk, Capital Costs, and Project Financing Decisions*. The Hague: Nijhoff.

Buckley, Peter J. and Mark Casson, 1976. *The Future of the Multinational Enterprise*. London: Holmes and Meier.

Davidson, William, 1980. "The Location of Foreign Direct Investment Activity: Country Characteristics and Experience Effects," *Journal of International Business Studies*, pp. 9–22.

Dunning, John H., 1977. "Trade, Location of Economic Activity and the MNE: A Search for an Eclectic Approach," in Bertil Ohlin et al. (eds.), *The International Allocation of Economic Activity*. London: Holmes and Meier.

———, 1979. "Explaining Changing Patterns of International Production: In Defense of the Eclectic Theory," *Oxford Bulletin of Economics and Statistics* 41, pp. 269–96.

————, 1981. "Explaining Outward Direct Investments of Developing Countries: In support of the Eclectic Theory of International Production," in *Multinationals from Developing Countries*. Lexington, Mass.: Maxwell G. McLeod.

Helleiner, Gerald K., 1979. "Transnational Corporations and Trade Structure: The Role of Intra-firm Trade," in H. Giersch (ed.), *On the Economics of Intra-Industry Trade*. Tübingen: J. C. B. Mohr.

Hirsch, Seev, 1976. "An International Trade and Investment Theory of the Firm," *Oxford Economic Papers* 28, pp. 258–270.

Hirschman, Albert O., 1970. *Exit, Voice, and Loyalty. Responses to Decline in Firms, Organizations, and States*, Cambridge, Mass.: Harvard University Press.

Katz, Jan Hack, 1981. "Does Foreign Direct Investment Theory Reflect Reality: The Case of the American Food Processors." Unpublished paper, October; to be published as a Sloan School of Management Working Paper, Massachusetts Institute of Technology.

Kindleberger, Charles P., 1969. *American Business Abroad: Six Lectures on Direct Investment*. New Haven: Yale University Press.

Lessard, Donald, 1976. "World, Country, and Industry Relations in Equity Returns: Implications for Risk Reduction through International Diversification," *Financial Analysts' Journal*, January/February, pp. 2–8.

————, 1979. "Transfer Prices, Taxes and Financial Markets: Implications of Internal Financial Transfers Within the Multinational Firm," in R. G. Hawkins (ed.), *Economic Issues of Multinational Firms*. New York: JAI Press.

————, 1980. "Evaluating International Projects: An Adjusted Present Value Approach," in R. Crum and F. Derkinderen (eds.), *Capital Budgeting Under Conditions of Uncertainty*. The Hague: Nijhoff.

McDonald, Robert, and Daniel Segal, 1981. "Options and the Valuation of Risky Projects," (unpublished paper), August, presented at the Finance Research Seminar of Sloan School of Management, Massachusetts Institute of Technology.

Magee, Stephan P., 1977. "Information and the Multinational Corporation: An Appropriability Theory of Direct Foreign Investment," in J. Bhagwati (ed.), *The New Economic Order: The North-South Debate*. Cambridge, Mass.: MIT Press.

Niehans, Juerg, 1977. "Benefits of Multinational Firms for a Small Parent Economy: The Case of Switzerland," in T. Agmon and C. P. Kindleberger (eds.), *Multinationals from Small Countries*. Cambridge, Mass.: MIT Press.

Robinson, Richard D., 1976. *National Control of Foreign Business Entry*. New York: Praeger.

Rugman, Alan M., 1980. "Internalization as a General Theory of Foreign Direct Investment: A Re-Appraisal of the Literature," *Weltwirtschaftliches Archiv* 116, pp. 365–79.

Solnik, Bruno H., 1974. "Why Not Diversify Internationally?", *Financial Analysts' Journal*, July-August, pp. 48–54.

Stopford, John, and Louis Wells, 1972. *Managing the Multinational Enterprise. Organization of the Firm and Ownership of the Subsidiaries*, New York: Basic Books.

Vernon, Raymond, 1971. *Sovereignty at Bay: The Multinational Spread of US Enterprises*. New York: Basic Books.

————, 1977. *Storm over the Multinationals: The Real Issues*. Cambridge, Mass.: Harvard University Press.

————, 1979. "The Product Cycle Hypothesis in a New International Environment," *Oxford Bulletin of Economics and Statistics* 41, pp. 255–267.

Wells, Louis, 1977. "Firms from Developing Countries," in T. Agmon and C. P. Kindleberger (eds.), *Multinationals from Small Countries*. Cambridge, Mass.: MIT Press.

3 The "New Theories" of International Trade and the Multinational Enterprise

Paul R. Krugman

I. Introduction

Ask a layperson what issues are interesting in international economics, and the answer will almost certainly include the role and effects of multinational enterprise. Yet the multinational firm has never been brought into the core of theoretical thinking in international economics. The theoretical models of trade, factor movements, and protection, which are the essence of standard trade theory, have no role for direct foreign investment. The multinational firm remains within the "penumbra" of international economic theory, one of those subjects, like the theory of international money, which is analyzed with educated guesswork and suggestive analogy rather than formal modeling.

The reason for this peripheral position is not hard to find. At the root of conventional models in international trade is the assumption of perfect competition; but any theory of the multinational firm must come to grips with imperfect competition. As Hymer and Kindleberger pointed out long ago, direct foreign investment must be a response to market failure. In essence the multinational firm provides a way of taking some transactions which the market does badly out of the market's province and placing then inside a hierarchical command economy. By and large, the market failures which can be corrected this way will involve oligopoly, bilateral monopoly, or some other breakdown in perfect competition. As an empirical observation, direct foreign investment generally occurs in oligopolistic markets. Thus a prerequisite to a formal model of multinational enterprise must be a tractable model of imperfect competition. Since this is hard to come by, until recently formal treatment of multinationals has seemed too hard to attempt.

In the last few years, however, a number of authors have begun to introduce imperfect competition into trade theory.[1] This development of "new theories" has in part been a response to growing dissatisfaction with standard theory, and growing doubt about the ability of conventional approaches to explain actual trade patterns. At least as important, however, has been the availability of new tools. Recent developments in theoretical industrial organization have provided a set of models—of monopolistic competition, of duopoly, of entry deterrence—that have proved easy and informative to apply to international trade.

The purpose of this paper is to use the same strategy—the borrowing of recent theory in industrial organization—to develop some simple theoretical models of multinational enterprise. The paper is in two parts, reflecting the observation of Caves (1971) that there are two main types of direct foreign investment: "horizontal" investment associated with product differentiation, and "vertical" foreign investment associated with backward integration into raw materials. Corresponding to this, the paper first presents a product differentiation model of DFI based on the recently developed theory of trade in differentiated products or "intra-industry" trade. Then an alternative model of DFI is presented in which vertical integration is the basic motivation; this model draws on the recent theory of monopsony and vertical integration developed by Perry (1978).

The models presented here are, of course, highly oversimplified representations of reality, and they undoubtedly miss many important considerations. They should be viewed as a first cut: an attempt to show that the theory of multinational enterprise can be made more formal, and integrated into the main body of trade theory.

II. A Product Differentiation Model

In recent years several models of trade have been developed that share certain basic features.[2] First, there are a large number of potential products that consumers would demand if offered. Second, there are fixed costs in production, so that the number of products actually produced is limited by the extent of the market. International trade creates a bigger market, so that firms can provide consumers with a greater variety of and/or cheaper products because of increased scale of production yielding lower average costs. Finally, the market structure is one of Chamberlinian monopolistic competition, with each firm a monopolist producing a differentiated product.

A slight twist on these models can convert them into models of multinational enterprise. Suppose that the fixed cost is not in production, but in R&D, interpreted broadly to include anything which creates a differentiated product. Then it need no longer be the case that each product will be produced in only one place. We will still have monopolistic competition among firms producing differentiated products, but each firm will be able to produce in a decentralized fashion—and, in particular, it can choose to produce abroad instead of exporting.

To develop this idea, we will begin by restating a simple model of trade in differentiated products which I have presented elsewhere (Krugman 1980), which in turn is based on the monopolistic competition model of Dixit and Stiglitz (1977). Then we modify the model slightly, turning it into a model of multinational firms. Simple (simplistic?) as the analysis is, it is enough to have some suggestive welfare implications, with which the section concludes.

A Model of Trade in Differentiated Products

Consider a world of two countries, Home and Foreign. Each country has only a single factor of production, which we will call labor. For simplicity, we will assume that the labor forces of the two countries are equal. Within each country labor can produce any of a large number of goods; because of fixed costs in production, however, not all goods will be produced. The technology of production is the same in both countries.

Consumers are assumed to have a taste for diversity; specifically, their tastes over the large number of potential products can be written as

$$U = \sum_i c_i^\theta, \qquad 0 < \theta < 1, \tag{1}$$

the same in both countries.

To produce a product requires a fixed start-up cost, with constant marginal cost thereafter. Thus the labor requirement for production of any good i is

$$l_i = \begin{cases} 0 & \text{if } x_i = 0 \\ \alpha + \beta x_i & \text{if } x_i > 0 \end{cases} \tag{2}$$

in both countries, where x_i is the output of good i. Both countries also face a full employment constraint,

$$\sum_i l_i = L. \tag{3}$$

Now in this model there is no comparative advantage, since the countries have identical tastes, technology, and factor endowments. Thus there are none of the usual reasons for trade. Further, we will assume that there are some costs to trade. Specifically, we will assume that there are transport costs of the "iceberg" type: whenever a good is shipped, part of it melts away en route, so that only a fraction g arrives.

In spite of this, there will still be trade and gains from trade. The reason is that the fixed costs prevent either country from producing the whole range of products, so the countries end by specializing in producing different things.

The market structure will be one of monopolist competition. First, consider the demand for any single product. The form of the utility function (1) implies a constant elasticity demand curve, with elasticity $1/(1 - \theta)$. Because of the type of transport costs assumed, this will also be true for export demand. Thus each firm will charge the profit-maximizing monopoly price given this elasticity,

$$p/w = \beta/\theta, \tag{4}$$

where w is the wage rate, which we use as numeraire. The price p is both the price on domestic sales and the f.o.b. export price. The symmetry of the countries assures that w will be the same in both; the symmetry of the products assures that p will be the same for all products actually produced.

The next question is the scale of production and the number of products actually produced. Entry will drive profits to zero, so that in equilibrium price will equal average cost. From (2) and (4) this means that the output of a representative product will be

$$x = \alpha\theta/[\beta(1 - \theta)]. \tag{5}$$

The full-employment constraint will then allow us to derive the actual number of products produced in each country,

$$n = L(1 - \theta)/\alpha. \tag{6}$$

What we have shown, then, is that each country will produce a distinct set of products, with all products produced at the same scale and sold at the same price. The output of each country can be regarded as a composite commodity; in effect, the two countries, though they start out identical, end by specializing in the production of two different goods.

The last remaining step is to determine the pattern of consumption and trade. It will be useful to think in terms of the composite commodities that the countries produce. Each country produces a composite of n differentiated products, with f.o.b. price p, and pays for the equivalent foreign composite the c.i.f. price $p = p/g$. The budget constraint is that spending on the two composites equal national income, or that

$$pC_h + \tilde{p}C_f = wL, \tag{7}$$

where C_h, C_f are domestic consumption of the home and foreign composites respectively. At the same time, the relative consumption of the two products will be determined by relative prices,

$$C_f/C_h = (\tilde{p}p)^{-1/(1-\theta)} \tag{8}$$
$$= g^{1/(1-\theta)}.$$

Thus the pattern of consumption in Home is determined in the way illustrated in figure 1. In Foreign, of course, the situation is a mirror image of what happens in Home.

Trade vs. Multinational Enterprise

A simple reinterpretation of the model we have just laid out suggests a theory of multinational enterprise. In the model the essential motivation for trade was the presence of fixed costs in production, which limited the variety of products any country could produce. Suppose now that we interpret these fixed costs as occurring not in production but in *development*. What we mean by this is that once the fixed cost has been incurred it need not be repeated even if production takes place in more than one location. The asset acquired by the fixed cost might be technology in the usual sense, or it might be less easily specified "know-how" in management, marketing, etc. The important assumption for our purposes is that the fixed costs are not tied to the location of production.

It is immediately apparent that this offers alternatives to trade in commodities. Foreign consumers can be provided with goods developed

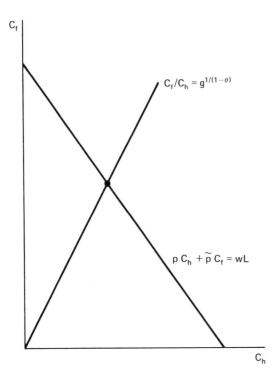

Figure 1

by domestic firms through exports; but they can also be supplied if the goods are produced abroad, either through licensing of the product to local producers or through the establishment of subsidaries. Note that this latter alternative is "direct foreign investment" only in the sense of establishing control; it is not a flow of capital, since there is no capital in the model!

We will rule out licensing of products by assumption. The reasons why licensing is relatively unimportant in practice have been extensively discussed, if not very carefully modeled, and lie outside the scope of our analysis. Caves (1971) offers a discussion which makes the main point, which is that the nature of product differentiation may not be tangible enough to specify in a contract.

There remains, then, the choice between production by overseas subsidiaries and export. The incentive to produce abroad is to avoid transportation costs—and tarriff barriers, as we will discuss below. If production abroad were as easy as production at home, it would clearly dominate trade in our model. However, it seems reasonable to suppose that there are also costs of overseas production. These may be due to unfamiliarity with language, customs, or legal system, or they may be due to the difficulty of controlling at a distance. Some of the costs of overseas operation are probably best modeled as fixed costs of entry, but for simplicity we will only consider those which raise average production costs. Specifically, let us assume that in foreign-controlled production labor is only a fraction k times as productive as it is in locally controlled production, so that for a firm producing both at home and abroad labor requirements are

$$l = \alpha + \beta x + (\beta/k)x',\tag{9}$$

where x' is production abroad.

It is immediately apparent what the consequence for trade will be. If $k > g$, so that it is cheaper to produce abroad than trade, trade in commodities will be replaced by direct foreign investment.

How should we view this latter situation? Nothing material is being traded, yet some kind of trade is going on—and it is a trade which the countries find mutually beneficial. It is easy to show that if there are no taxes on trade, the move from trade to multinational enterprise raises welfare in both countries; the budget constraint is shifted out to

$$pC_h + (p/k)C_f = wL,\tag{10}$$

which lies outside the budget line without multinationals. But what kind of trade produces these gains?

There are two answers here. First, in an accounting sense what we would see is that the countries trade in *services*; that is, each country's firms are earning profits in the other country, and the balance of payments would show equal and opposite entries in this line of the service account. In an economic sense, however, the countries are basically trading *information*. Each country has incurred the cost of developing a number of products; this is what enables its firms to collect from producing abroad. By allowing each other's firms to establish subsidiaries, the countries provide a channel for trading this information.

There is an interesting parallel between the view of trade and foreign investment here and Mundell's (1957) famous interpretation of factor proportions theory. As Mundell pointed out, in the Heckscher-Ohlin model what countries really want to trade is factor services, reflecting their different endowments. They can do this either by actual movement of factors or by trade in goods produced with different factor proportions. Which route is taken depends on the incentives: transportation costs or tariffs tend to promote factor mobility instead of trade; barriers to the movement of capital and labor push the world toward trade instead of factor movements.

In our model, countries want to trade because they have acquired different technologies, taking the form of the knowledge of how to produce different products. They can trade this knowledge either directly, through technology transfer within multinational firms (or by licensing, except that we have ruled this out); or they can trade it indirectly, through trade in commodities embodying their special technological advantages. The choice of method depends on the costs; transport costs encourage direct technology transfer, costs of multinational operation promote trade.

The "product differentiation" model suggests, then an interpretation of multinational enterprises as vehicles for trade in information. Trade and multinational enterprise are substitutes, just as trade and factor mobility are substitutes in the Heckscher-Ohlin model. As we argue in section III, however, this is not the only possible model of multinational firms; and as we will see, in a "vertical integration" model trade and multinational enterprise will be complements rather than substitutes.

Tariffs and Multinationals

We have just seen that barriers to trade can cause technology to be traded through direct foreign investment rather than embodied in exports. If the barriers to trade are natural, i.e., represent transport costs, this is beneficial. But what if multinational enterprise is a way of leaping over tariff barriers? Is it still a good thing?

Again there is a parallel with the factor proportions model which suggests that harm may result. Diaz-Alejandro and Brecher (1977) have shown that in the presence of a tariff foreign capital inflow can easily lead to reduced real income. Similarly, if direct foreign investment is caused by a tariff it may cost more in reduced tariff revenue than it is worth.

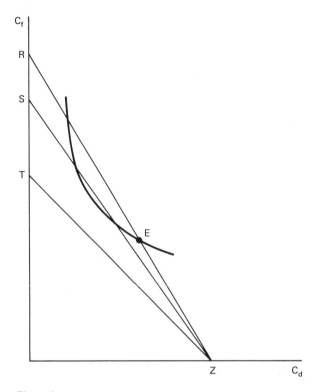

Figure 2

Suppose that in the absence of tariffs trade would dominate multinational enterprise: $k < g$. Suppose, however, that both countries have ad valorem tariff rate of t, sufficient to make multinational operation worthwhile: $k(1 + t) > g$. Then trade will be displaced by direct foreign investment.

The results are illustrated in figure 2. Before multinational operation is allowed, the budget constraint for each economy is

$$pC_h + (p/g)C_f = wL. \tag{11}$$

Consumption choices are distorted by the tariff, however, so that consumption is at a point like E, where the slope of the indifference curve II is flatter than that of the social budget line RZ.

What multinational enterprise does is, first, to shrink in the budget line to

$$pC_h + (p/k)C_f = wL. \tag{12}$$

At the same time, however, it removes the consumption distortion. Whether the net result is a gain or a loss depends on whether the new budget line contains points above II, like SZ, or lies entirely below it, like TZ. Obviously, the higher the tariff rate and the less the production inefficiency the more likely it is that multinational enterprise will be a good thing.

III. A "Vertical Integration" Model

In section II, we developed a model of "horizontal" multinationals, producing the same product in different countries. The other important form of multinational enterprise is the firm which is vertically integrated, controlling different stages of a production process which takes place in different countries.

Before proceeding to the model, it is worth noticing that there are two quite different kinds of vertical multinationals. One kind is the manufacturing firm with a marketing-and-distribution subsidiary. This is very common, and about half of US imports are transactions between such "related parties" rather than arms-length market transactions. But the employment and capital invested in such subsidiaries is fairly small. The other kind of vertical multinational is the refining or processing firm which controls its foreign sources of raw materials. This is a much more important type of integration, and it is on this that we will focus.

In modeling vertical integration, we will draw on the industrial organization literature on the subject. This literature falls into two parts. On one side is an informal and insightful, but not too rigorous, literature that attempts to explain why some transactions are mediated by markets while others take place within hierarchical organizations.

On the other side are formal models that pinpoint particular market failures. While recognizing the importance of studying the deeper questions, we will limit ourselves here to a model of the second type: Perry's (1978) model of vertical integration due to monopsony.

The Model's Assumptions

Consider a single industry, producing a single product, say kryptonite. Kryptonite is produced in a number of "mines", production units which are characterized by increasing marginal cost:

$$C_i = f_i(q_i); \quad f_i' > 0, \quad f_i'' > 0, \tag{13}$$
$$i = 1, \ldots, \mathrm{n},$$

where C_i is the cost of operating the ith mine, and q_i the output of that mine.

Raw kryptonite cannot be used directly. It must first be processed. We will assume that there is a single monopolistic firm which does this, and that it has processing costs

$$C_0 = \alpha + \beta Q_0, \tag{14}$$

where Q_0 is the quantity it processes, and

$$Q_0 = \sum_i q_i. \tag{15}$$

To make this a model of international trade, we assume that at least some of the mines are located in one country, called South, and that the demand for processed kryptonite lies in another country; call it North. Further, let us assume that processing must take place in North, so that to the extent that mining and processing are to be done by the same firm it must be multinational.

Demand for the processed product will be represented by a demand function relating price to deliveries:

$$P_F = D(Q_0). \tag{16}$$

Now consider the position of the processing firm. We will start from a situation where the industry is partly vertically integrated; the case of no vertical integration is just a special case of this. The processing firm also owns some of the mines: $1, \ldots, m$. Mines $m + 1, \ldots, n$ remain independent, and their output must be bought on the open market at a price P_I. The supply curve of the independents gives us P_I as an increasing function of purchases Q_I:

$$P_I = S(Q_I) \tag{17}$$

The multinational firm wants to maximize its profits, which are given by

$$\Pi = P_F Q_0 - \alpha - \beta Q_0 - \sum_{i=1}^{m} f_i(q_i) - P_I Q_I \tag{18}$$

subject to $\sum_{i=1}^{m} q_i + Q_I = Q_0$.

The first-order conditions are that

$$P_F + D'Q_0 - \beta = P_I + S'Q_I \tag{19}$$

$$= f_i, \qquad i = 1, \ldots, m.$$

These conditions have simple economic interpretations. The expression on the left is what we might call the "net marginal revenue" — marginal revenue net of processing costs. This must equal marginal cost of production for all the mines the firm controls. It must also equal the marginal cost *to the firm* of supply from the independents. But this is more than the price, because any attempt to increase purchases will increase the price on inframarginal sales. It is this wedge that will provide an incentive to extend vertical integration.

The profit-maximizing solution is illustrated graphically in figure 3. The line NMR is the processing firm's net marginal revenue schedule. MC is the marginal cost of supplies from owned mines. $MC + MC_I$ is the "social" marginal cost schedule, treating owned and independent mines alike. Finally, $MC + MC_I$ is the supply schedule the firm sees itself as facing. It lies above the social marginal cost schedule because of the monopsony effect: the firm realizes that purchases of independent output cost more than just the market price.

The result is that total output is Q_0^1, with net marginal revenue of MC^1 equal to marginal costs of production in owned mines. The marginal cost production in independent mines, however, is set equal to the market price P_I^1, which is lower than MC^1. And in this lies the incentive for integration.

The incentive to integrate

The essential explanation of the existence of vertically integrated multinationals must be that the profits of the vertically integrated firm will be larger than the combined profits of independent upstream and

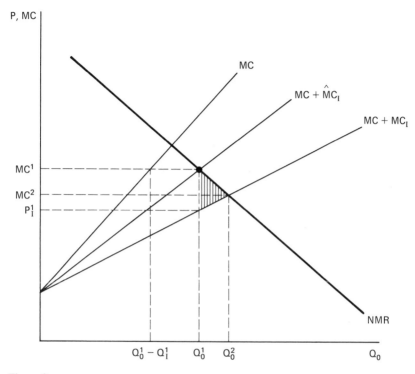

Figure 3

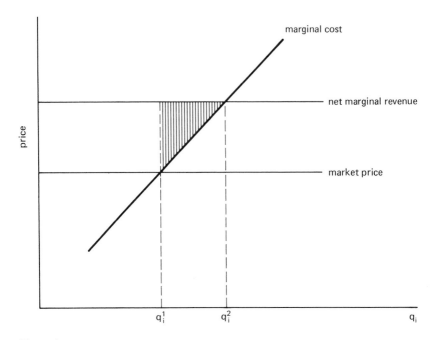

Figure 4

downstream firms. In our model this means that we must show that
each mine is worth more to the processing firm than it would be worth
to an independent owner.

Consider, for simplicity, a mine which is "small" in the sense that
its acquisition by the multinational will have negligible effects on both
net marginal revenue and the market price of kryptonite. The situation
of such a mine is illustrated in figure 4. We show the mine's marginal
cost curve and the levels of the market price and of net marginal
revenue. If the mine is privately owned it will be operated at the level
of production q_i^1 where price equals marginal cost. If owned by the
multinational, however, production will be raised until marginal cost
equals the shadow price of the mine's output, which is net marginal
revenue. There will be a net gain in the combined profits of the mine
and the multinational, equal to the shaded area in the figure.

The source of these gains is the correction of the monopsony distortion.
By holding down the price paid to independent mines, the multinational
leads them to produce too little. Once it need not worry that buying

more from a mine will raise the prices it pays, the vertically integrated firm can correct this distortion and appropriate the efficiency gains.

What happens when this process is completed is illustrated in figure 3 by the equilibrium at MC^2, Q_0^2. Vertical integration allows an increase in output from previously independent mines, serving partly to allow reduced output from already owned mines, reducing costs, and allowing also a profitable expansion in total output.

What we have just done is to show that monopsony provides an incentive for vertical integration. Since the different stages of production are assumed to be located in different countries, the result is multinational enterprise. In its effects, this kind of direct foreign investment is quite different from the product differentiation discussed in our first model. Instead of serving as a substitute for trade, DFI here encourages it; after the monopsony distortion is removed, output from the mines in South and thus exports to North are larger than before.

It should also be noted that the motivation for multinational enterprise comes out clearly here in a static model without uncertainty. It is sometimes argued, e.g., by Caves and Jones (1981), that vertically integrated multinationals are essentially created to reduce uncertainty. This may be true in practice, but the theory of vertical integration does not necessarily require uncertainty. Perhaps what is meant is that monopsony power only becomes important when capacity constraints are hit, an unpredictable occurrence; but it is still the monopsony power rather than the uncertainty which is the crucial element.

IV. Summary and Conclusions

This paper has presented two models of multinational enterprise in the spirit of the "new theories" of international trade. The basic innovation of the "new theories" has been to borrow models for studying the international economy from industrial organization rather than solely from competitive general equilibrium theory. The result of this innovation has been to allow imperfect competition into trade theory; we here have followed the same approach, and taken two simple models from industrial organization and applied them to international investment.

The first model attempts to explain "horizontal" multinationals as a response to product differentiation. Firms, by R&D spending, acquire the ability to manufacture different products; they can then export this technology either directly by establishing foreign subsidiaries or indirectly by embodying the technology in goods. Which route they take depends on economic incentives, incentives which may be distorted by tariffs.

The second model attempts to explain "vertical" multinationals using a standard model of vertical integration. A monopsonistic "downstream" firm keeps the price of its raw material down, but by so doing distorts the production decisions of its overseas suppliers, leading them to produce too little. By going multinational and integrating backward, the firm can eliminate the distortion and appropriate the efficiency gain.

Needless to say, these are very simplified, stylized models. They do not capture any of the richness of detail involved in real decisions to create multinational firms. On the other hand, models of this kind offer at least the possibility of discussing multinational enterprise with something like the clarity with which we discuss, say, comparative advantage. For a long time direct foreign investment has been a subject area in which anything goes; the typical trade textbook—or trade course—is rigorous and model-oriented until it reaches multinationals, then suddenly becomes a mixture of anecdote and loose, if valuable, insight. The main moral of this paper is that this need not continue to be the case. Once we are prepared to put imperfect markets into our models, we can use models to analyze problems which involve imperfect markets.

Notes

1. Recent contributions include Dixit and Norman (1980), Lancaster (1980), Helpman (1981), Brander (1981), Brander and Spencer (1981), Krugman (1980), and Ethier (1982).

2. This model is very similar in spirit to Feenstra and Judd (forthcoming), except that they assume that (i) technology is transferred through licensing, not DFI, and (ii) one country has a "comparative advantage" in innovation.

References

Brander, J., 1981. "Intra-Industry Trade in Identical Commodities," *Journal of International Economics* 11, 1–14.

Brander, J., and B. Spencer, 1981. "Tariffs and the Extraction of Foreign Monopoly Rents under Potential Entry," *Canadian Journal of Economics* 14, 371–389.

Brecher, R., and C. Diaz-Alejandro, 1977. "Tariffs, Foreign Capital and Immiserizing Growth," *Journal of International Economics* 7, 317–322.

Caves, R., 1971. "International Corporations: The Industrial Economics of Foreign Investment," *Economica* 38, 1–27.

Dixit, A., and V. Norman, 1980. *Theory of International Trade*. London: Cambridge University Press.

Ethier, W., 1982. "National and International Returns to Scale in the Modern Theory of International Trade," *American Economic Review* 72, 389–405.

Feenstra, R., and K. Judd (forthcoming). "Tariffs, Technology Transfer, and Welfare," *Journal of Political Economy*.

Helpman, E., 1981. "International Trade in the Presence of Product Differentiation, Economies of Scale, and Monopolistic Competition," *Journal of International Economics* 11, 305–40.

Krugman, P., 1980. "Scale Economies, Product Differentiation, and the Pattern of Trade," *American Economic Review* 70, 950–959.

Lancaster, K., 1980. "Intra-Industry Trade under Perfect Monopolistic Competition," *Journal of International Economics* 10, 151–175.

Perry, M., 1978. "Vertical Integration: The Monopsony Case," *American Economic Review* 68, 561–570.

II Industrial Organization and International Markets

4 Foreign Market Operations and Domestic Market Power

K. Celeste Gaspari

I. Summary

While traditional industrial organization theory has established that foreign investment and oligopolistic power go hand in hand, it has not been established how (or even if) oligopolistic power is affected by foreign investment. Since foreign operations provide an opportunity for the pooling of market risks, vertical integration, sharing of research and development technology, and advertising costs, as well as an additional tax advantage, the benefits from such positions can be used to strengthen domestic market positions. Taking into account these feedback effects from the foreign market indicates that traditional industrial organization theory has overcredited the importance of domestic barriers to entry by ignoring the role played by foreign investment.

These advantages, except for vertical integration, are enjoyed by both multinational corporations and domestic firms engaged in exporting. This work addresses the following question: Do foreign market operations themselves constitute a separate and significant barrier to entry in the domestic market? This problem is analyzed with two data sets. The first uses 75 IRS minor industries disaggregated into asset class divisions. The second set relies on IRS firm level data for 1974.

The results from regressions on both data sets indicate that export activity has a consistently strong impact on domestic profitability while foreign investment activity has an insignificant impact on domestic profitability. Traditional industrial organization studies that omit the impact of foreign operations on domestic profitability are misspecified; foreign market operations, specifically export operations, are the result of domestic elements of industrial structure and are themselves a determinant of domestic market power.

II. Introduction

The year 1971 saw the United States both as holding an overvalued currency and as a country steadily accumulating a large balance of payments deficit. To ameliorate the situation, Congress passed the Domestic International Sales Corporation (DISC) legislation as a way of promoting exports and discouraging the rising tide of foreign direct investment. The DISC program was seen as a means to partially offset certain features of the United States[1] and foreign tax system that tend to favor foreign production by US firms over production in the United States for sale abroad.

After 4 years of DISC operation, the (1975) statistics showed that large corporations were overwhelmingly reaping the benefits of the DISC program. Further inspection of these large beneficiaries showed that this program, aimed at promoting exports and discouraging foreign direct investment, was benefiting US multinational corporations.

At the same time Horst (1975) posed and found support for the hypothesis that multinational investments are not only profitable in their own right, but they lead to higher profits for the domestic parent. He estimated a simple recursive system[2] that (1) captures the traditional industrial organization causation between the firm's foreign investment levels and the elements of domestic industry structure; and (2) explains a firm's market performance in terms of conventional industrial organization variables and the level of foreign investment.

The traditional barriers to entry explanation of domestic profitability could now be viewed as the sum of two components: (1) the effect such barriers may have directly on domestic profitability; and (2) the effect such barriers have on foreign investment activity and then the effect of foreign investment activity on domestic profitability. The indirect effect of these various barriers to entry were found to be substantial.

Thus policies such as DISC, which primarily affect the foreign operations of US firms could also have spillover effects on US domestic market structure. Could export activity also be a cause of domestic market power? Could a program such as DISC have an unexpected cost in reducing competitive forces within the US economy? The overwhelming evidence of this study supports the hypothesis that export activity does indeed contribute to a firm's domestic market power.

III. Underlying Ideology: Prior Works

While few industrial organization works have addressed any aspect of foreign investment's effect on domestic profitability, two works that have, those by Benjamin Cohen (1972) and Alan Severn and Martin Laurence (1973), have lent credence to the above causal pattern. Cohen, in a study of American domestic corporations, found that fluctuations in earnings and sales were reduced for those corporations with foreign investment and concluded that foreign investment provided American firms with an effective way of stabilizing operations. Multinational operations enable the firm to smooth out such fluctuations through diversification; thus multinational firms gain a financial (stability) advantage over purely domestic firms.

Severn and Laurence found that foreign investors tended to spend more (on research and development) and earn more than firms without substantial investments abroad; foreign investment allows firms to spread research and development costs over a larger base.

More obvious industrial organization arguments have been advanced by Bain (1956) and Caves (1971). Bain divided barriers to entry into three classes: economies of scale; absolute cost advantages; and product differentiation advantages. In the first two of these categories, the multinational firm has distinct advantages over its purely domestic counterpart; advantages associated with product differentiation accrue to both the domestic and multinational firms equally. Since multinational firms are consistently the larger firms within an industry,[3] they enjoy various economies of scale as well as often being vertically integrated. Other cost advantages arise in the tax advantages the multinational firm enjoys through unrepatriated income, a range of options for computing its tax and the practice of transfer pricing.

In short, there are multiple opportunities for the firm to cut costs and establish various barriers to entry which are open to the firm that changes its operations from one of purely domestic to multinational. Hymer (1960), in fact, empirically demonstrated that such entry barriers provide a necessary basis for foreign expansion.

Hypothesis

These same barriers to entry aspects of multinational investment—the pooling of risks, sharing of costs of advertising, R&D, and technology—are also aspects of exporting.[4] The hypothesis posed in this paper is two-fold. First, elements of domestic market structure provide a basis for a firm's foreign market operations. Second, domestic firms engaged in foreign market operations, be they in the form of foreign investment activities or export operations, are twice blessed in that they receive profits from the foreign operations and these foreign operations indirectly increase domestic profits and enhance domestic market performance.

The testing of these two hypotheses allows a three-way separation of the roles played by elements of domestic market structure on the firm's domestic profitability:

1. the barrier to entry effect on the firm's foreign operations;
2. the barrier to entry effect on the firm's purely domestic profitability; and
3. the effect of the firm's foreign operations on its purely domestic profitability.

Model

The above hypothesis can be econometrically tested employing the following simultaneous equation model:

$$D = D(A, S, R\&D, H, MES, MDd, X, F), \tag{1}$$

$$X = X(A, S, R\&D, H, MES, TRANS, F), \tag{2}$$

$$F = F(A, S, R\&D, H, MES, VI, X), \tag{3}$$

where

A = advertising/sales,

S = log(10) total assets,

$R\&D$ = (scientists + engineers)/total employment,

H = the Herfindahl measure of seller concentration,

MES = a measure of minimum efficient scale,

MDd = a measure of per year market growth in the domestic market,

$TRANS$ = the mile radius within which 80% of an industry's shipments travel,

VI = a dummy variable to measure vertical integration,

D = a measure of domestic profitability,

X = a measure of export activity,

F = a measure of foreign investment activity.

Description and sources of the exogenous variables are given in the appendix (section IX); the endogenous variables are explained below.

IV. Hypothesized Relations

The following independent variables are hypothesized to be barriers to entry. An additional hypothesis is also tested: that the foreign and domestic market do not share the same barriers to entry.

Advertising

While Bain (1956) emphasized the barrier to new competition role played by advertising only with respect to domestic markets, the foreign operations of the firm can benefit in the same manner. To the extent that a firm exports or engages in foreign investment of consumer (rather than producer) products (Comanor and Wilson, 1969) advertising is seen as being a barrier to entry in foreign market operations. Thus, advertising is expected to positively affect a firm's domestic profitability, export activity, and foreign investment activities.

R&D

The importance of R&D as a determinant of a firm's foreign market operations is seen in the "New Trade Theories" literature. Gruber, Mehta, and Vernon (1967) found that US export performance was highly correlated with industrial R&D effort, which was in turn correlated with high seller concentration, large firm size, and the tendency to invest abroad. Vernon's product cycle (1966) emphasized the role of technological innovation and standardization in the decision to invest abroad. The impacts of R&D are posited to be positive on exporting and foreign investment activities and for domestic profitability.

Size

In broad, inter-industry studies, size is expected to affect profits "[S]ince large firms have (financial) access to a wider range of industries (some of which require a large financial commitment 'up front') than small and may be expected to invest in those industries with high prospective profits" (Weiss, No. 246). The advantage of size is expected to carry over to the export market.

Size has been established to be a significant factor in explaining the propensity to invest abroad in an intra-industry study by Horst (1972); across industries size was not an explanatory factor for foreign investment. Thus, multinationals are posited to be the largest firms in their particular industry, but they need not be the largest firms across all industries. Likewise, the coefficient on size need not be significant in the foreign investment equation.

Herfindahl

The classical hypothesis of monopoly dealt with profits (Bain, 1956); profit rates and collusion would increase as concentration became more successful. Both Hymer (1960) and Knickerbocker (1973) established that the level of industry concentration would also play a key role in determining who would invest abroad. They showed that multinationals were concentrated in oligopolistic industries, keenly aware of market shares, and likely to follow a chainlike reaction of foreign investment activity begun by rivals. In highly concentrated industries, expansion by one firm in the domestic, export, or foreign markets is likely to be viewed as an attempt to reapportion market shares. Thus, industry concentration should be significantly and positively related to domestic profitability, export activity, and foreign investment activity.

MES

Economies of scale may permit established firms to maintain artificially high price-cost margins without attracting new competition (Bain, 1956). Thus, *MES* imparts a positive effect on domestic profitability. Firms that engage in export activity (rather than foreign investment activity) should be characterized by high *MES*, captured by a single-plant production process, and are thus seeking an additional market for this high level of production.

MDd, TRANS, VI

Each market is also affected by influences which are unique to that market.

Market growth is considered to be an important measure of demand-side influences. While its overall effect on the price level is indeterminate, an increase in market demand should have an important positive influence on the profit rates of firms operating in the market.

Whether or not a firm exports is in part a function of the good that the firm produces. If the firm produces a good that has only local appeal, is highly perishable, or is bulky, i.e., has a low value/weight ratio, then it cannot export the good. The transportability variable controls for this aspect of the good.

One of the explanations of foreign investment is that firms desire to control their entire production process. US firms are likely to invest abroad in order to extract some natural resource used intensively in their domestic product, and to assure more certain access to it at favorable terms. Thus, vertical integration in the natural resource industries may be a strong motivation to invest abroad.

The type of interaction that exists between exports and foreign investment is also of interest as one could view exporting and investing abroad as alternative ways of servicing the foreign market. Although the question of complementarity or substitutability between export and foreign investment activity will not be directly addressed in this work (Gaspari, 1980) the existence of an option to the firm of servicing the foreign market through either or both is captured in the simultaneity of the model.

V. Variable Description

The following variables were created for two data sets: the 1965–1971 asset-class IRS data and the 1974 firm-level IRS data. Differences in the levels of aggregation, as well as differences in the availability of specific pieces of data made it necessary to change the forms of some variables between the data sets; such changes will be noted.

Domestic Profitability

1965-1971 Typically domestic profitability is measured by a firm's net income plus interest paid on debt as a rate of return on total assets. The inclusion of interest paid on debt in the net income figure captures a rate of return on resources available to the firm while correcting for distortions occurring in interfirm comparisons of profit rates resulting from different degrees of leverage.

The choice of the appropriate rate of return for the 1965–1971 data was predetermined by data availability to be the traditional measure of domestic profitability,[5] i.e., the pre-tax rate of return on assets. One objection to the use of this measure of profitability is its inclusion of foreign dividends and tax credits (the foreign investment proxy) and export profits, which make domestic profitability highly correlated correlated with both the foreign investment and export activity proxies. To eliminate such correlations both foreign dividends and tax credits and export profits[6] were subtracted from domestic net income plus interest on debt.[7]

Domestic profitability is measured as:

(1/parent's assets)

  × [(domestic sales)/domestic sales + export sales)

  × (net income before tax + interest paid)

  − (foreign dividends + foreign tax credits)].

Thus, the measure of a firm's domestic profitability is based on a firm's net income from only its domestic operations.

1974 Hall and Weiss (1971) have argued that the rate of return on equity is the appropriate measure of a firm's profitability on the grounds that managers would seek to maximize this rate of return rather than that based on total capital.

The 1974 micro data set made available sufficient information to allow construction of the preferred measure of domestic profitability,[8] i.e., the rate of return on equity plus long-term debt after tax. Due to differences in leverage, managerial ability (at tax avoidance) and industry-specific tax breaks, firms do not face the same effective rate of taxation. In a world of imperfect competition and immobility of capital the after-tax rates of return differ because of the immobility of capital; these differences are explained by industrial-organization variables.

For the 1974 data set,[9]

domestic profitability = (1/parent's equity + long-term debt)

$\times$ [(net income before tax + interest paid) − taxes paid

− $(1 - t) \times$ foreign dividends − foreign tax credits

− DISC actual distributions to parents

− $(1 - t) \times$ (DISC income to related suppliers)

+ $t \times$ (DISC deemed distributions to parents)

+ (gross export receipts/total business receipts) $\times$ cost of

production],

where t = effective tax rate. Note that net income[10] from foreign operations, is subtracted from the total net income of the parent to arrive at a measure of net domestic income.

Foreign Investment Proxy

For the hypothesis advanced in this study, the firm's measure of its foreign investment stock deflated by the parent firm's total assets would be an ideal measure of the firm's foreign investment position. Since this data is unavailable, the proxy used in this study is the product of the following three terms: (1) foreign investment/parent's assets; (2) the rate of return realized on this foreign investment; and (3) the dividend payout ratio.[11] What this product yields therefore is the foreign dividends of the parent, i.e., the repatriated profits from the foreign investments. Specifically the proxy is

$$\frac{\text{foreign dividends (from controlled foreign corporations)} + \text{foreign tax credits}}{\text{parent's assets}}.$$

The proxy for the 1974 data base is virtually identical to the above except for the addition in the numerator of includable income of controlled corporations.[12]

Export Activity

While data for the foreign investment proxy is available at the industry-size class level, data for the export activity variable is available only at the 4-digit SIC level. The export literature (Cavusgil, 1976; Bilkey and Tesar, 1976; Hirsch and Lev, 1974; and Hirsch and Adar, 1974), strongly supports the allocation of industry exports on the basis of firm size and sales.[13] This need not be a proportional allocation based on a firm's share of its industry's output.

Based on this export literature, the method of allocating an industry's exports to each of the industry-size class divisions is

$$X_{ij} = \left| \frac{\text{firm sales } i_j}{\sum_k \text{firm sales } j} \right|^{1/2} \left| \frac{\text{firm assets } i_j}{\sum_k \text{firm assets } j} \right|^{1/2} \times X_j,$$

where

X_{ij} = exports for asset-class i, in industry j,

k = number of asset-classes for industry j,

x_j = total exports for industry j.

The major advantage of the 1974 micro data set was the availability of firm-level export data from the annual DISC tax return, form 1120-DISC. This yields a firm-level proxy for export activity for the 1974 data set:

gross export receipts/parent's assets.[14]

VI. Data

The regression results cover three data sets. The first is the 1965–1971 asset-size class data for the full sample of US manufacturing firms. This data was obtained from the IRS Sourcebook of Statistics on Income-Corporations, which contains individual firm returns of US large corporations and a large sample of smaller firms. The number of observations varies over the years due to the change in the number of asset classes reporting income within an industry, as well as a change in the number of asset classes defined by the IRS.

The second set of data consists of the 1965–1971 asset-size class data for the "giant" US manufacturing firms; this sample included those firms with over \$250 million total assets. This data set presented problems of heteroskedasticity with respect to the F and D variables. Examination of the F variables indicated that they were highly skewed and asymmetric with the larger firms accounting for substantial foreign investment receipts, while the majority of firms, the smaller ones, possessed virtually none. A simple solution is to use $F^{1/a}$ rather than F, where a is greater than zero and chosen to best eliminate the problem;[15] $F^{1/2}$ was chosen as the best value over other nonlinear transformations.

For the D variable, the standard deviation of the residual varied inversely with the asset class's share of its industry's total assets. The simplest remedy to correct for this heteroskedasticity is to apply the weighted least squares method of estimation where the observations for each asset class were weighted in proportion to the class's contribution to its industry's total assets. The weight employed is $w_i = S_{ij}/S_i$ for group j in industry i, where S = total assets.

The third data set employed was the 1974 firm-level data. Since this data represented individual IRS returns, the majority of the firms have no export or investment receipts. Thus, in terms of the above simultaneous model, one or two of the dependent variables has a zero value. One method of dealing with a truncated dependent variable is to limit the sample to a subsample where the values of the dependent variables are greater than zero by sampling on a variable related to these zero-valued dependent variables. Such a subsample of 150 manufacturing firms was obtained by sampling on the size of total assets. This constituted the "giants" subsample of US manufacturing firms for 1974 of firms with assets over \$1 billion.

The question of generality of the model arises with respect to the 1974 "giant" data. To test this, the reduced form of the domestic profitability equation was estimated for the subsample of "giant" firms, the subsample of non-giant firms, and the sample of total firms. The results of the multiple F-tests (see Gaspari, 1979 for details) indicated that the two samples did not arise from the same population. The same multiple F-tests were constructed for the 1965–1971 data and again the "giant" and "non-giant" corporations were seen as arising from different populations. Results therefore will be given for three distinct populations.

Because the system of simultaneous equations contains both exactly identified as well as overidentified equations, the two-stage least squares instrumental variables method was employed.

VII. Results

Differences often distinguish the 1974 results from the 1965–1971 results. In specific instances a time-series explanation will be offered, but the frequency of such differences prompted a closer inspection of the 1974 "giant" subsample. This inspection involved a comparison of the 1974 "giants" to the 1965–1971 "giants" and to the 1965–1971 full sample. Such differences add support to Porter's (1974) hypothesis (see also Caves and Pugel, 1979) that the determinants of companies' profits rest on the structure within industries as well as on industry-wide traits of market structure.

As table 1 indicates, advertising, firm size, and R&D have a positive and significant impact on export activity and foreign investment activity over the 1965–1971 period. For the majority of the years, the Herfindahl index has a positive significant impact while MES is negative and significant. The activity-specific variables, both $TRANS$ and VI, performed erratically, being positive significant for only 4 years. The two foreign market operations appeared to share the same determinants of market structure.

The determinants of domestic profitability, however, differ substantially from the foreign operations' determinants. Firm size and advertising were positive and significant in only 4 years, and $R\&D$ had a negative, significant coefficient in 5 of the years. MES and MDd played a significant positive role for the majority of the years. There are indeed significant differences between the elements of domestic industry structure as incentives to operate abroad (either foreign investment or export) and as barriers to new domestic competition. Only advertising and size play generally significant positive roles in the foreign and domestic market; their role is more consistent in the foreign market than in the domestic. $R\&D$ and MES play opposite roles in the two markets; $R\&D$ provides a barrier to entry in foreign operations (a source of comparative advantage in exporting and a source of internationalization advantages in foreign investment activity) but is a handicap in the domestic market. MES is significant for more years in the foreign equations, but it detracts from these foreign activities, while it plays a predictable role in the domestic operation.

The "Giant" Subsample

As stated above, the 1974 results are often distinguished from the 1965–1971 results.

Advertising and MDd positively affected the 1974 "giants" domestic operations while $R\&D$ once again had a negative impact. The only significant coefficient in the foreign market operation equations was a positive coefficient on size in the foreign investment equation.

The 1965–1971 "giant" subsample yielded different results. Domestic profitability was positively affected by Herfindahl (4 years), MES (3 years), and advertising (3 years) and negatively by $R\&D$ (2 years). Advertising, size, and $R\&D$ again have significant positive coefficients in the foreign operation equations, but for fewer years than in the full sample. The only barrier to entry commonly shared by the "giant" domestic and foreign markets is advertising.

Some of the above results warrant closer inspection.

Advertising   The role played by advertising in 1974 differs from its 1965–1971 role. From 1965–1971 for both the full samples and giant subsample advertising was a barrier to entry in foreign and domestic markets; by 1974 advertising advantages had been neutralized (in the case of foreign investment) or almost negated (in the case of exporting). This coincides with the international trade climate of 1974 when exports of consumer goods increased very little, in contrast to the exports of foodstuff and raw materials, which increased markedly over their 1973 levels.

R&D   The R&D results for the 1965–1971 "giant" subsample are the same as those for the full sample. The negative impact of R&D on domestic profitability is supported by the 3 sets of data, but the 1974 results are insignificant for export and foreign investment. Since it is improbable that between 1971 and 1974 there was a shift from high to low R&D industries engaged in foreign operations, there is strong suspicion that highly intensive R&D industries retained their earnings abroad and thus decreased their dividend repatriation over this period. This would adversely affect the foreign investment proxy.

Size   Although the role of firm size as a barrier to entry is firmly established in traditional industrial organization literature, this role was only observed for the 1965–1971 sample in the foreign market oper-

Table 1
Cross-section regression across asset size.

Year		Constant	Advertising	Size	R&D	Herfindahl
1965 (547)	D	−0.0004 (−0.118)	0.984 (2.14)	0.023 (1.97)	0.076 (0.32)	0.139 (2.49)
	X	−0.001 (−0.149)	1.32 (1.14)	0.003 (0.12)	2.41 (4.83)	0.473 (3.58)
	F	−0.003 (−5.75)	0.568 (7.03)	0.014 (11.23)	0.26 (2.71)	0.042 (1.32)
1966 (704)	D	0.0025 (1.08)	0.259 (0.208)	0.004 (0.278)	−0.608 (−4.32)	0.076 (0.53)
	X	−0.012 (−2.57)	8.11 (4.29)	0.070 (2.99)	0.61 (1.55)	0.87 (3.89)
	F	−0.002 (−4.00)	1.07 (13.04)	0.010 (10.25)	0.045 (0.79)	0.108 (5.59)
1967 (638)	D	0.004 (2.95)	0.149 (0.264)	−0.001 (−0.230)	−0.562 (−2.13)	0.151 (2.66)
	X	−0.017 (−3.09)	8.17 (4.20)	0.063 (3.46)	3.70 (5.19)	0.652 (2.52)
	F	−0.002 (−5.77)	1.12 (13.50)	0.009 (8.71)	0.462 (7.21)	0.090 (3.06)
1968 (641)	D	0.0015 (1.39)	0.188 (0.280)	0.011 (2.88)	−1.47 (−2.40)	−0.077 (−0.679)
	X	−0.003 (−2.39)	2.96 (9.04)	0.012 (2.83)	2.19 (14.60)	0.432 (7.34)
	F	−0.002 (−3.80)	1.33 (14.65)	0.006 (5.17)	0.87 (9.15)	0.165 (5.66)
1969 (727)	D	0.002 (2.34)	0.616 (3.25)	0.005 (1.63)	−0.291 (−2.69)	−0.070 (−1.22)
	X	−0.015 (−3.77)	5.46 (5.01)	0.063 (3.66)	3.55 (7.84)	−0.167 (−0.916)
	F	−0.002 (−6.97)	0.880 (10.76)	0.012 (13.03)	0.444 (6.54)	−0.077 (−3.57)
1970 (729)	D	0.002 (1.59)	1.21 (4.02)	0.002 (0.496)	−0.406 (−1.27)	0.079 (1.89)
	X	0.017 (2.44)	0.223 (0.105)	−0.042 (−2.09)	4.86 (4.34)	−0.254 (−0.853)
	F	−0.002 (−5.35)	0.895 (6.94)	0.009 (6.15)	0.426 (2.25)	0.033 (1.35)
1971 (566)	D	−0.0009 (−0.217)	1.20 (1.34)	0.015 (1.45)	−1.02 (−0.680)	−0.647 (−0.604)
	X	0.004 (0.863)	0.599 (0.381)	−0.019 (−1.16)	2.29 (5.01)	1.32 (11.77)
	F	−0.003 (−6.20)	1.27 (12.90)	0.011 (8.86)	0.389 (4.48)	−0.040 (−0.852)
1974 (150)	D	−0.164 (−0.82)	0.99 (1.83)	0.036 (1.09)	−0.13 (−1.21)	0.006 (0.06)
	X	0.034 (0.18)	−0.37 (−1.01)	0.0004 (0.012)	0.057 (0.48)	0.097 (1.06)
	F	−0.124 (−2.72)	0.107 (0.55)	0.024 (3.47)	−0.0005 (−0.012)	−0.034 (−1.09)

MES	MD_d	TRANS	VI	F	X
0.002 (1.14)	0.114 (4.24)			−0.814 (−1.01)	0.035 (0.40)
−0.004 (−0.81)		0.00006 (3.70)		−2.04 (−1.04)	
−0.002 (−3.55)			0.0005 (−0.12)		−0.016 (−0.43)
0.003 (0.785)	0.202 (3.55)			0.790 (0.65)	0.200 (2.37)
−0.02 (−3.16)		0.00007 (2.07)		−7.64 (−4.33)	
−0.003 (−4.51)			0.004 (0.881)		−0.10 (−4.34)
0.003 (2.90)	0.064 (2.42)			0.779 (1.55)	0.518 (2.55)
−0.011 (−1.89)		0.00002 (0.636)		−7.37 (−4.38)	
−0.001 (−2.05)			0.004 (0.849)		−0.092 (−3.70)
0.005 (2.24)	0.204 (4.20)			0.275 (0.567)	0.826 (2.75)
−0.009 (−5.21)		0.000007 (0.645)		−2.19 (−8.04)	
−0.003 (−4.70)			0.013 (3.09)		−0.36 (−8.13)
0.004 (4.94)	0.153 (3.61)			0.211 (0.858)	0.174 (2.71)
−0.016 (−3.30)		0.001 (3.57)		−6.53 (−5.27)	
−0.002 (−2.52)			0.014 (3.39)		−0.062 (−3.04)
0.003 (2.12)	−0.059 (−2.30)			0.350 (1.35)	0.093 (1.83)
−0.005 (−0.587)		−0.002 (−2.59)		2.94 (1.44)	
−0.001 (−1.48)			0.008 (1.63)		0.013 (0.408)
0.005 (0.778)	0.185 (0.645)			0.107 (0.122)	0.539 (0.701)
−0.009 (−2.69)		−0.000002 (−0.114)		−0.550 (−0.423)	
−0.001 (−1.97)			0.015 (3.19)		−0.008 (−0.271)
−0.001 (−0.67)	0.069 (2.07)			−0.97 (−0.73)	1.91 (6.14)
0.0001 (0.061)		0.00002 (1.40)		−1.07 (−1.05)	
−0.0003 (−0.35)			−0.003 (−0.32)		−0.10 (−0.73)

ations. For the "giant" subsample, only the 1974 domestic equation felt the advantage of size. The insignificance of this variable for the "giant" subsamples is not a surprising result (see Horst, Bergsten, Moran for contradictory results), since the "giant" subsamples have to a large extent already controlled for size of the firm.

MES   Plant size as measured by minimum efficient scale underscores the differences in barriers to entry in the domestic and foreign markets. *MES* played a positive barrier to entry role in the domestic market equation (for 4 years) but a negative role in the foreign market equations (for a majority of the years). The results of the 1974 "giant" subsample are remarkably different; *MES* plays an insignificant role in all 3 equations. The only significance of the *MES* coefficient for the 1965–1971 "giants" is in the domestic equation and for only 3 years. Thus, the large scale of operations is seen as an advantage in the cross-sectional study of all firms, but it loses its significance in the subsample population. Porter's (1979) results differ from these; economies of scale in production are positively associated with the profits of large-size firms.

Herfindhal   The fact that scale economies exerted a negative impact on foreign market activities over the 1965–1971 period seemed counter-intuitive and at odds with the positive impact of the Herfindhal index. Scherer (1970) notes a study by Nelson, who observed a negative correlation between the fraction of all industry plants controlled by Big Four members and the ratio of average Big Four member plant size to average industry plant size.

The results of the Nelson work suggest that the giants appear to have low *MES* but engage in substantial multi-plant operations; such multi-plant operations could readily be established abroad. The multi-plant, low *MES* firms are more active in the foreign market, in both export and foreign investment, than are the high *MES* firms. Thus, it appears that exporters are not characterized by high *MES* captured by a single plant production process but by the same low *MES* multi-plant process as firms engaged in foreign investment.

This study has attempted to identify various firm and industry-level characteristics as barriers to entry in the domestic market and as determinants of activity in the export and foreign investment markets. The results indicate that there are significant differences between the elements of domestic industry structure as incentives to invest abroad or to export and as barriers to new competition.

VIII. The Impact of Foreign Market Operations on Domestic Profitability

This paper has posed the hypothesis that foreign market operations themselves constitute a separate and significant barrier to entry in the domestic market. The results of testing this hypothesis can be ascertained from tables 1 and 2; the regression coefficient on X and F in the D equation capture the barrier to entry effect of foreign market operations on the domestic market.

For the 1965–1971 sample, export activity exerted a significant positive effect on domestic profitability (5 out of 7 years) while foreign investment activity was positive and significant (otherwise it was insignificant) for only 2 years. The 1965–1971 "giant" subsample produced weak results; export activity is positive and significant for 2 years and foreign investment activity is significantly positive for 1970 only. The 1974 results are stronger but comparable; export activity has a positive significant impact on domestic profitability while foreign investment activity has an insignificant impact.

Although the benefits from export operations are translated into an increase in domestic market power, the impact of foreign investment on domestic market power is generally inconsistent and insignificant. Thus, export leadership roles are used to secure leadership roles in the domestic market but the same cannot be said about foreign investment leadership roles.

Some industrial organization specialists might interpret the positive sign on exports in the domestic profitability equation as an indication of industries which are not subject to the competitive pressures of imports. This argument follows the lines of Esposito and Esposito (1974) who found that the amount of industry-level imports exerted a negative impact on domestic profitability. This argument holds that imports (or exports) merely capture the role of foreign competition on a firm's profit rate.

If a negative relationship between industry-level imports and exports exists then all that either variable is capturing is the degree of potential foreign market competitiveness to which the industry is subjected. The

Table 2
Cross-section regression over "giant" firms.

Year		Constant	Advertising	Size	R&D	Herfindahl
1965	D	−0.0035	0.894	0.0136	−0.384	0.213
(53)		(−0.334)	(1.49)	(0.784)	(−0.749)	(1.64)
	X	0.0078	0.058	0.004	0.543	0.039
		(1.43)	(0.118)	(0.336)	(2.11)	(0.491)
	F	−0.0036	0.632	0.009	−0.068	0.0145
		(−0.247)	(0.912)	(0.767)	(−0.084)	(0.125)
1966	D	−0.001	1.50	0.009	−0.483	0.184
(79)		(−0.208)	(1.11)	(0.632)	(−1.57)	(1.17)
	X	0.009	−0.205	−0.004	0.468	0.046
		(3.13)	(−0.70)	(−1.00)	(5.60)	(1.35)
	F	−0.018	1.51	0.010	−0.783	−0.035
		(−1.49)	(3.50)	(1.75)	(−1.65)	(−0.352)
1967	D	0.001	1.07	0.003	−0.234	0.299
(78)		(0.308)	(2.45)	(0.669)	(−0.618)	(4.08)
	X	0.006	0.257	0.0007	0.477	0.069
		(1.82)	(0.488)	(0.158)	(2.54)	(1.13)
	F	−0.009	1.46	0.007	0.171	0.042
		(−1.33)	(5.30)	(1.53)	(0.557)	(0.455)
1968	D	−0.002	−0.248	−0.013	−0.996	0.250
(81)		(−0.162)	(−0.055)	(−0.316)	(−0.289)	(1.62)
	X	0.003	0.529	0.005	0.546	0.030
		(0.883)	(1.47)	(1.28)	(3.08)	(0.503)
	F	−0.003	1.42	0.008	0.605	0.098
		(−0.673)	(6.66)	(2.11)	(2.99)	(1.57)
1969	D	−0.005	−0.230	0.012	−1.09	−0.532
(90)		(−0.434)	(−0.143)	(0.954)	(−0.866)	(−0.782)
	X	0.0005	1.35	0.0005	1.05	0.431
		(0.056)	(1.90)	(0.041)	(3.68)	(3.04)
	F	−0.005	1.11	0.011	0.646	0.022
		(−0.916)	(2.81)	(1.88)	(1.42)	(0.069)
1970	D	0.002	1.15	−0.003	−0.190	0.153
(93)		(0.958)	(4.20)	(−1.32)	(−1.28)	(4.47)
	X	0.006	0.108	−0.0002	0.431	0.036
		(2.04)	(0.266)	(−0.073)	(2.09)	(0.812)
	F	−0.005	1.40	0.005	0.568	0.017
		(−0.997)	(5.07)	(1.36)	(2.56)	(0.261)
1971	D	−0.010	1.33	0.004	−0.605	0.070
(60)		(−0.868)	(1.41)	(0.460)	(−1.09)	(0.846)
	X	0.005	1.05	0.008	0.783	0.004
		(0.317)	(0.809)	(0.606)	(2.21)	(0.036)
	F	−0.012	1.62	0.011	0.275	−0.006
		(−0.929)	(4.76)	(2.35)	(0.613)	(−0.070)

MES	MD_d	TRANS	VI	F	X
0.003 (0.777)	0.091 (1.48)			−0.617 (−0.531)	1.41 (1.93)
0.0004 (0.124)		0.000008 (0.547)		−0.366 (−0.370)	
−0.002 (−0.863)			0.032 (0.429)		0.916 (0.405)
0.001 (0.176)	0.117 (0.661)			−0.069 (−0.060)	0.559 (0.942)
0.001 (0.795)		0.000002 (0.281)		0.139 (0.612)	
−0.003 (−0.938)			0.060 (1.42)		1.81 (1.40)
0.002 (1.59)	0.120 (1.42)			0.052 (0.162)	0.408 (1.06)
−0.000006 (−0.004)		0.000007 (0.613)		−0.194 (−0.504)	
−0.002 (−0.819)			0.042 (1.62)		0.823 (1.16)
0.007 (0.641)	−0.175 (−0.178)			1.21 (0.295)	2.13 (0.384)
−0.0009 (−0.508)		0.000008 (0.663)		−0.395 (−1.67)	
−0.003 (−1.90)			0.025 (1.63)		−0.179 (−0.433)
0.009 (1.42)	0.108 (0.634)			0.458 (0.538)	1.16 (0.841)
−0.006 (−1.85)		0.00002 (0.482)		−0.825 (−1.02)	
−0.002 (−0.724)			0.019 (0.956)		−0.315 (−0.566)
0.003 (2.82)	−0.005 (−0.127)			0.277 (1.44)	0.274 (1.02)
0.0001 (0.090)		0.00001 (0.980)		−0.118 (−0.398)	
−0.001 (−0.815)			0.027 (1.67)		0.457 (1.03)
0.001 (0.504)	0.020 (0.466)			(0.081) (0.122)	1.03 (1.49)
−0.001 (−0.363)		0.00002 (0.739)		−0.807 (−0.911)	
−0.002 (−1.02)			0.030 (1.32)		0.317 (0.380)

theoretical trade model of Heckscher-Ohlin would support this negative relationship, but the empirical results of the New Trade Theories (Grubel and Lloyd, 1971); Ohlsson, 1975; and McAleese, 1976) provide proof that the correlation between industry-level exports and imports is indeed positive. Thus, the impact of X on D is an issue separate from that of foreign competitive pressures felt by the industry. Rather, the results of this paper indicate that the firm's export operations fuel its purely domestic profitability.[16]

Given the result of this work, the traditional barriers to entry explanation of domestic profitability can really be viewed as composed of two components: (1) the direct effect such barriers may have on domestic profitability; and (2) the effect such barriers have on foreign market activities and then the effect of foreign market activities on domestic profitability, i.e., the indirect effects.

For example, the direct effect of advertising on domestic profitability, $\partial D/\partial A$, is obtained in the D equation. The indirect effect of advertising on domestic profitability (through its impact on export activity and foreign investment activity) is not so easily discernible. The indirect effect of advertising on domestic profitability is composed of: (1) the impact of advertising on foreign investment activity, and then the effect of foreign investment activity on domestic profitability; (2) the effect of advertising on export activity, and then the effect of export activity on domestic profitability; and (3) the interaction between export activity and foreign investment activity.[17]

Traditional industrial organization studies would define the combined direct and indirect effects as the domestic barrier to entry effect. While it is indeed this total effect that is felt in the domestic market, omission of foreign activity variables as determinants of domestic profitability camouflages the feedback effect of these foreign market operations on domestic market structure.

IX. Conclusion

This paper has addressed the following question: Do foreign market operations themselves constitute a separate and significant barrier to entry in the domestic market? The answer to this question is twofold. First, it was shown that there are significant differences between the elements of domestic industry structure as incentives to invest abroad or to export and as barriers to new domestic competition. While some determinants of domestic market power and foreign market operations may coincide, the coincidence is not so strong as to frustrate attempts to differentiate between the two. Second, the benefits of foreign market sales, particularly through export sales, can be used to strengthen domestic market positions. This second tier of benefits to the parent (the first tier being foreign dividends and tax credits and export profits) indicates that industrial organization studies which ignore foreign market activities as determinants of domestic market power are misspecified. These studies have thus overemphasized the role played by traditional barriers to entry.

It should be noted that different results were obtained for the "giant" subsample versus the full sample; this is especially evident for the years 1965–1971. This is not a surprising result as: (1) the subsample does not preserve the full cross section of industries; (2) the subsample controls for size of the firm; and, to the extent that other variables are correlated with size, these other variables have been controlled; (3) the subsample often has less variation in the observations than does the full sample. In fact, the F-test results indicated that the "giant" and non-giant firms were two distinct samples from different populations. These results are in keeping with the inter- and intra-industry studies conducted by others (Porter, 1979; Caves and Pugel, 1979).

This finding has an importance for policymakers; a change in legislation need not affect all firms in the manufacturing population in the same way. Within the US market itself, at least two distinct groups of firms are evident and oftentimes two distinct reactions to the economic environment are present.

All populations, however, lent evidence to the misspecification of industrial organization studies that omit the impact of foreign operations on domestic profitability. Policymakers oblivious to this feedback effect of foreign market operations on domestic power, have used instruments aimed at affecting these foreign market operations with no regard to the effect on the domestic market. And foreign market operations, specifically export operations, appear to be a cause of domestic market power.

X. Appendix. Exogenous Variables

Variable	Definition and Source
A	Level of advertising per sales; this varies between asset classes and over years. (IRS)
R&D	Level of technology as measured by the ratio of engineers and scientists employed to the total industry employment. This variable is held constant within a particular industry and over the years but not across industries. (OI)
S	Size denoted by $\log_{10}$ Size. Size is measured as the total assets per firm average for the group and takes on a potentially unique value for each industry asset class and each year. (IRS)
H	Herfindahl index of industry concentration computed as $H = \sum_i^N s_i^2$, where s_i is firm i's share of the industry's total assets and n is the number of firms in the industry. H had the same value for all groups within the same industry, but could vary between industries and across years. (IRS)
MES	Minimum efficient scale as measured by the average plant size among the largest plants that account for 50% of industry output. This varies across industries but remains constant over time. (CM)
MDd	Growth in domestic market demand as measured by the change in dollar value of sales. This varies between industries and across years. (IRS, EX, EI)
VI	The dummy variable signifying vertical integration within an industry. This variable takes on the value of zero for no vertical integration and the value of unity for the following industries: paper, wood, petroleum, non-metallic mineral products, basic metals, and rubber and other miscellaneous plastics products. This variable has a unique value per 4-digit SIC but remains constant over asset classes and years.
TRANS	Transportability of a product. This variable represents the mile radius within which 80% of an industry's shipments travel (Weiss, 1972). (CT)

Appendix table (continued)

Note: Data sources are shown in brackets.
CM: *Census of Manufacturing*, 1967 and 1973.
IRS: *Internal Revenue Service Sourcebook*, 1965–1971.
OI: US Bureau of the Census, *Occupation by Industry*, 1970.
EX: *US Exports-Value and Percent of Domestic Output for 5-Digit SIC Based Commodities, 1965–1971*, Dept. of Commerce.
EI: *US Commodity Exports and Imports as Related to Output, 1965–1971*, table 2A, Dept. of Commerce.
CT: US Bureau of the Census, *Census of Transportation*, vol. III Commodity Transportation Survey, part 3, Commodity Groups, 1967, 1972, Dept. of Commerce, Bureau of the Census.

Notes

1. The most important of these are the deferral of US income tax on unrepatriated income from foreign subsidiaries; in the foreign tax system, border tax adjustments made foreign products more attractive than US exports.

2. Horst took $F = F(A, T, S, \ldots)$,   (1)

$D = D(A, T, S, F, \ldots)$,   (2)

where

$F =$ a foreign investment proxy,
$D =$ measure of domestic profitability,
$A =$ a measure of advertising,
$T =$ a measure of research and development,
$S =$ a measure of size,
$\ldots =$ other structural variables.

3. Horst (1972).

4. Vertical integration is the only exception to this statement as it applies to multinational operation but not to exporting.

5. See Hall and Weiss, (1971), for objections to various measures of profitability.

6. Thus (domestic profits) × (domestic sales/total sales) implicitly omits any profits accruing directly to export sales from the measure of domestic profitability.

7. An unfortunate consequence of such subtractions is that our tests are biased against the hypothesis that foreign investing and exporting augment the parent's domestic rate of return.

8. The 1974 data set also permitted linking the parent to its DISC and thus calculating firm level export profits.

9. For a detailed explanation of the construction of this and other variables, see Gaspari (1979).

10. Because this analysis is interested in net numbers, export related production costs are added to the parent's net income.

11. A deficiency of this proxy arises from the effect of the dividend payout ratio on this measure of foreign-investment activity. A change in the dividend payout ratio could occur without any change in the parent's foreign-investment activity, yet the proxy for

foreign-investment activity will be affected. Until better data exists, the choice of a better foreign-investment proxy will be curtailed.

12. See *Internal Revenue Service Sourcebook*, 1968, p. 159, for an explanation of includable income of controlled corporations.

13. Some literature also supported an allocation based on R&D, as evidenced by royalty payments. Examination of the data indicated that within an industry the lower asset classes occasionally have substantial royalties while the upper asset classes have none. Since this seemed anomalous, royalties were omitted from the calculation.

14. For further detail on the DISC program, intercompany pricing methods, and construction of DISC variables, see Gaspari (1979), appendix D.

15. The Box-Cox technique estimates *a*. See G. E. Box and D. R. Cox, "An Analysis of Transformations," *Journal of the Royal Statistical Society,* series B, pp. 211–243, 1974. An application of the Box-Cox technique can be found in: D. Caves, L. Christensen, M. Tretheway, "Flexible Cost Functions for Multiproduct Firms," University of Wisconsin, SSRI No. 7818, August 1978.

16. The reader should bear in mind that D in this study is defined *only* in terms of the *domestic* market whereas other works (Esposito and Esposito, 1971; Pugel, 1978) define it to include profits from non-domestic sales.

17. Thanks to the referee and Dr. Alan Schucat for pointing out the differences between the indirect and total-effects in this simultaneous model and those in the Horst et al., recursive model. In Horst et al., the total effect was simply:

$$\frac{dD}{dA} = \frac{\partial D}{\partial A} \cdot \frac{\partial D}{\partial D} + \frac{\partial F}{\partial A} \cdot \frac{\partial D}{\partial F}.$$

The simultaneous system presented here has the following solution

$$\frac{dD}{dA} = \frac{-\Delta_1}{\Delta_2},$$

where

$$\Delta_1 = \begin{vmatrix} \dfrac{\partial D}{\partial A} & \dfrac{\partial D}{\partial X} & \dfrac{\partial D}{\partial F} \\[2mm] \dfrac{\partial X}{\partial A} & -1 & \dfrac{\partial X}{\partial F} \\[2mm] \dfrac{\partial F}{\partial A} & \dfrac{\partial F}{\partial X} & -1 \end{vmatrix} \quad \text{and} \quad \Delta_2 = \begin{vmatrix} -1 & \dfrac{\partial D}{\partial X} & \dfrac{\partial D}{\partial F} \\[2mm] 0 & -1 & \dfrac{\partial X}{\partial F} \\[2mm] 0 & \dfrac{\partial F}{\partial X} & -1 \end{vmatrix}.$$

While these calculations appear "messier" than those obtained from the recursive model, the presence of indirect effects is still observed.

References

Bain, Joe S., 1956. *Barriers to New Competition, Their Character and Consequences in Manufacturing Industries.* Cambridge, Mass.: Harvard University Press.

Bilkey, W., and G. Tesar, 1978. "The Export Behavior of Smaller-Sized Wisconsin Manufacturing Firms," unpublished.

Caves, Richard, 1971. "International Corporations: The Industrial Economics of Foreign Investment," *Economica*, February, pp. 1–27.

Caves, R., and T. Pugel, 1979. "Intraindustry Differences in Conduct and Performance: Viable Strategies in US Manufacturing Industries." Discussion Paper No. 734, December, HIER.

Cavusgil, S. T., 1976. "Organizational Determinants of Firms' Export Behavior: An Empirical Analysis." Ph.D. thesis, University of Wisconsin Business School.

Cohen, Benjamin I., 1972. "Foreign Investment by US Corporations as a Way of Reducing Risk." Economic Growth Center Discussion Paper No. 151, Yale University.

Comanor, W. S., and T. A. Wilson, 1969. "Advertising and the Economies of Scale," *American Economic Review* 59, no. 2 (May), pp. 87–98.

Esposito, Frances F., and Louis Esposito, 1971. "Foreign Competition and Domestic Industry Profitability," *REStat* 53, pp. 343–353.

Gaspari, K. C., 1979. "Exporting, Foreign Investment, and Domestic Market Power." Ph.D. thesis, University of Wisconsin.

————, 1980. "Exporting and Foreign Investment: Are They Substitutes or Complements?" Wellesley College Working Paper No. 33.

Grubel, H., and P. Lloyd, 1971. "The Empirical Measurement of Intra-Industry Trade," *Economic Record* 47, pp. 494–517.

Gruber, W., D. Mehta, and R. Vernon, 1967. "The R&D Factor in International Trade and International Investment of the United States Industries," *Journal of Political Economy* 75, no. 1, pp. 20–37.

Hall, M., and L. Weiss, 1967. "Firm Size and Profitability," *REStat* 49, no. 3 (August), pp. 319–331.

Hirsch, Seev, and Zvi Adar, 1974. "Firm Size and Export Performance," *World Development* 2, no. 7 (July), pp. 41–46.

————, 1974. "Protected Markets and Firms' Export Distribution," *World Development* 2, no. 8 (August), pp. 29–36.

Hirsch, Seev, and Baruch Lev, 1974. "The Firm's Export Concentration: Determinants and Applications," *World Development*, 2, no. 6 (June), pp. 27–33.

Horst, Thomas, 1972. "Firm and Industry Determinants of the Decision to Invest Abroad: An Empirical Study," *REStat* 54, no. 3 (August), pp. 258–266.

————, 1975. "American Investments Abroad and Domestic Market Power," unpublished.

Horst, T., I. Moran, and F. Bergsten, 1978. *American Multinationals and American Interests*. Washington, D.C.: Brookings Institution.

Hymer, Stephen, 1960. "International Operations of National Firms: A Study of Direct Foreign Investment," Ph.D. thesis, Massachusetts Institute of Technology. Published in 1976, MIT Press.

Knickerbocker, 1973. *Oligopolistic Reaction and Multinational Enterprise*. Boston: Harvard University Graduate School of Business Administration.

McAleese, D., 1976. "Industrial Specialization and Trade: Northern Ireland and the Republic," *Economic and Social Review*, 7, no. 2 (January).

Ohlsson, L., 1975. "Specialization Tendencies in Swedish Trade and Production of Fabricated Metal Products in the 1960s," *Swedish Journal of Economics* 77, pp. 338–350.

Porter, Michael, 1974. "Consumer Behavior, Retailer Power, and Market Performance in Consumer Goods Industries," *REStat* 56, no. 4 (November), pp. 419–436.

Scherer, F. M., 1970. *Industrial Market Structure and Economic Performance.* Chicago: Rand McNally.

Severn, A., and M. Laurence, 1973. "Direct Investment, Research Intensity, and Profitability." Division of International Finance Discussion Paper No. 30, May 31, Board of Governors of the Federal Reserve System.

Vernon, Raymond, 1966. "International Investment and International Trade in the Product Cycle," *Quarterly Journal of Economics* 80, no. 2 (May), pp. 190–207.

Weiss, Leonard, 1978. "Quantitative Studies of Industrial Organization." Social Systems Research Institute, Reprint No. 246, University of Wisconsin.

Weiss, Leonard, 1972. "Geographic Size of Markets in Manufacturing," *REStat* 54, no. 3 (August), pp. 245–257.

5 Entry, Exit, and the Theory of the Multinational Corporation

Daniel M. Shapiro

I. Introduction

This paper uses the industrial organization approach to the study of multinational corporations (MNCs) to test two related hypotheses:

1. that subsidiaries of MNCs possess advantages relative to domestic firms in overcoming barriers to entry in the host market; and
2. that subsidiaries of MNCs are, relative to domestic firms, less encumbered by barriers to exit in the host market.

Together, these hypotheses imply that foreign firms are more mobile than domestic firms and, ceteris paribus, find it easier both to enter and to exit an industry.

The first hypothesis was explicitly posited by Richard Caves (1971) in his influential article on the industrial organization approach to the MNC. It has been directly tested but once, by Paul Gorecki (1976), who was able to provide supporting evidence using Canadian data. In retesting this hypothesis, Canadian data are again employed, but for a larger sample over a more recent time period (1972–1976), and with a more appropriate definition of entry.

The second hypothesis is new and arises from recent contributions to the industrial organization literature by Caves and Porter (1976) and Eaton and Lipsey (1980, 1981) on the nature of barriers to exit. However, these contributions have not previously been related to the theory of multinational investment.

In section II, the industrial organization approach to the theory of the MNC is briefly reviewed, along with some recent literature on barriers to entry and exit. The two hypotheses are derived in this context. It is recognized that the industrial organization approach does not provide a comprehensive theoretical framework for the study of the MNC. A recent survey by Calvet (1981) points out its limitations, and discusses the alternatives. However, given the nature of the problem at hand, reliance on this approach seems appropriate since previous applications have been successful in explaining the related question of inter-industry differences in foreign ownership (Caves, 1974; Saunders, 1982).

Given the hypotheses, the model used to test them is presented in section III, while the results are discussed in section IV. The results are summarized, with concluding remarks, in section V.

II. Entry, Exit, and the Multinational Corporation

The industrial organization approach to the MNC began with Stephen Hymer's 1960 thesis, which was belatedly published in 1976. Since that time a large literature has emerged based on Hymer's insights. The essence of this approach is that MNCs are characterized by the ownership of specific assets, unique to the firm, which can be transferred relatively costlessly within the firm, but which cannot easily be acquired by other firms, because markets for the asset are either imperfect or nonexistent. This allows the firm which owns the asset to exercise monopoly power at home and to exploit its advantage abroad. The assets in question are usually cited as being technological expertise in product or process development, a successfully differentiated product, or managerial skills. Caves (1971) recognized that in the industrial organization literature these same factors are typically considered to represent barriers to the entry of new firms.[1] Thus, factors which represent an incentive to foreign entry represent a barrier to domestic entry, and the first hypothesis follows: foreign firms are advantaged in overcoming barriers to entry because they already possess those assets which preclude the entry of domestic firms.

There are, however, other barriers to entry. The traditional Bain-Sylos model also identifies economies of scale and capital requirements as impediments to the entry of new firms.[2] Caves also argued that MNCs possess advantages in overcoming these barriers. However, in order to defend this position he was forced to go beyond the framework outlined above. Capital cost barriers are overcome because the foreign entrant is able to take advantage of its parent's retained earnings, credit rating, and world-wide sourcing ability. Economies of scale barriers are less binding to the extent that they prevail at one stage of the production process, thus allowing the subsidiary to engage in limited operations in the host market.[3] There is, however, another reason why foreign entrants may not be deterred by economies of scale. In their widely cited study of Canadian industries, Eastman and Stykolt (1976) argued that in a tariff-protected small-market economy there is an incentive to produce at less than optimal scale. This tendency is reinforced when economies of scale at the firm level can offset the inefficiency resulting from the operation of suboptimal plants. Since foreign entrants are likely to possess the advantage of firm-level economies of scale, they can still profitably construct plants of inefficient size.[4]

The result of this analysis is the hypothesis that foreign entrants enjoy advantages over domestic entrants in overcoming *all* barriers to entry. This hypothesis has been explicitly tested with Canadian data by Gorecki (1976), using an empirical model of entry developed by Orr (1974). Gorecki was able to provide evidence consistent with the hypothesis. Recent developments in the industrial organization literature suggest, however, that the analysis may be taken further. It has been argued by Caves and Porter (1976) as well as Eaton and Lipsey (1980, 1981) that barriers to entry also serve as barriers to exit. This symmetrical relationship arises from the characteristics of the assets involved. If symmetry does indeed obtain, and if it applies to both foreign and domestic firms, then foreign firms may not only find it easier to enter, but to exit as well.

Both the Caves-Porter and Eaton-Lipsey analyses focus on the effects of investments in assets that are durable and/or firm- or product-specific. Caves and Porter (1976) refer to such assets as DSAs (durable and specific assets) while Eaton and Lipsey (1981) prefer PSC (product specific capital). The assets which they have in mind are, however, the same: durable plant and equipment, advertising expenditures, firm-specific human capital, and expenditures on product and process development (R&D).[5] Durability and specificity combine to create barriers to entry because entrants must duplicate assets which are expensive and for which markets are limited. In addition, specificity limits the scrap value of the asset and thus increases the risk of entry. However, these same characteristics also make the assets barriers to exit, since the committed assets represent nonrecoverable costs to existing firms because of their limited marketability. Simply stated, the firm is bound to its market owing to an inability to divest. Specificity thus appears to be more important than durability. Caves and Porter cite the case of advertising expenditures as being assets which are firm specific, but not necessarily durable, yet act as a barrier to exit nonetheless.[6] This analysis therefore suggests that commonly used empirical proxies for barriers to entry such as R&D and advertising expenses should also constitute barriers to exit.

Caves and Porter further argue that economies of scale, and their associated capital requirements, also represent a barrier to exit since it is their view that large-scale production depends on durable and specific capital. The symmetry between entry barriers and exit barriers is therefore complete, covering both absolute cost differences and economies of scale.

The evidence relevant to the "symmetry" hypothesis is limited. Caves and Porter do provide empirical results, but they are based on firm-level data, and do not include many of the industry-level variables commonly used as measures of barriers to entry (exit) in the industrial organization literature. Thus, measures of economies of scale, capital requirements, and R&D are not included. Their evidence does suggest that advertising represents a barrier to exit, although proxy measures for the durability of capital do not perform well.

The analysis of barriers to exit has not been related to the theory of the MNC. The unifying element in the preceding discussion is the existence of firm- or product-specific assets for which markets are non-existent or inefficient means of transferring the assets. For potential domestic entrants, such assets represent barriers to entry because the asset cannot be purchased and must therefore be replicated, often at substantial cost. For existing domestic firms, or domestic firms which do enter, the same assets represent a barrier to exit because it is difficult to liquidate the asset. The foreign entrant, on the other hand, is characterized by its ability to deploy the assets created by its parent. The MNC is able to internalize markets and thereby transfer the assets relatively costlessly. Hence, foreign entrants are able to overcome barriers to entry, as Caves (1971) hypothesized. However, once established the foreign firm is less restricted by barriers to exit. This follows from the fact that the asset was deployed relatively costlessly, thus reducing the necessary recoverable costs. In addition, the assets may be transferred within the multinational system, thus using internal markets as a means to effect the transfer. This reasoning leads directly to the second hypothesis: subsidiaries of MNCs are less affected by barriers to exit in the host market.

The two hypotheses may not be symmetrical. Whereas Caves argued that foreign entrants are better able to overcome *all* barriers to entry, it is not clear that foreign firms are immune from all barriers to exit. The analysis above is confined to certain assets. It is relevant to economies of scale or capital requirements only to the extent that they embody durable and specific capital. A large amount of sunk physical capital may be a barrier to exit for foreign as well as domestic firms if the former cannot transfer the asset. Thus the second hypothesis may be more limited than the first.

In the next section, the model used to test the two hypotheses is discussed.

III. The Model

The test methodology is as follows. We first specify a model of the inter-industry determinants of entry. This model is then estimated for both domestic and foreign entrants, thus testing the first hypothesis. Using the symmetry hypothesis, the same independent variables are then used to model the determinants of exit for both foreign and domestic exits. This tests the second hypothesis.

The entry model is specified along the lines suggested by Orr (1974) and employed by Gorecki (1976) in his test of the first hypothesis. Orr's specification is chosen to ensure comparability in the results and because it has certain desirable properties, to be discussed below.

Orr's specification is characterized by equations (1) and (2), with error terms omitted:

$$E = \alpha_0 e^{\alpha_1 ITE} e^{\alpha_2 BTE} S^{\alpha_3}, \tag{1}$$

or

$$\ln E = \ln \alpha_0 + \alpha_1 ITE + \alpha_2 BTE + \alpha_3 \ln S, \tag{2}$$

where

E = absolute entry;

ITE = incentives to entry (past profit and growth rates);

BTE = barriers to entry (estimates of minimum efficient plant size, capital requirements to build an MES plant, advertising, R&D, industry risk, industry concentration);

S = industry sales.

This specification is somewhat unusual. In most studies, the *rate of entry* is regressed on the incentives and barriers to entry.[7] Orr, on the other hand, employs the logarithm of absolute entry and corrects for inter-industry differences in size by including the logarithm of industry sales on the right-hand side. He defends this specification on a priori grounds, arguing that since his explanatory variables are all expressed as percentages, his transformation leaves "the relationship between entry and each of the independent variables in percentage terms" (p. 62). His results suggest that the coefficient of the logarithm of size is significantly different from 1.0, thus indicating that the correction for industry size is most appropriately introduced on the right-hand side.

The independent variables are standard to the literature. Entry is induced by above average profit and growth rates in the previous period and is deterred by the various barriers to entry. The only variable which requires additional explanation is the concentration variable. It is included to account for the possibility that existing firms will collude to deter entry. Concentration thus acts as a barrier to entry and the sign of its coefficient is expected to be negative.

As will be seen below, each of these independent variables can be used to explain inter-industry differences in exit, thus allowing the use of the same model for both entry and exit.

With respect to the dependent variable, both Orr and Gorecki employed *net* entry, which is calculated as the difference between the number of firms in time t and time t − 1. Evidently, this is a biased measure, since net entry measures the effects of entry, exit, reclassifications, and mergers. What is required is a measure of gross entry (or exit) of firms, excluding reclassifications and mergers.

Thus, in estimating the entry (and exit) model, the Orr/Gorecki specification is employed with some changes and modifications. The most important of these is that the data allow the measurement of gross entry and exit of both foreign and domestic establishments. Second, included are certain independent variables not included by them. Third, the sample size is nearly double theirs and, finally, the sample period is updated from 1964–1967 to 1972–1976.[8]

The dependent variables are therefore the births and deaths of domestic and foreign manufacturing establishments in Canada over the period 1972–1976. These numbers represent "pure" births (entry) and deaths (exit) in that they are gross measures and exclude reclassifications and mergers. These measures will reduce the measurement errors associated with the use of net entry.

The independent variables are, with two exceptions, the same as those employed by Orr/Gorecki. These variables, with the signs their estimated coefficients are expected to take in the various equations, are summarized in table 1. Following Orr, the incentives to entry are modeled by growth ($GROW1$) and profitability ($MARG1$) in the previous period. It is expected that above average growth and profitability will attract entrants, while below average growth and profitability will encourage exits. These incentives should operate in the same way for both foreign and domestic firms. There is an additional incentive which neither Orr nor Gorecki considered, but which is highly relevant in the Canadian context. It is a widely held belief in Canada that tariffs have represented an important incentive to foreign entry, as foreign firms substitute production in Canada for exports which are precluded by the tariff.[9] Thus, it is important that any model of foreign entry (exit) include the tariff as an explanatory variable. The coefficient on this variable ($TARN$) is expected to be positive for foreign entry and negative for foreign exit.[10] The same rationale suggests that the tariff be included in the domestic equations. High (low) tariff protection precludes (encourages) foreign import competition and induces domestic entry (exit).

The barriers to entry (exit) may be classified as arising from three sources: specific capital, economies of scale, and associated capital requirements, and entry risk. The type of specific capital which lies at the heart of the present analysis is measured by investments in advertising (ADV), product and process development ($R\&D$), and human capital (scientists and engineers) devoted to product and process development (SAE). As the last two probably measure the same thing, they are not included together in any estimated equation. In their role as barriers to entry these variables are expected to carry negative signs in the domestic entry equations. However, the first hypothesis suggests that this will not hold, or will hold to a lesser extent, in the foreign

Daniel M. Shapiro

Table 1
Independent variables.

Independent Variable	Description	Year	Expected sign			
			Domestic entry	Foreign entry	Domestic exit	Foreign exit
MARG1	Past profit margin (average)	1968–1972	+	+	–	–
GROW1	Past rate of growth of shipments	1968–1972	+	+	–	–
KI	Capital requirements (fuel and electricity) to build an MES plant (logarithm) (see text note 11)	1972	–	0	–	?
RISK1	Variance of past profits	1968–1972	–	–	+	+
RD	R&D/sales ratio	1972	–	0	–	0
SAE	Scientists and engineers as a percentage of total employment	1972	–	0	–	0
MOS	Minimum efficient plant size as a percentage of market size (see text note 11)	1972	–	0	–	?
ADV	Advertising/sales ratio	1971	–	0	–	0
CR472	4-firm concentration ratio	1972	–	–	–	–
LS72	Logarithm of industry shipments	1972	+	+	+	+
MOS × CDR	MOS interacted with the cost disadvantage ratio (see text note 11). MOS × CDR = 0 if MOS was less than its mean plus one standard deviation	1972	+	0	+	?
TARN	Nominal tariff rate	1972	+	+	–	–

Notes: The data base on which this study is based has been compiled from various published and unpublished sources. The data base was compiled as part of a larger study on entry and exit on which the author is collaborating with R. S. Khemani. Details are available on request.

0 implies either that the coefficient is expected to be statistically insignificant, or that it will be lower in the foreign equations.

entry equations. As barriers to exit, the same variables will carry negative signs in the domestic exit equations, but the second hypothesis is that the relationship will not hold in the foreign exit equations.

The economies of scale variables include an estimate of minimum efficient plant size as a percentage of the market (*MOS*), the capital required to build such a plant (*KI*), and an estimate of the effects of the steepness of the declining portion of the long-run average cost curve (*MOS* × *CDR*).[11] *MOS* and *KI* were employed by Orr and Gorecki, while *MOS* × *CDR* is included here to account for the ease of entry at suboptimal scale. The inclusion of the interactive term allows the entry-deterring effects of *MOS* to vary with the ease of entry at suboptimal scale. Since the effects of *CDR* are likely to be important only when *MOS* is high, *MOS* × *CDR* was constrained to equal zero when *MOS* was less than its mean plus one standard deviation; otherwise it assumes its own value.[12] As barriers to entry, the coefficients of *MOS* and *KI* are expected to be negative in the domestic entry equation, but not necessarily in the foreign entry equation, given Caves's argument that foreign firms can overcome *all* barriers to entry. Since *CDR* is an inverse proxy for the cost disadvantage of entry at suboptimal scale, *MOS* × *CDR* should carry a positive sign in the domestic entry equation, i.e., the higher the measured *CDR*, the lower the cost disadvantage, thus reducing the entry-deterring effect of *MOS*. For the reasons suggested above, this term is not expected to have the same effect in the foreign entry equation. As barriers to exit, the signs of these terms are expected to be the same in the domestic exit equations. However, as the previous discussion indicated, there is some doubt as to whether foreign firms will be affected by these barriers to exit. The expected signs in the foreign exit equations are therefore in doubt.

The last group of variables measures entry (exit) risk. *RISK1* measures the variance of past industry profits. Entry into high-risk industries is expected to be low, while exit would be high, and this should hold for both foreign and domestic firms. *CR472* is the four-firm concentration ratio and was included by Orr to measure the possibility of active collusion to prevent entry. The possibility of post-entry retaliation increases entry risk and the expected sign in the entry equations is negative. To the extent that foreign entrants are better placed to counter such actions, this relationship may be weaker in the foreign entry equation.

High concentration may be expected to deter exit to the extent that excess profits shelter firms from the urgent need to liquidate assets.

LS72 is the logarithm of industry shipments and is included in all equations to account for industry size. Accordingly, the coefficient should always be positive.

Finally, it should be noted that relevant barriers to entry (exit) may be omitted. The most likely candidates are those resulting from various government policies such as R&D incentive grants, subsidies to failing firms, and restrictions on foreign ownership, all of which may affect the decision to enter (exit). While it was not possible to measure these factors, it is useful to speculate on their potential impact.[13] For this study, the most important omissions are those affecting foreign entry and exit. Popular opinion in the United States notwithstanding, Canada has no coherent policy regarding foreign investment. Much publicity accompanied the National Energy Program (NEP), but its impact is limited to the energy sector, and it was enacted after the period relevant to this study. The Foreign Investment Review Act (FIRA) was enacted in two phases, the first in April 1974, and the second in October 1975. The first phase applied only to takeovers of existing Canadian firms, while the second phase broadened the screening powers of the agency to include new businesses. Only the second phase would affect the present results since entry (exit) through mergers is not included. However, Phase II came near the end of the sample period and, in any event, it is widely acknowledged that FIRA's impact has been minimal (see Rugman, 1980, chapter 10). To the extent that the debate over foreign ownership in Canada creates uncertainties for foreign firms, there may be hidden barriers to entry and incentives to exit, but there is no reason to believe that these were particularly strong over the sample period, or in any way related to the included variables. Thus, one can be reasonably confident in the unbiasedness of the estimated coefficients.

IV. Estimation and Results

Four basic sets of equations have been estimated by ordinary least squares on a common set of exogenous variables. The four sets of equations are defined by four different dependent variables: domestic entry, foreign entry, domestic exit, and foreign exit.[14] There may be a systems relationship among the dependent variables, but Zellner (1962) has shown that under these circumstances ordinary least squares is an appropriate technique when the exogenous variables are all the same. Investigation of possible simultaneous relationships seems warranted in future research.[15]

The results are reported in table 2. The odd-numbered columns present the results using the same independent variables as were used by Orr/Gorecki; the even-numbered columns present additional independent variables. Like Orr and Gorecki, some multicollinearity was detected, most seriously between $CR472$ and all the barriers to entry. $CR472$ is therefore omitted from the results reported in the even-numbered columns. We first consider the entry equations, columns (1)–(4).

It is seen that regardless of the specification, the entry model is more successful in explaining inter-industry differences in domestic entry. This is so because most of the barriers to entry are not significant in the foreign entry equations. These broad results are the same as those reported by Gorecki, and provide further evidence in support of the hypothesis that foreign firms are not as disadvantaged as domestic firms in overcoming barriers to entry. Closer examination of the entry equations reveals that most of the estimated coefficients bear the expected signs. One prominent exception is the risk variable, which has the wrong sign, but is not significant in any of the entry equations. Gorecki reports this same result, for foreign entrants only, and justifies it on the grounds that multinationals may enter high-risk industries if this results in a diversified "portfolio" which reduces overall risk.

Concentration appears to deter the entry of domestic firms, but not foreign firms, a result similar to that of Gorecki. However, it is difficult to interpret this finding because the concentration variable is highly collinear with most of the barriers to entry, but particularly with MOS. Hence, the latter was omitted in other runs, a procedure which made the MOS coefficient significant in the domestic entry equations. An important difference between the present results and those of Gorecki relates to the R&D variable RD. This variable is commonly employed as a barrier to entry and is usually found to act as such. Orr found it to be significant (negative) while Gorecki reports the same result for domestic entrants, and a negative, but insignificant, coefficient for foreign entrants. Table 2 reveals a negative, and insignificant, relationship for

Table 2
Regression results for entry and exit models.

Independent Variable	Domestic entry (logarithm)		Foreign entry (logarithm)		Domestic exit (logarithm)		Foreign exit (logarithm)	
	(1)	(2)	(3)	(4)	(5)	(6)	(7)	(8)
MARG1	0.022** (0.012)	0.024** (0.012)	0.019** (0.010)	0.021* (0.010)	0.012 (0.013)	0.020*** (0.012)	0.011 (0.011)	0.013 (0.010)
GROW1	0.021* (0.009)	0.021* (0.009)	0.011*** (0.008)	0.011*** (0.008)	-0.002 (0.009)	-0.003 (0.009)	-0.002 (0.007)	0.000 (0.007)
KI	-0.377** (0.085)	-0.451* (0.083)	-0.029 (0.073)	-0.102*** (0.069)	-0.440* (0.088)	-0.543* (0.081)	-0.036 (0.072)	-0.106*** (0.065)
RISK1	0.276 (0.737)	0.359 (0.711)	0.156 (0.634)	0.032 (0.593)	0.113 (0.769)	0.050 (0.723)	0.447 (0.628)	0.486 (0.581)
RD	-0.000 (0.000)		0.002* (0.001)		-0.001 (0.001)		0.001 (0.001)	
SAE		-0.001** (0.000)		0.001* (0.000)		-0.001* (0.000)		0.001** (0.000)
MOS	-0.015 (0.028)	-0.156* (0.042)	-0.021 (0.025)	-0.041 (0.035)	-0.011 (0.029)	-0.132* (0.043)	0.004 (0.024)	-0.060** (0.034)
ADV	-0.010* (0.005)	-0.007*** (0.005)	-0.006 (0.004)	-0.004 (0.004)	-0.001 (0.005)	0.001 (0.005)	0.003*** (0.002)	0.005 (0.004)
CR472	-0.025* (0.006)		-0.003 (0.005)		-0.027* (0.006)		-0.008** (0.005)	
LS72	0.587* (0.109)	0.583* (0.118)	0.240* (0.093)	0.219* (0.099)	0.522* (0.114)	0.606* (0.116)	0.347* (0.093)	0.329* (0.093)
MOS × CDR		0.082* (0.028)		0.014 (0.024)		0.068* (0.030)		0.045** (0.024)
TARN	-0.004* (0.001)	-0.004* (0.001)	-0.002** (0.001)	-0.002** (0.001)		-0.005* (0.001)		-0.002** (0.001)

Constant	-1.952^{***}	-1.714	-2.370^{*}	-1.780^{***}	-0.186	-0.926	-3.126^{*}	-2.705
	(1.290)	(1.396)	(1.111)	(1.165)	(1.347)	(1.379)	(1.100)	(1.106)
$\bar{R}$	0.654	0.653	0.168	0.211	0.647	0.666	0.238	0.292
F	27.43	25.50	3.83	4.47	26.61	26.91	5.37	6.36
n	127	131	127	131	127	131	127	131

*, Significant at the .975 level, one tailed test.
**, Significant at the .95 level, one tailed test.
***, Significant at the .90 level, one tailed test.
Standard errors in parentheses.

domestic firms, but a positive and significant one for foreign firms. However, the former result changes when SAE replaces RD as a measure of investments in technology: SAE in the domestic equation has a coefficient which is negative and statistically significant. Apparently, in the technological environment of the 1960s investments in such assets deterred the entry of domestic firms, but not foreign firms; in the 1970s the same investments may have deterred domestic entry, but they induced foreign entry. Both sets of results suggest an advantage for foreign firms, albeit under different circumstances.

The new variables introduced in columns (2) and (4) are of interest. As expected, domestic entry is deterred by severe cost disadvantages associated with production at suboptimal scale, i.e., the $MOS \times CDR$ coefficient is positive and significant. The same is not true for foreign entrants, thus suggesting either that foreign firms can enter at suboptimal scale or do not need to, i.e., they are large-scale entrants. The tariff variable ($TARN$) provides surprising results. Tariffs actually deter both domestic and foreign entry, although the effect is weaker for foreign entrants. These results suggest that tariffs, rather than providing an incentive for new entrants, actually serve to protect existing firms, both foreign and domestic, and provide yet further refutation of the widely held view that Canadian tariffs act to encourage foreign entry.

Two final comments are in order. First, the coefficient of $LS72$ (industry size) is always significantly different from one, thus suggesting that this variable serves as more than a simple deflator: large markets facilitate entry, but the elasticity is less than one. Second, there is a high positive correlation between foreign control and the barriers to entry across industries. The result is that domestic entry into industries with high foreign control is impeded, while foreign entry into the same industries is facilitated. Thus, the industrial system is such that continued foreign control of high-technology, large-scale industries is probable.

The exit equations provide support for both the hypothesis that barriers to entry also act as barriers to exit, and the hypothesis that foreign firms are relatively immune to barriers to exit. As was the case with the entry equations, the domestic exit equations are more successful in explaining inter-industry variations in exit. However, the specific results do not entirely parallel those in the entry equations.

One important asymmetry which arises is that advertising expenditures do not act as a barrier to exit for either foreign or domestic firms. Caves and Porter found advertising to be an important barrier to exit, and this was expected to hold for domestic firms. The advertising coefficient for foreign firms is not significant in the extended equation, as hypothesized. Investments in technology, on the other hand, do deter the exit of domestic firms, but facilitate the exit of foreign firms. This is as hypothesized, although the positive sign on the technology term for foreign firms is somewhat surprising. Foreign firms apparently have high turnover rates (entry and exit) in high-technology industries; domestic firms, once in, tend to stay.

While the evidence on the role of specific capital (ADV, RD, SAE) in deterring exit is mixed, the economies of scale variables (MOS, $MOS \times CDR$, KI) seem to deter both domestic and foreign exit. However, the deterrent effect is lower for foreign firms. This would seem to confirm Caves's and Porter's suggestion that economies of scale are achieved through durable and specific capital which make exit difficult for domestic firms. Foreign firms are less constrained, for all the reasons relating to their ownership of specific capital.

High tariff industries are characterized by low exit. Thus, tariffs do not provide any incentive to entry, but do serve to protect existing firms, foreign or domestic.

Paralleling the entry case, foreign exit is highly positively correlated with foreign control. However, the relationship between domestic exit and foreign control is negative, but weak and not significant. Thus, domestic firms that find it difficult to enter industries with high degrees of foreign control, find it considerably easier to leave such industries. Put another way, when foreign firms are competing in a predominantly Canadian-controlled industry, they are less likely to leave, while domestic firms are as likely to leave any industry, regardless of the ownership composition of its firms.

V. Summary and Conclusions

Evidence has been presented in support of the hypotheses that foreign firms possess advantages over domestic firms in overcoming both barriers to entry and barriers to exit. Foreign firms are therefore more mobile than their domestic counterparts. This is not surprising, given the notion that MNCs are characterized by the ownership of specific assets which are easily and relatively costlessly transferable world-wide through internal markets.

One must exercise caution in drawing policy conclusions from these results. The purpose of this paper has been to point out the relationship between the MNC and elements of the industrial structure in the host market. The analysis has not been framed in a welfare context and the results leave some questions unanswered.

In finding that foreign firms are better able to overcome barriers to entry in Canada, Paul Gorecki, working within the standard structure-performance-conduct paradigm, was led to the conclusion that foreign entrants represent a pro-competitive force, and thus provide benefits in static allocative efficiency. While our entry results confirm those of Gorecki, the exit results suggest that his conclusion is based on incomplete information. Because foreign firms are also better able to overcome barriers to exit, their pro-competitive tendencies are mitigated. However, this line of thinking should not be overemphasized. If profitable foreign entry occurs at suboptimal scale, then productive efficiency is lost, and industrial rationalization prevented. On the other hand, the ability of foreign firms to exit may encourage rationalization by removing redundant and inefficient capacity. Furthermore, recent theoretical developments cast doubts on the traditional interpretation of the effects of barriers to entry/exit. The theory of contestable markets (Baumol, 1982) suggests that in markets where barriers to entry and exit are low, static efficiency is ensured, even when the industry is characterized as oligopolistic. However, contestable markets may suffer from dynamic inefficiencies. In addition, to the extent that barriers to entry are endogenous, arising from the need to create credible threats against potential entry (Dixit, 1980), then the interpretation of the effects of high exit barriers becomes problematic. Clearly, further research on these issues is warranted.

Since the results of this study suggest that the mobility of foreign firms is highest in those industries with high barriers to entry, and since the mobility of domestic firms is restricted in these same industries, the dualistic nature of Canadian industry becomes clear. In the high-technology, large-scale industries, foreign firms come and go, while Canadian firms find it relatively difficult to enter, although once in they are more likely to stay, unless faced by foreign competition. The consequence is likely to be the continued foreign domination of such industries, unless explicit policy measures are taken. It should be noted, however, that there is some evidence that the technological environment in Canada changed between the 1960s and 1970s. Canadian firms found it easier to enter high-technology industries in the later period, although they were still disadvantaged relative to foreign firms. Exactly what caused this change remains a matter of conjecture.

The tariff has always been at the center of policy controversies in Canada. The evidence presented here suggests that tariffs serve to protect existing firms, foreign and domestic, but do not act as an incentive to entry for either foreign or domestic firms. Indeed, entry into high-tariff industries is impeded. Thus, attempts to lower tariffs would result in the exit of both foreign and domestic firms, but could, paradoxically, induce entry. The latter outcome may result from the diminution of market power attendant upon tariff reduction, and the consequent reduction in entry risk.

One obvious implication to emerge from this study is that the high mobility of foreign firms may result in policy asymmetries. Foreign firms are likely to be more sensitive to policy initiatives which they view with disfavor, and thus more likely to scrap plants. They may therefore react differently than domestic firms to tax changes, interest rate changes, or elements of the domestic government's industrial strategy such as nationalization or Canadianization. Foreign firms thus gain considerable leverage in negotiations with governments. They possess a credible threat against policies to which they are opposed; a power not shared by most domestic firms, which are generally not as mobile internationally.

Future research should be directed towards a more detailed analysis of the relationships among foreign entry and exit, and domestic entry and exit. For example, does the knowledge that foreign firms are more advantaged in overcoming barriers to entry act as a deterrent to domestic entry? In addition, the impact of foreign mobility on host-country economic policy requires further analysis. These are problems we hope to address in our on-going study of entry and exit.

Notes

This study derives from a larger project being undertaken with R. S. Khemani, Bureau of Competition Policy, Ottawa. The assistance, in various forms, of R. S. Khemani, the

Social Sciences and Humanities Research Council, and the Bureau of Competition Policy is gratefully acknowledged. I am indebted to Ralph Bradburd, Lynne Pepall, Morton Stelcner, and the participants of the Middlebury Conference for valuable comments on an earlier draft of this paper.

1. The basic argument is that new firms are disadvantaged by the need to incur additional costs to overcome the cumulated expertise or brand loyalty of existing firms. The relevant empirical evidence is surveyed in Scherer (1980, ch. 9).

2. For more recent theoretical analyses confirming the role of economies of scale as a barrier to entry, see Dixit (1980) and Schmalansee (1981).

3. This implies that subsidiaries of foreign firms are likely to be less integrated than domestic producers. For a further discussion, with supporting evidence, see Caves (1975).

4. While Caves did not fully consider this argument in his 1971 paper, the role of multi-plant economies was given greater prominence in his 1974 paper, which attempted to test the theoretical arguments outlined above. For more recent evidence on the role of multi-plant firms, see Saunders (1982).

5. See Eaton and Lipsey (1981, p. 594) and Caves and Porter (1976, pp. 40–41).

6. They also point out that assets can be durable, but not specific (computers, for example), and not act as a barrier to exit.

7. The rate of entry is defined as absolute entry divided by the number of firms, thus deflating for industry size. For a recent example, see Hirschey (1981).

8. The basic sample comprises some 160 four-digit Canadian manufacturing industries. After the elimination of industries for which data was unavailable or unreliable (miscellaneous industries) the final sample numbers 127 when concentration is included and 131 when it is not. The results are not sensitive to changes in sample size.

9. The most widely cited source of this argument is Eastman and Stykolt (1967). Despite its popularity, there is little evidence to support the hypothesis that tariffs induce foreign ownership. For example, see Caves (1974) and Saunders (1982). However, the direct relationship between tariffs and foreign entry has not been tested. This is a preferred test since current tariffs are related to current entry, and not the stock of foreign owned assets.

10. Nominal tariffs were used, as effective tariff data for the entire sample were not available. The reported results do not change when effective tariffs are employed in a restricted sample.

11. MOS is measured by the average plant size of the largest plants accounting for 50% of industry employment, divided by industry size. KI is derived by multiplying the industry capital-output ratio by the estimate of minimum efficient size. Data for capital were not available, so that expenditures on fuel and electricity were used as a proxy. As this is the only variable measured in absolute terms (the others are percentages), it is converted to logarithms. CDR is computed as the ratio of the value-added per worker in the smallest plants accounting for 50% of industry employment to the value-added per worker in the largest plants accounting for the other 50% of industry employment. It is therefore an inverse proxy. See Caves et al. (1975).

12. This is not the usual treatment of CDR. Most typically, CDR is used to "switch on" the MOS term. In the present case, MOS switches on CDR. This formulation was chosen because it seems more reasonable to suppose that suboptimal scale is only a problem at high MOS, and because it relies less on the measurement of CDR which is not necessarily reliable (see Caves et al., 1980).

13. Other omitted variables which could not be measured, but which would be of interest, would be measures of the existence of second-hand markets.

14. As the dependent variables are measured in logarithms, all observations were increased by one before the transformation to avoid zero values.

15. Preliminary investigation suggests that even if entry and exit are simultaneously determined, identification may be difficult. The reported equations may be interpreted as reduced-form estimates of an unidentified system. It can be shown that even if the system is simultaneous, the predicted signs are expected to hold, under reasonable assumptions. For a similar problem with a similar solution, see Hirschey (1981).

References

Baumol, W. J., 1982. "Contestable Markets: An Uprising in the Theory of Industry Structure," *American Economic Review* 72 (March), pp. 1–16.

Calvet, A. L., 1981. "A Synthesis of Foreign Direct Investment Theories and Theories of the Multinational Firm," *Journal of International Business Studies* 7 (Spring/Summer), pp. 43–59.

Caves, R. E., 1971. "International Corporations: The Industrial Economics of Foreign Investment," *Economica* 38, (February), pp. 1–27.

———, 1974. "Causes of Direct Investment: Foreign Firms' Shares in Canadian and United Kingdom Manufacturing Industries," *REStat* 56 (August), pp. 279–293.

———, 1975. *Diversification, Foreign Investment, and Scale in North American Manufacturing Industries*. Ottawa: Economic Council of Canada.

Caves, R. E., J. Khalilzadeh-Shirazi, and M. E. Porter, 1975. "Scale Economics in Statistical Analyses of Market Power," *REStat* 57 (May), pp. 133–140.

Caves, R. E., and M. E. Porter, 1976. "Barriers to Exit," in R. T. Masson and P. D. Qualls (eds.), *Essays on Industrial Organization in Honor of Joe Bain*. Cambridge, Mass.: Ballinger.

Caves, R. E., M. E. Porter, A. M. Spence and J. T. Scott, 1980. *Competition in the Open Economy*, Cambridge, Mass.: Harvard University Press.

Dixit, A. K., 1980. "The Role of Investment in Entry-Deterrence," *Economic Journal* 90 (March), pp. 95–106.

Eastman, H. C., and S. Stykolt, 1967. *The Tariff and Competition in Canada*. Toronto: Macmillan.

Eaton, B. C., and R. G. Lipsey, 1980. "Exit Barriers Are Entry Barriers: The Durability of Capital as a Barrier to Entry," *Bell Journal of Economics* 11 (Autumn), pp. 721–730.

———, 1981. "Capital, Commitment, and Entry Equilibrium," *Bell Journal of Economics* 12 (Autumn), pp. 593–605.

Gorecki, P. K., 1976. "The Determinants of Entry by Domestic and Foreign Enterprises in Canadian Manufacturing Industries: Some Comments and Empirical Evidence," *REStat* 58 (November), pp. 485–488.

Hirschey, M., 1981. "The Effect of Advertising on Industrial Mobility, 1947–72," *Journal of Business* 54, no. 2, pp. 329–339.

Hymer, S. H., 1976. *The International Operations of National Firms: A Study of Direct Foreign Investment*. Cambridge, Mass.: MIT Press.

Orr, D., 1974. "The Determinants of Entry: A Study of the Canadian Manufacturing Industries," *REStat* 56 (February), pp. 58–66.

Rugman, A. M., 1980. *Multinationals in Canada: Theory, Performance and Economic Impact.* The Hague: Nijhoff.

Saunders, R. S., 1982. "The Determinants of Interindustry Variation of Foreign Ownership in Canadian Manufacturing," *Canadian Journal of Economics* 15 (February), pp. 77–84.

Scherer, F. M., 1980. *Industrial Market Structure and Economic Performance*, second edition. Chicago: Rand McNally.

Schmalansee, R., 1981. "Economies of Scale and Barriers to Entry," *Journal of Political Economy* 89 (December), pp. 1228–1238.

Zellner, A., 1962. "An Efficient Method of Estimating Seemingly Unrelated Regressions and Tests for Aggregation Bias," *Journal of the American Statistical Association* 57 (June), pp. 348–368.

6 The Multinationals in the World Oil Market: the 1970s and 1980s

Morris A. Adelman

I. Multinational Corporations: The Necessary Conditions

Adam Smith says somewhere that if there were no barriers to trade, the nations of the world would resemble the provinces of a single great empire. In fact, a century ago, in the United States, interregional trade and multiregional corporations were an important economic novelty and political issue, as witness the Sherman Antitrust Act of 1890. This has now been repeated world-wide in the long economic boom which followed on World War II.

Why should there be multilocation and multiplant firms? Or, as a special case, vertically integrated firms, operating at the successive stages of production? If there were no economies or diseconomies of scale or of vertical integration, then multiplant firms and multiregional corporations would exist by chance.

We should in fact expect more horizontal and vertical integration than by chance alone. First, customers, suppliers, and rivals are much better informed on the prospects and profitability of any given plant or firm. Hence, if it is available for purchase they will offer a higher price for it than will unaffiliated persons upon whom ignorance enforces caution. There is another, and perhaps more important factor: the replication of a successful formula. Given some competitive advantage, however derived, a firm will seek to exploit it elsewhere. Even under pure competition we have quasi-rents, and they may be enormous.

Hence a particular kind of market failure may explain a particular case, but market failure in itself is neither necessary nor sufficient for multiregional operations. A local monopoly may be altogether quiescent. We need some firm-specific competitive advantage, which generates expected above-normal profits, but cannot be sold. A patent permits a firm to collect royalties on its knowledge, and many firms do. But where the knowledge cannot be separated from its use, and cannot be sold but must be practiced, there is an incentive for direct foreign investment. This is perhaps as far as general reasoning takes us.

II. World Oil before OPEC; The Multinational Hunting Ground

The world oil market is the outstanding example of multinational corporations, and indeed dwarfs all others. Its current condition is traceable to before the turn of the century, when Royal Dutch was already operating in Russia and Indonesia, BP was looking around at the Persian Gulf, and others in Mexico. Outside the United States, oil was found mostly in less developed countries where there were special problems and risks atop the usual uncertainties. A company needed a large bankroll to avoid gambler's ruin. Few were called, fewer chosen. At the same time, the refining industry showed economies of scale over a size range which would strike us today as ridiculously small. But these tiny economies of scale were great relative to the very tiny markets. Hence, refiners were few.

Refiners did not relish buying from oil producers, who were few enough to keep the price quite high above competitive levels, and make supply insecure. (In 1914, just before the outbreak of World War I, Winston Churchill set out very clearly that insecurity was a special case or aspect of monopoly. Our statesmen have not yet understood that.) Hence, refiners might either themselves become producers, or seek to acquire a producing affiliate. Similarly, the producers did not like to sell into highly concentrated markets, where they feared the same kind of abuse by their customers. Thus from both sides there was an incentive to integrate by direct investment or by acquisition. Hence the Royal Dutch–Shell merger of 1907, based avowedly on the economies of vertical integration; and the formation of Cal-Tex in 1935. In the late 1970s, some of these economies of vertical integration were "proved" by calculations I regard as highly ingenious and unconvincing. Last year, the senior Shell managing director said that maybe there wasn't much to these economies after all. But once established, the concentrated integrated market structure perpetuated itself.

The few companies who produced and refined the great bulk of the oil moving in international trade could protect their very high prices and profits without much formal collaboration before World War I, and for the first decade afterward. Yet despite a permissive legal environment, they could not prevent all competitive erosion. To block it, they made the famous 1928 Achnacarry agreement. They had a sound distaste for detailed regulation. Settle strategy and let tactics be flexible. But with a varied product mixture and with many product dimensions offering as many new channels for competition as were dammed up elsewhere, the companies found themselves writing more and more detailed specifications. Something of the same kind has happened recently, as we will see.

The cartel ended with the outbreak of war in 1939 and was never revived. After World War II, the companies' obvious strategy was an orderly retreat: do nothing that would tend to lower the price. To do nothing was to do much—but even so, from 1945 to 1970, the real price of international oil fell about 65%. Yet in early 1970, the Persian Gulf price, at about $1.20, was still 6 to 12 times the full cost (including a 20% return on investment) of producing oil in the great Persian Gulf concessions. Who was to get that surplus?

III. Enter OPEC

It was the companies' retreat in the face of competition and the threat of ever-lower prices which led directly to the formation of the Organization of Petroleum Exporting Countries in 1960. In itself OPEC is only a forum, but the OPEC nations acting in concert have been extremely effective. The income tax was soon converted into an excise tax in fact if not in form, by following the principle that posted prices were not to be reduced, regardless of what happened to actual market prices.

With a slowly rising tax and slowly falling price, the host governments' share of the net profits rose to about 85%. There is a wonderful French phrase, "grande firme, petite nation." But in aphorisms as in cooking, the French must yield to the Chinese: "Power grows out of the barrel of a gun." With the end of colonialism the small nations have the guns, and they can handle the big companies.

Accordingly, the 1968 OPEC resolutions recognized no limits to the governments' authority, and stated that contracts would not bind them. Their actions had already shown that this was no empty boast. This excise tax acted as a floor to price, as an excise tax always does. Prices kept declining toward that floor, however, at the expense of the companies' profit margin. It was up to the OPEC nations now to do something about prices.

Since mid-1970, when they began to act, the cartel of the OPEC nations has been a colossal success, increasing prices by a factor of approximately 13, real, from 1970 through 1980. There has been only a small relapse since, which I think they will reclaim in the months to come.

But before looking more closely at the cartel and the multinational companies in relation to it, we will have to clear the ground of an influential but I venture to say mistaken non-cartel theory, which is that the OPEC governments do not act like private firms, and try to maximize neither revenues nor the present value of future revenues. All they want to do is have "enough for their revenue requirements." They produce more than suits their economic interest. They would prefer to keep their oil in the ground for future generations. Sheik Yamani has told us many a time that his country was making great economic sacrifices by producing more than it wished. Nobody laughs. But that's no wonder, for the US government was saying so over a decade ago, before he did.

Furthermore, if exporting governments follow their interests and produce less, this of course increases the price, which increases the undesired revenues, which makes them cut the production again, which raises the price . . . hence there is a backward-sloping supply function. So the big question is: aside from physical shortage, which by now is generally acknowledged not to exist, how much of their oil will they "permit us to have," and will it be "enough for our needs?" (This was the theme of the 1978 report of the Workshop on Alternative Energy Systems, the so-called WAES Report, which, like the Club of Rome Report, was also known for a time as the "MIT Report.")

The "revenue requirements" theory confuses getting with spending. Governments, like private individuals, want money for many diverse reasons, many of which they don't know themselves. But the more money the better, whatever the recipients want to buy: investment, consumption, influence, armaments, or anything else. The more money a private company makes, the better for the individual stockholders; and the more money a publicly owned business makes, the better for the owners, whether a family of three thousand adult males, or a whole nation. There is no conflict or tradeoff between more wealth and other purposes. The mullahs' Iran was the one big exception, for a year or two. Today it is a nightmare from which they are trying to awake.

This influential fiction of "revenue requirements" has lost some popularity during the past two years, as the squabble among OPEC nations for markets which they "really didn't want" became more and more overt. But its falsity was evident years ago. The OPEC current-account surplus went from $84 billion in 1974 to zero in 1978, largely because of surging imports of goods and services which they "really didn't want." Even Saudi Arabia managed a budget deficit in 1978. The 1980 OPEC surplus was about $130 billion; Morgan Guaranty expects a deficit for 1982. I cannot tell the "needs" of the Saud Family. But their budgeted expenditures were just under $3 billion in fiscal 1972/73, before the price explosion, and $88 billion in 1981/82. Making a rough allowance for price changes, there was an increase of roughly 1500% in nine years. Common sense ought to tell us that "needs" are what people think they can get.

If we go back only as recently as 1980, there was a "gentlemen's agreement" to cut output, which was aborted by the outbreak of the Persian Gulf war. There was a Saudi warning in March 1981 that nobody should depend on them automatically to cut back from 10 mbd to 7 mbd. Less than a month ago there was finally an explicit agreement on production, and the Saudis agreed to that 7 mbd, but only on the condition that everybody else hold their place. All this makes perfectly good sense under a theory of a collusive cartel doing its best to restrain production, and preferring to defer as long as possible the difficult divisive job of explicit production control and market allocation. It refutes the "revenue requirements" theory of output and price determination.

The formal pro-rationing scheme may act as did the informal pro-rationing scheme in early 1979. Then, Saudi Arabia twice cut back too far too fast, and thereby tripled the price of oil. There is always a good chance that the mechanism will again be wound too tight, and short-term fear of scarcity will create short-term scarcity. When that happens, undoubtedly the story about revenue requirements will be resuscitated.

IV. Cartel Prospects and Hidden Strength

The cartel will continue raising toward the optimal level, i.e., the one which maximizes net revenues or wealth. The word "toward" is used advisedly. Nobody knows where that optimum lies. One nation's optimum is not another's. They will ultimately raise the price, I believe, too far for their own good because the market response is so slow and uncertain. Moreover, quarrels among members are most easily resolved by raising the price. They will not soon know that they have overshot. And as with singing and mountain climbing, it is easier to go up than to come down. Indeed, they may already have surpassed the optimum, and Sheik Yamani has been plainly worried about it this past year.

I do not believe that the cartel is about to collapse. They have run into serious difficulties, largely because of Saudi Arab dilatoriness in cutting back production. But they have great reserves of strength. First, they are sovereign states. No antitrust law or policy influenced by consumer interest has any power over them. Second, their accumulated assets protect them against a great danger to any cartel, the reluctant price cutter. Nigeria has come closest to the position of the cartelist who does not want to cut prices, knows how dangerous this is for the group, but has no choice because he must pay his bills. Accumulated wealth and high credit standing permit them to hold out until the ranks can be reformed, and each individual can do what is best for the group as a whole.

Both these great assets, sovereignty and accumulated wealth, are seen in the Iran-Iraq war. This has put about nine mbd out of action. Had it not been for large foreign assets, the war would be over. For the cartel, it has been a piece of great good fortune. But, to draw four aces takes gook luck, to keep drawing them requires good management. It is costing Saudi Arabia, Kuwait, and the UAE $20 billion a year to keep the war going, but they have it and will spend it as needed.

Moreover, the cartel has a great source of strength in the toleration of the consuming country governments, whose interests it has greatly injured. When Libya made demands upon oil companies in 1970, at least one oil company (Shell) knew it meant "an avalanche of escalating demands," and they wanted to resist. The oil companies were divided but the US government strongly favored giving the Libyans what they wanted, for reasons never explained then or since. Mr. Kissinger advocated "cooperation," "dialogue," and "interdependence," and this is still policy. He also echoed the call of Saudi Arabia and Iran for world-wide agreements to fix "a just price." I do not think we have heard the last of it. If the world price is in serious danger, or falls significantly, the OPEC nations will call on non-OPEC producers to join in output limitation and price maintenance. I think that Britain, Norway, and Mexico and the United States will lend a sympathetic ear, but will not guess at the outcome.

V. The Multinationals in the New International Economic Order

There has been a massive vertical dis-integration. The companies' production interests in the OPEC nations have been practically all expropriated. Remnants of ownership under severely limited conditions survive in Nigeria, Libya, and Indonesia. In Saudi Arabia, Aramco is a contractor for a service fee of 20¢ per barrel, plus profits of construction. But a much bigger reward in the last three years has been the so-called Aramco advantage. During 1979–1981, Saudi Arabia squeezed production to make the price shoot up but maintained its sales, and profited greatly, by always charging about $2 less than the prevailing price. Competitors complained bitterly of the Aramco advantage, which has more recently become the Aramco albatross. When oil product prices fell in late 1981 and early 1982, the $2 advantage became a $5 loss because the companies were told that they would either fulfill their buying requirements at the official price or be expelled altogether. These are the same Saudis who loved to tell us that they really would prefer not to produce so much. The Aramco companies have stayed and lifted Saudi oil at a $5 loss, hoping for the best, but obviously some of the fervor with which they cling to their position has been eroded.

Compensation for the expropriated investments has been trifling. This is a special case of a wider rule. In international mineral development, contracts have no force. Recall the 1968 OPEC resolution. The Tehran agreements between the Persian Gulf producers and the oil companies were signed in 1971 with great acclaim from our State Department, who assured the world that "the previously turbulent oil market would now quiet down." It was of these agreements (repeatedly

violated) that Sheik Yamani said in September 1973, a month before
the Arab-Israeli war: "We in Saudi Arabia would have like to honor
and abide by the Tehran agreement but. . . ." Changing circumstances
and all that. (Since then there has been a succession of promises to our
government, all broken, all part of "cooperation, dialogue, and
interdependence.")

An oil company knows that if it explores and finds nothing, it is out
of pocket. If it finds something worth finding, the host government will
claim most of the rent, and perhaps more than all of it. Overreaching
is likely, even to the injury of the host itself, because of normal uncertainty, normal human greed, and the normal attitude that plundering
the transnational corporation is either a minor vice or a major virtue.
Hence even with astronomical oil prices, the rate of exploration in
LDCs around the world has grown only modestly. Things may change
in this respect, but slowly at best. The World Bank is trying to evolve
some new institutions, whereby companies may find it worthwhile to
invest, and LDCs to grant concessions or contracts. All persons of
goodwill must wish them success.

Oil as a Declining Industry, OPEC's Declining Share

Also blunting the edge of exploration is the state of the oil market.
There have been innumerable warnings from on high of dreadful scarcity
looming ahead. Oil production would peak in the 1980s or 1990s. In
fact it has peaked already, for lack of market. Noncommunist consumption in 1982 will be rather less than in 1972. Nothing like this
has ever been seen before. In 1930–1933, when GNP in the United
States fell by one-third and other nations did almost as badly, world-
wide oil consumption fell by only 5% and was again at a record high
in 1935.

Not so this time. In the United States, the real price of energy has
about doubled since 1973. Long-term elasticity of demand seems to
lie somewhere between 0.5 and 1.0, which would point to an eventual
reduction in the energy used per unit of output of something between
30 and 50%. It is actually down by about 17% since 1973, and in my
judgment has a long way still to go. Oil use per unit of national output
has of course diminished more, about 25%. These responses to higher
prices are like a glacial drift—imperceptible in the short run, and irresistible in the long run. For this decade at least, oil is a declining

industry. This weakness of demand of course makes oil companies more reluctant than ever to explore outside of North America and the North Sea, which are too small to make much of a difference in a world picture. Still, non-OPEC production has slowly crept up. Therefore as total oil consumption has declined, OPEC exports have declined more. In 1973, they were 31 mbd. The official truth from the CIA in 1977 and the Energy Information Administration in 1978 was that 44 mbd would be "needed" by 1985. In the opening months of 1982, OPEC exports were around 15. OPEC exports will, I am sure, revive considerably this year or next, but the revival will be only a wave on the long downward sweep, which is the slow reaction to the price explosions of 1973 and of 1979.

Oil Companies and the Supply-Demand Balance before 1979

During the early 1970s the OPEC nations used the multinational companies as their tax collectors when the revenues were in the form of a tax. Later, when the concessionaires had been reduced to the status of producing contractors, customers, and sales agents, the companies could still be used to match production with market demand. There was no collusion among companies, who had no market power anyway. But each producing company would lift only what it could sell at the current price. Their total liftings equaled their total estimated sales, whether they numbered seven or 700. This was an odd, haphazard way to set market shares among governments, but it was effective. The producing nations entrusted market sharing to a mechanism which was outside their control and which they did not need to control.

But the system allowed small amounts of competition to seep into the market. The trouble was and is that the relative values of crude oils are constantly changing, moving up and down because of constant changes in relative demands for the various petroleum products. But since the crude oil prices are rigidly set out in advance, crudes yielding higher fractions of some products became better buys while other crudes became worse buys. As companies gradually became buyers, they gradually became less reliable off-takers because they would to some extent shift to the better buys. Thus fixed prices meant fluctuating market shares. Since there was a surplus of capacity, as is usual in a cartel, some governments were seriously embarrassed by unexpected market-share losses. Millions of dollars and many hours of computer time were spent in the vain attempt to arrive at a "right" set of differentials. The failure was generally acknowledged by 1978, and a movement began toward direct production control to keep market shares, if not completely stable, at least predictable.

Thus small amounts of inter-company competition in buying, exacerbated by sluggish demand, led directly to the price explosion of 1979. In consequence, there was a near complete ejection of the companies, and still more competition. That is how an unstable system works.

The 1979-1980 Price Explosion and After

The legend of a shortfall caused by the Iranian revolution in not even a half truth. Oil consumption never greatly exceeded production; it stayed within the range of variation which inventories cover. Moreover there were several million daily barrels of unused producing capacity. But they were not to be used. In January and again April 1979, there were two production cuts by Saudi Arabia and—worse yet—complete uncertainty as to how much would be available from month to month. There was therefore an abrupt rightward shift of the short-term demand curve because of demand for hoarding over and above consumption. This drove up spot prices and soon official government prices. In the general scramble for short-term gains, the governments cut the multinational companies out of third party sales, and permitted them to buy only for their own use.

The output-price developments in 1979 and 1980 are consistent with the theory that the Saudis and partners aimed to raise prices by a factor of 2.5, and did so. But the facts are equally compatible with a less demanding theory: the Saudis et al. aimed to raise prices, but never were in full control of the situation, and never could predict the precise effects of one or another step. Thus they lived from day to day; they did not intend to raise prices by 2.5 times but at every point they were willing to risk a probable shortage in order to head off a possible glut. The outcome had to be higher prices.

At any and every moment, the Saudis could have turned the market completely around, and brought the price down, by letting it be known that they would produce at capacity, for an indefinite period. That would have increased supply, by one or two mbd. It would have lowered demand, probably, even more since it would have checked the demand for hoarding. The price soared because the Saudis were ready and willing to let it soar, and to disregard their promise to the United States to maintain production.

Today the OPEC governments directly control production. Each government sets out in advance the amount it will be producing in the next month. Moreover, in late March 1982 they took the additional step of formally limiting total output and sharing it among themselves. I think they will succeed in holding production to demand, and restoring the recent price cuts. But successful or not, production control can drastically destabilize the market, as in 1979.

The trouble is, nobody can fine-tune a market with coarse instruments. Production figures are a month or more late, and their accuracy is diminishing. Consumption data even for the OECD nations are six months or more out of date. Even there, nobody knows the inventories in the hands of distributors and consumers.[1] Thus estimated short-term changes in consumption are not only imprecise but can show increases when there are really decreases and vice versa. Furthermore, outside of the OECD nations there is almost complete statistical darkness.

Accordingly, the decisions of the Saudis and their colleagues are made in ignorance. Moreover, an undershoot is more likely than an overshoot. They will do all they can to avoid a glut, and are willing to risk a shortage. Even the fear of a shortage produces a shortage and sends up the spot price. In 1979 a group of EEC commissioners toured the Persian Gulf and pointed out that the aim of the producing nations was to maintain a chronic small deficit. One comissioner called this "brinkmanship," a word which some thought in bad taste.

Oil Companies as Customers

Vertical dis-integration in world oil has now gone so far that the multinational companies have become largely buyers of oil, even when they do the work of production. Most crude oil is today being sold directly by the OPEC national oil companies to a variety of multinationals, traders, independent refiners, and governments who partly use, partly sell it. With more surpluses and deficits, oil is traded and sold around as never before. Heating-oil futures are being routinely traded. Term contracts have lapsed, at least for the moment, and it is not clear how many will be restored. We have the beginning of a wide decentralized oil market.

Previously, a few companies were tied to particular concessions. There were only a few prices to watch. Producing profits were high enough to make it better to produce oil than to buy it, even when market prices did not match product prices. Today, all companies are net buyers, and they actively look for even a slightly better deal. During the current surplus, oil companies have learned to terminate contracts and even to bargain over prices.

In Nigeria, where production had dropped by three-fourths, customers shrank to a reluctant dozen. This would have been unthinkable in other years. Saudi Arabia has tried to support Nigeria on the cheap. They have through a friendly publication warned the oil companies that their supplies of Saudi oil could be cut if they did not buy enough from Nigeria at current prices. Mobil Oil quickly squeaked, "Yes boss," but by this time their lawyers have probably told them of the dangers of even indirectly agreeing with other companies on prices or outputs.

In April 1981, the Kuwait oil minister accused Gulf Oil and BP— he must have blushed pronouncing it—of "haggling." Tradesmen, not gentlemen! Buyers free to roam the market and take advantage of better offers are destabilizers of any collusive price. They have the potential to become what they are not yet, and do not wish to be, so many loose cannons on the deck.

US price controls are gone, and American production is now integrated into the world market, where it is now a fifth of the total. American producers have long been accustomed to respond quickly to price signals and force a response on their rivals. American importers now make constant comparison of prices from various sources, and a few cents too many means no sale. Therefore the government sellers know not on whom to align, and some find themselves reducing prices to maintain output because they cannot see their rivals, hence cannot exchange reassurances that they will not cut prices.

I do not think we are approaching the demise of the OPEC cartel; far from it, so long as consuming governments remain anxiously deferential. But it is an interesting scene.

In the meantime the multinationals still lift the oil for their decreasing refining and marketing. In 1981, despite some shutdowns, excess refining capacity was about 25% in the United States, and 40% in Europe and

Asia. Losses are horrendous and will continue until the shakeout is over. Some fortunate companies can sell a loss-making refinery to a government, as in Italy or Canada, which draws spiritual sustenance from being "in oil." Oil companies made huge inventory gains during the two price explosions, and as producers in safe areas are of course immensely better off at the higher price levels.

The multinationals will survive and prosper, though not as much as in the past, because their know-how is, and will remain, a valuable asset. The myth of their tremendous power still lingers, and hence they will be resented, for how long I cannot say.

Notes

The research underlying this paper has been supported by the National Science Foundation under Grant No. DAR 78–19044, and by the MIT Center for Energy Policy Research. I have benefited much from a long collaboration with Henry D. Jacoby and James L. Paddock, and from the comments of Michael Lynch.

1. In a newly completed MIT doctoral thesis, Ellen Burton estimates that these inventories in the United States can expand or contract by an amount equal to about 10% of annual consumption. Focused into a short period, such an increment can have an explosive effect on prices.

III Country Studies

7 Performance of the Multinational Drug Industry in Home and Host Countries: A Canadian Case Study

Myron J. Gordon and David J. Fowler

I. Introduction

In Canada the markets for high technology, manufactured products are dominated to an extraordinary degree by subsidiaries of foreign corporations—through both their imports to Canada and their production in Canada. This state of affairs is not peculiar to Canada, and there is wide disagreement in other countries as well as in Canada on the consequences for host countries of such foreign control. There is general agreement, however, at least in the popular literature, on how any industry should be judged: the lower the prices charged for its products, the better its performance. In addition, the higher the quantity, skill content, and compensation rates of the employment provided; the higher the taxes paid; and the greater the quantity of products purchased domestically—the better the industry's performance. These two criteria may be called, respectively, the price and the expenditure performance of an industry.

The disagreement on the welfare consequences for a host country of foreign control is over the price and expenditure performance of a foreign-controlled industry in the host country by comparison with its performance in the home country. One view, which may be called the multinationalist position, is that subsidiaries improve the performance of the host country's industry (to the extent that is economically feasible) through "technology transfer." The sense in which the term is used here implies that technology transfer is *complete* if a subsidiary (1) sells its parent company's products in the host country at prices comparable to those charged in the home country, and (2) provides a market in the host country for employees, materials, and services that is comparable in scale to the market provided by the parent company at home. Just how complete the technology transfer actually becomes depends both on the actions of the parent company and on the economic environment provided by the host country. Multinationals argue that a host country should have *no* policy regarding foreign ownership and control, since multinational corporations would then find it profitable to enter a country only to the degree that their presence served the country.

By contrast, the nationalist position is that the presence of multinational corporations in a host country is due not to technology transfer but to their monopolistic power—to their acquisitions, patents, predatory pricing, marketing practices, etc.—and replacing them with national firms would not only have strategic and psychological benefits, but it would improve the economic welfare of the host country through some combination of lower prices and higher employment income. Nationalists argue that the industries dominated by multinationals are, in fact, characterized by a large number of small plants that use inefficient methods of production and limit their production either to the final assembly of components or to the mixing of ingredients—with the production of components/ingredients taking place abroad. In addition, much of a subsidiary's product line is imported as finished products. The nationalists maintain that as a result of these various practices, foreign ownership raises prices in the host country and reduces both the level of employment and its skill content.

When the financially rewarding and intellectually stimulating employment in managerial and professional activities is considered, nationalists claim that the performance of subsidiaries in host countries compares even less favorably with that of the parent companies. In Canada a government study[1] characterized subsidiary corporations as "truncated" branch plants because their role is confined to the limited production described above, to sales, and to their immediate supervision. Top management responsibilities and staff functions—such as investment decisions, research and development (R&D), market research, and systems development—remain abroad. It was further claimed that these truncated plants are also prohibited from serving export markets and from introducing new products initially into Canada.

This paper has two related purposes. One is to provide some factual evidence relevant to the above debate by comparing the performance of the multinational drug industry in a home and a host industry, namely, in the United States and Canada, and the other is to examine various policy options open to government in the host country for improving the price and expenditure performance of its drug industry.

The drug industry was selected because of its high technology, its high degree of foreign ownership, and the good data available (census and related government statistics) for carrying out the comparison. Furthermore, the drug industry is of special interest because Canadian governments adopted measures around 1970 to reduce drug prices by increasing competition.

It may be noted that there has been considerable research by economists on the comparative performance of manufacturing industries in Canada and the United States, but the development and interpretation of their data has been carried out within the framework of the neoclassical theory of perfectly competitive markets.[2] Within the theory there are no rents in employment income and the value of output is exhausted by its cost of production, so that labor productivity has been taken as the measure of performance. Productivity has been found to be lower in Canada, and—as a consequence of the neoclassical basis of the research—the difference has been attributed largely to tariffs and other barriers to free trade.

II. Description of the Drug Industry

The multinational drug industry enjoys an exceptionally large gross margin—the margin between the value of its output and its labor and material costs of production. For example, the US drug industry as a whole—which includes over-the-counter drugs and non-drug products made by drug firms as well as prescription drugs—had production costs that were only one-third the value of its output in 1968. However, this large gross margin is absorbed for the most part by overhead costs (R&D, marketing and selling, etc.), which are incurred to maintain the large gross margin and increase the volume of sales.

Production in the drug industry is classified as either primary or secondary manufacturing. The former comprises the manufacture of the active ingredients, while the latter comprises the mixing of the active ingredients with inert filler materials, the putting of the mixture into dosage form, and the packaging of the end product. Secondary manufacturing involves little or no economies of scale; hence, it may be located in each of the host countries where the product is sold. On the other hand, the technology involved in the primary manufacture of the active ingredients is not trivial, and economies of scale make it advisable to satisfy the world-wide demand for these ingredients with the output of only one or a few plants. Even so, production technology is a relatively unimportant factor in the size and profitability of a drug firm when compared with its R&D and marketing activities.

Because large fixed overhead costs are incurred in the development of new drugs, in establishing their safety and therapeutic value, and in gaining initial consumer acceptance, world-wide distribution of a drug is essential if its full profit potential is to be realized. The relative unimportance of production technology in the profitability of new drugs is evidenced by the fact that the socialist and some underdeveloped countries can and do produce drugs at costs that are only a small fraction of the prices charged by the multinational firms. However, their generic substitutes can only compete in those countries where legislation has eliminated the R&D and marketing advantages of brand-name drugs.

III. Price Performance

Although both the Canadian and US governments publish wholesale price indices, these indices are not comparable, and the underlying price-quantity data from which a comparative index could be constructed is not publicly available. We were able, however, to obtain comparable price-quantity data for 1968 and 1976 for both Canada and the United States from IMS of Canada Ltd., a subsidiary of a world-wide organization that specializes in the collection of pharmaceutical industry data (including prices). The IMS data appears to be exceptionally reliable, since it is taken from customer invoices, not from manufacturers' price lists.[3]

We found that in 1968 Canadian drug prices (weighted by quantity sold) were only 94.0% of their US level—somewhat surprising since a significant fraction of the Canadian market was satisfied by imported drugs that were subject to tariff. It was also surprising since production costs were probably higher in Canada despite the considerably lower wage rates there. On the other hand, a number of plausible reasons can be advanced to explain the lower Canadian price index. In the drug industry, production cost is only a small fraction of sales price and so has little influence on price. Furthermore, Canadian pharmacists typically buy through cooperative purchasing organizations that may be able to obtain lower prices than US pharmacists can. Finally, it should be noted that the margin of error in our price index makes it possible that the average level of prices was in fact the same in the two countries.

During the sixties the Kefauver Committee in the United States, the Harley Committee in Canada, and similar government bodies in England and elsewhere, publicized the enormous spread between the price of a prescription drug and its cost of production. In Canada the Harley Committee also publicized instances where drug prices were higher than in the United States, but it ignored or failed to recognize the parity that existed in the general level of drug prices. Perhaps because the Canadian drug industry was owned for the most part abroad, the legislative response to its investigation was stronger in Canada than elsewhere.[4]

Around 1970 the federal and various provincial governments in Canada adopted competition policies designed to eliminate the large spread between price and cost of production. These policies had two prongs: compulsory licensing and product selection. Federally, legislation was passed to compel a drug's patent holder to license generic producers at a modest royalty. Some provinces, including Ontario, then enacted legislation which *allowed* the pharmacist to substitute (with no legal liability) the generic for the brand-name drug, the one usually specified on the doctor's prescription. In Ontario and elsewhere such substitution was, in effect, compulsory on prescriptions paid for by the province, since pharmacists were only reimbursed their prescription fee plus the price of the "least-cost" product (usually generic) on the official list of approved drugs. Note that on prescriptions paid for by the consumer the pharmacist received—in addition to the prescription fee—the manufacturer's *list* price for whichever product (brand-name or generic) he actually dispensed to the consumer.

The above legislation encouraged generic competition in Canada, and generic substitutes for drugs under patent came on the market at prices that were one-half or less—in some cases as little as one-fifth—the prices of the brand-name drugs. However, the overall impact of these competition policies was far less impressive when the 1976 quantity-weighted price index for Canada relative to the United States is compared with the 1968 index. For the drugs that became subject to compulsory license, the relative price index fell from 93.3 in 1968 to 74.0

in 1976. For all drugs in our sample, however, the Canada/US price index was practically unchanged: 94.0 in 1968 and 93.6 in 1976.

If prices in Canada (relative to the United States) on drugs *not* under compulsory license were raised in order to offset the fall in prices for drugs under compulsory license, the competition policies of the federal and provincial governments would not have benefited Canada. However, there is good reason to believe that the drug firms did not act in this way. Wage rates and other costs rose more rapidly in Canada than in the United States between 1968 and 1976, so that it is quite likely that without the legislation to encourage competition, the index for all drugs would have been up sharply, as it was for drugs not under compulsory license. Canada benefited from these competition policies, but that benefit was quite modest, and it is of interest to consider why.

By 1976 only 27 of all drugs produced in Canada were produced under compulsory license: the brand-name producers had maintained a solid front against taking out compulsory licenses from each other, and the few, small generic producers[5] had only found it profitable to compete with the brand-name producers on a few high-volume drugs. Even though spared the R&D costs of the original developer, a generic producer faces high fixed costs when bringing a substitute drug on the market. In addition, for reasons to be explained shortly, the generic producer is confined to a very small fraction of a drug's total market. Hence, with production costs that are substantially higher than those of the brand-name producer, and with a price substantially lower to assure some share of the market, the generic producer cannot compete on the very large number of low-volume drugs.

Even though the average prices paid for drugs under compulsory license fell from 1968 to 1976, the government's competition policy was a disappointment in that the fall was not to the prices charged by the generic producers. The brand-name producers kept their dominant share of the drug market with prices that were two to five times higher than those of the generic producers. Recall that on prescriptions paid for by the consumer, the pharmacist is allowed to charge a prescription fee plus the manufacturer's *list* price for the product dispensed to the consumer. In this situation, if the pharmacist were actually to pay the list price, he would be indifferent as to the product dispensed and might very well dispense the least-cost product instead of the brand-name product prescribed by the doctor. However, the brand-name producers give the pharmacist "quantity discounts," and these discounts can be as much as 50% of inflated list prices.

In Ontario this "discount competition" confines generic sales almost exclusively to hospitals and to prescriptions paid for by the province, and it allows the brand-name producers to keep drug prices in the remainder of the market at a high, noncompetitive level. Although most of the other provinces also have product-selection legislation, the legislation is commonly even more favorable than Ontario's for nonprice competition on the part of the brand-name producers. Consequently, generic producers have a smaller share of the market for the drugs under compulsory license, and these provinces are even less favorable than Ontario for obtaining compulsory licenses on small-volume drugs. In Saskatchewan, by contrast, the province is, in effect, the purchasing agent for the drug stores and hospitals, and the least-cost supplier captures the entire market. However, Saskatchewan is too small a market to have much impact on the national level of demand and industry structure.

Thus we see that compulsory licensing and product selection have not imposed on the multinational corporations either a serious fall in prices or a material reduction in market share. It is clear that the market power of the multinationals is truly formidable, and that little short of complete government control of distribution can materially change their domination of the Canadian drug industry.

IV. Expenditure Performance in 1968

Government action to achieve better price performance in Canada may have been motivated in part by the expenditure performance of the multinational corporations, which was perceived to be unsatisfactory. To compare expenditure performance in Canada and the United States in 1968, table 1 presents the distribution of sales revenue between production costs (broken down into the components) and gross profit, and table 2 presents the distribution of gross profit among its components. In considering this data it should be kept in mind that the sales figures are comparable in real terms since product prices were on average about the same in the two countries. Table 1 reveals that production costs were 33% of sales in the United States and 47% (or

Table 1
Income statements for the Canadian and US drug industries, 1968 (millions of Cdn. $s).[a]

	Canada		United States	
	$	%	$[a]	%
Sales	368.5	100.0	6,103.0	100.0
Production costs:				
Material—Domestic	71.1	19.3	1,331.9	21.8
Material—Imports	73.0	19.8	99.6	1.6
Fuel and Electricity	2.0	0.5	45.7	0.8
Labor	27.0	7.4	534.5	8.8
Total	173.1	47.0	2,011.7	33.0
Gross profit	195.4	53.0	4,091.3	67.0

Source: Myron J. Gordon and David J. Fowler, *The Drug Industry: A Case Study in Foreign Control* (Toronto: Lorimer, 1981), pp. 45 and 111–112.
[a]US dollars have been converted to Canadian dollars @ 1.08108.

42.4% higher) in Canada, with the difference due to higher material costs in Canada.

Material Cost

Domestic expenditures for materials were actually lower in Canada than in the United States (19.3 versus 21.8% of sales), but import costs were about equal to domestic costs in Canada, so that *in total* material costs were 39.1% in Canada compared to only 23.4% in the United States. The US drug industry was vertically integrated in 1968, with practically no imports. By contrast, manufacturing in Canada was basically confined to secondary manufacturing, and finished products were imported to a significant degree. It is true that reliance on imports does substitute material cost for labor cost, but that explains only a small fraction of the large difference in material costs between the two countries.

Why was there such a significant difference in material costs between the two countries? The primary reason was the use of transfer pricing to reduce taxable profits in Canada. For instance, on the finished products imported in 1968, material costs were 82.5% of their sales value,[6] and the 17.5% gross profit margin allowed to Canadian subsidiaries

Table 2
Distribution of gross profits for the Canadian and US drug industries, 1968 (millions of Cdn. $s).[a]

	Canada		United States	
	$	% of Sales	$[a]	% of Sales
Gross Profit	195.4	53.0	4,091.3	67.0
Overhead Costs:				
R&D Expenditures				
—Domestic	7.1	1.9	457.6	7.5
—Imported	3.8	1.1		
Salary Compensation Other Than R&D	54.8	14.9	640.2	10.5
Nonpayroll Selling Expenses	54.1	14.6	746.9	12.2
Purchased Business Services				
—Domestic	6.7	1.8	243.7	4.0
—Imported	10.8	2.9		
Other Overhead Costs	31.2	8.5	520.3	8.6
Total Overhead Costs	168.5	45.7	2,608.7	42.8
Income Taxes	13.8	3.7	667.1	10.9
Net Profit	13.1	3.6	815.5	13.3

Source: Myron J. Gordon and David J. Fowler, *The Drug Industry: A Case Study in Foreign Control* (Toronto: Lorimer, 1981), pp. 52 and 115–117.
[a]US dollar amounts have been converted to Canadian dollars @ 1.08108.

was far short of the margin they needed merely to cover their selling expenses. A secondary reason for the higher level of material costs in Canada was the inefficiency of the small-scale production that was scattered over a large number of plants, thereby increasing material usage per unit of output. In addition, the prices of raw materials purchased domestically may have been higher, and imported materials were in part subject to a modest tariff. In conclusion, it is our estimate that about 60% of the difference in material costs between the two countries was due to transfer pricing.

Labor Cost

The cost of production labor was a slightly lower percentage of sales in Canada than in the United States, but it does not follow that labor productivity was higher in Canada. Recall that a substantial fraction of sales in Canada was of imported finished goods, and on the remainder there was only secondary manufacturing. Hence, if wage rates and labor productivity were the same in the two countries, then labor cost should have been a much smaller percentage of sales in Canada. Actually, the average hourly wage rate was 68% higher in the United States, so that the slightly lower Canadian labor cost per unit of output implies that labor productivity was higher in the United States by a very large margin.[7]

Such large differences in productivity and in the average wage rate per production worker were not due to any differences in the inherent skills or diligence of the Canadian and US labor forces. Rather, they were due to differences in the technology and scale of production between the industries of the two countries. It is our conclusion that up through 1968 the large presence of multinational drug firms in Canada did not benefit the country's production methods or compensation rates. The multinationals provided no technology transfer to Canada in the area of production.

R&D Expenditures

Turning to the distribution of the 1968 gross profits of the Canadian and US drug industries that is shown in table 2, we see that the US expenditures for R&D were 7.5% of sales, while in Canada they totaled 3.0%—with the *domestic* expenditures on R&D only 1.9% of sales. Actually, we had expected the last percentage to be even smaller, since we had been told that only a few of the multinational corporations did any primary R&D in Canada. R&D in the drug industry falls under four major headings: (1) the discovery of new drugs—or of improvements to existing drugs—and their testing on nonhuman subjects; (2) an initial program of human testing that is extremely careful and highly controlled to detect any undesirable health effects; (3) an extensive program of human testing to secure approval of the new drug by an appropriate government agency in some major country; and (4) additional testing to secure adoption of the drug in other countries.

The last type of R&D is certainly trivial in nature, and we understand that it is typically all the R&D done in Canada by the multinationals. The point is emphasized by the fact that the one important Canadian-owned firm in the industry, Connaught Laboratories, spent $2.1 million on R&D in Canada, which was actually 29.6% of the total R&D expenditure in Canada by *all* drug firms. Also, most of the remaining $5 million was accounted for by two subsidiaries of foreign companies that were formerly Canadian-owned and that had, therefore, well-established R&D organizations in Canada. Practically no R&D activity was introduced into Canada by the multinational corporations through the subsidiaries they had established there.

The view of people in related sciences in Canada is that the country has the infrastructure—hospitals, medical schools, universities—necessary to achieve a level of R&D activity comparable to that in the United States. It follows, then, that the small amount and the trivial character of the R&D done in Canada is due to the foreign ownership and control of the country's industry.

Salary Compensation Other Than R&D

Percentage-wise, salary compensation other than R&D was much higher in Canada—42% higher—than in the United States. This is somewhat surprising, since the subsidiaries of multinational corporations are given limited management responsibilities. It appears that for salaried employees, as well as for production workers, a large number of small firms reduces their productivity. In fact, although the world-wide sales of the US industry in 1968 were 16.6 times those of the Canadian industry, the number of salaried employees in the United States was only 9.2 times larger, meaning that output per salaried employee (measured by sales) was 72% higher in the United States. The much higher sales per salaried employee in the United States was not matched by a corresponding difference in salary compensation as a percentage of sales. The latter was only 42% higher in Canada, because compensation per employee was 58% higher in the United States.

Differences in the employment structure of the Canadian and US drug industries are revealed further by the 1970/1971 data in table 3. The percentage of persons in sales and in clerical jobs was much higher in Canada, while the percentage of persons in skilled, technical jobs— both white collar and blue collar—was much higher in the United States. Although the percentage of persons in management positions was only slightly higher in the United States, it should be remembered that their responsibilities were much greater than in Canada.

Table 3
Distribution of employees by type of occupation in the Canadian (1970) and US (1971) drug industries (%).

Type of Occupation	Canada	United States
Engineers, Scientists, and Technicians	14.14	21.16
Managers	9.10	10.96
Salespersons	18.20	9.74
Clerical Persons	25.16	20.12
Production Workers	23.72	23.15
Craft, Service, and Other Workers	9.68	14.87
Total	100.00	100.00

Source: See Myron J. Gordon and David J. Fowler, *The Drug Industry: A Case Study in Foreign Control* (Toronto: Lorimer, 1981), pp. 56 and 118.

Non-payroll Selling Expenses

Non-payroll selling expenses were a larger percentage of sales in Canada than in the United States in 1968. From sources other than those used to arrive at table 2, we estimated that *total* selling expenses were 15% of sales in the United States and 20% in Canada.[8] The Canadian figure was down from a 1964 trade association figure of 30%.[9]

The higher Canadian selling expenses (as a percentage of sales) can be attributed to a number of causes: the large number of firms participating in a small market spread out over a large territory; the burden of regulation on both the federal and provincial level; and, perhaps most important, the large number of firms that had entered the Canadian market after World War II and—as late as 1968—were still competing vigorously to establish their positions in that market.

We see that when expenditure performance is expressed as a percentage of sales, the performance of the multinational corporations was better in Canada than in the United States for selling expenditures. However, these expenditures represented little by way of technology transfer, since marketing strategy and techniques were developed in the United States, and the marketing organizations in Canada were merely comprised of the persons who implemented the policies and practices developed abroad.

Remaining Overhead Costs

The cost of purchased business services in 1968 was a larger percentage of sales in Canada than it was in the United States. However, 62% of the Canadian services represented payments to parent companies abroad. Finally, other overhead costs (including depreciation) are almost the same percentage of sales in the two countries.

Income Taxes and Profits

Perhaps the most striking difference between the industries of the two countries in 1968 was in the comparative figures for profit before taxes and income tax expense. Profit before taxes was 24.2% of sales in the United States, but only 7.3% in Canada. Consequently, income taxes were also very much larger in the United States, specifically 10.9% of sales to only 3.7% in Canada. The difference in profit before taxes was due in part to higher production and overhead (particularly selling) costs in Canada. The major reason, however, was the high prices used in transferring products and services from the parent company. Although some part of the gross profit of the Canadian industry was attributable to the activities of the parent companies, and transfer prices could legitimately be used to capture an equitable share of the industry's profits, it remains true that Canada did not share very generously in the tax revenues of the drug industry.

Domestic Share of Sales Revenue

The percentage of the Canadian industry's sales revenue that accrued to foreign recipients may be determined by taking the sum of the imported components of production and overhead costs in tables 1 and 2, adding to it all of the industry's net profit given in table 2, and subtracting the tariff on imports.[10] The calculation reveals that slightly more than 25% of Canada's sales revenue was distributed to foreign recipients. This figure may be considered low enough to support the view that the Canadian industry's expenditure performance was quite good in 1968. However, some of the reasons why 75% of Canada's sales dollar was spent domestically are not very satisfying. One is the high level of selling expenditures that were incurred in Canada during the year. Another is the low level of technology in the Canadian plants, requiring the employment of a relatively large number of unskilled, low-paid workers. Finally, the large number of truncated branch-plant operations in Canada resulted in an excessive employment of clerical and other low-paid persons in overhead activities.

Table 4
Income statements for the Canadian and US drug industries, 1976 (millions of Cdn. $s).[a]

	Canada		United States	
	$	%	$[a]	%
Sales	865.7	100.0	12,834	100.0
Production Costs:				
Material—Domestic	171.0	19.8	3,760	29.3
Material—Imports	212.1	24.5		
Fuel and Electricity	7.0	0.8	178	1.4
Labor	74.0	8.5	1,038	8.1
Total	464.1	53.6	4,976	38.8
Gross Profit	401.6	46.4	7,858	61.2

Source: Myron J. Gordon and David J. Fowler, *The Drug Industry: A Case Study in Foreign Control* (Toronto: Lorimer, 1981), pp. 72 and 111–112.
[a]US dollar amounts have been converted to Canadian dollars @ 0.98603.

V. Expenditure Performance in 1976

Table 4 presents condensed income statements for the Canadian and US drug industries in 1976. The figures for Canada reflect, among other things, the impact of the federal and provincial competition policies— five to seven years after they were adopted. Of course, there were other developments between 1968 and 1976 that also influenced the figures for the two countries.

Material Costs and Tax Havens

In both Canada and the United States, production costs rose as a percentage of sales between 1968 and 1976, due largely to increased material costs. The latter increased from 39.1 to 44.3% in Canada and from 23.4 to 29.3% in the United States. In Canada the rise in material costs was due primarily to a more rapid rise in the genral price level than occurred in the United States—at a time when product prices were rising at about the same rate in the two countries. Furthermore, the rise in Canadian drug imports and the higher transfer prices on them may also have contributed to the rise in Canadian material costs.

In the United States, on the other hand, the rise in material costs appears to have been due to the transfer of production abroad and to the use of transfer pricing in order to reduce reported profits in the United States. In order to stimulate employment in Puerto Rico, the US government had made tax exempt the profits on subsidiaries located there, and during the late 1960s and early 1970s US drug firms began to take advantage of this tax haven. So much so, in fact, that by 1978 a *Business Week* article reported that the US government was considering closing this tax loophole for the drug industry: too many drug firms were using transfer pricing to report 50% or more of their total profits in their Puerto Rican subsidiaries.[11]

Some idea of the use of Puerto Rico as a tax haven is provided by the *US Economic Census of Outlying Areas for 1977*. The Puerto Rican drug industry had shipments of $1,350 million, cost of materials of $327 million, and compensation of *all* employees of $96.6 million. Consequently, if all other expenses were as much as $100 million, the Puerto Rican subsidiaries had a reported, tax-free profit of over $800 million. By comparison, the *entire* US industry had a pretax profit on its US operations in 1976 of only about $1,700 million. Furthermore, the above census reported that 71% of the Puerto Rican drug shipments were to the United States, and only 27% went to foreign countries. It seems reasonable to conclude that the rise in material costs for the United States between 1968 and 1976 was in no small part due to the transfer of production to Puerto Rico and the high transfer prices on shipments to US parent firms from their Puerto Rican subsidiaries.

Labor Costs and Tax Havens

Production labor fell in the United States between 1968 and 1976 from 8.8 to 8.1% of sales, probably because of the transfer of production abroad. In Canada production labor rose during the same period from 7.4 to 8.5% of sales, due to a more rapid rise in Canadian wage rates. In 1976 the US wage rate of production workers in the drug industry was only 22% higher than in Canada, whereas in 1968 it had been 68% higher. If the technology of production in Canada had improved relative to the United States, the relative rise in the Canadian wage rate might have been due in some part to a rise in the skill content of employment in Canada. However, output per production worker (without adjustment for the greater degree of fabrication in the United States) was 55%

Table 5
Foreign trade statistics for drug products.

	1968		1976		1979[a]	
	$	%	$	%	$	%
Sales	368,511,000	100.0	865,595,000	100.0	1,085,000,000	100.0
Net imports	51,272,000	13.9	166,704,000	19.3	285,538,000	26.3
Net exports	15,350,000	4.2	43,975,000	5.1	67,849,000	6.3
Trade deficit	35,922,000	9.7	122,729,000	14.2	217,689,000	20.1

Source: Statistics Canada. *Trade of Canada: Imports, Merchandise Trade* (Ottawa: various years).
[a]The sales figure for 1979 is our estimate.

higher in the United States than in Canada—still the same as it was in 1968.

A widely held view of the multinational corporation is that it first enters a foreign country through exports, and then, with the passage of time and with its increased sales in and knowledge of the country, it expands production and improves the technology of production in the country. This pattern of development, however, was reversed for the Canadian drug industry during the period from 1968 to 1976, when the fraction of the Canadian market served by imports originating from parent countries or other subsidiaries abroad increased, while the fraction of the market served by Canadian subsidiaries fell.

This substitution of imports for domestic production continued at an accelerated rate from 1976 to 1979 (the last year for which data could be obtained), as shown in table 5. We see that in the eight years from 1968 to 1976 net imports rose from 13.9 to 19.3% of sales, and in only three more years they rose further to 26.3%. Over the same two time spans, net exports rose much less rapidly, so that the trade deficit as a percentage of sales rose from 9.7 to 14.2 to 20.1.

The large increase in drug imports into Canada may have been due in part to the government's competition policy, which the multinational drug firms viewed as an expression of hostility, making them less inclined to follow policies designed to secure the government's goodwill. However, other developments during the period may have actually played a larger role in the transfer of production abroad. Prior to the mid-1960s, a multinational's alternative to producing in Canada was producing in its home plant in the United States, England, Germany, or the like. The comparative advantage of producing in its home plant was relatively small and declining, certainly for high-volume drug products, while the various advantages (especially goodwill) of producing in Canada were considerable and led to the gradual growth of production over time. However, by the 1970s, the much lower production costs and considerable tax advantages of producing in Puerto Rico, Ireland, Portugal, or similar places, persuaded the multinational drug firms to transfer production to these countries. The advantages were even substantial when compared to production at home. The initial transfers were on an experimental basis, but as experience increased and as the benefits became obvious, transfers to these low-wage, low-tax havens increased — not only from the high-cost Canadian subsidiaries but also from the lower-cost plants at home.

R&D Expenditures

Table 6 presents the distribution of gross profits for the Canadian and US drug industries in 1976. We see that in the United States R&D increased from 7.5% of sales in 1968 to 9.2% in 1976. In Canada the total remained unchanged at 3.0%, but domestic R&D expenditures increased from 1.9 to 2.9% of sales. This shift of R&D expenditures to Canada was probably in some measure a response to the increasing expression of concern about its low level in Canada that was associated with the rise of nationalist sentiment. However, although R&D in relation to sales was unchanged in nominal terms from 1968 to 1976, it fell in real terms, since compensation rates in Canada had risen sharply during the period.

Foreign control of the drug industry would seem to be the only explanation for the continued low level of R&D in Canada. As noted earlier, the country had the human resources and institutional infrastructure to support a much higher level. In addition, compensation rates were still relatively quite low in 1976 for doctors and scientists, and regulations on human testing made the country an attractive place to carry on R&D. It is true that industry representatives had made a number of announcements over the years to the effect that programs to expand R&D in Canada were not adopted because of the government's competition policy, but these announcements were unsupported by concrete commitments on what they would do if the legislation were repealed. It should be added that the multinationals also made vague

Table 6
Distribution of gross profits for the Canadian and US drug industries, 1976 (millions of Cdn. $s).[a]

	Canada		United States	
	$	% of Sales	$	% of Sales
Gross Profit	401.6	46.4	7,858	61.2
Overhead Costs:				
R&D Expenditures				
—Domestic	24.8	2.9	1,184	9.2
—Imported	1.1	0.1		
Salary Compensation Other Than R&D	120.9	14.0	1,327	10.3
Nonpayroll Selling Expenses	87.0	10.0	1,797	14.0
Purchased Business Services				
—Domestic	16.9	2.0	930	7.3
—Imported	22.8	2.6		
Other Overhead Costs	74.6	8.6	995	7.7
Total Overhead Costs	348.1	40.2	6,233	48.5
Income Taxes	24.1	2.8	585	4.6
Net Profit	29.4	3.4	1,040	8.1

Source: Myron J. Gordon and David J. Fowler, *The Drug Industry: A Case Study in Foreign Control* (Toronto: Lorimer, 1981), pp. 79 and 115–117.
[a]US dollar amounts are converted to Canadian dollars @ 0.98603.

promises to expand production in Canada, notwithstanding the fact that doing so would be quite unprofitable for them.

Salary Compensation Other Than R&D

From 1968 to 1976 salary compensation other than R&D fell marginally as a percentage of sales in both the United States and Canada. However, the underlying reasons were quite different in the two countries. In Canada the number of salaried persons rose by only 8.6%, while their average rate of compensation rose by 103%. In the United States the number of salaried persons rose by 35.9%, while their average rate of compensation rose by 61%. By 1976 compensation rates for given job categories were about the same in the two countries, but the higher level of management responsibilities in the United States kept the average rate of compensation there still higher than it was in Canada—26% higher.

The very small absolute growth in non-R&D salaried employees in Canada was due in part to a reduction in selling activity per dollar of sales that will be discussed shortly. However, employment in the remaining categories of salaried persons also rose very little in Canada. No doubt the sharp rise in Canadian compensation rates stimulated a more rational and efficient organization of management functions. It also stimulated the transfer of work from Canada to headquarters abroad. The dramatic progress in travel, communications, and information processing during the postwar years made this feasible and economical.

Remaining Overhead Costs

Between 1968 and 1976 nonpayroll selling expenses rose slightly—from 12.2 to 14.0—as a percentage of sales in the United States, while in Canada they fell sharply from 14.6 to a more reasonable level of 10.0%. This reduction in selling activity in Canada was due in part to the government's competition policy which had made selling activities less profitable.

Purchased business services in the United States increased sharply from 4.0 to 7.3% of sales, while they fell slightly in Canada, notwithstanding the rise in compensation rates over the period. Here again we have evidence that the movement in management responsibilities from 1968 to 1976 was out of—not into—Canada.

Finally, total overhead costs in the United States rose from 42.8% of sales in 1968 to 48.5% in 1976, due largely to increased R&D, sales promotion, and other such overhead activities undertaken to improve gross profit margins and sales volume. In Canada, total overhead expenditures fell from 45.7 to 40.2% of sales, notwithstanding the sharp relative rise in compensation rates. The fall was made possible by the rationalization and curtailment of some overhead activities, including in particular marketing activities.

Income Taxes and Profits

The combination of higher overhead costs and transfer pricing reduced profits before taxes sharply in the United States from 24.2% of sales in 1968 to 12.7% in 1976, and income taxes fell by more than one-half—from 10.9 to 4.6%. In Canada the rise in material costs more than offset the fall in overhead costs, so that profits before taxes fell from 7.3 to 6.2% of sales, and tax revenues fell from 3.7 to only 2.8% of sales.

Domestic Share of Sales Revenue

Allocating the distributive shares in sales revenue for 1976 between domestic and foreign recipients, as we did earlier for 1968, reveals that the share to domestic recipients fell from 75 to 71% between the two years. However, these figures understate the curtailment of production and overhead activities that actually took place in Canada. As shown above, the sharp rise in wage and salary rates in relation to the United States and in relation to Canadian drug prices, masked the sharp fall in Canadian employment relative to sales. These developments could have taken place as a consequence of a sharp rise in productivity, but the analysis carried out earlier would indicate that production and overhead activities were transferred abroad.

VI. Conclusion

The long-term tendencies in the behavior of the multinational corporations that dominate the drug industry may be summarized as follows. R&D and general administration tend to be centralized in a corporation's *home* country. Sales tend to take place in *host* countries to the extent that the latter provide profitable markets, with each host country participating in marketing and distribution activities in accordance with the size of its market. Finally, corporations tend to locate their production activities and—for tax purposes—their profits in *haven* countries that offer low wage rates and freedom from taxation. These developments have been accelerated by the postwar progress in travel, transportation, communication, and information systems and by the current resurgence of the ideology of free trade.

It is beyond the scope of this paper to consider all of the policy options that might be open to a host country that wishes to improve the price and/or the expenditure performance of its drug industry. However, without going too far afield, we can examine the consequences of a free-trade policy that includes nonintervention beyond the prevention of monopolistic combinations in restraint of trade. Without doubt, our conclusions can have some relevance for other high-technology industries that are dominated by foreign multinational corporations.

We have seen that the price performance of the Canadian drug industry was improved by the compulsory licensing and product selection that was legislated in the early 1970s by the federal and various provincial governments. This improvement was limited, though, by the countervailing marketing strategies adopted by the industry, and an aggresive government response to these strategies is needed if a significant improvement in price performance is to be obtained. It is clear that Canada's pursuit of a free-trade policy implies abandonment of these competition policies, a drastic reduction in generic competition, and a rise in drug prices—particularly in the prices of hospital purchases and of prescriptions for individuals paid for by provincial governments.

While a free-trade policy would do no more than *impair* the drug industry's price performance, it would be quite *disastrous* for its expenditure performance. Production employment in the industry (and in the industries that provide filler, packaging, and other materials) would continue to decline in the host country as tariffs were completely eliminated and as the expansion of modern capacity in haven countries increased their competitive advantage. Finally, a laissez-faire environment would eliminate the need for multinationals to be "good corporate citizens," so that a host country's tax revenues and expenditures on R&D, administration, and other staff functions would also decline.

In view of the fact that Canada has the human resources and the institutional infrastructure required, one may wonder why it has not and why—under a laissez-faire policy—it undoubtedly could not become the home country for a reasonable share of the world-wide drug industry. Prior to World War II, domestic firms were an important presence in the Canadian drug industry, but by 1965 all but one of these firms had been acquired by foreign multinationals.[12] The reason why this took place is illustrated most vividly by Ayerst, the most promising of the privately owned Canadian firms. Between the wars Ayerst engaged in an ambitious R&D effort, which culminated in a number of important and potentially profitable discoveries. To realize that potential and to continue supporting its large R&D organization required the acquisition of foreign markets. However, the size and risk of the investment needed for the approval and marketing of its products abroad were prohibitive for an independent Ayerst. The company was worth far less as an independent than as a subsidiary of a large multinational drug firm. In 1943 Ayerst was acquired by American Home Products, and the subsequent growth in its world-wide sales has been outstanding.

The probability that domestically owned, research-based companies would appear and grow in Canada under a laissez-faire policy is practically zero. Required first of all is the discovery of important and patentable new drugs, which is most unlikely, since research on new products in Canada would be small in amount and confined to subsidiary companies. Of course, research in universities and hospitals—supported by government and by foundations—might give rise to new drugs. However, the investment required to perfect a new drug, to secure government approval, and to market it extensively abroad would preclude any other course of action by a wealth-maximizing person or firm than selling the discovery to one of the multinational drug firms.

Notes

1. Canada, Privy Council, *Foreign Direct Investment in Canada* (Gray Report) (Ottawa, 1972). A summary is in the *Canadian Forum* 51 (December 1971).

2. See, e.g., R. J. Wonnacott and Paul Wonnacott, *Free Trade Between the United States and Canada: The Potential Economic Effects* (Cambridge, Mass.: Harvard University Press, 1967); and E. C. West, *Canada-United States Price and Productivity Differences in Manufacturing Industries, 1963,* Staff Study No. 32 (Ottawa: Economic Council of Canada, 1971).

3. The development of the index is explained further in Myron J. Gordon and David J. Fowler, *The Drug Industry: A Case Study in Foreign Control* (Toronto: James Lorimer, 1981), pp. 43–4, 68–72, and 109–11.

4. An excellent review of the developments leading up to the legislation can be found in Ronald W. Lang, *The Politics of Drugs* (Farnborough: Saxon House, D. C. Heath, 1974). He concluded that the Canadian industry's trade association was dominated by the foreign parents of its member firms, and that the association's efforts to influence legislation were uninformed and unresponsive to the Canadian situation.

5. To this date, there are only four generic producers of any consequence in Canada, and two of these are subsidiaries of US corporations. Each of the two Canadian-owned companies survives by virtue of the exceptional ability of its owner-manager.

6. Here and in what follows, data without specific reference are obtained from Gordon and Fowler, op. cit.

7. Shipment of goods of own manufacture per production worker were 55% higher in the United States. Since the US plants carried out both primary and secondary manufacturing while the Canadian plants only performed the latter, the actual difference in output per worker was far greater than 55%.

8. The sources used to arrive at table 2 provided R&D salary compensation and salary compensation other than R&D (both of which were discussed earlier), but they did not provide the salary compensation of salespersons, which we, therefore, had to estimate from other sources in order to arrive at total selling expenses.

9. See Pharmaceutical Manufacturers Association of Canada, *Background Information on the Canadian Pharmaceutical Manufacturing Industry* (Ottawa, October 1979), appendix 7(E).

10. Our estimate of the tariff on imports in 1968 was $7.5 million, roughly 2% of Canada's sales revenue for the year.

11. See "Closing in on Puerto Rico's Tax Haven," *Business Week* (May 22, 1978), p. 154.

12. The one remaining Canadian firm, Connaught Laboratories, was established by the University of Toronto in 1920, and, as a consequence of government intervention, it has remained Canadian-owned.

8 Multinationals and Marketplace Magic in the 1980s

Richard S. Newfarmer

On October 15, 1981, President Ronald Reagan unveiled his program for developing countries. It revolves around three themes closely related to multinational corporations: (1) Reliance on markets to stimulate growth and development; (2) reliance on the private sector to lead development; and (3) minimizing government "interference" in the market. The president put the matter succinctly: "The societies which achieved the most spectacular, broad-based economic progress in the shortest period of time are (those that) . . . believe in the magic of the marketplace."

Certainly a principal actor in the Reagan program is the multinational corporation. By reducing the official development assistance efforts, his program implicitly places a heavy burden on their corporate shoulders. But will unfettered markets and MNCs produce the most rapid and broadly shared development? In addressing this question, this paper first looks at international markets, including the flows of foreign direct investment to developing countries and then the more complex question of the distribution of gains from multinational investment. Second, it examines the effects of multinational investment on the pattern of development. The discussion suggests that powerful economic and political forces usually trigger government intervention in MNC activities and the administration program will probably be received coolly in most developing countries. Since intervention usually results in bargaining between host government and MNCs, a final section speculates on MNC-host government relations in the 1980s.

I. International Markets and Growth of Developing Countries

President Reagan stated his position with eloquence in the Philadelphia speech: "Free people," he said, "build free markets that ignite dynamic development for everyone." But it is not always clear that market-led development always does benefit everyone—at least with the sense of equity and fairness implicit in orthodox trade theory. The issue of the distribution of gains from MNC-related trade and investment between host country and home country as well as the internal distributional effects have been the subject of heated political[1] and academic[2] controversy during much of the 1960s and 1970s. Two lines of argument suggest that the international markets in which MNCs operate will not produce growth as rapidly as some more preferable mixture of host-government intervention and market functioning.

The first line of argument focuses on the workings of international capital and technology markets, and points out that the flows in these markets are highly uneven. That is, foreign direct and indirect investment goes to the richest of poor nations and not to the nations which need it most. This is borne out in tables 1 and 2, which show that 87% of investment is concentrated in 14 of 132 developing countries—almost all of them oil exporters or wealthy semi-industrialized countries. This is a fair indication that technological transfers associated either with MNCs or sold independently are also quite concentrated.

The poorest 36 countries experienced economic growth rates of 1.6% during the 1960–1979 period, well below those of both the semi-industrialized countries (3.8%) and developed countries (4.0%) (World Bank, 1981, pp. 134–135). Moreover, World Bank projections show that the current account deficits of oil-importing countries will be between $70 and $85 billion over the next five years, of which $40 to $50 billion may be financed through private lending or direct investment (World Bank, 1981, pp. 60–63). The shortfall must be financed largely through concessional aid. A policy which relies solely on private international capital and technology markets to produce growth in the poor countries will certainly accentuate the pain of their structural adjustment and not ameliorate poverty for much of the 1980s.

In fairness to the administration, there is some ambivalence among its spokesmen on the degree to which private markets are expected to fill the void created by cuts in development assistance. Some officials seem to see foreign investment as a substitute for development assistance while others see it as a complement.[3] In either case, the aggregate numbers indicate that markets alone will not do the job.

Even if markets' capital and technology were perfectly competitive, laissez faire policies would undoubtedly produce similar flows. This is because the distribution of world wealth generates patterns of effective

Table 1
Direct investment stock in developing countries, by host country or territory
characteristics.

Host country, territory, or group	1967		1975	
	$ billions	%	$ billions	%
Total stock	32.8	100.0	68.2	100.0
OPEC countries[a] of which:	9.1	27.7	15.6	22.9
Venezuela	3.5	10.6	4.0	5.9
Indonesia	0.2	0.6	3.5	5.1
Nigeria	1.1	3.3	2.9	4.3
Iran	0.7	2.1	1.2	1.8
Tax havens[b]	2.3	7.0	8.9	13.0
All other developing countries and territories of which:	21.4	65.3	43.7	64.1
Brazil	3.7	11.3	9.1	13.3
Mexico	1.8	5.5	4.8	7.0
India	1.3	4.0	2.4	3.5
Malaysia	0.7	2.1	2.3	3.4
Argentina	1.8	5.5	2.0	2.9
Singapore	0.2	0.6	1.7	2.5
Peru	0.8	2.4	1.7	2.5
Hong Kong	0.3	0.9	1.3	1.9
Philippines	0.7	2.1	1.2	1.8
Trinidad and Tobago	0.7	2.1	1.2	1.8
Total above ten countries.	12.0	36.5	27.7	40.6

Source: Adapted from United Nations Center on Transnational Corporations, based
on Organization for Economic Cooperation and Development, *Development Cooperation* (Paris, various years).
[a]Algeria, Ecuador, Gabon, Indonesia, Iran, Iraq, Kuwait, Libyan Arab Jamahiriya,
Nigeria, Qatar, Saudi Arabia, United Arab Emirates and Venezuela.
[b]Bahamas, Barbados, Bermuda, Cayman Islands, Netherlands Antilles and Panama.

Table 2
Direct investment by GNP of host economy (non-OPEC).

Per capita gross national product	1967		1975	
	$ billions	%	$ billions	%
$1,000 or more	9.3	43.4	21.6	49.5
$500 to $999	5.0	23.4	9.7	22.3
$200 to $499	3.5	16.4	5.8	13.3
Less than $200	3.6	16.8	6.5	14.9
Total	21.4	100.0	43.6	100.0

Source: As table 1.

demand that create the most profitable business opportunities in the wealthy countries. Greater wealth means larger markets, greater opportunities for specialization, and economies of scale in production. To the problem which income distribution poses for free-market development, one must add another market failure: the positive externalities associated with higher levels of production and wealth. Income distribution and market failures indicate that free-market policies will probably not produce sufficiently rapid growth in the poorest countries to narrow the gaps in per capita income separating rich and poor countries in the coming decades.

A second line of argument is more complex and requires greater elaboration, for it lies at the root of many MNC-host government conflicts as well as the ill-fated North-South dialogue during the 1970s. The argument is that international markets are systematically biased against developing countries in their distribution of gains from trade and investment. These biases are traceable in part to the very existence of nation-states, which put restrictions on the movement of products and factors, and to the failure of markets to be competitive. This is not to say that trade and investment do not produce economic gains for buying and selling countries. At issue is the distribution of gains between developing and developed countries. G. K. Helleiner in his review of several international markets concluded that "There does seem to be a strong presumption that the developing countries do rather badly under the existing market system" (1979, p. 383).

The remainder of this section expands Helleiner's argument to MNC-related trade and investment. The contention is that imperfect international markets associated with MNC investment bias the distribution of gains against developing countries, ultimately requiring some government intervention for maximum growth.

Most economists in both the North and South give some credence to the fundamentally oligopolistic character of the MNCs. The theoretical underpinnings come from the pioneering work of Hymer (1960), Kindleberger (1969), and Richard Caves (1971).[4] This view starts with the insight that the MNC brings not only capital or technology to developing countries, but a *package* of tangible and intangible assets. The package is unique to each firm and thus not readily imitated by would-be competitors, especially domestic firms whose superior knowledge of the local business environment would in other instances give them a competitive edge. MNC control of this unique bundle therefore gives them a monopolistic advantage in all markets and, together with their ability to raise barriers to entry to further protect their advantage, creates a market with a limited number of sellers—oligopoly.

Oligopoly may in certain circumstances be associated with increases in global welfare, such as when it leads to economies of scale, economies of internalization, or increases in innovation. On the other hand, individual countries are not concerned about global welfare, but national welfare, and desire to accumulate benefits locally. From the perspective of developing countries, oligopoly raises the possibility that the costs of obtaining the package of MNC-provided assets is higher than would occur under workably competitive conditions—or if the package were de-bundled and the assets bought separately.

Even viewed more narrowly from the vantage of the product cycle—thought of as "cycles of monopoly" rather than as markets ineluctably working toward greater competition (Streeten's interpretation of Vaitsos' (1974) study)—successive waves of MNC market power may put developing countries at a distinct disadvantage in unregulated market transactions. This is because developing countries more often sell their products or factors in competitive markets in their dealings with developed countries or MNCs, while MNCs presumably sell in oligopolistic markets.

Impacts on Market Structure

There is in fact considerable evidence that MNCs operate in oligopolistic markets. For example, Fajnzylber and Martinez Tarrago (1976) found that in Mexico, MNCs sold 61% of their total sales in markets where the leading four plants accounted for 50% or greater and less than 10% in markets where the four leaders held less than 25% of the market; by comparison, Mexican firms sold only 29% in the highly concentrated markets and 33% in the low-concentration industries. More sophisticated econometric studies have found a strong correlation between concentration and various indicators of foreign participation (see Newfarmer and Marsh, 1981b for Brazil; Lall, 1979 for Malaysia; Tironi, 1978 for Chile; Cory, 1979 for Mexico; Connor and Mueller, 1977b for Brazil and Mexico). These facts, together with studies showing strong correlations between market structures internationally (Bain, 1966; Mellor, 1977; Connor and Mueller, 1977b), suggest that foreign direct investment is the bridge that links concentrated market structures in various countries—except perhaps where the state intervenes to proscribe multinational investments as in Japan.

These indicators of oligopoly—four-firm concentration ratios and the like—miss another important deviation from workable competition, market power attributable to conglomerate organization. A conglomerate is a firm which operates in several product and geographic markets. Almost by definition then, MNCs are large multi-market firms and have at their disposal discretionary power unavailable to single-market firms. This includes the ability to cross-subsidize growth in one market with profits from another, to manipulate transfer prices on in-house product and factor flows between markets, to allocate production among alternative countries, and engage in international price discrimination (see Newfarmer, 1980, pp. 21–30). Differences in relative size of MNCs and their domestic competitors also creates asymmetry in competition. This power may or may not be used in ways which correspond to the dictates of workably competitive markets.

The mere presence of these industrial structures, however, is not sufficient to support the argument that MNC-related trade and investment are biased in favor of the home country. It could be argued that new multinational investment reduces over time the level of concentration and barriers to entry facing potential entrants. In fact, Vernon (1977) has argued that an increasing number of cross-penetrating investments in European markets is evidence of the pro-competitive impacts of MNCs. On the other hand, there are some reasons to look closely at this finding.[5] For example, Connor and Mueller (1977a) found that between 1966 and 1972 the average share of the market held by

US subsidiaries in both Brazil and Mexico did not decline as Vernon's theory would suggest; to the contrary, it increased slightly.

Case studies of several industries in Latin America show that new MNC investment did indeed reduce concentration in certain high barrier-to-entry import-substitution industries (e.g., autos, heavy electrical equipment, tractors, tires), but only from a situation of a dominant firm to a more equally balanced oligopoly (Newfarmer, 1982a). (An exception was oligopolistic reaction in autos.) A second pattern—found in cigarettes, electronics, food, and to a lesser extent pharmaceuticals— was a process of MNC entry into highly concentrated industries dominated by a mixture of foreign and national firms, a short period of deconcentration through merger and shake-out, followed by a new consolidation in an MNC-led oligopoly. In virtually no case did market structure undergo a transition from monopoly to workable competition.[6]

Underlying this association between MNCs and oligopoly is a blend of behavioral and technological causes. Technologies of many modern MNC products play a dual role: Patented technology forms part of the unique package of assets that is the monopolistic advantage of MNCs in the market, and thus accords MNCs an absolute cost advantage over potential competitors. Also, production technologies generate economies of scale which create a scale barrier to entry and limit the number of producers a market can efficiently support. Economies stemming from the internalization of international flows of information may also act as a scale barrier. Although the international patent system is certainly important as a determinant of concentration (and arguably biased against developing countries, as Penrose (1973) and Vaitsos (1976) have contended), the scale barrier is more intractable from the perspective of the host government, since remedial policies to affect structure would undermine technical efficiency. Econometric studies of Mexico (Cory, 1979), Malaysia (Lall, 1979), Brazil (Newfarmer and Marsh, 1981b; Mooney, 1982) and the Philippines (Manrique, 1982) find that proxies for scale barriers are strongly associated with domestic levels of concentration.

But technology and economics of internalization are far from the sole source of MNCs' monopolistic advantage. Company behavior in advertising, acquisitions, and restrictive business practices are probably as important as technology in creating concentrated domestic market structures. Advertising (discussed further below) has been shown to have a positive association with concentration in econometric studies of Brazil, Malaysia, Mexico, the Philippines and other countries. UNC-TAD's several studies on restrictive business practices serve to illustrate the importance of interlocking directorates, cross-subsidization, local cartels, and foreclosure of supplies. Unlike patent or scale barriers associated with technology or information transfers, these sources of monopolistic advantage do not usually carry the social benefits that might otherwise offset their effects on market structure. In most cases, their net effect is to restrict competition and raise prices to consumers with little or no efficiency gains.

Another behavioral determinant of domestic market structure stems from the fact that domestic oligopolies dominated by subsidiaries are linked to a larger global network of rivalry. As a newly studied phenomenon, "international oligopoly" merits detailed consideration.

International Oligopoly?

As foreign direct investment has grown, MNCs in the same industry find themselves in competition with ever more frequency with the same rivals in several national markets. "This creates the possibility," wrote Richard Caves (1974) "that oligopolistic patterns of behavior found at home will spill over into the international markets." Raymond Vernon put the case more strongly: "Concepts of oligopoly pricing behavior, which heretofore have been treated within a singly national market, must be applied in an international setting" (1974, p. 100). This is, there may be only a few large companies in an industry so that one firm may look out across the international market and recognize its strategic interdependence with a firm based in another industrialized country, eventually facilitating collusive or parallel actions in markets around the world.

One can imagine several kinds of international oligopolistic behavior, including the formation of cartels, spheres of influence, and joint ventures to share markets, as well as oligopolistic reaction in investment strategies; one can also imagine local market effects stemming from international business practices. Let me recount briefly Shepherd's (1982) analysis of the history of the international cigarette industry to show how a few of these forms have direct consequences for market structure and performance in developing countries.

In the 1880s, mechanization provided the initial dynamism for consolidation and concentration in the United States. James Duke formed the powerful American Tobacco Company (ATC) and introduced "demand creation" marketing. He turned to foreign investment when it appeared in the 1890s that a wave of quasi-moralistic anti-cigarette publicity and the flood of machine-made cigarettes had led to stagnation in the US market. ATC tried to penetrate the British market where 10–15 small domestic firms competed. These firms, fearing the powerful ATC, banded together to form the Imperial Tobacco Co. (ITC). The resulting struggle among equals eventually ended in truce when in 1903 ATC and ITC decided to establish a world cartel to limit their competition and share markets in the world. They allocated to each other their home territories and established a joint venture to control markets in the third world, called British American Tobacco (BAT). This cartel lasted until US antitrust authorities required its dissolution in 1911. The divestiture arrangement severed management ties among the three companies, though it left some minority equity holdings in place.

But the story of international oligopoly in cigarettes hardly ended there. American producers continued to produce primarily for the US market, comprising perhaps one-half of world demand. ITC continued to produce in England and some European markets, and BAT continued to have free rein in the developing world. With minor deviations, these "spheres of influence" evolved and lasted with surprising durability until the mid-1960s. Then, the Surgeon General's Report in 1964 and subsequent consumer awareness in the United States that cigarettes were linked to cancer and other diseases caused a dramatic fall in the growth for US producers. They could only react by diversifying within the United States and by investing in foreign markets. This precipitated a wave of foreign investment that impinged on traditional BAT territory. Thus, in sharp contrast to BAT, over 90% of the 150 overseas affiliates of US cigarette manufacturers were established after 1965. Yet the point is that for nearly seven decades some loose form of international oligopolistic behavior determined the number and source of producers in the major cigarette markets of the developing world.

(Nor did the post-1965 entry of the US producers into Latin American markets have a particularly salutary effect on local market structure and performance. Generally, Shepherd finds that the dominant position of BAT in Argentina, Brazil, Mexico, and elsewhere was eroded somewhat, but the new foreign entry had greater impact on local firms which had existed under BAT's umbrella. These domestic firms were either acquired by incoming American investors or pushed out of the market altogether. What emerged was a new foreign dominated oligopoly.)

Market Structure and Profitability

A final link in the argument from imperfect international markets to uneven distribution of gains is profitability. Two questions about profitability are relevant: If our concern for the determinants of structure is sound, then structure should be a determinant of profitability. Second, MNCs should be related to higher profitability.

Although widely studied in the industrialized countries,[7] the market structure-profits relationship is only now becoming a concern for development economists. The 15 studies[8] that exist for developing countries are of varied sophistication and use disparate data sets, but they have surprisingly consistent results: Nearly all show a fairly strong positive relationship between imperfect market structures—market concentration, product differentiation, relative market share, and to a lesser extent barriers to entry—and profitability.

The evidence comparing the profitability of MNCs to local firms is mixed. The econometric studies find either no difference or that MNCs in fact report lower profits.[9] Concentration and other market imperfections may thus be the prime factor determining profits, not "foreignness" per se. It is also possible that foreign firms are in fact more profitable but that transfer pricing reduces downward profits reported in the host country.

This evidence is by no means conclusive in proving the assertion that the international system is biased in favor of home countries in the distribution of the gains from MNC-related trade and investment in favor of developing countries. One always wishes for more reliable data, more widely accepted assumptions, and fewer exogenous influences. But the evidence is persuasive that (a) foreign investment is strongly and persistently linked to domestic oligopoly in the host country, and (b) that domestic oligopoly generates high profits for those fortunate enough to operate in these markets. The evidence is sufficiently strong, in my opinion, to throw the burden of proof on those in the administration and in academia who hold that this distribution of gains from MNC-related trade and investment is fundamentally "fair."

Ironically, domestic market structure is a variable that host governments are in a position to influence—through domestic antitrust policy, tariff policy and other industrial policies. This raises the critical question of the role of the state, addressed in detail below. The point to be made here, however, is that any policy of letting "free markets work" will probably produce uneven growth among countries and relegate to developing countries a smaller share of the gains from MNC-related trade and investment than would occur in the presence of government bargaining or de-packaging of MNC assets.

II. MNCs and the Path of Development

The consequences of a policy that relies on MNCs as a prime mover of growth extend beyond the consideration of the international distribution of gains. One of the most important consequences to analyze is their dynamic effects on the nature of growth itself—which products are produced, which technologies are employed, and how industries are to fit themselves into an increasingly interdependent global system. MNCs, of course, are not the sole actors in the growth process. But a policy which accords MNCs a central role must recognize their influence in forging the path of development.

The way economies grow, as distinct from the growth rate itself, has an impact on economic sovereignty and national income distribution. From the perspective of a host country, the path that will permit the greatest flexibility and control in dealing with the constraints imposed upon internal growth by the international economy is to be preferred, ceteris paribus, over alternatives. These constraints include the effects of cyclical fluctuations in demand for host country exports associated with growth or recession in the industrialized world, as well as the perennial foreign exchange shortages and technology deficiencies stemming from the process of late-starting industrialization itself. The long-term distributional effects of the way an economy grows are also important from a host-country perspective. The evolution of factor shares over time will depend on changes in relative factor quantities, changes in demand, the elasticity of substitution between factors, and the factor bias in technical change. Government policy and institutional factors, such as the distribution of land or political power, are no less important in affecting income distribution. It is of more than passing interest to planners in host governments how MNCs affect these relationships and with them the path of development.

One approach to the obviously difficult measurement problems in addressing this issue is to study how MNCs "grow differently" from domestic firms in an industry. Holding industry constant (and therefore government policy to the extent it is nondiscriminatory among ownership groups), this comparison can often place differences in behavior in stark relief and we can see how the differences in firm behavior affect development.[10] Let us consider five aspects of firm behavior: advertising, technological appropriateness, technological dependence, trade propensities, and transfer prices. All have implications for economic sovereignty and income distribution.

Advertising

There are several reasons to suspect that MNCs may be associated with increasing levels of advertising. The promotion of certain products over others ultimately influences consumer choices and the mix of products available locally. First, an important monopolistic advantage of many MNCs is their differentiated products coupled with their superior marketing skills. These skills are usually employed to mount substantial advertising campaigns. Second, an element of differentiation in many consumer goods is constant change of model and product design, regardless of the actual usefulness of the change. Sometimes these costs are quite expensive, as in the auto industry. MNCs are the unquestioned leaders in this process as they ride the crest of the product-cycle wave, another element of their monopolistic advantage. Third, many of the new products are designed in the first instance for the mass markets of the home country, markets where wealth and consumer awareness are much higher, and where poverty is far less widespread, leading to questions about the appropriateness of products for poor countries.

Evidence on the issue of advertising is of three types: The first links MNCs to the parallel rise of the multinational advertising agencies.[11] Both are seen as promoting the technology of inefficient consumption. These studies are not particularly helpful in isolating the role of MNCs from domestic actors, who after all use the same foreign advertising agencies. Second, some anecdotal and econometric evidence does seem to indicate that MNCs change promotional norms within an industry.

For example, MNCs sponsored 75–80% of radio and newspaper ads in Swahili and English in Kenya and were responsible for 45% of all advertising placed (quoted in Helleiner, 1975, p. 174). Econometric findings for Brazil, Mexico, Malaysia, and the Philippines show that the level of foreign ownership was positively correlated with the level of industry advertising (Connor and Mueller, 1977b; Newfarmer and Marsh, 1981b; Lall, 1979; Manrique, 1982), though one study for a more limited sample in Colombia found no difference (Lall and Streeten, 1977).

The third variety of evidence is case studies, and is perhaps the most persuasive because it charts the dynamic relation between increases in foreign ownership and changes in promotional norms and product quality. American firms entering Argentina's cigarette industry were responsible for a quadrupling of the advertising expenditures to sales in the three years after their entry in 1966 (Shepherd, 1982). Other cases are also reported in Mexico's food industry (Whiting, 1982) and in pharmaceuticals for Argentina (Gereffi, 1982).

The much-discussed case of infant formula offers the clearest case of the link between the growth of multinationals, changes in promotional norms, and the link to inappropriate products. Nestlé's activities in much of the Third World drew attention because the company used saleswomen dressed in white coats to promote sales of infant formula in rural areas. It became popular in several communities to switch from breast-feeding to formula, even at the increased cost to poor consumers. An adverse side consequence in many areas, however, was an increase in infant mortality and malnutrition because mothers mixed the formula with polluted water; they were not able to sterilize their feeding implements; or they cut down the amount of milk powder in the formula mixture to save money. This illustrates the more general point that consumer ignorance is much higher in developing countries, consumer protection laws much weaker, and so the net distorting effects of MNC advertising in "consumption technology" may be greater (see Helleiner, 1975).

While the evidence is not conclusive, the development implications of increases in advertising associated with foreign investment are extremely important. First, advertising appears to increase industrial concentration in developing countries (e.g., Newfarmer and Marsh, 1981b; Lall, 1979; Manrique, 1982), with attendant consequences for income distribution and economic efficiency. Second, advertising appears to influence profitability, as discussed above, channeling more resources for investment into the differentiated consumer goods industries— industries that tend to produce goods serving the relatively wealthy. Third, advertising does appear to direct consumer choice towards the advertised products and therefore shift consumption patterns to mirror those in the North, shaping the "ideology of consumption" (see Barnet and Muller, 1974, and Galbraith, 1973). Advertising levels in developing countries are now comparable to those in the developed countries (James and Lister, 1980).

The possibility that products may not be "appropriate" to poor countries should not be dismissed. The difficulties in defining "appropriate" render any conclusion subjective, but I find Helleiner's (1975) extension of Lancaster's work a promising neoclassical avenue to explore as a way around this problem.

Product choice has a strong impact on the path of development because it influences which industries are established and, to the extent that elasticities of substitution between labor and capital are less than one, which technologies are employed. This has direct implications for distribution and economic sovereignty.

Technological Appropriateness

Because MNCs create technology in an environment where capital is cheap relative to labor, it has been argued that their technology is probably more capital-intensive than is appropriate to developing countries. The transfer of their technology on the heels of their products, the argument runs, creates a bias in growth towards a capital-intensive technology with its adverse effects on employment and income distribution. Despite the large number of studies on the relative labor intensity of multinationals and domestic firms, there are to date few definitive results.[12] Sanjaya Lall is probably correct when he writes,

The mass of conflicting evidence, the occasional use of imprecise methodology, the inherent problems of definition and measurement, all do not support any strong statement about the relative performance of MNCs and local firms. (1978, p. 241)

The absence of consensus is reason enough to undertake further, more detailed research. Our recent study for Brazil used a matched sample of firms in 30 four-digit industries (Newfarmer and Marsh, 1981b).

Controlling for market structure, firm size and other characteristics, multinationals were found to be consistently more capital-intensive as measured in the total employment to fixed asset ratio (table 3). These findings are consistent with Morley and Smith's (1977) study based upon census data, and indicate the continued importance of the question.

There is some evidence that market structure, including the degree of concentration, barriers to entry, and relative market share, also influence technical choice. Yeoman (1968) and Wells (1973) have found that firms in less competitive market structures tend to be less responsive to local factor prices then when in competitive markets. Yeoman (1968) found that subsidiaries in concentrated markets made less of an effort to modify the techniques they brought from the home country, while Wells found multinationals made only weak efforts to use the more efficient labor-intensive technology. Our study for Brazil using cross-sectional data found that measures of imperfect market structures, including concentration and relative market share, were found to be positively associated with lower labor capital ratios, although the results were not as consistent as the effects of ownership and scales of production (both negative).

One reason why this question is so difficult to resolve is that technological change is bound up closely with changes in products. Cutting in at any point in time for measurement probably misses imitation effects among ownership groups when a new product or technology is introduced, diluting any statistical results. Also, controlling for product mix and quality is extremely difficult in cross-sectional studies. The most promising area of further research is that of case studies linking the introduction of new products and advertising with changes in technology and market structure.

In conclusion, it should be noted that variation in capital-labor ratios is far more sensitive to industry than to ownership group, suggesting the policy instrument of greatest importance is the selection of which industries are to be established, and only secondarily who produces within any given industry.

Technological Dependence

Technological dependence refers to the continuing inability of a developing country to generate the knowledge, inventions, and innovations necessary to propel self-sustaining growth (Furtado, 1970). If a country

Table 3
Number of jobs created with Cr$1 million invested in fixed assets, by size,
concentration, and ownership category of investing firm.

	Brazilian	Foreign
Firm Size and Ownership		
Size class of firm (Cr$1,000)		
10,000	18.33	14.33
100,000	18.09	14.09
1,000,000	15.69	11.69
2,500,000	11.69	7.69
5,000,000	5.02	1.02
Concentration and Ownership		
Four-firm concentration ratio		
10	16.49	12.49
20	16.29	12.29
30	16.09	12.09
40	15.89	11.89
50	15.69	11.69
60	15.49	11.49
70	15.29	11.29
80	15.09	11.09
90	14.89	10.89
100	14.69	10.69

Source: Newfarmer and Marsh, 1981b; this table is calculated from the estimations
contained in the regression equation

$$LKR - 0.021 - 0.004OWN - 0.02ITR - 0.002CR4 - 2.678SIZE + 0.003VERT,$$
$$\quad\quad\; (5.38)\quad (-2.62)\quad\quad (-5.09)\quad\quad (-0.673)\quad (-2.74)\quad\quad (0.534)$$

$DF = 222$, $R = 0.18$, F ratio = 9.49,

where

$LKR \equiv$ labor/capital ratio,
$OWN \equiv$ dummy variable, one if MNC, otherwise zero,
$ITR \equiv$ index of technical rigidity,
$CR4 \equiv$ Four-plant concentration ratio, 1973, weighted by product sales,
$SIZE \equiv$ Size of firm measured in revenue; rescaled by multiplying coefficient $\times$ 10^{-9},
$VERT \equiv$ Vertical integration, measured by value-added to sales.

does not produce its own technology in at least some industries, it is argued, it will suffer slower growth and more disadvantageous terms of trade in the long run. As the product-cycle model suggests, technological prowess is often the secret to large shares in fast-growing export markets and to some degree of market power, and hence high prices. Developing countries have long recognized that the inability to produce local technology can hamper economic growth. Fajnzylber (1981) recently extended this argument to the capital-goods industry by arguing that developing countries must learn the design and engineering skills required in capital goods production or face not being able to create the "critical mass" of innovation necessary to spur development. Technological dependence may mean slower or "distorted" growth and reduced economic sovereignty.

Magee (1977), for one, sees MNCs as behaving differently in their approach to local knowledge creation. MNCs create "information" with the hope of appropriating some portion of the prospective monopoly rent associated with the application of the patented information in production and marketing. Since patent protection is imperfect, MNCs are predicted to develop technology for markets where barriers to entry may be expected to supplement patent protection. It follows from Magee's argument that MNCs will transfer technology to developing countries within those institutional frameworks that maximize "appropriable" rents (most desirably the wholly owned subsidiary) and when business conditions make such a transfer the most profitable (usually in response to tariffs, government demands, or threats to the local markets formerly served by exports). It also follows that MNCs will generally prefer to tightly control research and development activities, the source of new information, in the home country. Centralization of the R&D activities of the global company conflicts directly with the interests of developing countries in domestic technological "parity" or independence.

It does appear that domestic firms are more aggressive in their knowledge-creating attempts. West (1982) found that an independent firm in Argentina, FATE, was able to develop its own technology, in part adapted from foreign licenses, and use this to expand its position in the tire industry. FATE spent 0.4% of its sales on R&D, compared to zero for subsidiaries of MNCs. In fact, when local manufacturers established a research and development institute in the industry, MNCs offered no support. Gereffi (1982) found that in Mexico's steroid industry local firms also invested heavily in R&D, and that this produced significant benefit to the industry's development. R&D expenditures in Brazil's electrical industry were virtually unknown in the mid-1970s; the bulk of expenditures was found in one national firm (Newfarmer, 1980).[13]

Perhaps the most persuasive case for seeing MNCs as the institutionalization of technological dependence comes from the experience of Japan, which did not permit the establishment of MNC subsidiaries. After World War II, the Japanese continued their policy of not permitting foreign direct investment but of spending liberally for imported licenses technology (see Tsurumi, 1976). Their purchases of technology from abroad were considerable, yet at the same time they spent more than four times that amount on domestic R&D. Within the relatively short period of two decades they transformed themselves into aggressive world leaders in many industries. It is arguable that this would not have occurred had US and European MNCs been allowed to control technology-intensive industries in Japanese manufacturing.

Trade

MNCs' international trade behavior appears to be different as well. With import substitution industrialization, MNCs may initiate local production through the assembly of imported components and then gradually shift to local inputs as supplier industries develop and relative costs shift in favor of local purchase. However, MNCs may lag domestic firms in the process of domestic integration for several reasons: Local inputs may entail risks in quality and supply; parents profit on the export of parts to captive subsidiaries; costs may be different due to economies of scale; exports to subsidiaries from the parent facilitate the accumulation of profits abroad through transfer pricing; and exports from the home country please home governments worried about trade deficits and employment. Domestic firms have different interests in nearly all of these areas. On the other hand, if wide cost differences between local and foreign inputs persist, local producers may join foreign producers in opposing domestic vertical integration (see Hirschman, 1968).

These dynamics do appear to lead to higher import propensities for foreign subsidiaries than for domestic firms, even among firms in the same industry. Although some studies have shown no difference, the majority point to higher import propensities.[14]

One might expect that any elevated import propensity for MNCs would in some measure be offset by higher export propensities. MNCs have marketing channels in place, know foreign markets better than domestic competitors, and may be better able to take advantage of inter-country difference in costs of production. On the other hand, it could be that with production facilities already in place in several markets, parents would discourage subsidiary exports on the ground that such exports would be competitive with existing operations.

A review of the several studies[15] of relative export performance supports only weak generalizations. Several show that domestic firms perform somewhat better. An exception is when the government has taken carrot-and-stick measures to create incentives for MNCs to export. Thus, Jenkins shows that MNCs have a high export propensity in engineering industries in Mexico although a lower one in traditional industries. Bennett and Sharpe (1979a and 1979b) recount the successful government measures in autos which led to an increase in MNC exports. Another important variable influencing MNC exports from developing countries is the degree of competition experienced in the home country. The aggressive Japanese entrance to the US electronics industry, for example, led American firms to respond by setting up "export platforms" in several developing countries to take advantage of lower labor costs (see Newfarmer, 1980; Flamm, 1982). These situations illustrate the importance of MNC links to the home market in determining firm behavior in the developing country.

Transfer Pricing

Since the sale of a good or a service from one affiliate to another is not subject to the discipline of the market, the appropriate authority in the corporate hierarchy is free to set prices at the most advantageous level for maximizing corporate profits, subject to effective constraints imposed by governments. Intra-firm trade of MNCs account for a significant share of manufactured imports and exports of most developing countries. There are several reasons why MNCs might find it advantageous to manipulate transfer prices by overpricing imports to host countries or underpricing exports: to avoid controls on profit repatriation, on royalties payments and on local prices (because inflated import prices show up as higher costs), or to circumvent local tax rules, tariffs, exchange rate controls (see Vaitsos (1974), Lall (1973 and 1977), Robbins and Stobaugh (1973), and Horst (1971)). The incentives are usually present to use transfer prices against developing countries because taxes in developing countries are often higher, import duties on intermediate goods lower, currencies are less stable, and controls on profit remittances more stringent (Lall, 1973, p. 179). The recent precipitous cuts in US corporate taxes under the Reagan administration have probably widened the tax rate differences.

Since Vaitsos' seminal study (1974) that found that overpricing of intra-firm exports to affiliates amounted to more than 15% of the world prices in four Colombian industries, a few other studies have indicated that MNCs do indeed take advantage of the mechanism. Robbins and Stobaugh (1973) developed an optimization model of MNCs operating under different tax regimes and found that manipulating transfer prices could increase global profits as much as 15%. Their interviews of several companies found that managers of large MNCs were not taking full advantage of transfer prices, though medium-size companies tended to be more aggressive in seeking out transfer pricing profits. More recently the Greek government, for example, found that foreign subsidiaries on average paid 20% higher than the world market price in their sample of metallurgical imports and 25.7% for chemical imports (Roumeliotis and Golemis, 1978). Other recent examples can be found among a set of studies edited by Robbin Murray (1981).[16]

With the increasing importance of overseas banking, the possibility arises that financial corporations may engage in transfer pricing on foreign exchange transactions, accentuating the difficulty of controlling nonmarket financial transactions (see Bartlett, 1981). The *New York Times*, for example, reported that the enforcement staff of the Securities and Exchange Commission, after a three-year investigation, concluded that Citicorp "had directed a scheme for seven years that had circumvented and at times violated other countries' tax and currency laws." Between 1973 and 1980, "at least $46 million in profits . . . had been improperly shifted from the bank's branches in Europe, where taxes are high, to other branches in the Bahamas, where taxes on profits are much lower." The practices were not limited to Europe. In October 1979, Citibank's comptroller reported to the audit committee of the bank's board of directors that transfer prices — called "off-market rates"—were used in foreign exchange transactions in Japan, Hong Kong, the Philippines, Malaysia, Indonesia, India, and Saudi Arabia. Citicorp does not deny the facts or evidence in the case, according to the *Times*, though it maintains its transactions were "basically proper" (*New York Times*, February 18, 1982).

This cursory review of five important dimensions of MNC behavior suggests that there is a strong reason to believe that MNCs alter the character of growth in ways that do not always promote broadly shared development. It is entirely possible that their effects on changing the aggregate pattern of demand through advertising, combined with their effects in biasing the factor-intensity of technologies and in shaping market structures that accompany the new products, aggravate income inequities. These tendencies probably more than offset any tendencies in the opposite direction that come through the addition of capital to domestic stocks and hence lower returns to capital relative to labor. Similarly, there is reason to believe that the trade effects do not contribute to greater economic sovereignty or to structures of trade likely to produce the greatest gains in development.

All this is not to say that MNCs do not have a contribution to make to development. To the contrary, often they represent the most immediately available combination of valuable resources. Rather, the conclusion to be drawn from this discussion is that there is much legitimate and well-founded concern about the influence of MNCs on market-led development, and, from the host government's perspective, much to be gained from bargaining vigorously with MNCs.[17]

For that reason, host governments will in all likelihood continue to pressure MNCs for a greater share of the gains from their activities and for changes in their behavior. A US policy that asks host governments to reduce their regulatory role vis-à-vis MNCs thus flies in the face of some powerful political-economic forces.

III. MNCs and the State: A New Era of Peaceful Coexistence?

Administration initiatives towards developing countries come at a time when the conflicts over MNCs within developing countries and between North and South have apparently abated. How does one explain this apparent quiet in MNC-host country relationships? Does the new calm auger an era of peaceful coexistence in the 1980s, in which MNCs and host governments will work together to maximize the mutual gains from MNC-related trade and investment?

A strong argument can be made for the idea that the era of nationalism and MNC-host government conflict is passed. Some authors (e.g., Frank, 1980) have suggested that bargaining power in the bilateral negotiations between states and MNCs has swung irreversibly in favor of host governments, producing a new, more equitable distribution of gains—and with it a new stability. Indeed, several studies of the natural resource industries show that after the huge fixed costs of investments in resource installations are sunk, the host government can in effect "hold the company hostage." Bargains made at entry become obsolete as power shifts from the companies to the state (Vernon, 1971; Moran, 1974, 1977).

At the same time, the technical expertise within the governments to negotiate beneficial contracts has strengthened the governments' bargaining hand. Governments have learned to play off one oligopolist against another. Governments in the Caribbean succeeded in getting Kaiser to break the united opposition of the larger aluminum companies to government participation in their bauxite operations. The Brazilians were able to set up an aircraft industry by creating a state enterprise and buying licenses from Piper, the weaker competitor of Cessna. Cessna had dominated the Brazilian market but it refused government demands to take on domestic partners and begin local production with international technology (Baranson, 1982).

Also, the explosion of international liquidity as petrodollars were recycled through the Eurodollar markets has given host governments and alternative to MNC-provided capital. Between 1970 and 1980, foreign direct investment fell from 34% of nonconcessional flows going to developing countries to 77%, while private bank and bond lending rose from 30% to 36% (DAC, 1981, p. 172). In the short period between 1978 and 1980, the claims of American banks on Third World nations rose from $78 billion to $137 billion (Mathieson, 1982). It is argued that this has strengthened the hand of host governments in dealing with MNCs.

MNCs, for their part, have demonstrated a new flexibility in their dealings with host governments. This has given rise to unprecedented arrangements in technology transfer and ownership arrangements. One indication of this is the trend toward joint ventures. It is probable that the increase in joint ventures is largely attributable to post-1973 increases in Japanese foreign investment in natural resources in partnership with governments. Joint ventures in manufacturing, undoubtedly more common than a decade ago, are still by and large majority-controlled, with stock dispersed on incipient local capital markets or in the hands of weak joint-venture partners. Nonetheless, the importance of joint venture should not be overlooked because in the industrialized countries these have historically provided a stepping-stone to full domestic control later. The same could be said for other "new forms" of multinational activity, such as management contracts and engineering and services.

Yet it would be a mistake to infer from these changes a new era of peaceful coexistence in MNC-host country relations. The thrust of the analysis in the first part of this paper suggests that governments will continue to apply pressure to MNCs to increase their share of the gains from multinational investment, to overcome foreign exchange and technology constraints, and, perhaps with less urgency, to spread the benefits of development. Measures taken range from regulating firm conduct, such as in the transfer of patented technology and requiring exports as a condition for importing, to squeezing MNCs out of industries by systematically favoring domestic or state enterprises over foreign subsidiaries.

To be sure, the parameters of bargaining are considerably narrower than in the 1960s from the viewpoint of both host countries and MNCs. Host countries are more appreciative of the full costs of nationalization (see Kindleberger, 1977) and less disposed to rapid expropriation. Companies, for their part, realize that a piece of the market is better than none at all; it may even be embarrassing when a hardline stance by one oligopolist is broken with a concession of a competitor, who then enjoys the more limited fruits of the bargain; and collusive stances vis-à-vis an aggressive government are arguably more difficult to forge in an international (as opposed to an American) oligopoly. The massive expansion of private international debt has undoubtedly reinforced this parameter on the company side. The international banks, many of which have intimate ties with industrial companies, have a vested interest in the overall macroeconomic success of the developing country. They cannot simply shut down a plant and pull out in a dispute over a single investment or policy; rather they must rely on negotiated outcomes or risk losing an entire portfolio. But the underlying drive within the narrower bargaining parameters continues to be for developing countries to change the structure of their economies, compelling most host country to pressure the MNCs.

In this view, the primary reason that MNC-host conflicts have abated in the late 1970s is the weakened (not strengthened) position of many states brought about by the abrupt price increases in oil. Developing countries which coped with the oil-induced problems of structural adjustment by borrowing recycled petrodollars were soon dealt a second blow—abrupt increases in world interest rates. These two events have turned terms of trade sharply against oil-importing developing countries, and their current-account deficits moved deeply into the red. Thus, even though commercial bank lending increased in relative share of capital inflows into these countries, foreign investment inflows are no less important for their contribution to capital-account balances. (In fact, with the abrupt rise and instability in international interest rates, governments may well prefer equity over debt as a source of capital.) Any government action to undermine the position of foreign investors during this period jeopardizes this thin stream of inflows.

These events weakened major nationalistic initiatives to change ownership and other relationships with MNCs in Latin America and elsewhere. Brazil, the largest single recipient of foreign inflows among developing countries and one of the most sophisticated regulators of multinational investment, slowed its attempts to leverage industries out of MNC control.[18] The Andean Pact abandoned its Article 24 agreement requiring a fade-out of foreign investment for a mixture of reasons: Chile's withdrawal from the pact after the military coup in 1973, the impact of the foreign exchange shortage induced by the deterioration in terms of trade, and finally the political difficulty of implementing the accords in multiple countries. The change in governments in Peru after 1975 in the face of severe economic recession, together with the change in Chilean policy and the subsequent defeat of Manley in Jamaica, gave rise to the feeling that, among their other "mistakes," the nationalistic regimes in these countries had pressed their bargaining position vis-à-vis the companies too far.[19] Their experience argued for subtlety in negotiation.

Besides the weakening of states attributable to the international economy, the very spread of MNCs in manufacturing has also had an impact upon the internal politics of the state in a way that places new constraints on the "political will" to bargain, and thus requires technocrats use greater finesse in future bargaining. Contrary to the case in raw-materials production, MNCs in manufacturing have far greater linkages to local interest groups—MNCs employ a larger labor force (per unit of capital) than most raw-materials ventures, they usually create a larger network of white-collar employees, and they usually have at least a few domestic competitors who share broad class interests (though not without conflict at the margin). These social groups have much deeper roots in civil society than do elites traditionally associated with raw materials. This makes "foreigners" much less obvious targets of nationalistic forces on the one hand, and on the other, accords them some influence in policy-makers' circles.

Some examples illustrate the point: The spread of MNCs in Brazil's electrical industry in the 1960s and 1970s had an important impact upon the manufacturers association, the Brazilian Association of the Electrical and Electronics Industry (ABINEE). Founded in 1962 to represent industry's interests to the government, the association's officers were primarily from local firms. By 1975, their share of official positions had fallen from 65% in 1962 to 40% while the MNC share increased from 35% to 60% (Newfarmer, 1980, pp. 173–175). ABINEE's voice is known in the halls of government. In the cigarette industry, MNCs in Latin America collect a high percentage of tax revenues for host governments, so the government is more likely to see itself as an ally of the industry than adversary. In Argentina's tire industry, MNCs in the first Peron era did not impede the entry of a domestically owned competitor (FATE), so that the new firm could represent more per-suasively the industry's interest to the government.

Also contrary to the raw-materials case, a continual flow of new products and technology emanates from the home country so that the subsidiaries' continued growth and prosperity is contingent to some degree upon its links to the parent. This works to strengthen the hand of multinational manufacturers of differentiated products over time.

These characteristics of manufacturing industries lead Bennett and Sharpe (1982) to conclude, on the basis of their analysis of the Mexican auto industry, that the bargaining-power dynamic in manufacturing is exactly the reverse of the raw-materials case: The host government's power is greatest just prior to MNC entry; after the investment has been made, social groups dependent on the new industry as well as negotiators themselves come to support the MNCs' interests and the government's position becomes weaker.

A final change in business organization in the 1970s also places a new parameter on the political will of the state: Many advanced developing countries have sired their own multinationals, giving their governments a new stake in an open international commercial system. This tendency is rapidly growing but small in relative importance and so is not yet strong enough to dampen the overall impulse of host governments to bargain.

These two socioeconomic dynamics—a drive for host governments to change the structure of their economies in the face of market pressures to the contrary and narrowing bargaining parameters—will undoubtedly play themselves out differently in each country. Given the narrow parameters of bargaining in manufacturing, government strategies will probably be more subtle, more piecemeal, and slower than the overt conflicts of the past that sometimes ended in nationalization or the toppling of a regime—or both. Mexico perhaps offers a paradigmatic example of the hard bargaining to come. In food, the new Mexican Food System program contains counter-advertising measures that will undermine the position of multinational manufacturers of baby formula. (A lovely, nationally known actress is shown breast-feeding her newborn infant under the voice-over, "Mother's milk is pure, secure, and contains love.") In electrical equipment, the government is seeking domestic vertical integration with partial government ownership based upon the bargaining strength of the state-owned electrical utility. In autos, performance requirements compelling exports were introduced in the late 1970s and have recently been reaffirmed. In pharmaceuticals, the government continues to put pressure on patent policies of the companies by reducing patent life from 15 to 10 years and by requiring patent exploitation within four years, on penalty of forfeiture. The Social Security Administration, the country's largest buyer of drugs, have moved to bulk purchasing of basic drugs. In petrochemicals, Pemex has laid out plans to build an industry through negotiation with the petrochemical multinationals based on limiting their share to minority holdings. Mexico, like many other developing countries, will continue to welcome foreign investment, but the welcome will be contingent upon ever more exacting conditions designed to achieve national goals.

One element in the 1980s may figure prominently in MNCs-host country relations and is wholly unpredictable: the politics supporting the regimes in advanced developing countries. The current path of development continues to leave large numbers of people isolated from the benefits of development. Unemployment, malnutrition, and low productivity continue to characterize large segments of the population, even in advanced developing countries. To be sure, these groups are not wholly unaffected by growth; the better off among them are not infrequently able to climb above some line of absolute poverty during their lifetimes. Nonetheless, concepts of social justice and human rights to the basic necessities of life often precede the economic model's capacity to deliver them, sowing the seeds of political change. This is especially true of the urban poor, who are most susceptible to the new aspirations for consumption introduced by advertising and most vulnerable to downturns in growth rates. These politics may interact with slow real growth in many developing countries during the 1980s to produce a volatile mixture of political instability. In some countries, these politics will certainly reshape the parameters of negotiation between the state and multinational companies in the coming years.

Notes

This paper has benefited from the thoughtful comments of Richard Feinberg, G. K. Helleiner, Bruce Kogut, Saul Schwartz, and others at the Middlebury Conference on MNCs in the 1980s.

1. Tensions sown by the expansion of MNCs in the 1960s in many developing countries exploded in a storm of conflict ushering the 1970s. ITT was discovered to be linked to a plan to "create economic chaos" as a way of destabilizing constitutionally elected Salvador Allende in Chile. This set off investigations in the US Senate. The Senate Foreign Relations Committee founded a Subcommittee on Multinational Corporations, which went on to investigate corporate payoffs of Lockheed, alleged destabilizing effects of MNC behavior about the time of the second dollar devaluation, etc. Other countries conducted similar investigations. Questionable payments, analyzed thoroughly by Gladwin and Walters (1980), came under scrutiny of the SEC and Congress. These events prompted developing countries to demand international action. The activity later culminated in the formation of the UN Center on Transnational Corporations, and a new concern for MNCs in halls of UNCTAD, UNIDO, and even the OECD.

Of lesser drama but perhaps greater consequence were changes in the bilateral relations between MNCs and host governments. Several governments introduced legislation aimed at reducing the influence of MNCs in their economies. Mexico in 1972 passed stringent legislation requiring minority ownership for foreign investors and regulating the flow of technology; Brazil adopted a strong technology law; the Andean Pact, then comprising Peru, Chile, Bolivia, Equador, and Colombia, required a 15- year fade-out provision for foreign investors with its article 24. India, South Korea, and even Taiwan enacted strong regulatory measures governing the behavior and ownership of subsidiaries during the period. For analyses of legislation change in the period, see Robinson (1976) and Wallace (1976).

2. Several excellent reviews of these contrasting perspectives are available; see Chilcote (1974) and Valenzuela and Valenzuela (1978) for superb discussion. One of the best reviews of dependency theory is Palma's (1976).

3. AID Administrator McPherson seemed to see private flows as a substitute for development assistance when he said in congressional testimony: "Less emphasis will be placed on the transfer of funds, of taxpayers' dollars. Greater emphasis will be placed on the transfer of those things that generate resources—the technology skills, know-how and capital of the US private sector." Then, asked in an interview on October 22, whether the United States should follow the Brandt Commission Report's recommendation to nearly double developmental assistance, Treasury Secretary Regan responded in the clearest possible manner: "We cannot afford to give any more. . . . There's certainly no more room for more aid from us." The president, for example, seemed to favor the private-foreign resource-flows as a substitute position when he juxtaposed the two in Philadelphia: "The financial flows generated by trade, investment, and growth far exceed official development assistance funds provided to developing countries."
Secretary of State Haig seemed to hold the foreign assistance-as-complement perspective. In his September speech before the IMF/World Bank directors in Washington, Secretary Haig stated that "the poorest developing countries require long-term and generous concessional aid. . . ." Asked in Cancun whether his statements disavowing the term "Marshall Plan" for developing countries meant "no more foreign aid," Secretary Haig replied: "No, not at all. I think I said precisely the opposite of no foreign aid. It (my statement) means not only foreign aid in a bilateral sense; it also means continuing support for the multilateral institutions. . . ." Secretary Baldridge, after affirming the policy of relying on the private sector in a speech to the UNA, said "Don't draw the conclusion that the Reagan administration is pulling in the reins on foreign aid. The reverse is true." It is probably no accident that Haig and Regan appeared jointly at several press briefings at Cancun.

4. For a thoughtful and assiduous review of these, see John Connor's (1977) opening chapter.

5. The method used to support this claim is flawed in some important respects: (a) A mere increase in the number of firms is not an indication of erosion of concentration, since high prices may produce a large competitive fringe; (b) the industries are three-digit SIC industries, usually too broad to capture the effects of market power in particular product classes, and (c) the effects of acquisitions do not appear to be wholly considered.

6. Also, MNCs are likely to be associated with persistently high concentration, rather than be a force promoting competition, through their effects on barriers to entry. MNCs can raise entry barriers facing domestic firms through the financial ties they establish with subsidiaries (facilitating cross-subsidization), through advertising behavior, and by producing excess capacity through investment in large- scale production (often pari pasu with new technologies) or investing "ahead" of demand.

7. Weiss (1974) reviews 56 econometric studies for the United States alone, and concludes that ". . . our massive effort to test these predictions [i.e., oligopoly is associated with higher prices and profits] has, by and large, supported them. . . . (1974, p. 231).

8. These include House (1973, 1976) on Kenya, White on Pakistan (1974), Sawhney and Sawhney (1973) on India, Amjad (1977) on Pakistan, Nam (1975) for Korea, Fajnzylber and Martinez-Tarrago (1976) for Mexico, Gan and Tham (1977) on Malaysia, Connor and Mueller (1977a) on Brazil and Mexico, Gupta (1968) on India, Lall and Streeten (1977) for Colombia and India, and Newfarmer and Marsh (1981a) for Brazil's electrical industry.

Newfarmer and Marsh's (1981b) study for all Brazilian manufacturing is one of the more detailed, finding strong influences for concentration and relative market share, and a less strong influence for product differentiation. Barriers to entry, found to be strongly associated with concentration, are not found to be directly related to profitability.

Perhaps the most sophisticated study is Mooney's (1982) for Brazil, which used both ordinary least squares and three-stage least squares multiple regression analysis with concentration and profitability endogenously determined. He finds positive correlation between measures of imperfect markets and profitability.

Manrique's (1982) study of the Philippines is one of the more recent. Using OLS procedures, his measures of market structure and profits have the predicted sign, but are not significant.

9. Reuber (1973) Found slightly higher rates of profitability for MNCs than domestic firms and took this as an indication of superior efficiency, though he did not control for domestic market structure. Fajnzylber and Martinez-Tarrago (1976), Cross-tabulating industry level data, found that industrial profitability was markedly higher in industries with 75% of sales or more controlled by MNCs; some of this was due to the effect of concentration, since most sales in foreign-dominated industries were also in highly concentrated, highly profitable industries (1976, p. 238). Lall and Streeten (1977) in their sample of Colombian and Indian firms found no significant differences in profitability, though their data were limited and did not include complete structural measures. Newfarmer and Marsh (1981a) presented 1972 and 1974 data for Brazil's electrical industry showing higher rates of profitability for domestic firms than for foreign subsidiaries, after controlling for measures of imperfect market structures (which are also positive and significant). This same pattern was found in their much larger study for all Brazilian manufacturing (1981b), and in Mooney's (1982) study.

10. There are some obviously important caveats to this methodology. First, in comparing the behavior of the two ownership groups, there is no guarantee domestic firms will behave "any better" by development criteria than MNCs. Is a local pharmaceutical firm which manufactures an ineffectual drug an adequate standard against which to compare MNCs? Presumably only if MNCs perform better; but difficulty arises when the two are indistinguishable. Second, there are often dynamic interactive effects among firm strategies that are difficult to detect, especially through econometric tests. For example, if an MNC enters the market and advertises unusually heavily, other firms may be forced to respond; a cross-sectional snapshot in the second phase would have blurred result. (This may plague many studies of technological choice.) Third, there may be vertical links among industries which are not analyzed sufficiently. Finally, there may be no domestic firms against which to measure MNC performance. The final-stage assembly operations in autos are almost always 100% in the control of MNCs in developing countries. In this case, counterfactual assumptions can be employed — asking how the industry would perform under alternative industrial organizations. Or, cross-national comparison might be used. Case studies, especially when combined with econometric tests with cross-sectional data, can help remedy many of these drawbacks.

11. Often this evidence is anecdotal and focuses on the "cultural imperialism" dimensions of advertising (e.g., Barnet and Muller, 1974; Schiller, 1971; Roncaglioli and Janus, 1978). These studies commonly link the transnational influence to the spread of foreign advertising agencies such as J. W. Thompson, McCann-Ericsson, etc. A recent study from the Latin American Institute of Transnational Studies (ILET) shows the parallel expansion of transnational advertisers, foreign subsidiary advertising, and stories in local newspapers of Latin America adapted from the major transnational wire services (Roncaglioli and Janus, 1978). Useful as they are, these studies do not tell us whether MNCs advertise more (or differently from) their national counterparts or whether increases in foreign direct investment are associated with increases in promotional outlays of firms.

12. There are several studies that have found MNCs do employ less labor per unit of capital than domestic firms (e.g., Radhu, 1973; Cohen, 1975, for Malaysia; Wells, 1973;

Morley and Smith, 1977). Some others find no conclusive results (such as Mason, 1973, and Lall and Streeten, 1977). Yet others, such as those of Pack (1976) and Strassman (1968), have found that MNCs are in fact more labor-intensive than domestic firms, apparently because they are more alert to ways of cutting costs, especially in peripheral processes.

13. Other studies of subsidiary behavior in developing countries also tend to confirm the proposition that MNCs would rather not invest heavily in local R&D. Jorge Katz (1973) found that local expenditures on R&D in Argentine manufacturing, where foreign investment is prevalent, are about 1/20 of the expenditures on imported technology (0.03% of sales versus 1.5% of sales respectively) and are only about 1/5 of US R&D investments on sales. Moreover, much of the local expenditure is devoted to product differentiation, such as researching consumer tastes and redesigning products accordingly. Perhaps for this reason and the fact that payments for technology are often used to transfer profits abroad, Katz found no statistical association between unit royalties paid abroad and observed technological progress (1973, p. 216). Morley and Smith (1974), who studied the capital goods industry in Brazil, found most multinational research was to modify production techniques to suit local scales and inputs.

14. Using a variety of methodologies, such findings are reported for Canada (Safarian, 1966), Korea (Cohen, 1973), Costa Rica (Wilmore, 1976, although the differences in import propensities were not statistically significant), Peru (Vaitsos, 1978), Taiwan (Riedel, 1975), India (Subrahamanian and Pillai, 1977 for the engineering industry), Mexico (Jenkins, 1979), and Brazil (Fajnzylber, 1970); Newfarmer and Marsh, 1981a and b). Some studies have reported no significant differences in import propensities. These include Lall and Streeten (1977) for a sample drawn from India, Kenya, Jamaica, Iran, Colombia, and Malaysia; Reuber (1973) for a sample from Indonesia; and Cohen (1975) for Singapore. Only in Taiwan are foreign firms reported to have a lower import propensity than domestically controlled firms (Cohen, 1975); yet there is reason to doubt this finding: Cohen's sample is small (10 foreign, 5 local firms) and it conflicts with Riedel's study for Taiwan based on a larger sample.

15. These include Brazil, Argentina, Mexico, Colombia, Peru, and Venezuela (Vaitsos, 1978), Taiwan (Cohen, 1975), Jamaica, Kenya, India, Iran, Colombia, Malaysia, and India (Lall and Streeten, 1977), and Mexico (Fajnzylber and Martinez-Tarrago, 1976). Nayyar (1978) concluded that the share of manufactured exports of US subsidiaries from all developing countries has fallen from nearly 20% in 1966 to about 9% in 1974, though it was not clear if domestic firms or other MNCs have made up the difference.

There are some exceptions to the findings that domestic firms have a higher export propensity than foreign firms. Cohen (1975) and Jo (1976) both found that in Korea MNCs exported notably more than their local counterparts, though when the effects of industrial location were taken into account the differences narrowed. This was attributed, in part to generous tax incentive schemes, profit repatriation rules, and import licensing.

Two studies for Central America (Wilmore, 1976, in Costa Rica, and Rosenthal, 1975, in Guatemala) found that MNCs exported slightly more than domestic firms. These firms generally exported to neighboring regional markets.

Newfarmer and Marsh's (1981b) study for Brazil found no significant difference, when controlling for industry through matched samples.

16. There are other studies: Lall (1973) provided some additional information for the pharmaceutical industry, finding extensive overpricing on UK MNCs' sales to affiliates. The Monopolies Commission indicted Hoffman La Roche of Switzerland for overpricing its intrafirm sales to its affiliates in the United Kingdom and was ordered to reduce prices by an average of 30% or greater (Monopolies Commission, 1973). The US IRS examined prices on intrafirm trade of several thousand firms, found potential transfer pricing cases in over 700 firms, and ordered the reallocation of earnings back to the United States in over 400 cases. Because the IRS is concerned only with US tax revenue, it does not (and

perhaps legally cannot) compel reallocation of profits to other countries. This is recounted in Murray (1981), one of the most thorough empirical treatments of transfer pricing to date.

17. This situation has commonly been likened to a bilateral monopoly in which the companies monopolize their package of assets and the countries monopolize access to the host market or resources. Kindleberger (1977) argued that the solution to the bilateral monopoly would be political, that is, settled on the basis of which side has more power. The lower boundary on costs of direct investment to developing countries is determined by the rate of returns just necessary to produce the investment; the upper bound, or most developing countries would pay, is determined by the scarcity value of the resource— that price at which developing countries would forgo the investment altogether.

18. The government has forged a larger, domestically controlled position in sectors formerly dominated by foreigners, such as in electrical generation, petroleum refining and distribution, steel, aircraft, some pharmaceuticals, and petrochemicals.

19. For a broader discussion of the many other elements influencing US relations with nationalistic regimes, see *From Gunboats to Diplomacy* (Newfarmer, 1982b), particularly the papers on Chile, Brazil, Nicaragua, and Guatemala, as well as on US economic policy.

References

Amjad, R., 1977. "Profitability and Industrial Concentration in Pakistan," *Journal of Development Studies*, April, pp. 181–198.

Bain, Joe S., 1966. *International Differences in Industrial Structure*. New Haven, Conn.: Yale University Press.

Baranson, J., 1982. *North-South Technology Transfer: Financing and Institution Building*. Mt. Airy, Md.: Lomond Publications.

Barnet, R. S., and R. E. Muller, 1974. *Global Reach: The Power of Multinational Corporations*. New York: Simon and Schuster.

Bartlett, S., 1981. "Transnational Banking: A Case of Transfer Parking with Money," in R. Murray (ed.), *Multinationals Beyond the Market*. London: Harvester Press.

Bennett, Douglas, and Kenneth E. Sharpe, 1979a. "Transnational Corporations and the Political Economy of Export Promotion: The Case of the Mexican Automobile Industry," *International Organization*, Winter.

————, 1979b. "Agenda Setting and Bargaining Power: The Mexican State vs. Transnational Automobile Corporations," *World Politics*, October.

————, 1982. "The World Auto Industry and Its Implications for Developing Countries in Latin America," in R. Newfarmer (ed.), *International Oligopoly and Development*.

Business International, 1973. *Setting Intercorporate Pricing Policies*. New York: Business International.

Caves, R. E., 1971. "International Corporations: The Industrial Economics of Foreign Economics of Foreign Investment," *Economica* 38, p. 149.

————, 1974. "International Trade, International Investment, and Imperfect Markets." Special Paper in International Economics No. 10 (November), Dept. of Economics, Princeton University.

Chilcote, R., 1974. "Dependency: A Critical Synthesis of the Literature," *Latin American Perspectives* (Spring), p. 1.

Cohen, Benjamin I., 1973. "Comparative Behavior of Foreign and Domestic Export Firms in a Developing Economy," *REStat* 55, pp. 190–197.

————, 1975. *Multinational Firms and Asian Exports.* New Haven: Yale University Press.

Connor, John M., 1977. *The Market Power of Multinationals: A Quantitative Analysis of US Corporations in Brazil and Mexico.* London: Praeger.

Connor, John M., and Willard F. Mueller, 1977a. *Market Power and Profitability of Multinational Corporations.* Report to the Senate Subcommittee on Multinational Corporations. Washington, D.C.: Government Printing Office.

————, 1977b. "The Shaping of Market Structures by Multinationals, Brazil, Mexico, and the US," Staff Paper Series No. 120, *Agricultural Economics*, University of Wisconsin.

Cory, P., 1979. "The Pattern of Foreign Subsidiary Production in Mexican Industry." Paper presented to the North American Economic Studies Association, Atlanta, Georgia, November.

DAC (Development Assistance Committee), 1981. *Development Co-operation: 1981 Review*, Paris: OECD.

Fajnzylber, Fernando, 1970. "Sistema Industrial e Exportacao de Manufacturas." Rio Economic Commission for Latin America, Instituto de Planejamento Economic e Social.

————, 1980. *The Industrial Dynamic in Advanced Economies and Semi-industrialized Countries.* UNIDO/NAFINSA Paper Presented to the Eleventh Pacific Trade and Development Conference, Seoul, Korea, September 1–4.

Fajnzylber, Fernando, and Martinez Tarrago, Trinidad, 1976. *Las Emprasas Tranacionales.* Mexico City: Fundo De Cultura Economica.

Flamm, K., 1982. "Off-shore Production in the International Semi-conductor Industry," in J. Grunwald and K. Flamm, The Internationalization of Industry (mimeo).

Feinberg, Richard E., 1983. *The Intemperate Zone: Third World Challenge to US Foreign Policy* (mimeo).

Frank, I., 1980. *Foreign Enterprise in Developing Countries.* Baltimore: Johns Hopkins University Press.

Furtado, Celso, 1970. "The Concept of External Dependence in the Study of Underdevelopment," in Charles Wilber (ed.), *The Political Economy of Development and Underdevelopment.* New York: Random House.

Galbraith, J. K., 1973. *Economics and the Public Purpose.* New York: Signet.

Gan, W. B., and S. Y. Tham, 1977. "Market Structure and Price-Cost Margins in Malaysian Manufacturing Industries," *The Developing Economies* 15, no. 3, pp. 280–289.

Gereffi, G., 1982. "The Global Pharmaceutical Industry and Its Impact on Third World Countries," in R. Newfarmer (ed.), *International Oligopoly and Development.*

Gladwin, T. N., and I. Walters, 1980. *Multinationals Under Fire.* New York: Wiley.

Goodsell, C. T., 1974. *American Corporations and Peruvian Politics.* Cambridge, Mass.: Harvard University Press.

Gupta, V., 1968. "Cost Functions, Concentration, and Barriers to Entry in Twenty-Nine Manufacturing Industries of India," *Journal of Industrial Economics* 17–18, pp. 57–72.

Helleiner, G. K., 1975. "The Role of Multinational Corporations in the Less Developed Countries' Trade in Technology," *World Development* 3, no. 4, pp. 161–189.

————, 1979. "World Market Imperfections and the Developing Countries," in W. R. Cline (ed.), *Policy Alternatives for a New International Economic Order.* New York: Praeger.

Hirschman, A., 1968. "The Political Economy of Import-Substituting Industrialization in Latin America," *Quarterly Journal of Economics*, February.

Horst, Thomas, 1971. "The Theory of the Multinational Firm: Optimal Behavior under Different Tariff and Tax Rates," *Journal of Political Economy* 79, p. 5.

House, W. J., 1973. "Market Structure and Industry Performance: The Case of Kenya Revisited," *Oxford Economic Papers* 25, pp. 405–419.

————, 1976. "Market Structure and Industry Performance: The Case of Kenya Revisited," *Journal of Economic Studies*, November, pp. 117–132.

Hymer, Stephen, 1960. *The International Operation of National Firms: A Study of Direct Foreign Investment*. Published in 1976, MIT Press.

James, L., and S. Lister, 1980. "Galbraith Revisited: Advertising in Non-Affluent Societies," *World Development* 8 January, p. 1.

Jenkins, Rhys, 1977. *Dependent Industrialization in Latin America*. New York: Praeger.

Jo, Sung-Hwan, 1976. "The Impact of Multinational Firms on Employment and Incomes: The Case of South Korea." World Employment Programme Research Working Papers WEP2-28, WP12. Geneva: International Labour Office.

Katz, J. M., 1973. "Industrial Growth, Royalty Payments and Local Expenditure on Research and Development," in V. Urquide and R. Thorp (eds.), *Latin America in the International Economy*. New York: Wiley.

Kindleberger, Charles P., 1969. *American Business Abroad: Six Lectures on Direct Investment*. New Haven, Conn.: Yale University Press.

————, 1977. *Economic Development*. New York: McGraw-Hill.

Lall, Sanjaya, 1973. "Transfer-Pricing by Multinational Manufacturing Firms," *Oxford Bulletin of Economics and Statistics* 35, p. 3.

————, 1977. "Transfer Pricing in Assembly Industries: A Preliminary Analysis of the Issues in Malaysia and Singapore." Commonwealth Secretariat, London (mimeo).

————, 1978. "Transnationals, Domestic Enterprises, and Industrial Structure in Host LDCs: A Survey," *Oxford Economic Papers* 30, no. 2, pp. 217–48.

————, 1979. "Multinational and Market Structure in an Open Developing Economy: The Case of Malaysia," *Weltwirtschaft Archiv*, June.

Lall, Sanjaya, and Paul Streeten, 1977. *Foreign Investment, Transnationals and Developing Countries*. Boulder, Colo.: Westview Press.

Magee, Stephen P., 1977. "Information and Multinational Corporations: An Appropriability Theory of Direct Foreign Investment," in J. Bhagwat (ed.), *The New International Economic Order: The North-South Debate*. Cambridge, Mass.: MIT Press.

Manrique, Gabriel, 1982. "Multinational Corporations, Advertising and Industrial Organizations in Economic Development; A Case Study of the Philippines." Ph.D. thesis, University of Notre Dame.

Mason, R. Hall, 1973. "Some Observations on the Choice of Technology by Multinational Firms in Developing Countries," *REStat* 55, pp. 349–355.

Mathieson, J., 1982. "The Development Role of the Private Sector." Overseas Development Council (mimeo).

Mellor, Patricio, 1977. *The Pattern of Industrial Concentration in Latin America*. CIEPLAN-CHILE, and National Bureau of Economic Research (mimeo).

Monopolies Commission, United Kingdom, 1973. *Report on the Supply of Chloradiazepoxide and Dizepam*. London: HMSO.

Mooney, J., 1982. *Profit and Concentration in Brazil.* Ph.D. thesis, University of Notre Dame.

Moran, Theodore H., 1974. *Copper in Chile: The Politics of Dependence.* Princeton University Press.

————, 1977. "The International Political Economy of Cuban Nickel Development," *Cuban Studies/Estudios Cubanos* 7, no. 2.

Morley, Samuel A., and Gordon W. Smith, 1977. "The Choice of Technology: Multinational Firms in Brazil," *Economic Development and Cultural Change* 25, no. 2, pp. 239–264.

Murray, R., 1981 (ed.). *Multinationals Beyond the Market.* London: Harvester Press.

Nam, Woo H., 1975. "The Determinants of Industrial Concentration: The Case of Korea," *Malaysian Economic Review* 20, no. 1, pp. 37–48.

Nayyar, D., 1978. "Transnational Corporations and Manufacturers Exports from Poor Countries," *Economic Journal* 88.

Newfarmer, Richard, 1980. *Transnational Conglomerates and the Economics of Dependent Development.* Greenwich, Conn.: JAI Press.

————, 1982a (ed.). *International Oligopoly and Development: Case Studies of Transnational Industries and their Growth in Latin America.* (mimeo, February)

————, 1982b (ed.). *From Gunboats to Diplomacy,* New US Policies for Latin America. Washington: Senate Democratic Policy Committee.

Newfarmer, Richard, and Lawrence Marsh, 1981a. "Foreign Ownership, Market Structure and Industrial Performance: Brazil's Electrical Industry" *Journal of Development Economics* 8, pp. 47–75.

————, 1981b. *International Interdependence and Development.* Report to the US Department of Labor, July 31 (mimeo).

Pack, Howard, 1976. "The Substitution of Labour for Capital in Kenyan Manufacturing," *Economic Journal* 86, pp. 45–58.

Palma, Gabriel, 1976. "Dependency: A Formal Theory of Underdevelopment or a Methodology for the Analysis of Concrete Situations of Underdevelopment," *World Development* 6, no. 2, pp. 881–925.

Penrose, Edith, 1973. "International Patenting and the Less-Developed Countries," *Economic Journal* 83.

Radhu, Ghulam M., 1973. "Transfer of Technical Know-How Through Multinational Corporations in Pakistan," *Pakistan Development Review* 12, no. 4, pp. 361–374.

Reuber, Grant L., H. Crookell, M. Emerson, and G. Gallais Hamonno, 1973. *Private Foreign Investment in Development.* Oxford: Clarendon Press.

Riedel, J., 1975. "The Nature and Determinants of Export-Oriented Direct Foreign Investment in a Developing Country: A Case Study of Taiwan," *Weltwirtschaft Archiv* 3.

Robbins, Sidney M., and Robert B. Stobaugh, 1973. *Money in the Multinational.* New York: Basic Books.

Robinson, R. D., 1976. *National Control of Foreign Business Entry.* New York: Praeger.

Roncaglioli, Rafael, and Norean Janus, 1978. "A Survey of the Transnational Structure of the Mass Media and Advertising." Instituto Latinoamericano de Estudios Transnacionales, Working Paper.

Rosenthal, Gert, 1975. "The Expansion of the Transnational Enterprise in Central America: Acquisition of Domestic Firms" (mimeo).

Roumeliotis, Panayotis V., and Charalambos P. Golemis, 1978. "Transfer Pricing and the Power of Transnational Enterprises in Greece," Paper presented to the UNCTAD-IDS Conference on Transfer Pricing, November, Brighton, England.

Safarian, A. E., 1966. *Foreign Ownership of Canadian Industry.* Toronto: McGraw-Hill of Canada.

Sawhney, P., and B. Sawhney, 1973. "Capacity-Utilization, Concentration, and Price-Cost Margins: Results on Indian Industries," *Journal of Industrial Economics* April, pp. 145–153.

Schiller, H., 1971. "Madison Avenue Imperialism," *Transaction,* March–April.

Shepherd, P., 1982. "Transnational Corporations and the International Cigarette Industry," in R. Newfarmer (ed.), *International Oligopoly and Development.*

Strassman, P., 1968. *Technological Change and Economic Development: The Manufacturing Experience of Mexico and Brazil.* Ithaca: Cornell University Press.

Subrahamanian, K. K., and P. Mohana Pillai, 1977. "Transnationalisation of Production and Marketing Implications of Trade: Some Reflections on Indian Experience." Paper presented to IDS/UNCTAD seminar, Intra-firm Transactions and Their Impact on Trade and Development.

Tironi, E., 1978. "Latin American Economic Integration." Paper presented to UNCTAD Conference on TNCs and Economic Integration, Lima, Peru, June.

Tsurumi, Yoshi, 1976. *The Japanese Are Coming.* Cambridge, Mass.: Ballinger.

Vaitsos, Constantine V., 1974. *Intercountry Income Distribution and Transnational Enterprises.* Oxford: Clarendon Press.

————, 1976. "The Revision of the International Patent System: Legal Considerations for a Third World Position," *World Development,* February, pp. 85–99.

————, 1978. "The Role of Transnational Enterprise in Latin American Integration Efforts: Who Integrates and with Whom, How and for Whose Benefit?" Prepared for UNCTAD Secretariat and Presented at Conference on TNCs and Economic Integration, Lima, Peru, June.

Valenzuela, A., and J. S. Valenzuela, 1978. "Modernization and Dependency: Alternative Perspectives," *Comparative Politics,* Summer.

Vernon, Raymond, 1966. "International Investment and International Trade in the Product Cycle," *Quarterly Journal of Economics,* pp. 190–207.

————, 1974. "The Location of Economic Activity," In J. H. Dunning (ed.), *Economic Analysis and the Multinational Enterprise.* Praeger Special Studies in International Economics and Development. New York: Praeger.

————, 1977. *Storm over the Multinationals: The Real Issues.* Cambridge, Mass.: Harvard University Press.

Wallace, D., 1976. *International Regulation of Multinational Corporations.* New York: Praeger.

Weiss, Leonard, 1974. "The Concentration-Profits Relation and Anti-Trust," in H. J. Goldschmidt et al. (eds.), *Industrial Concentration: The New Learning.* Boston: Little, Brown.

Wells, L., 1973. "Economic Man and Engineering Man: Choice of Technology in a Low Wage Country," *Public Policy,* Summer, pp. 319–342.

West, P., 1982. "International Expansion and Concentration of the Tire Industry and Its Implications for Latin America," in R. Newfarmer (ed.), *International Oligopoly and Development*.

White, Lawrence J., 1974. *Industrial Concentration and Economic Power in Pakistan*. Princeton University Press.

————, 1976. "Appropriate Factor Proportions for Manufacturing in LDC's: A Survey of the Evidence." Princeton: Woodrow Wilson School, Research Projects in Development Studies No. 64.

Whiting, V., 1982. "Transnational Enterprise in the Food Processing Industry," in R. Newfarmer (ed.), *International Oligopoly and Development*.

Wilmore, Larry, 1976. "Direct Foreign Investment in Central American Manufacturing," *World Development* 4, no. 6, pp. 499–517.

World Bank, 1981. *World Development Report*. Washington, D.C.: World Bank.

Yeoman, W. A., 1968. "Selection of Production Processes for the Manufacturing Subsidiaries of U.S.-Based Multinational Corporations." D.B.A. thesis, Harvard University.

9 The Community and the Corporation

Eric W. Kierans

When geometric diagrams and digits
are no longer the keys to living things

"1800," Novalis, translated by Robert Bly

There are men of the East, he said,
Who are the East.
There are men of a province
Who are that province
There are men of a valley
Who are that valley

"Anecdote of Men by the Thousand," Wallace Stevens

In a thoughtful article, "Economic Sovereignty at Bay," Raymond Vernon noted that "The persistence of man in reaching out beyond his national boundaries to exploit the economic opportunities in other lands is amply documented by history, from the Phoenicians' investments in the tin mines of Cornwall to Fiat's commitments in the Soviet Union."

Having no knowledge of the terms that the Phoenicians negotiated with the Cornwallians a thousand years before Christ, I cannot judge who made the better deal. The Fiat–Soviet Union arrangements, however, would be much more interesting to Canadians since it is highly unlikely that the Russians suffered any decline in economic control and political authority over their own affairs. Undoubtedly Fiat invested in strict accordance with Soviet priorities and objectives, and this is really all that most nation-states would like to achieve.

As Professor Vernon points out, attempts at economic domination are nothing new. Aristotle cited approvingly the quick political response of Dionysius, the tyrant of Syracuse, to the threat of economic monopoly. Dionysius had given short shrift to a Sicilian who had cornered the iron market, by expelling him from Syracuse, reasoning that budding monopoly profits would soon master political authority. Aristotle, of course, considered politics to be the master science, by means of which the members of a community or nation-state declare their priorities and order their policies and laws.

I suppose that the simplest way of reaching to the heart of the topic, the Multinational Corporation in the 1980s, would be to ask if the Aristotelian belief in politics as the master science is still valid. George Ball would say no and he openly calls for the modernization of political structures, to evolve units larger than nation-states and better suited to the present day. Kindleberger is much more blunt when he writes, "The nation-state is just about through as an economic unit."

The theme of this paper holds the contrary—that the trend to economic globalism has peaked and that the current decline of the political role, of politics, cannot endure so long as there is freedom to associate for the broader political purposes that include social, intellectual, and cultural objectives. The symbiosis between economic policy and corporate power, central governments and international institutions, is widely recognized. The natural response for those with values to defend will be to strengthen the political roles of state, provincial, and community authorities. In other words, a return to community.

Kindleberger and I are observing the same process applied to different subjects. An idea or an institution is not for eternity. Time will sap the strength and thrust of any theory, idea, or institution. An apt example for economists would be the waning influence of Keynesianism. At the very moment that President Nixon was reputed to have said that "we are all Keynesians now," economists were scattering into monetarism or post-Keynesianism. An institution can wither by the very use or extravagant growth of its first principles. Where Kindleberger is thinking in terms of the nation-state, I would suggest that the vulnerable institution is the cosmocorporation.

To predict the position of the multinational corporation at the end of the 1980s is really to predict which of two political philosophies shall prevail—unity and order imposed on the world by those pursuing the dream of the greatest wealth for the smallest number, or the resurgence of the plural community. This is a debate that has been going on at least since Plato and Aristotole.

Plato, frustrated by the corruption that he found in political life, the crafty schemes of leaders and their advisers, the self-seeking, the obsessive search for increasing wealth and power, argued for institutions that would impose unity on the diverse elements within a nation. Consistent with his philosophy of ideas, Plato held that such a community could only be put together by a thinking leader who has grasped the pure idea of the political bond, who is able to impose order and unity where anarchy and disorder exist and to substitute for a rampant self-seeking individualism the collective interests and objectives of the ideal community. The theory of the unitary (global) state demands a reduction of the sensible differences in traditions, cultures, languages, and social values that have arisen in the long struggles of communities with their environments. The political task of Plato's philosopher king, whether democratic or authoritarian, would require the suppression of all other influences—including the religious, the military, the cultural and, of course, the commercial.

Aristotle, rebelling against the theory of the all-embracing state, espoused a thoroughgoing pluralism with full freedom for diversity and division. With faith in the political community and politics as the arbiter, he warned against the folly of attempting an overall unity, a unity that would reduce individual freedoms, a unity that would ignore regional characteristics, differences and challenges, a unity that could turn into a mindless conformity. The Aristotelian version of the political bond included responsible roles not only for regions, provinces, and municipalities, but also for non-political bodies such as the family, church, unions, economic associations, and professional interests.

In the 1980s, the internalizing instrument that people fear is not the philosopher king but the industrial-military complex that President Eisenhower first singled out and that Prime Minister Trudeau described as the helplessness of national governments before giant corporations.

Do the enormous clusters of wealth and market power pose a threat to political sovereignty? It is my belief after many years in politics that they do. We will not be concerned in Canada and the United States during the 1980s with religious, military, or revolutionary attempts to diminish the authority of our political institutions; but the awesome concentrations of corporate wealth can be and are a threat to the sovereignty of elected governments. In short, the threat that Dionysius faced 2,400 years ago.

A community, a region, is a given number of people, gathered together in a particular part of the world who create institutions and forms of government that are commonly accepted. A community is unique. While the people themselves will have had their own reasons for settling in a region—a simple search for new directions and opportunities, a flight from discrimination or prejudice, a moving towards preferred institutions or climates or places—it is certain that over time there will be in the region a gradual harmonization of values, of expectations, of viewpoints and of purposes. In short, a community has no problem with its identity.

To a great degree, this correspondence will be imposed by nature itself; for the possibilities inherent in the environment and the resource base determine the scope if not the limits of man's contributions. The challenges facing the Northern Ontario miner are not causes of concern to the Prairie farmer or the East Coast fisherman, nor would the responses to similar challenges in those regions be the same. Each accepts his environment for what it is, each strives to shape it and to use it rationally and consistently within the limits that nature itself imposes. In this harmony of man and nature, one finds the continuity that survives social and political upheavals. A better example of such survival than the preservation of French Canadian identity and nationalism, after military defeat and political subjection, would be difficult to find. As Canon Groulx has written: "La même entité humaine continue sa vie, sur la même terre, dans le même environnement géographique." The strength of the French-Canadian culture lies in the historical fact that the outlook, the language, the spiritual beliefs, the social institutions, and the political forms remain rooted in the soil of past generations. Wherever one finds a strong community, one always find a solid attachment of man to his environment, to his region, to his land.

The roots of any region are two: the people and the land. These are the basic factors, with capital, entrepreneurship, knowledge, and technology being derived from or through them. If the land is not attractive or yields but little, few will come or stay. If the land yields much and if this is retained, the community will grow and prosper. If, however, the surpluses are drained away, the community stagnates in an accelerating dependence.

It is in the very nature of the commercial corporation, large or small, to drain a market or an environment. Just as plants suck up moisture from the earth, so do corporations draw out and drain the surpluses inherent in the contributions of labor and the resources of nature. The primary objective of the corporate invader is to increase its own wealth and assets, not the level of community income. When communities enter into arrangements with corporations, it is important that the nature of the corporation be clearly understood.

The corporation is the dominant and dominating institution of our time. Governments identify growth and development with commercial corporations and shower them with subsidies, tax privileges, appropriate labor legislation, and market protection to attract a commitment and investment. Peter Drucker has accurately reflected the euphoria with which we have covered corporate institutions when he wrote: "Multinationals, whether corporate or communist, put economic sovereignty ahead of political nationality; the multinational corporation is by far our most effective economic instrument today and probably the one organ of economic development that actually develops. It is the one non-nationalist institution is a world shaken by nationalist delirium. It puts the economic decision beyond the effective reach of the political process and its decision makers, national governments."

However much one may be appalled by Drucker's justification of corporate domination over the political process, what he is saying is for all practical purposes the simple truth. Few suspected, when the act of incorporation for commercial purposes became, in the nineteenth century, a simple right, that the chartered company would ever attain its present importance and strength.

The classical economists from Adam Smith through to John Stuart Mill had based their theories of competition on large numbers of firms. Firms were individuals, proprietors, or partners; persons who were mortal. The early economists could legitimately think in terms of large numbers, free entry, and inevitable exit as mortality took its toll. Firms, like the persons who were their animating spirits, came and went. The real significance of the act of incorporation is that a new person is created: a juristic, legal entity endowed with continuity and immortality, the capacity to grow, to accumulate, and to compound forever.

Until the last century corporations were formed generally for public and specific objectives—the building of roads and canals, the creation of muncipalities, universities, and religious institutions. Such corporations provided continuity and extension to social, cultural, and religious purposes. They made possible the grouping of human and material resources to satisfy community needs and were generally oriented to nonprofit objectives. The major exceptions—East India Co., Hudson's Bay, etc.—served national and imperial objectives.

The clamor for the right to incorporate for commercial purposes became irresistible in the early and middle nineteenth century. Incorporation meant limited liability, which encouraged investment by enlarging the numbers of those willing to risk specified sums. Incorporation permitted the grouping of hundreds of investors and thus the accumulation of much greater sums and the building of much larger enterprises. The success of professional, managerial classes refuted the claims of economists from Adam Smith to Alfred Marshall that the new corporations would be limited by the absence of ownership and entrepreneurial direction to routine activities and modest growth.

In 1888, the State of New Jersey, anxious to become the home of corporations, enacted legislation that expanded the powers of corporations and opened up avenues of growth virtually without limit. Corporations, henceforth, could own and dispose of stocks and bonds of corporations of other states. The corporation was no longer simply a form of organizing land, labor, and capital to produce a greater flow of goods and services. It became the cathedral repository of the gold, incense, and myrrh of a commercial and industrial age—portfolios of stocks, bonds and marketable paper. The corporation was more than a simple means to greater efficiency; it became its own end and purpose.

It is ironic that the New Jersey initiative should have come at the very time that American pluralism, concerned by the growth of private corporate power, had sought to contain that challenge by the passage of the Sherman Antitrust Act of 1890. As J. P. Morgan and others quickly grasped the advantages of consolidations and takeovers, the first great merger movement of 1898–1902 got under way. The newly incorporated conglomerates were a great improvement over the uncertain legal status, the limited life, the surrender of voting rights, and the incessant quarreling inherent in the trust structure. Few realized, however, the explosive potential for compounding growth and wealth that would be the outcome of extending expanded corporate status to institutions for purely commercial purposes.

Today as we witness the wave of billion-dollar mergers with the resulting concentration of economic power, we understand better the import of Lord Acton's warning that every institution will finally collapse under the weight of its own basic principle. The single-minded accumulation of material wealth compounded indefinitely must inevitably arouse the opposition of those who wish to maintain the integrity of their community, their culture, their language, traditions, and values. The extension of the corporate institution to the private sector occurred without sufficient social and political safeguards, as men thoughtlessly substituted "the wealth of the nation for the commonwealth of their society."

Classical trade theory dealt with the mobility of goods and services and assumed the free movement of labor and capital within domestic borders only. Ricardo was certainly not unaware of the outflows of capital and heavy emigration from England but he and later classicists did not incorporate these facts in their theory. Even if conditions deteriorated in England and profits fell, it would not follow that capital and population would necessarily move from England to Holland, or Spain, or Russia, where profits might be higher, and he wrote approvingly of the "natural disinclination which every man has to quit the country of his birth and connexions, and intrust himself with all his habits fixed, to a strange government and new laws. . . ." It might have occurred to Ricardo, in his celebrated example of the English bolt of cloth and the Portuguese pipe of wine, that English capital could take over the Portuguese vineyards and that English managers could administer and control the output; but he would have dismissed this course of action as the flouting of a nation's political sovereignty and counterproductive in the long run both politically (ally) and economically (customer).

Nations gained from trading the goods and services in the production of which they excelled, i.e., had a comparative advantage, not from draining each other. Adam Smith wrote of the wealth of all nations and his principles were to be applied in all economies; they were not a tract pointing the way to England's economic dominance, even through her traders and industrialists were driving towards that goal.

At the heart of classical trade theory lies a political philosophy. Men and women were something more than mere tools, factors of production to be transported to foreign locations decreed by capital flows and technical requirements. They were citizens, possessed of all the advantages of that citizenship—laws, customs, culture, language, beliefs, roots, and traditions. Trade in goods, unlike trade in persons, would add to the level of real income in a nation which in turn led to increased wealth and/or improvement in the standard of living. In other words, the classicists were political economists who say the state as the political force, obligated to provide a framework of justice, freedom and stability—an environment in which the individual could work toward his personal goals and objectives. It is this belief in the dominance of politics over economics that led to their violent attacks on the crown-chartered monopolies of the mercantile system and the joint-stock giants of their time which were threatening the political role.

The theory of international specialization as outlined by Ricardo, is basic but not absolute. "Each country naturally devotes its labour and capital to such employment as are most beneficial to each. . . . It is this principle that determines that wine shall be made in France and Portugal, that corn shall be grown in America and Poland and that hardware and other goods shall be manufactured in England."

The theory, however, has its limitations. It is not a theory for all seasons and under all circumstances. In attempting to strengthen trade flows and development after World War II, the United States might have proposed the freeing of trade barriers with Europe and Japan and made it a condition of Marshall Plan aid. Such a policy, given the overwhelming wealth and productive superiority of the United States at the time, could only have served to keep Japan and Europe in colonial dependency for an extended period. As Bismarck had observed, "free trade is the policy of the strong," suitable for nations which are strong but not necessarily for nations which want to be strong. Infant-industry protectionism can also be made to work if it is accompanied by strong-industry creation, as Germany and the United States have shown.

Realism and relevance in international trade relations require adaptation. Sweden has always insisted that the ownership and control of national resources, land and forests, markets and manufacturing must remain firmly in Swedish hands. Such a policy would have led to the exploitation of consumers by Swedish monopolists, but the opening of her borders to the goods of other nations forced her industrialists to meet the standards of world competition.

Germany, like Great Britain, had witnessed extensive emigration during the greater part of the nineteenth century, a circumstance which did not suit her strategic ambitions. As Great Britain had become a heartland via free trade, so Germany sought the same status via Friedrich List's scientific tariff, which, in concert with policies of nationalization of the railways, subsidization of shipping, control of the banks, and cartelization of industry, enabled her to force her way into the markets of Eastern Europe and weakened British economic supremacy abroad.

The United States grew even more rapidly, aided by the heavy flows of British capital in the form of bonds and debentures placed by the wealthy and their private investment trusts. Ownership and property rights to perpetual revenue flows were not incorporated in the capital imported into the United States, which meant that the surpluses and rents as well as the equity and control of the successful enterprises remained firmly in the hands of American (host country) entrepreneurs and promoters.

The United States never lost control of its own economy nor was it drained of the surpluses needed to maintain and expand its domestic market as is so often the case with the developing countries of our time as they sell the equity in their inheritance and the rights to the streams of future revenues. Until the rules of the game are changed, and this inevitable, developing countries must live with the knowledge that they have bartered away future prospects for short-lived gain.

An inevitable result of the policy of international specialization is to make growth lopsided. Further, such specialization requires global markets if the nation is to earn the exchange receipts that will enable it to purchase the raw materials, capital, and consumer goods in which trading partners have the advantage. Thus, specialization leads to trade integration but also to vulnerability. The overdeveloped export sector is able to exert strong pressure on domestic fiscal policies and thus strengthen the distorted growth patterns to the detriment of any efforts to create a more balanced economy at home, e.g., Canada. An economy without balance cannot offer its citizens career options across the broad spectrum of economic activity but must limit them to specific roles. The free movement of persons does not solve the problem, for it is a contingent freedom—the freedom to follow the movement of capital in its geographical flights at the expense of citizenship and heritage.

By incorporating the movement of persons and capital into international trade theory, we are, of course, only taking into account what has been taking place for two centuries, heavy capital movements and surging population migrations. This present reshaping of the doctrine of comparative advantage does not simply mean the bringing-up-to-date of classical trade theory. It necessitates the dropping of basic classical assumptions, foresees the decline of the nation-state, and the domination of political objectives and national priorities by economic considerations. A nation, in the modern economist's or corporation president's view, becomes simply an artificial and accidental construct, a political edifice without economic significance.

To replace the classical doctrine of international specialization we need, we are told, a theory of international production that will aim for a gross global output of goods and services, produced by the land and resources of one nation, the capital investment of another and the labor of a third—all factors being perfectly mobile. Our very survival, it is said, depends on an optimal global allocation of resources, and this requires the most perfect mobility and deployment of all factors of production. Regional groupings are more efficient markets than national, and the global economy must logically be more productive than a number of regional blocs. At least, so the argument goes. The basic economic unit should be the Western world. The corollary, of course, is the erosion of community and the political bond and the acceptance of economic efficiency as the criterion motivating human behavior.

For centuries, democratic nations have been very sensitive to the possible accession to power of military or religious forces. Where this has happened, and it occurs frequently, the experience has generally been an authoritarian militarism or an unyielding fanaticism. And yet, quietly at first but now with an accelerating rush, we are witnessing the increasing dominance of the commercial role and power over political institutions, a condition which will inevitably lead to a dictatorship of the left or right.

If the world is to be considered the basic economic unity, technical principles of industrial location theory will assign resources according to the demands of the global economy. Regional significance is eliminated and the political region, i.e., the nation, makes no economic sense. Economically, a nation will be defined as a source of cheap labor, a supplier of capital, or a reservoir of raw materials and will be expected to fulfill this specific and restricted function. Global allocation suppresses national prejudices, pride and priorities, and the natural desire for a balanced national growth that will provide a full range of career choices.

Persons are free to move, of course, and to follow the new geographical flow of capital; but this is a very peculiar definition of freedom in that it takes no account of the costs of giving up one's heritage, culture, language and community of friends and family.

It is said that what is good for the world, the greater output, will somehow filter down and become good for the community that one has left behind. Build houses for the rich and the poor will get the tenements. Critics who resist this trend to economic globalism and who assert the value of national groupings are called parochial, which translates into nationalists, protectionists, chauvinists, xenophobes, and worse.

The method by which this greater global output is to be achieved will be the creation of a new class of citizens of the world, an artificial class called the global corporations. The parochial interests and narrow views of governments attempting to carry out the objectives and priorities of the voters who elected them will be denied by an international-companies law that will rank ahead of federal or regional legislation and that will protect the international company from the particular demands and restrictions that national governments might impose. This is the opposite of classical political economy.

An increased world output? Unobjectionable. But who will decide how the annual world output is to be divided up? What proportion will go to an immediate improvement in the standard of living against the proportion set aside for a better life tomorrow? What happens to the political principle if a supranational body makes the crucial investment-consumption choice for a whole host of countries in various stages of development? Can anybody do this? Can the corporation with the direct aim of increasing its assets, wealth, in conflict with society's demands for security, justice, and a normal life be entrusted with such choices? Which countries will share, which will have to wait another day?

The Hymer-Kindleberger-Caves theory of international trade has always bothered me. By making foreign direct investment a response to market failure in less sophisticated economies, multinationals have been made to appear as Galahads invading backward territories with the pure and noble motives of implanting the Holy Grail of unrestricted competition upon a population gasping for free consumer choice. The so-called market failure may have more to do with stages of development, propensities to save, social attitudes, political choices, environmental impediments, human values, and order of priorities than to industrial structure. There are many in Canada who believe, with the benefit of hindsight, that a slower rate of growth based on domestic savings, a greater control over the pace of resource development with less emphasis on foreign investment would have produced a more productive and better-balanced economy and a more confident and vigorous nation.

Theories of multinational enterprise would be more rewarding, in my view, if research were directed to developing a behavioral theory of the firm. It might be useful to begin with the principle that multinationals, like all firms, are primarily out to make a buck, not to resolve some nation's problems with an arthritic manufacturing sector.

The firms which lead in the investment and control of foreign markets and resources are, almost by definition, those which possess monopolistic power in their domestic markets. This control of markets yields cash flows which then have to be used. The decision to be made is created by that very flow of surplus income which is ignored in the theory of the firm. What to do with the flow of funds? Dividends? And spoil shareholders who would only add to their conspicuous consumption! Plant and equipment at home? And by expanding capacity spoil the domestic market! Add to working capital? A target for takeover artists, and dissident shareholders, and an invitation to entry by new firms. There is a large area in which decisions relating to the use of continuing and assured (oligopoly) income flows need to be explored. Does oligopoly in one nation breed oligopoly across the world? Is this not the final outcome of the Hymer-Kindleberger-Caves thesis? And what should public policy do about it?

It is worth reflecting on whether or not current economic theories of international trade via multinational enterprises are rationalizing the reorganization of the world along corporate lines. A nation is no longer to have control over its own factors, land, and labor, but must yield to superior concentrations of capital and/or knowledge which then take over. Presumably, the nation is not thought capable of resolving its own market imperfections or accumulating sufficient savings in the course of time. Implicit in the analysis is the assumption (fact) that each nation is riddled with oligopolistic structures. Further, that public policy dictates that each nation favor its large oligopolies with appropriate tax concessions, investment allowances, depreciation deductions, etc., and that it then inspire the firms to go forth and appropriate shares of foreign resources and markets. If all this can be tied into one giant conglomerate, e.g., Japan Inc., so much the better.

The trouble with all this is that it is not economics, not politics, not democracy. It is planning, regimentation, bureaucracy. It eliminates initiative, and the entrepreneur. One is reminded of the resolution drafted by Mussolini and read by him before the Assembly of the National Council of Corporations, Nov. 13th, 1933—"The National Council of Corporations defines Corporations as the instrument which, under the aegis of the State, carries out the complete organic and to-talitarian regulation of production with a view to the expansion of the wealth, political power and well-being of the Italian people." For Italian, substitute Canadian, American, Japanese, German, etc.

Canada is an example par excellence of a nation organized along oligopolistic lines by multinationals, both domestic and foreign. Statistics Canada noted a population of 413,034 corporations for the year 1979. Revenue Canada found that 200,825 firms had a taxable income base, amounting to $24.9 billion. Some 2,290 companies (.55%) in the $1,000,000 and up taxable income group earned $16.2 billion or 65% of total corporate profit. These are the firms whose control of markets or resources in Canada provides them with the continuing streams of income that enable them to finance penetration of foreign markets. The decision to invest directly in other nations signifies the rejection of other options such as increasing the returns to the owners (dividends), reducing prices to increase demand (excess profits), expanding domestic plant capacity to achieve economies of scale, etc. Our classical forbears would have considered the choice of any of these options to be more in tune with the principles of economic science than the decision to spread oligopolistic properties to other communities. This makes the international theory of industrial organization more realistic than the freedom of trade theories based on pure competition; but economics loses all claim to being an objective science, becoming the mere apologist for corporate accumulators.

The multinational does not transfer knowledge and technology in its foreign activities. There is no export or sale of these assets to an arm's length entity. The specific advantage together with the invested capital remain the property of the parent as the parent ingests foreign assets (resources and/or markets) via its branch plants. What happens is not a transfer but an extension of the firm's existing right to and control over a stream of revenues to new markets and political jurisdictions. The economist and the multinational president then assert that the superior efficiency (unproved) of a global allocation and investment of resources denies to national governments the right to intervene in the name of the priorities and preferences of their citizens. In other words, the nation-state has no place in the boardrooms of the global corporation.

The United States can afford to take a relaxed view of the foreign direct investment problem since the total sales of foreign subsidiaries in the United States would amount to approximately 2% US GNP. Even so agencies in the area of trade and commerce, banking, oil and gas, justice, securities and exchange commission, communications, and defense are becoming increasingly restive as the findings of various research groups, e.g., the Committee on Foreign Investment, are publicized and debated in the media.

Compare this 2% with the situation in Canada where, in an analysis of the sales and profits of 343,500 nonfinancial corporations, it was shown that 34% of all sales and 37% of all profits in 1978 accrued to foreign-controlled companies; Canadian firms produced 61% of the sales and 59% of the profits with 5% and 4% respectively unclassified as to ownership.

Consider the propensity to import of foreign-controlled firms and the consequent difficulty in building domestic industries. In 1978, the rate of imports to sales of foreign-controlled firms in the manufacturing sector in Canada was almost 30%, or nearly 4 times larger than that of domestic firms in the same sector. In the wholesale trade sector, foreign-controlled firms imported 25% of their sales while their Canadian competitors imported approximately 9%.

Reflect upon the balance of payment difficulties that face a nation that has permitted the measure of foreign control of its economy that exists in Canada if that nation decides to repatriate parts of its economy. Preliminary estimates indicate that Canada had a net outflow of $13 billion on interest, dividend, and commercial services for the year 1981. Repatriation of subsidiaries (mainly petroleum) located in Canada and net direct investments abroad added another outflow of funds of $10 billion. Since our surplus on merchandise trade amounted to $6.5 billion, the external borrowing, of both long- and short-term capital, exceeded

$16 billion. The interest costs of such borrowing can only serve to deepen Canada's long-run problems and particularly its dependence on the US economy. The lesson is that a nation without a strong and independent base is at the mercy of external forces, the sudden cessation of capital inflows, the imposition of trade sanctions, restrictions on the activities of subsidiaries, etc.

Growth in the mercantile system had meant power and plenty for the ruling class with little benefit to the community as a whole from the increased income. This accounted for the classical animus against mercantilism. The classical concept of growth and development was based on the principle of large numbers, a constant flow of new men entering the economy to push to one side the older, established firms or, at least, to cut down the surpluses inherent in the control of markets and resources.

Growth via large numbers of new firms fiercely competing is certain to be slow and laborious. New firms are initially financed by personal savings and these take time to accumulate. Profits are small or non-existent in early years, and competence and confidence are not built up overnight. "Natura non facit saltum," wrote Alfred Marshall and he was right. In today's environment of growing government deficits, inflation, and high interest rates, the classical dream of a continuing flow of new entrants has all but disappeared, and personal savings are channeled into government bonds rather than the expansion of the private sector and a competitive economy.

Net capital formation comes not from personal savings via the capital markets but from the consumer's dollar, the profits accumulated by corporations in control of markets and/or resources. The consumer pays not only for the cost of goods but also for the investments in research, development, and advertising that determine the products and technology of tomorrow and that dictate his need for them. The oligopoly firm, successful in its home market, then demands "access on equal terms, to such trade, raw materials, and industry" as exist in other nations. The multinational corporation now demands not merely access to export markets for its goods and services but the ownership and control of such markets and resources as exist abroad to provide it with an unending stream of revenues. Little enough would be left for the nation so controlled to assert its own priorities or ever to break the circle.

Capital is the means by which the two principal factors of production, land and labor, are organized. Where capital is raised at home via the surpluses inherent in an efficient use of people and resources, the nation remains sovereign and in control of its own priorities. So also with the capital that is borrowed and used effectively, permitting the repayment of principal and interest and leaving the ownership of markets and resources in domestic hands. US expansion in the nineteenth century was financed mainly with debt instruments.

When capital insists on the rights and privileges of absolute ownership as a condition of investment, the host country surrenders the value of its lands, resources, and markets in perpetuity. Although it benefits from an increase in labor income and that proportion of taxes that it has not bargained away as incentives to attract the foreign investment, the surpluses in the form of management fees, royalties, licensing charges, and interest and dividends swell the outflows of funds while the additions of retained earnings increase the volume of domestic assets controlled abroad. As the powerful industrial nations of the world gradually expand their control and ownership of foreign markets and lands, it is difficult to see how the system of global corporatism can avoid the consequences of growing hostility and repudiation.

Multinationals export their own technology or a scaled-down version thereof. Many of the claims made for the spread of technology throughout the less-industrialized economies assert too much. Technologies that fit the advanced economies will rarely be suitable for developing nations. Since the supply of factors in the two economies will be different by definition, the most appropriate capital-labor mix will inevitably vary. As Schumpeter has pointed out, it is bad economics to substitute advanced technologies for "technically backward methods of production" in economies where labor is plentiful and cheap and capital is scarce or nonexistent and dear. "The technically most perfect method of production is so often a failure in economic life." Again, one must refer to Alfred Marshall's dictum, "Natura non facit saltum," and recognize that growth in the poorer nations must proceed slowly and on a broad front.

A slow development of indigenous technologies does not provide a profitable market for the multinational corporation. Its own mass production techniques demand a great leap forward in mass consumption and the homogenization of new tastes and needs that the developing nation is ill-equipped to finance or to digest without uprooting existing traditions and culture. A bursting resentment towards the agents of change, the multinationals, will inevitably result in confrontation between the industrial nations determined to protect the markets and privileges of their corporate citizens and the governments of the host countries.

Are there new trends in international investments that will reduce the role of the multinationals? I believe that there are, and that these new directions spring from the increasing awareness by the nations of the world that the essence of sound economic policy for them is that they retain control of their own lands and resources, the full values and rents, that they never give them up but use them for their own purposes and objectives. By such a conviction communities would give priority to their own interests, surely the measure of sovereignty, and would do more for themselves in the long run than all the corporate direct investment that buys up their lands and resources has ever done. Perhaps this is chauvinism, nationalism, xenophobia. On the other hand it is consistent with the philosophy expressed by the authors of the Paley Report: "The overall objective of a national materials policy for the United States should be to insure an adequate and dependable flow of materials at the lowest cost consistent with national security and with the welfare of friendly nations." It is my belief that resource-hungry nations will be forced to trade their capital (loans) and technology for the energy and raw materials that they need and that there will be less acceptance by their allies and partners of takeovers of existing resource firms or the granting of outright licenses and rights to explore and exploit. Trade in goods and services is a measure of the respect which each partner has for the other. It is not clear that the "new theories" recognize that each partner has the same right to give priority to its own interests.

The "new theories" lead to economic centralism or economic sponsored supra-national integration. Heartlands are created and, by definition, peripheries, i.e., fringe regions and nations that are unbalanced, specialized, and dependent. For economists, this is the natural and predictable course of events. Concentration brings economies of scale which rest upon mass production. Is the distribution of the mass production between consumption and investment a political or an economic decision? Who will handle the political problems as some nations become heartlands and others exist on the fringe?

As corporate oligopolies, supported, financed, and encouraged by their respective governments, become ever greater compounds of wealth and economic power, political confrontation becomes inevitable both within and between nations. A prime target will be the corporate form itself and questioning about the capacity of our political institutions to maintain and to safeguard the human dimension in the face of an expanding corporate bureaucracy is bound to dominate the decade of the 1980s. The force and the power of this commercial institution is derived from within, the internal flows that is generates from the control of resources and the direction of markets along lines that best fit, not real needs but its own capacities. As it grows, it affects people more and is less affected by external forces, i.e., people and markets.

The inordinate size, concentration, and increasingly conglomerate nature of the corporate form led Henry Simons, a founder of the Chicago school, to write in 1945, "Having perhaps benefited briefly by corporate organization, America might now be better off if the corporate form had never been invented or never made available to private enterprise." Again, he states categorically, "Some direct dismantling of corporate empires seems indispensable." What would that ardent defender of free enterprise and the market say if he were alive today and particularly of the new theories of international trade based on oligopolistic actors in global markets? The legitimation that the multinational enterprise seeks far exceeds that which people, nations and communities, are prepared to grant. A resolution of the conflict will be an issue in the 1980s.

IV International Finance

10 Appraising Corporate Investment Policy: A Financial Center Theory of Foreign Direct Investment

Howard Curtis Reed

I. Introduction

The theory of foreign direct investment during the past twenty years has grown in its coverage and in its ability to explain why firms invest in markets alien to their decision-making centers. These theories have examined the determinants of foreign direct investment and corporate behavior by providing insight into how corporations appraise investment alternatives. Earlier studies of foreign investment activity (Behrman, 1960, Kindleberger, 1965, and others) identified interest rate differentials or capital (movement and formation) considerations as the principal determinants. In these studies, the impact of capital on foreign investment decisions centered around whether international investment took place as a result of the movement of capital from one country to another, usually from the firm's home country to the country where the investment was taking place; or as a result of capital being generated at the site where the investment was being made.

Stephen Hymer's pioneering work in 1960 used the theory of industrial organization to explain international investment behavior.[1] Hymer argued that direct investment is determined primarily by corporate organizational structure and behavior, and not by capital movement or capital formation. His central point was that if a firm is to operate in an unfamiliar political and legal jurisdiction at a long distance from its decision-making center, it will demand to be compensated with a clear operating advantage over other firms competing for a share of that market. He further argued that if capital were the principal determinant, it would move through the world's principal financial markets instead of through firms that specialize in—and seek control of—the sourcing, producing, and marketing functions.

Kindleberger in 1969 observed that multinational corporations are engaged in a wide variety of activities (i.e., managing and allocating resources, developing new products and processes, etc.), all of which are intended to enhance the firms' *growth* prospects. And in growing, these firms may invest their resources in familiar surroundings or they may choose to venture out by investing in foreign places. The investments may be the result of differences in existing levels of profits and profitability or they may be due to the plowing back into the firm of excessively large amounts of its earnings in hopes of an even larger return. The growth of the firm, it was further argued, has two dimensions. One dimension emphasizes the markets for the firm's products, and the other dimension emphasizes the firm's capacity and ability to finance a substantial percentage of its growth from profits. Businessmen, it was noted, rejected the argument that direct investment was due primarily to internally generated sources of finance. It was their contention that such investments were the results of expected levels of sales, because the firm's profit level will justify the necessary investment. Kindleberger, to a large extent, also agrees that direct investment is more closely linked to the market dimension than to the internal financing dimension. The theory offered is that "direct investment is tied to markets. If markets grow, the firm must grow. If the firm stops growing, it dies. Anything that interferes with growth of the firm, such as balance-of-payments restrictions, while the organic life of the market goes its way will kill the firm."[2]

In 1970, a paper written by Robert Aliber was published, and for the first time foreign exchange risk and currency valuation were seen as being significant determinants of foreign direct investment.[3] Aliber believed that foreign direct investment could be best explained by understanding the interrelationships between, and the behavior of, capital and foreign exchange markets. He argued that foreign direct investment is influenced significantly by the fact that the source-country firm capitalizes the same income stream of expected earnings as does the host-country firm, but at a higher rate. The difference in the capitalization comes about because the capital markets establish different capitalization rates, on debt and equity, for income streams denominated in different currencies. In his view, the difference in capitalization rates are explained by two factors. First, the market will demand a premium for accepting the exchange risk. Thus, the difference in interest rates on fixed-price securities can be expected to exceed the anticipated change in the exchange rate. Second, the market does not attach a currency premium to the foreign income of the source-country firm because the market for equities is biased against the host-country firm. The source-country firm may therefore issue securities in its market and use the proceeds to acquire the host-country firm. This argument leads Aliber to conclude that direct investment flows can, generally, be expected to flow from strong-currency areas to weak-currency areas.

In studying the movement of portfolio and direct investment capital between the United States and Western Europe during the 1960s, Ragazzi (1973) discovered that the large flow of US direct investment in Western Europe was matched by sizable purchases of US long-term portfolio assets by private European residents. He attributed the large outflow of portfolio capital to two characteristics of the European securities markets (the United Kingdom excepted). First, the European portfolio investor does not receive continually updated information. Public auditing of corporations is not as well developed in Europe as it is in the United States. This lack of information theoretically increases the risk of possible deviation from the expected rate of return for the portfolio investor. On the other hand, because the direct investor is in control of the company and therefore has immediate and direct access to all information, his risk is limited to the "industrial" risk inherent in the operations of the company. A second factor is the narrowness of the European securities market, again with the exception of the United Kingdom. This contracted state makes the fluctuations in prices of securities much larger than justified. Ragazzi concluded:

Even if the determinants of portfolio and direct investments are different, flows of the two forms of capital are likely to be partly substitutes. Thus, an outflow of portfolio capital, for instance, will discourage direct investment abroad and might encourage an inflow of foreign direct investments. This could happen to the extent that: (a) it reduces the supply of risk capital to local firms and increases that supply to foreign firms; (b) it pushes up the market value of securities of foreign firms, increasing the cost of take-overs of foreign firms by domestic firms; and (c) it pushes up the exchange rate of the foreign country, increasing the cost of direct investment in that country.[4]

Magee (1977) combined the neoclassical theories of creation and appropriability with the theory of industrial organizations to explain why firms engage in foreign direct investments. Magee argued that industries with a high derived demand for information (technology) must continually make investments that produce five specific types of information: (1) creation; (2) development; (3) production functions;

(4) markets; and (5) appropriability. He hypothesized that multinational corporations are specialists in the production of these five specific types of information because duplication by other market participants is difficult, and as a result this information is transmitted more efficiently through the firm's internal channels as opposed to the market's mechanisms. In addition, the multinational corporation produces such information because the level of appropriability increases as the information's level of sophistication increases. This combination of actions prescribes what the firm's optimum size should be throughout its technology life cycle. As the firm's international activities grow, and it enters the mature stage of the cycle, its optimal size begins to decline in conjunction with a like decline in the generation of new information.

The foreign direct investment theories cited here are representative, to a large extent, of the evolution of ideas and the thinking that has taken place during the 1970s. All of these theories, as well as the theories that they evolved from, provide valuable insight into how and why foreign investment takes place. The focus, however, is directed primarily toward the theory of industrial organizations and microeconomics. When the macroenvironment of foreign direct investment is discussed, the focus is either on (1) arbitrage activities available in the foreign exchange and credit markets (Aliber, 1970), or (2) some form of risk reduction through diversification. The portfolio approach to foreign direct investment hypothesizes that a multinational corporation can experience a significant reduction of risk by pursuing a growth strategy of international geographic diversification. This strategy allows the multinational corporation to offset lower rates of return in some countries by simultaneously reducing the firm's risk and enlarging its markets. As a result, the firm will be attractive to investors, which will increase the supply of funds available and in turn reduce its capital costs.

Missing from these discussions and explanations is the role of the *financial center* in determining the location, magnitude, and type (direct or portfolio) of investment activity. Financial centers, in general, are important to international investment activity. Financial centers that impact on foreign investment activity can be classified and grouped into three broad categories:[5] (1) *Host International Financial Centers* enhance their financial infrastructures and capabilities by attracting relatively large numbers of foreign financial institutions from a large number of countries. (2) *International Financial Centers* are host to a large number of foreign financial institutions; headquarters for a small number of internationally active banks that tend to follow the lead of the larger international financial institutions; and they possess a limited capacity to influence events that pertain to global asset and liability management. (3) *Supranational Financial Centers* are headquarters for a large number of large internationally active banks that are well connected (directly) to other centers throughout the world; managers of large amounts of foreign financial assets and liabilities; net supplier of foreign direct investment capital to the rest of the world; located close to a large number of large (measured by assets) industrial corporations; active users of global communication facilities (airplanes, telephone, telex, etc.); and management meccas, that attract and generate ideas and information in ways that eventually establish the organizational and operating norms that govern internationally active organizations (private and governmental).

The argument put forth in this paper is that the underlying determinants of foreign direct investment activity are best explained (and understood) by determining the motives and methods of evaluation employed by the supranational financial centers as they appraise, on a continuing basis, the activity of internationally active institutions. It is presumed that institutions actively engaged in foreign investment are firms whose equity is traded on at least one major stock exchange, and whose capital structure consists of publicly held debt securities that are also traded in secondary markets. Information about the operations, policies, and strategies of these firms, their competitors, their markets, and their sources of supply are continually scrutinized and factored into the centers' evaluation of the securities of these institutions. The functional relationship between the internationally active firm and the supranational financial center is essentially one of operating efficiency and not the commonly held view of revenue maximization and cost minimization. In this context the internationally active firm seeks to maximize its operating efficiency. The operating efficiency maximum, as used here, purports that the internationally active firm continually seeks to enhance its competitive position in its product markets by maximizing its price-earnings multiple on equity, and the price paid for its publicly traded debt securities. The firm wants to maximize operating efficiency by improving its competitive status (in its product market and in the capital markets) relative to other firms in the into organize the sourcing, reformulation, and marketing of resources in a clearly defined manner; a manner that lends itself to standardization and eventually the adoption of these practices on a wide scale. The supranational centers, it is argued, provide the environment, the mechanism, and the competence for evaluating on a continual basis the policies and activities of the institutional components of the global political economy. These centers are important for financial sourcing and allocations; evaluating the policies, strategies, and activities of nations;[8] industrial project evaluation and pricing; monitoring the activities of the institutional components of the political economy; and providing money and capital management services. Without question, the level of efficiency with which a center can perform these functions is dependent on its astuteness in gathering, evaluating, and utilizing information from around the world. Additionally, a center's astuteness is largely dependent upon the number (and size) of its locally headquartered banks, the acumen (management) of these institutions, the collective connections (to other centers) of these institutions, and the industrial power (and reach) of the nation's corporations.

Contemporary Measures

The earlier study of financial centers using traditional variable measures was quite valuable. It provided considerable insight into what is required to build financial center infrastructure over time (institutions, connections, markets, etc.), and into the organization, distribution, and influence of these centers. On the other hand, a study using only traditional measures leaves unexplored a whole range of factors that have emerged in the past ten to fifteen years that may have a significant influence on the building of financial center infrastructure, organization, and influence. Building on the information and conclusions generated in the earlier study, and in hopes of providing additional information that could be used in developing the arguments for this paper, a sixteen variable (as opposed to nine) analysis for 1980 was performed. Thirty-six financial centers were included in the analysis. The variable measures are:

1. Capital/deposit ratio of the large internationally active banks headquartered in the center.
2. Capital/asset ratio of the large internationally active banks headquartered in the center.

3. Pre-tax earnings/capital ratio of the large internationally active banks headquartered in the center.

4. Pre-tax earnings/assets ratio of the large internationally active banks headquartered in the center.

5. Revenue/asset ratio of the large internationally active banks headquartered in the center.

6. Total international currency clearings (daily average) of the center.

7. Size (liabilities) of center's Eurocurrency market.

8. Total amount of international bonds issued in the center during the year.

9. Foreign financial assets held in the center.

10. Foreign financial liabilities residing in the center.

11. The daily average of the center's stock exchange activity (sales value).

12. The number of large internationally active commercial banks headquartered in the center.

13. The number of large internationally active foreign banks with offices (agencies, branches, or subsidiaries) in the center.

14. The number of foreign financial centers with direct links, provided by the foreign internationally active banks, to the local center.

15. The center's airline passenger traffic (yearly total).

16. The center's airmail/airfreight volume (yearly total).

The thirty-six centers were divided into five distinct groups,[9] at four hierarchical levels (figure 1). The Five-group organizational structure is determined primarily by the amount of international currency clearings, the size of the Eurocurrency market, foreign financial assets, and headquarters for the large internationally active commercial banks.

If these contemporary measures are viewed as an extension of the traditional analyses, then the supranational centers can be characterized as centers whose principal operating currency(ies) is widely used for international trade and capital transactions; and whose financial infrastructures (primarily the large commercial banks) are developed to the extent that they are entrusted with the management of the world's foreign financial liabilities and assets. The large internationally active commercial banks have the primary responsibility for facilitating international clearings (daily) which in 1980, amounted to a US dollar equivalent of $236 billion. US dollars accounted for $178 billion of

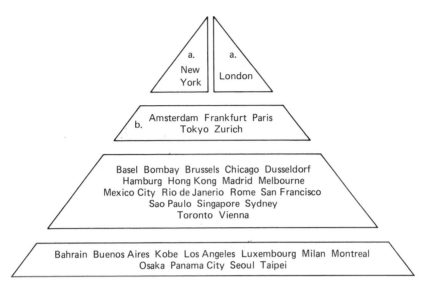

Figure 1
The hierarchy of financial centers. a, Supranational centers of the first order. New York and London differ in two variable measures: (1) total amount of international clearings (New York's dominant measure), and (2) size of the Eurocurrency market (London's dominant measure). b, Supranational centers of the second order. The magnitudes of their variable measures are less than those of the first-order centers, but their infrastructures are well-developed and well-balanced.

the total, and New York was clearing approximately 90 percent of these dollar transactions. In addition to the currency transactions, the clearing infrastructure is also used for coupon, dividend, and interest payments on securities; and it is used to facilitate the transfers and registration of securities.

It is widely believed that the large internationally active commercial banks have grown in size, reach, and scope as a result of the demands of their corporate customers. The argument is usually supported by citing examples that purportedly show that corporations establish foreign operations first, and in an effort to maintain their close ties to these corporations the banks follow this lead by establishing their own foreign offices. If this argument is accepted, then another important question must be answered: What factors explain the existence of a large number of internationally active banks (with substantial foreign office networks) during the first half of this century, when direct investment was minimal?

In the years preceding World War I, private banks and the links to other financial centers provided by the large internationally active banks (i.e., the number of foreign centers in which these banks had branch or subsidiary offices) were important determinants of financial center structure. Throughout the 1920s the number of foreign bank offices in the center was the most important determinant. During the 1930s the principal determinant was the number of large internationally active banks headquartered in the center. From the end of World War II until the late 1950s, financial center structure was determined principally by the foreign financial assets and the links to other financial centers provided by the large internationally active banks. From the late 1950s until the present, the principal determinants have been the number of large internationally active banks headquartered in the center, and the amounts of foreign financial liabilities and foreign financial assets. The contemporary analysis reveals that international currency clearing activity is the measure most responsible for financial center structure.

III. Determinants of Financial Center Structure

International Clearing Activity

It seems quite reasonable to argue that international currency clearings have throughout this century been an important determinant of financial center structure (even though comparable data for all of this period is not available). New York clears approximately $160 billion daily. Of the major centers London is next, clearing (in dollar equivalents) approximately $17 billion daily. Frankfurt and Paris follow with $12 billion each. Tokyo, Zurich, and Amsterdam clear approximately $7, $4, and $2 billion, respectively. The significance of clearing activity to the status of a financial center becomes clearer when the ancillary activities of currency clearing are examined.

In the United States, the 12 settling banks of the Clearing House Interbank Payments System (CHIPS) account for more than 70% of the annual increase in correspondent bank balances.[10] The increase in bank correspondent balances is directly attributable to increasing activity in foreign trade, foreign exchange, and capital flow activity (primarily short-term flows which include all Eurocurrency flows). The extent to which a center's principal operating currency is used in these international transactions determines the importance of that center as an international clearing center. In addition to the 12 settling banks of CHIPS, there are 87 associate member banks (an increase of 22 since January 1978).[11] These associate members, prior to 1980, were required to maintain a correspondent relationship with the 12 settling banks in order to have access to the CHIPS transaction processing mechanism.[12] Foreign bankers that have recently opened offices in New York (since 1978) readily admit that having access to CHIPS was an important consideration in deciding whether to open offices.[13] Virtually all of the Edge Act subsidiaries operating in New York are there because of the access to CHIPS.[14]

In the case of New York, there is strong evidence to indicate that international clearing activity increases the size and leveraging capacity of the banks headquartered in the clearing center by increasing the correspondent balances (deposits) of the local institutions. The level of international currency clearing in a center reflects, to a large extent, the overall importance of that center's indigenous currency in international financial transactions. Therefore it can be expected that the clearing center's large clearing banks would have foreign offices in other centers for the purpose of financial sourcing in their home currency, and for the purpose of facilitating international transactions that use their home currency. Furthermore, access to the clearing mechanism of a center is an important consideration for institutions headquartered in other centers, when deciding whether to open an office in another center, and what type of office to open in that center (e.g., a representative office or a full service banking office).[15]

Global Portfolio Management

In order for a center to be an active and influential participant in managing the world's portfolio of financial liabilities and assets, the center must be successful in attracting relatively large amounts of foreign financial liabilities. These resources can then be employed as the center sees fit, domestically or internationally. As the size, scope, and reach of the center's asset portfolio is increased, the need to enlarge its direct links to other centers is also increased. It is a natural evolution for foreign lending by the locally headquartered banks to be followed by an expansion of their overseas office network to supervise and better manage their foreign asset portfolios. The financial sourcing and allocation function demands that the center have a sufficient and well-managed infrastructure to provide liquidity and a competitive return on investments. Since there are never enough liquid reserves to cover all liabilities at any given time, the quality (risk vs. return, and maturity schedule) of a center's asset portfolio is paramount to the investor, governments of the investors, and the host nation government. Evaluating the policies, strategies, and activities of nations is necessary for several reasons. Nations (including their firms and citizens) are active users of the products and services of centers, and, as a result of the highly interdependent nature of the industrial country's markets, a shift in policy, strategy, or predicted activity could substantially alter the portfolio quality of the center, and in turn, of its investors. Accurate evaluation is also essential to evaluating and pricing industrial projects that are targeted for investment in foreign countries or projects that are dependent upon cash flow emanating from that country. Industrial project evaluation is also important for the initial pricing of the borrowed capital. Monitoring the progress of the projects is necessary so that the current value of the outstanding principal can be assessed. The quality of the money and capital management services offered by the center is largely a function of how well these other functions are managed.[16]

Communication (the Hidden Measure)

All sectors of the global political economy are heavily dependent on the medium of communication for successful performance and attainment of their operating objectives. And finance is perhaps the most dependent sector. The communication function is two-dimensional. In order to provide for a useful and continual exchange of ideas, fast and efficient communications, on a personal (face-to-face) as well as a non-personal (telephone, telex, etc.) basis, must be made available to the center.

Jet travel has made it possible to move important people and documents from one location to another, anywhere in the world, within 24 hours. This quick and relatively inexpensive means of moving highly skilled people is perhaps the single most important factor in diminishing the need for financial centers to be expert in a number of ancillary activities (i.e., accounting, advertising, law, printing, etc.). The supranational centers can export much of the needed ancillary services to other centers at substantially lower costs than would be incurred if each center had to generate these skills internally.

The nonpersonal form of communication may involve air mail or telephone, telex, or sea mail. Important documents such as letters of credit, trade bills, term loan agreements, and checks can now be moved overnight by air courier. This has improved the operating efficiency of centers and their clients in those matters that require the movement of a physical document. Telephone, telex, and other types of transmission make it possible to send and receive instructions almost instantaneously. The risk of error or misunderstanding is increased, perhaps significantly, when these nonpersonal means of communication are used. Face-to-face contact is, of course, the preferred method of communication but it is not always possible or practical. And I am told by bankers and corporate executives that the error rate of nonpersonal transmission is surprisingly low.

The importance of communications in the infrastructure of the financial center is clearly recognized, but it is difficult to measure because data on nonpersonal communications is difficult and costly to compile, and as a result most institutions make no attempt to get this data. Country data is available, but not city or center data. The absence of hard data on nonpersonal communication does not preclude the researcher from clearly seeing the connections and the relationships. The importance of direct links between centers (provided by the local and foreign banks) and the international telex activity clearly indicates that the information infrastructure is a significant determinant of financial center structure.[17] The basis for this contention is twofold. First, the greater the number of direct links, the greater the quality of unfiltered information available to the center.[18] Furthermore, unfiltered information presumably is transmitted at a greater speed and at higher levels of accuracy and quality than is filtered information. Therefore, direct links can be viewed as indicators (if not measures) of the speed with which information is transmitted between centers and the accuracy and quality of that information. Second, the volume of international telex activity is an indicator of a center's international influence as a financial and information center. Bankers, businessmen, and, to a lesser extent, international trade specialists use international telex facilities to the exclusion of nearly all other communications systems.[19]

Supranational Banks or Supranational Centers

The critical role played by the large internationally active commercial banks in the development, growth, and management of financial centers is clearly evident. The preeminent role of these banks naturally leads to an interesting question. Is it the banks or is it the centers that are the "real" preeminent actors in international finance? Or, to put it another way: Do the centers' infrastructures produce synergism? This question is perhaps best answered by examining the comprehensive character of the financial center.

Financial center eminence affects and is affected by the various commercial, monetary, industrial, and political systems of the world.[20] The centers' role in synthesizing these four systems lies in their ability to effectively gather, analyze, and disseminate information. The commercial, monetary, and industrial sectors rely on the centers' global network of offices, correspondents, customers, and suppliers for much of their information, much as political units (nation-states) rely on their diplomatic corps and intelligence agencies. The information network for commercial activities is located primarily in the major port cities of the world. Networks for industrial activities are widely dispersed, depending on the economies of location of the particular industry (should the location be nearer the supply source, the market, or somewhere in between?). Nation-states, naturally, have their information networks centered primarily in the various administrative capitals. The information network for the monetary infrastructure is located in the international financial centers.

The information generated independently by these four sectors is supplemented, in varying degrees, by the public media (the press, radio, television, and wire services). The major news (and wire) services have their international networks centered in the financial center of the nation when it is different from the administrative capital (New York instead of Washington, DC, Frankfurt instead of Bonn, and Zurich instead of Bern). The organizational structure of each individual organization (an export broker, a corporation, a bank, a nation-state, a wire service) is probably very efficient in managing information for internal purposes. With the exception of the public media, the internally generated information is usually not for horizontal distribution. As a result, there is no formal coordination and distribution of this information. The public media make a gallant attempt to perform this service. But because most of the important information must be discovered and/or uncovered, and because it requires considerable technical expertise to analyze, synthesize, and properly report, the attempt frequently falls considerably short of the objective. In an informal way the financial centers (particularly the supranational centers) perform this coordination and distribution function with considerable efficiency, a feat which seems to have been overlooked.

The centers' information systems (and networks) are important to multinational corporations, central bankers (and their governments), international organizations (i.e., the International Monetary Fund), and a number of other financial participants such as brokers, accountants, and attorneys. Multinational corporations use these information networks to assist them in their cash management activities and in transmitting information to their subsidiaries. Central bankers and international organizations find it necessary from time to time to intervene in the financial markets of the world. The questions that must be answered by these organizations are: Where should the intervention take place? Should the intervention be in more than one center? Which markets and institutions should the intervention directly affect?

The preeminence of these centers is perhaps best seen when the attributes of the large internationally active banks are examined. In Japan, the large internationally active banks headquartered in Osaka (Sumitomo, Sanwa, and Daiwa), Kobe (Taiyo), Nagoya (Tokai) have their "top" international people in Tokyo and have recently split their top domestic people between their home office and Tokyo. Similar activities have taken place in California; the Bank of America has officially split its headquarters into a northern division in San Francisco (the original headquarters), headed by the president (chief executive officer) and a southern division in Los Angeles, headed by the chairman of the board (chief operating officer). The two other large San Francisco banks—Crocker National and Wells Fargo—now have their chief executive officers spend 40 to 50% of their time in southern California. This reflects the growth of Los Angeles as a significant financial center. Also note the arguments opposing the establishment of international banking facilities in New York (see note 15).

Another action which appears to clearly favor the importance of the center over the bank is the behavior of the Organization of Arab Petroleum Exporting Countries (OAPEC) in 1973–1974. When OAPEC quadrupled oil prices in late 1973 and early 1974 its members initially chose to employ their cash reserves (billions of new dollars) in London even though comparable deposit rates in New York were 50 to 75 basis points higher in New York. The branch and subsidiary offices of the large New York banks were the principal recipients (receiving more than 70% of the total) of these funds. If the supranational banks were preeminent, then why not take advantage of the higher yields being offered in New York since the London affiliates of the New York banks were the principal depositories for these OAPEC funds? This example points to the significance of politics and confidence, in addition to the more quantifiable variables, as important determinants of financial center structure—particularly the perceived willingness of a center to use economic means to achieve a political objective. As important as the banks are, the evidence appears to clearly show that the large internationally active banks are not more important than the centers. The evidence also appears to clearly show that the reach, scope, and influence of the centers is far greater than the total reach, scope, and influence of its various institutions when measured independently.

IV. Multinational Corporations, Supranational Financial Centers, and Foreign Direct Investments

Beginning with Hymer's pioneering work in 1960, the growth of multinational activity has been well documented, and to a large extent chronologically. The "real" growth in multinational industrial activity began in the early 1950s. Between 1950 and 1965 US direct investment abroad increased nearly fivefold, from $12 billion to $55 billion. At year end 1980 the total was approximately $220 billion. Most of the early studies (prior to 1970) examined US foreign investment activity, mainly because American firms (during this period) were the dominant force in foreign investment activity. It is not surprising that Hymer found that the principal reason for foreign direct investment was monopoly power. He noted that firms operating at a distance from their decision-making center are operating at a substantial "cost" disadvantage: the cost of travel and transmitting information; the time lost in travel; and the costs associated with errors which results from misunderstandings in the absence of face-to-face communications.

Hymer's research covered the period of time when operating in foreign environments was a relatively new experience for most US firms. Most of these firms, naturally, relied on New York and its resources to assist in their overseas expansion. Even though New York emerged from World War II as the world's preeminent financial center, its direct links to other centers (its information network) never equaled or seriously challenged London's, in scope or in depth. For much of this time (prior to 1970), New York's capability in providing unfiltered information about product markets, and the legal and political environments of a large number of countries, was quite limited. It seems appropriate to argue that New York's limited knowledge about foreign places would cause it to view any substantial commitment of resources, by US-based firms, to overseas expansion in markets that did not appear to offer monopoly (or near monopoly) profits as being relatively risky. This would result in a lower price-earnings multiple for the firm's shares and a lower price for its debt.

Throughout the 1960s New York broadened and deepened its direct links to other centers. As New York's connections grew, its knowledge about foreign places grew. It was during this period that the so-called "growth" strategies and policies of the multinational corporations (MNCs) were rewarded. Some MNCs saw the price-earnings multiple for their shares soar to three-digit levels. It was during this period, when MNCs were emphasizing growth, that the so-called "two-tier" stock market developed. It was observed that the large institutional investors (i.e., bank trust departments, mutual funds, insurance companies, etc.) tend to buy and actively trade the stocks of a relatively small number of firms. These firms were usually one of the dominant firms in their respective industry, or they (and their industry) were seen as growth oriented. As a result of these activities of the institutional investors, the price-earnings multiple of the shares of these firms were far higher than the multiple for the rest of the market. Thus the firms whose shares were part of the "upper-tier" group of stocks had a substantial advantage in accessing new capital as well as in the cost they had to pay for that capital.

New York's increasing knowledge about foreign places apparently led it to conclude that it was capable of managing a much larger and more complex portfolio of activities. As the efficiency of its global information network increased, the investment opportunities available in foreign locations were more clearly seen. This understanding was made possible by having first-hand unfiltered information to corroborate, and enhance, the filtered information that had been received earlier via London. New York's view at that time was, apparently, that the product markets of the world were broad and deep enough to accommodate any market structure short of perfect competition. It therefore appears that through its appraisal machinery New York rewarded firms that retained (and reinvested in foreign locations) a large portion of their earnings. This type of foreign investment strategy meant that the MNC was also enlarging its portfolio of investments through geographic diversification. Theorists studying this phenomenon argued that geographic diversification of the MNC lowered the risk to the investor by reducing the impact of a potential loss of any single investment project. As a result, the shares of the MNC will be more attractive to the risk-averse investing public, which will increase the MNC's supply (and decrease its costs) of capital. Note that the portfolio theory of foreign direct investments places considerable emphasis on the risk of doing business within sovereign political jurisdictions, and somewhat less emphasis on the risk of competing in the marketplace.

The portfolio theory of foreign direct investment was followed by explanations based on internalization and appropriability motives. These theories argued that due to imperfect knowledge in the marketplace the MNC develops its own internal markets in intermediate products, such as marketing, personnel management and training, foreign exchange arbitrage, and capital market arbitrage. It should be noted that the emphasis at this juncture was not on capital movement, capital formation, expanding existing facilities, or building new facilities. The emphasis was on vertical integration—increasing control over all activities taking place within the firm, and particularly on activities that generated new information. As less and less of the MNC's internally generated knowledge is made available to the markets (the public), the issue then becomes appropriability of this information.

The growth of the modern MNC during the postwar period has led to the generation of hypotheses and arguments that increasingly call upon the MNC to organize and manage its resources in ways that are primarily beneficial to society. The MNC's direct concern for society must be limited, by the invisible-hand doctrine. It should presumably conduct its affairs in ways that optimize the interest of its shareholders, creditors, and management. This is best done by it maximizing its competitive position in the markets in which it operates and by maximizing its competitive position within the supranational financial center, in which it is continually being evaluated, by having the center optimally price its securities. The proposition then is to reject the arguments that have been put forth in the past, suggesting that the MNC should include as part of its objective the welfare of society.

The welfare of society is looked after by the supranational financial center (SFC). The SFC is a synthesized infrastructure of institutions and markets whose function it is to evaluate the operating efficiencies of those financial, industrial, commercial, and political organizations that utilize its capital, information, and management resources. The SFC's objective, with respect to the MNC, is to maximize the welfare of all society by optimally distributing multinational activity (i.e., sourcing, production, marketing, and information) throughout the world.

In a world divided up into developed countries (DCs) and less-developed countries (LDCs), it is the SFC's task to optimally allocate multinational activity in a way that approaches Pareto optimality. That is, if we have two multinationals, a consumer-product firm and an electronics firm, it is the SFC's responsibility to evaluate each MNC's operating efficiencies in a way that optimally distributes their resources between the LDCs and the DCs. This means that an LDC's marginal rate of substitution of the electronics MNC investment for the consumer-product MNC investment must be the same as that of the DC. That is, the ratio of the marginal utilities of the two investments must be the same. Figure 2 shows the Pareto optimal solution (curve CC') to the problem of multinational resources allocation. The contract curve CC' represents the locus of points of tangency between the indifference curves of the DCs and the LDCs.

When the SFC evaluates the securities (operating efficiencies) of the MNC, its actions are constrained by the function it must perform. For example, if an MNC's leverage is too high (in the SFC's view) the center cannot take steps to reduce its holdings of that firm's securities because it is acting for all of society. Thus, the center's only option is to reduce the value of the firm's securities. The response of the MNC to the center's appraisal of its securities is of great interest to the SFC because if the firm does not respond to the center's signals and continues to maintain a highly leveraged structure, the center must further reduce

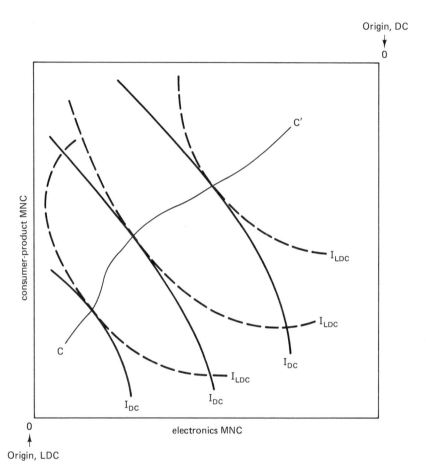

Figure 2
Funds available for foreign investment.

the value of the MNC's securities, which lowers the overall value of the center's portfolio. This means that capital is not distributed as efficiently (optimally) as it might be, which causes the cost of capital to rise for all. In addition to the issues of leverage, the SFC is continually evaluating the MNC on its other operating and performance dimensions (earnings, market share, location portfolio of investments, etc.).

When the SFC's evaluation of MNC activity suggests some adjustments be made, the center's objective is usually not to undo management's decisions but rather to alter the decision.[21] For example, when the center is continually decreasing the value of the shares of a firm, relative to its industry, the center will not be simultaneously engaging in activities that will increase the value of that firm's debt securities. The center will either take action that is designed to inform another firm, operating within that industry, that its leverage should be higher. Or, if the industry's capital structure (as determined by the center) is in balance, the SFC could purchase an amount of equity and debt securities of the other industry participants in proportions equal to their share of stocks and bonds outstanding.

When the focus is on earnings, the center must first take steps to ensure the success of its multinational clientele. This means that the SFC is concerned foremost with the earnings and overall value of the portfolio of its clients and less concerned with its own earnings and investment portfolio. The reason for this is twofold. First, the center operates as an intermediary providing capital, information, and management products and services. And second, the center's total portfolio of clients (society) represents the center's investment.[22] The financial center is unlike the corporation, in that the lower the expected risk the greater the return for the center. The center's primary concern, at all times, should be to reduce the expected risk of return on its portfolio of activities. For example, in cost-of-capital considerations and where interest rates are important, the center's behavior should be to bid down the amount it pays for funds so as to minimize what it must charge for funds. The higher the capital-servicing requirements for the borrowing firms, the greater the probability of problems occurring with the SFC's portfolio. Figure 3a shows the financial center's risk-earnings possibility curve. The center's earnings are derived principally from fees and the spreads received between bid and ask on a wide range of intermediary activities. The negative slope of the curve suggests that

a. supranational financial centers   b. multinational corporations

Figure 3
Risk-earnings possibility curves.

along with the benefits derived from an increase in the volume of
activity, the center could widen the spread between bid and ask, and
increase the base rate of its fee schedules without significantly increasing
risk or reducing volume of activity. Figure 3b shows the MNCs' risk-
earnings possibility curve. These curves depict the expected *rational*
behavior of the SFC and the MNC. The SFC wants to enhance the
quality of its asset portfolio by providing capital to users at a cost that
minimizes the risk of capital depreciation (being unable to service debt
obligations, omitting or reducing dividend payments, etc.) and capital
destruction (being unable to repay the principal from debt obligations,
having the value of stockholders' equity reduced, etc.). The MNC, on
the other hand, seeks to increase its return on capital employed as the
risk associated with employing that capital is increased. This attitude
has led the MNC to pursue, at times, relatively more risky investments,
in hopes of increasing revenues, or cash flow, or profits, or market
share, or some combination of the four.

  Developing a theoretical framework to explain behavior is not only
important because it may explain the events that have already taken
place, but also because it may explain future events. Theory is also
important because it is useful in identifying those factors that may be
impeding the more "logical" or more "rational" behavior of financial
centers. Since the early 1970s financial center behavior has been at

odds with the theoretical framework argued for in this paper. A case in point, since the initial quadrupling of oil prices in 1973–1974 the global economy has generated virtually no real growth, unemployment has more doubled, inflation has increased threefold, corporate bankruptcies have more than doubled, and the international financial system is precariously plodding along without a clear plan for solving the problems associated with prohibitively high capital costs.

A question that remains unanswered, in my mind at least, is: Why did interest rates not fall precipitously (perhaps as much as 300 to 400 basis points) in the weeks and months following the oil price increase of 1973–1974? At the time of the oil price increases, the international financial system was still adjusting to the consequences of the demise of the fixed exchange rate system that had been in existence since the conclusion of the Bretton Woods conference following World War II. Worries about rising unemployment and inflation, and the economic health of LDCs, were also being voiced. In early 1974 the magnitude of the shift in wealth from the industrialized Western nations to the oil-exporting countries was becoming quite clear. OPEC oil revenues were in 1973 a mere $22 billion. Early estimates of 1974 OPEC revenues ranged from $100 to $115 billion (the actual revenues were slightly less than $90 billion). Armed with this information it seems reasonable to have expected that London, the principal beneficiary of OPEC funds, would have bidded down substantially the price it was willing to pay for new deposits. New York being the only other center capable of handling such a large influx of funds was not receiving, directly, any of these new deposits from OPEC—for obvious reasons. It was clear at the time that these new liabilities accruing to London would be converted into assets by primarily increasing loans made to developing countries, which were already having difficulty meeting their financial obligations. It should have also been clear that rising interest rates have a destabilizing effect on the world's equity markets, which make it difficult for corporations to maintain the appropriate debt/equity mix in their capital structure, which is vitally important to investor confidence. London, and the American banks which dominate the Eurocurrency market, should have realized that rising interest rates increase the general level of uncertainty, which in turn tends to slow capital investments in favor of short-term cash management, which puts additional upward pressure on inflation and unemployment.

The results of London's actions to increase interest rates has led to a continual deterioration in the quality of the asset portfolios of the community of financial centers. There are at least two factors which may explain why London did not take steps to reduce the interest rate paid on deposits. First, floating interest rates were becoming the accepted practice for banks in the management of their asset portfolios. This meant that any increase in cost associated with their liabilities could be passed on to the borrower by adjusting the interest rate charged on their asset portfolios. As a result, there apparently was little or no incentive to aggressively manage the liability side—as is the case when fixed interest rates are the practice. Second, the world's principal central banks agreed to become lender of last resort for the international financial centers. This meant that any major default by a developing country, for example, would be covered by the community of central banks, and this apparently reduced the incentive of the financial centers to emphasize asset portfolio quality and prudence.

It appears that the fixed-interest-rate philosophy, policy, and practice offers some hope of a less volatile and more efficient international financial system. The practice of central banks proclaiming themselves as lenders of last resort for the community of international financial centers, particularly as it relates to LDC credits, has the disruptive effect of diverting capital away from the more efficient users such as the MNCs—which are also important contributors to the economic development process. I agree that the world financial system should in fact have a lender of last resort, but the provider of this type of insurance requires that the insurer charge a premium that must be factored into the cost of the insured credits. In most domestic financial systems reserves held against deposits act as insurance premiums; but such a system is deficient in that it is directed exclusively at the liability side and principally ignores asset quality. Perhaps a more efficient method for assessing insurance premiums for domestic as well as Eurocurrency credits, would be for the central banks to classify assets in much the same way as insurance companies classify life and casualty risks. Based on the various asset classifications, an insurance premium should be charged or a reserve requirement should be imposed. Since the primary purpose of this paper is not prescriptive, a detailed discussion of how and why these actions should be taken is inappropriate.

Notes

1. Stephen H. Hymer, *The International Operations of National Firms; A Study of Direct Investment* (Ph.D. thesis, Massachusetts Institute of Technology, 1960; published 1976, MIT Press).

2. Charles P. Kindleberger, *American Business Abroad* (New Haven: Yale University Press, 1969), p. 90.

3. Robert Z. Aliber, "A Theory of Direct Foreign Investment," in C. P. Kindleberger (ed.), *The International Corporation* (Cambridge, Mass.: MIT Press, 1970) pp. 17–34.

4. Giorgio Ragazzi, "Theories of Determinants of Foreign Direct Investments," *Staff Papers* (International Monetary Fund), July 1973, pp. 476–481.

5. Howard Curtis Reed, *The Preeminence of International Financial Centers*, (New York: Praeger, 1981), pp. 60–61.

6. Ibid., p. 10. The centers were measured in five-year intervals covering the period 1900 to 1980. The ninve variable measures were (1) the number of large internationally active commercial banks headquartered in the center; (2) the number of foreign financial centers with direct links to the local center and the links are provided by the local center's internationally active banks; (3) the number of private banks (including investment and merchant banks) located in the center; (4) the number of large internationally active foreign commercial banks with a banking office in the center (representative offices are excluded); (5) the number of foreign financial centers with direct links to the local center, with the links provided by the foreign internationally active banks; (6) the total amount of foreign financial assets held in the center; (7) the total amount of foreign financial liabilities residing in the center; (8) the number of foreign financial centers with direct links to the local center, with the links provided by the foreign internationally active banks (agency, branch, representative, and subsidiary offices); and (9) the number of large internationally active foreign commercial banks with agencies or branches, or representative or subsidiary offices in the center. In addition to these measures, another 41 variables were used to measure various dimensions of each center's country. These variables examined capital and trade flows, inflation and capital formation, industrial activity, and international communication activity.

7. Hierarchical cluster analysis was used to determine the structure of financial centers over time. Stepwise multiple discriminant analysis was then used to verify the cluster-analysis grouping (organizational structure), and determine what factors (variables) caused the particular grouping.

8. This evaluation is reflected immediately in the foreign exchange (spot and forward) market value of currencies, and later on, in the nation's collective cost of capital.

9. "Distinct" means that statistically significant separation between the groups of centers is at the .001 level of significance.

10. The 12 settling banks are all headquartered in New York and are the 12 members of the New York Clearing House Association.

11. Associate members are New York-based Edge Act subsidiaries of US banks, and New York agencies, branches, or subsidiaries of foreign banks.

12. This practice was relaxed in 1979. Today, any institution can open a CHIPS settlement account at the Federal Reserve Bank of New York, if it wants to operate independently of the New York settling banks. As of February 1982, only two banks had done so— the New York-based Edge Act subsidiaries of Bank of America and Continental Illinois. Non–NewYork settling banks with less than $250 million in capital must have their parent banks guarantee their CHIPS-related obligations.

13. Recently opened offices include foreign banks that have upgraded their representative offices to an agency or branch. This information is based on a series of wide-ranging interviews with New York-headquartered, foreign and Edge Act bankers during 1979 and 1980. Four were New York settling banks, four were Edge Act subsidiaries, and seven were foreign banks.

14. Edge Act as well as foreign bankers, while not giving exact figures, make mention that their clearing activities are one of the most profitable areas of their New York operations.

15. A group of large US banks (headquartered outside of New York), led by Bank of America and Continental Illinois, attempted to delay and perhaps prevent New York from receiving final approval from the Federal Reserve to establish International Banking Facilities (IBFs). The support of this group was contingent upon their being given direct access to the CHIPS computer from their home offices outside of New York. It was argued that with IBFs and CHIPS at their disposal, the 12 settling banks headquartered in New York will be able to obtain deposits at lower costs and make loans more profitably, thus giving the New York banks an unfair competitive advantage. Apparently, the ploy did not work. New York's IBFs began operating on December 1, 1981, and the non–New York banks do not have direct computer access to CHIPS.

16. It may also be of interest to note that large internationally active financial institutions have a tendency to assign their "best" people on the basis of a center's perceived status; see Reed, op. cit., pp. 69–74.

17. International telex emerges as the single most important determinant of financial-center structure when country variable measures are used. See Reed, op. cit., p. 48.

18. Unfiltered information refers, in this instance, to the information transmitted between centers through direct banking links; filtered information refers to the information transmitted between centers through relatively public networks. Unfiltered information is not necessarily transmitted directly from one center to another; it may be processed through an intermediary office (a regional office, or the corporate headquarters, or both), but the processing takes place within a single institution.

19. International currency clearing institutions are heavy users of personal communication facilities. CHIPS, for example, is primarily a confidence-based system where payments are made via an electronic funds transfer mechanism. The daily transactions are presently in excess of 60,000.

20. See Reed, op. cit., chapter 2.

21. The undoing of a decision would occur only in extreme cases (e.g., when, in the center's opinion, an MNC's action(s) would clearly jeopardize the future of the firm).

22. The center's portfolio of clients includes multinational corporations, nonmultinational corporations, governments, and international organizations; in other words, all of society.

11 Money, Multinationals, and Sovereigns

Robert Z. Aliber

Within the last several hundred years numerous innovations have threatened established business and financial arrangements. Some innovations were technological: the railroads displaced the canals, which in turn were displaced by motor and air transport. Frequently the introduction of labor-saving devices has appeared threatening; a generation ago the railroads debated whether they needed firemen on diesel locomotives, while now the airlines debate whether three pilots and engineers are needed or whether two will do. Sometimes the innovation may be organizational: the ability to coordinate the management of selling units across large distances led to chain stores and legislation designed to protect the Ma and Pa stores from the predatory out-of-towners. Smaller banks have sought to limit the expansion of the branch systems of the large banks. When the innovations develop abroad, latent xenophobia may surface; foreign competitors are charged with being unfair (they dump or they discriminate) or with having a factor price advantage, or with acting in their own interests rather than in someone else's interest.

Within the last several decades, the expansion and increased attention to multinational enterprises (MNEs) has led to numerous charges that they pursue antisocial and/or predatory behavior. Thus MNEs manipulate transfer prices to shift income to low-tax jurisdictions. Or the MNEs shift production to low-wage countries. The MNEs shift their foreign exchange profits from centers where they are earned to centers where they are taxed less heavily. Or the MNEs shift funds to high interest rate centers, or from currencies which are likely to be devalued or to depreciate; indeed the shift of funds from one currency to another by the MNEs was said to have caused the breakdown of the Bretton Woods agreements.

The difficulty with assessing these claims about the impacts of the multinationals is that the counterfactual cases are rarely specified. Systems of pegged exchange rates broke down long before there were significant numbers of MNEs. Production traditionally has flowed toward countries and areas with lower production costs, which is what international trade theory is all about. Moreover, the shifts of income to low-tax jurisdictions occurs without multinationals; tax avoidance is pervasive among doctors and bakers and candlestick makers. The difficulty of specifying and measuring the counterfactual cases does not obviate the need to evaluate the allegations about the impacts of MNEs—although the evaluation requires a theory or a model that explains why firms grow across national borders.

The concern with multinationals would be redundant in a world without nation-states, or in a world with only one-nation state. So, presumably, would much of the concern about the shifts of factors of outputs, or income, and of funds from one jurisdiction to another, although there obviously would be factionalism of the Sunbelt-Frostbelt variety. By definition, an MNE is involved in a range of functional business activities—marketing, production, finance—that are coordinated or integrated across the borders between nation-states.

The necessary condition for the emergence of multinationals is that the borders among nation-states are associated with the segmentation of product or factor markets. National markets for factors and for products are segmented by economic distance, by market imperfections, by various policy measures like tariffs and quotas that are congruent with national borders, and by policy measures like minimum wages or income taxes or interest rate ceilings that differ among countries. Firms— both national firms (NFs) and MNEs—arbitrage differences across borders in the prices of products and of factors, and thus limit the deviations of prices of factors and of products in one national market from those that prevail in other national markets.

The ability of MNEs to arbitrage across national markets is discussed in the various theories of the multinationals—hypotheses developed to explain why firms headquartered in one country have both a financial or economic *incentive* to expand abroad *and* an advantage relative to their host-country competitors. A decade and more ago, a number of different theories were developed to explain the advantage of the source country firms (Hymer, Kindleberger, Caves, Vernon, Aliber). The theories sought to explain both the nature of the advantage of the source-country firm and why these firms sought to exploit these advantages on their own rather than sell these advantages to host-country competitors. Some hypotheses focused on firm-specific advantages, others involve locational advantages, and a third, much smaller group, involves advantages in the asset or ownership market. Each of these theories relies on certain stylized facts, mostly of an anecdotal quality. Several efforts have been made to synthesize these hypotheses into a comprehensive or eclectic theory (Buckley and Casson, Dunning).

Within the last few years—indeed almost since the shift to floating exchange rates early in the 1970s—there have been significant changes in the patterns of direct foreign investment. While US firms continue to expand their ownership interests abroad, the striking development is the very sharp increase in direct foreign investment in the United States by European and Japanese firms. Much of this investment involves takeovers of established US firms, although there is some "greenfield" investment. Moreover, there are a significant number of cases in which firms headquartered abroad have purchased offshore productive facilities of US firms; thus Peugeot bought British and French facilities from Chrysler. A key question is how well the theories developed with the rapid surge in US direct foreign investment in the 1950s and 1960s in mind can explain the turnabout in the geographic pattern of direct foreign investment. The answer may help focus attention on the robustness of the theories proposed a decade ago.

This paper argues that the shortcoming of most theories of direct foreign investment produced a decade ago and the synthetic inclusive theories is that they are "under-determined." Three different questions are answered by "theories" of direct foreign investment—one is why firms grow and expand beyond the size of the competitive firm identified in Alfred Marshall's *Principles of Economics*; the second is why production of certain goods occurs in particular countries rather than in other countries; and the third is why productive facilities located in particular countries are owned by firms headquartered in other countries. This last question is the key question, and it has two aspects—one is why firms expand across national borders, while the second is whether the distribution of ownership of productive facilities in particular countries is random or nonrandom with respect to the location of the headquarters of the firms that own these facilities. Traditionally, these theories seek to answer at least two of these questions with one proposition— thus the story of why firms grow and expand is sometimes used to answer why firms acquire productive facilities abroad. This paper asserts that the central question to be addressed by the theory of direct foreign investment is not which firms from a population of firms invest abroad, but rather the distribution of the ownership of productive facilities in particular countries by domestic firms and by foreign firms.

Section I of this paper discusses some general propositions about the incentives for the growth and expansion of multinationals in terms of the operations of the international economy. Section II deals with the impacts of the growth of the multinationals on national monetary independence and on the stability of exchange rates. Section III deals with the impact of the segmentation of national financial markets on the patterns of direct foreign investment, especially which countries are the source countries and which are the host countries and why this pattern changed in the 1970s.

I. The Segmentation of National Markets and the Growth of Multinationals

This section deals with three related questions that derive from Ronald Coase's insight that firms expand and grow because the costs of avoiding the use of the market are less than the costs of using the market (Coase). The first is how this insight might be applied to explain the growth of the multinationals. Then the incidence of the benefits of the growth and expansion is discussed. Finally, the factors that MNEs "internalize" are examined, especially the financial factors.

Coase postulated that the expansion in the size of firms beyond Marshall's small competitive firms reflects that the costs of using the market can be avoided or reduced by internalizing certain transactions; these costs are those of search, transactions, contracting, and uncertainty (Williamson). The greater the costs of using the market, the greater the incentive for firms to expand to reduce these costs. And to the extent that these costs are higher at national borders than within individual countries, the incentives for firms to internalize certain transactions across national markets will be strong; indeed, firms might have greater incentives to expand across borders rather than within individual countries if these costs are substantially higher at national borders than within particular countries.

Moreover, the Coase argument about limits to the expansion of the size of the firm within a national economy because of the difficulty of coordinating activities in space can be extended to firms in the international context. MNEs encounter costs of coordinating production and marketing activities in foreign countries that NFs do not encounter, and these costs of economic distance may limit their growth.

Hence just as the ability to reduce these costs by internalizing them may explain why firms grow, so the ability to internalize the costs associated with transactions across national borders may explain why firms become multinational. If the necessary condition for the growth of multinationals is that national markets for goods and factors are segmented at the borders, the sufficient condition is that the firms can reduce their costs by internalizing certain transactions. That is, there are certain cost savings from undertaking particular types of transactions within firms that might otherwise occur as a series of transactions between national firms headquartered in different countries.

For the world economy as a whole, the growth of MNEs is cost-efficient just as the expansion of firms within the national market is cost-efficient. That these firms are cost-efficient means that they are able to sell their output for a lower price than the output of the domestic firms. These cost savings are partly passed on to consumers in the form of lower prices, to workers in the form of higher wages, to investors in the form of higher returns, and to governments in the form of higher taxes. So these firms, both within countries and across countries, increase their market share and displace smaller national firms because they are able to charge lower prices, or because they are able to pay factors more. The displaced factors move the MNEs. Some individuals and some governmental units are better off, others are worse off, as is the case with virtually all technological and competitive change.

The segmentation of national markets for products and for factors may result from the costs of economic distance or from market imperfections or from various policy actions, both those expressly adopted to segment markets and those adopted for other reasons. The costs of economic distance include those of transportation, communication, and search. These costs are important for particular products and for various types of capital. But these factors probably are not significant in the markets for money and finance, for the costs of moving funds from one jurisdiction to another—say from a New York dollar deposit to a London dollar deposit—are trivial, as are the costs of changing the currency denomination of funds, say from a London dollar deposit to a London sterling deposit. The market imperfections in the financial context involve uncertainty, especially about changes in exchange rates, changes in exchange controls, changes in tax rates, and the various other financial measures that segment national markets for money and finance. Some of these measures can be converted into a price-effective equivalent; for example, the interest rate equivalent of reserve requirements can be readily computed. Other policy measures that segment the national markets limit the quantity of funds that may be shifted abroad; in this case the interest rate differential or the yield differential adjusts to the quantity limitation. Differences in national tax rates on corporate income and personal income establish incentives to shift income to low-tax jurisdictions; because the costs of shifting income are so low, the return almost always exceeds the costs.

Both casual empiricism and numerous studies indicate that there are substantial differences among countries in nominal interest rates and real interest rates. Given that transactions costs are so trivial, the difference in nominal interest rates might reflect anticipated changes in exchange rates. Nominal interest rate differentials, however, are poor forecasts of future changes in exchange rates, although (together with forward exchange rates) they may not be significantly inferior to other forecasts. The large forecast errors provide one dimension of exchange rate uncertainty. Moreover, the substantial differences in real interest rates confirm the proposition that national money and capital markets are segmented significantly (Aliber). While some investors arbitrage funds across national borders to profit from the anticipated difference in interest rates and yields, the volume of such transactions is not sufficient for the differentials in interest rates and yields to become nontrivial.

These differences in nominal and real interest rates and yields can be considered a market imperfection. One consequence of this market imperfection is that a wedge is introduced between returns on similar securities denominated in different currencies. Firms and investors are reluctant to arbitrage funds across the borders between currency areas because of the uncertainty about possible changes in the exchange rates or changes in exchange controls, with the result that anticipated returns on assets denominated in one currency might differ significantly from the anticipated returns on comparable assets denominated in other currencies. If the difference in the anticipated returns approaches or exceeds the economic value of the wedge, then the investors would "arbitrage" any difference in anticipated yields. A second consequence of these imperfections is that investors may prefer to have assets denominated in some currencies rather than others, with the consequence that interest rate differentials would be biased predictors of future spot exchange rates. That the interest rate differentials are "biased" relative to future spot exchange rates does not necessarily mean that the international money market is inefficient; the "return" from the forecast error may be a return for holding "risky assets." But even if the market is not deemed inefficient, the differences in interest rates on similar assets denominated in various currencies may have significant economic consequences.

The wedge and the forecast error are related in the following way. The larger the risk aversion of the portfolio investors, the more likely that interest rates and yields on assets denominated in one currency may move independently of interest rates and yields on assets denominated in other currencies. The larger the size of the economic wedge, the less likely that the interest rate differentials will be biased predictors of future spot exchange rates. In contrast, the smaller the segmentation of national financial markets because of a concern with uncertainty, the more likely that interest rate differentials might be biased predictors of future changes in exchange rates. If the wedge or buffer is small, then real interest rates within each country might not differ significantly. If, however, real interest rates differ significantly, then the cost of capital to firms headquartered in different countries also may differ.

If investors believed that the interest rate differentials are unbiased predictors of future changes in exchange rates and they are not concerned with exchange risk, then the choice of currency of denomination for assets and liabilities would be redundant. If instead investors believe interest rate differentials are unbiased on average but they are nevertheless concerned about the impacts of exchange rate uncertainty in the short term, they would be reluctant to take on foreign exchange exposures unless they were adequately compensated for the risks.

Portfolio investors who shift funds across the borders among currency areas incur a set of risks that they do not incur on domestic transactions. In the absence of these risks, real interest rates in various countries would equalize; because of risk of changes in exchange rates, differences in real interest rates are significant. Moreover, the divergences among real interest rates in different countries that might be evident if countries follow similar monetary policies are almost certain to be exacerbated because they follow dissimilar monetary policies.

The segmentation of national financial markets does not necessarily establish an incentive for firms to internalize the flow of funds. The managers of firms respond to the interest rate differentials established by portfolio investors. If portfolio managers had "perfectly" priced exchange risk, then the corporate managers would be reluctant to have their firms incur foreign exchange risks. A very large part of direct foreign investment involves intercompany loans from parents to foreign subsidiaries. The parents of the subsidiaries take on the foreign exchange exposure because the corporate managers believe that the interest rate differentials are significantly larger than from the anticipated rate of change of the exchange rate. If instead corporate managers believed that the interest rate differentials fully and only reflected the anticipated rate of change of the exchange rate, they would not take on the foreign exchange exposure.

Thus, at the financial level the reason that firms internalize the flow of funds is that the corporate managers believe that the interest rate differentials are large relative to the anticipated change in the exchange rate and the appropriate payment for risk. In effect, the managers of the firm believe that portfolio investors demand too high a return for taking on the exchange risk and other risks associated with foreign investments. The magnitude of the minimum threshold return required by portfolio investors relative to that required by managers of MNEs for taking on the same set of risks is not readily measured, for the corporate managers have effectively displaced the portfolio investors; ex poste, the interest rate and yield differentials have become smaller as a result of the transactions of the MNEs. But the difference is probably small—probably no more than one or two percentage points.

The expansion of firms across national borders is consistent with the view that corporate managers internalize the costs and risks of foreign exchange exposures at lower costs than portfolio investors. The impact of their ability and willingness to internalize the flow of funds is to increase the magnitude of the flow of funds from countries where interest rates and yields are high to areas where interest rates and yields are low. The presence of these financial barriers creates an incentive for firms to expand across national borders by internalizing transactions rather than by borrowing funds within each country. However, this incentive affects firms headquartered in the low interest rate countries much more than firms headquartered in the countries with the higher interest rates. And this incentive may explain why firms headquartered in some countries choose to expand by ownership rather than by selling licenses.

II. Monetary Independence and the Multinationals

The MNEs respond to differences in interest rates on similar assets denominated in different currencies; they continually adjust the currency mix of their assets and liabilities as interest rates and anticipated exchange rates change. The MNEs react to the efforts of national monetary authorities to pursue policies that they believe will enhance attainment of their national objectives monetary policies. If the authorities set interest rates—or if they seek to set interest rates—at levels inappropriate with the anticipated exchange rates, the MNEs, like the NFs, will seek to take advantage of any spread between the interest rate differential and the anticipated spot exchange rates. The MNEs may be quicker than the NFs in seeking to take advantage of this apparent profit opportunity, perhaps because their information network may be more comprehensive, or because they have better access to sources of credit in different countries. Yet the difference or the advantage of the MNEs is likely to be modest, and it is likely to be limited to differences between the willingness of portfolio investors to acquire risky positions in foreign exchange and the willingness of corporate managers to take on similar positions. Almost certainly the minimum threshold return required by portfolio investors is larger—but the argument of the previous section is that it is modestly smaller. The source of the problem is not that MNEs speculate in the foreign exchange market, but that in a world in which costs of communication are declining rapidly, the national authorities cannot pursue monetary policies which are inconsistent with the monetary policies abroad without inviting significant changes in exchange rates. The hedging and speculative transactions undertaken by the MNEs may have quickened the demise of the pegged exchange rate system; a system of pegged exchange rates cannot survive long if inflation rates or interest rates differ sharply among countries.

Whether these exchange rate changes triggered by changes in interest rates are desirable can be determined only ex poste. If domestic monetary policy is constrained, it is because the segmentation of national financial markets has declined, not that MNEs are behaving in an antisocial way. In this sense the problem is with the complex of the exchange market arrangements and the monetary policies, not with the behavior of individual firms.

To the extent that multinational firms can internalize the transfer of funds at lower cost than national firms, then the expansion of the MNEs may restrain monetary independence. Thus the segmentation which provided the incentive for the growth and expansion of the MNEs becomes somewhat self-limiting—the firms shuffle funds and so limit the ability of monetary authorities to pursue independent policies.

For years, the national authorities benefited from the segmentation of national markets. As MNEs have become more experienced, the ability of the authorities to pursue policies that lead to the significantly different anticipated returns has declined.

III. The Theory of Direct Foreign Investment and the Changing Patterns

The theory of direct foreign investment seeks to identify the advantage of source-country firms that enable them to compete effectively with host-country firms on the latter's own turf. The industrial-organization hypothesis explains the expansion of firms abroad in terms of the desire to exploit a firm-specific advantage and the reluctance to sell this advantage. Firms expand abroad for the same reasons they expand at home. Taken literally, this theory of direct foreign investment is really a theory of why firms grow and expand, not why firms have an advantage in acquiring productive assets abroad relative to their host-country competitors. These approaches provide no special significance to the segmentation of the national product and factor markets. Moreover, these theories provide no insight into whether there are country-specific patterns to direct foreign investment—why some countries are source countries for direct foreign investment and others are host countries. Nor is there any indication why there might be changes in this pattern, and especially why the foreign companies became so aggressive in buying US firms in the last several years. Consider how this theory might explain why British firms buy US firms—is it because British firms now are generating much more firm-specific knowledge? This seems unlikely, since much of British investment in the United States is in standard industries, such as banking, retail food chains, and hotels.

The three variables to explain are the incentives of firms to grow and expand, the location of the productive investments, and the ownership of the productive assets. Many firms have an economic incentive to grow and expand, within countries and across national boundaries, to the extent that they can internalize certain costs and this incentive to expand will be true for firms in most countries. Where production can occur at low cost will be determined by the usual arguments that involve factor productivity, factor costs, and the real exchange rate. The arguments that explain why firms grow and expand, and why production occurs in some countries and not in others, cannot be used to explain the geographic patterns in the international ownership market. It may be that there are no geographic patterns—that the country mix of direct foreign investment is random; if so, there is no need for a theory of direct foreign investment. If there are patterns—if the country mix is not random, then a theory is needed to explain these patterns.

The arguments used to explain why firms grow cannot be used to explain why firms headquartered in particular countries may have an advantage in the ownership market, any more than the arguments that explain why firms grow and expand can provide an answer to the question of where production can occur at low cost. The issue of ownership is critical if the geographic patterns of direct foreign investment—which countries are the source countries and which are the host countries—is deemed relevant.

A decade ago, the hypothesis was that US firms had an advantage in the capital market or the ownership market; this advantage derived from the preference that investors in the United States and abroad had for dollar-denominated debt. The evidence for this preference was that interest rates on dollar-denominated debt were low relative to interest rates on debt denominated in various foreign currencies, after adjustment for any anticipated changes in exchange rates. The derived argument was that investors would pay a higher price for a $1 of equity income of US-headquartered firms than for the equivalent equity income at the prevailing exchange rates of firms headquartered in other countries. (In effect, the Q ratio for US firms was higher than for non–US firms.)

The willingness of investors to pay a higher price for $1 of equities of US firms meant that the US firms in turn were willing to pay a higher price for any given income stream than were firms headquartered in most other countries. In effect, US firms bid away foreign income streams from foreign firms.

The surge in US direct foreign investment in the 1960s, especially toward the latter part of the decade, reflected that the US dollar was becoming increasingly overvalued. The range of products in which the United States had a comparative advantage was declining. And since US firms were preferred by investors, the US firms implicitly were willing to pay a higher price for these income streams than host country firms.

With the move to floating exchange rates a decade ago and especially with the sharp decline in the foreign exchange value of the dollar in the late 1970s, real exchange rates changed sharply. The US comparative advantage increased in a wide range of products; once again the United States became a low cost (or lower cost) source of supply. This change in comparative advantage does not explain why firms headquartered in Western Europe and Japan became so aggressive in the international market for ownership; a change in advantage in the production market is different from a change in advantage in the ownership market. The change in the real exchange rate meant that the profits on US production increased relative to the profits on foreign production. Yet US equity prices fell, while the equity prices abroad increased. The Q ratios for US firms were falling; those for European and Japanese firms were increasing.

The increase in the aggressiveness of firms headquartered in Western Europe and Japan relative to the aggressiveness of US–headquartered firms reflects that the market values of the firms headquartered abroad have increased relative to the market values of US firms. The firms headquartered abroad have been willing to pay more for $1 of earnings in the United States or its equivalent abroad because investors in the United States and abroad have been willing to pay a higher price for the shares of these foreign firms than for the shares of US firms. The arguments that the aggressiveness of British firms in the market for ownership of assets in the United States reflects the very low levels of profitability in Great Britain is not convincing (although it satisfies the necessary condition for a direct foreign investment); instead what must be explained is why $1 of US earnings is more valuable to a British firm than to a US firm.

If the direct and immediate answer is that the price that firms headquartered in each country will pay for $1 of earnings reflects the price that investors will pay for each of these firms, the next question is why investors will now pay so much more for the earnings of the foreign firms. The apparent answer is that the interest rates on dollar assets increased sharply relative to interest rates on comparable assets denominated in the German mark, the Swiss franc, the British sterling, and the Japanese yen. Thus corporate managers believed that the portfolio investors demanded too high a risk premium to hold dollar-denominated assets.

Thus the change in the country pattern of direct foreign investment can be explained by the decline in the market values of US firms relative to the market values of firms headquartered abroad. These changes in market values of firms headquartered in different countries are a response to the complex of changes in nominal exchange rates, inflation rates, and monetary policies. Whether the change in the portfolio investors' demands for assets denominated in the dollar relative to assets denominated in the currencies of other industrial countries will persist is conjectural.

IV. Summary and Conclusion

The segmentation of money and capital markets at national borders provides an incentive for firms to grow and expand across national borders. In effect the risk premium required by portfolio investors to take on foreign exchange exposures is higher than that deemed appropriate by corporate managers; by internalizing the flow of funds, they reduce the costs of funds available to their foreign subsidiaries. That corporate managers require a lesser return for acquiring foreign exchange exposures means that the scope for national monetary independence has been reduced, for in effect the borders among currency areas have been lowered. The empirical significance of the increased integration of national money and capital markets is difficult if not impossible to evaluate; the offset to the possible welfare from the decline in monetary independence is the welfare gain from the more effective allocation of capital on a world-wide basis.

A major assertion of this paper is that the theory of direct foreign investment should deal with the question, "Is the distribution of source and host countries random or is there a pattern, and, if there is a pattern, how might it be explained?" The question which has received so much attention in the last decade, "What are the characteristics of firms that invest abroad?" in an attempt to explain direct foreign investment is really no more than the international extension of the question raised by Coase, "Why do firms grow?" Perhaps there are advantages to considering the international version of this question to be the theory of direct foreign investment; if so, those advantages have yet to be demonstrated.

If the exception tests the rule, the power of each theory might be evaluated in terms of its ability to predict the turnabout in the direction of direct foreign investment in the last decade. The shortcoming of these eclectic type theories is instructive; there are three questions to answer (why firms grow, where production occurs, and who owns the assets) and only two explanatory variables. The thrust of this paper is that if the theory of direct foreign investment is to be concerned with the geographic distribution of direct foreign investment, then international capital market phenomena are central. And this approach, more than any other, can provide insights into the recent changes in the pattern of direct foreign investment.

Moreover, the segmentation of the financial markets affects the market values of firms as a group. The multipliers within each currency area differ substantially and from one period to another; and there are significant country-specific or currency-area-specific effects. Thus the changes in the market values of headquartered in different countries affects the takeover patterns. In the 1960s, US firms had the highest market values, and were in a position to take over or buy out firms in other countries. In the late 1970s, firms in Europe and Japan had the highest market values, and were well placed to acquire productive facilities and established firms in the United States.

Note

I am greatly indebted to Charlie Kindleberger for his initial invitation more than a decade ago to write an article on why firms invest abroad. This paper is one more attempt to convince him of the soundness of that argument. Cole Kendall has been a helpful reader of this draft.

References

Aliber, Robert A., 1970. "A Theory of Foreign Direct Investment," in Charles P. Kindleberger (ed.), *The International Corporation*. Cambridge, Mass.: MIT Press.

Buckley, Peter J., and Mark Casson, 1976. *The Future of the Multinational Enterprise*. New York: Holmes and Meier.

Caves, Richard E., 1973. *Canadian Economic Policy and the Impact of International Capital Flows*. University of Toronto Press.

Coase, Ronald H., 1937. "The Nature of the Firm." *Economica* 4, pp. 386–405.

Dunning, John H., 1981. *International Production and the Multinational Enterprise*. London: Allen and Unwin.

Hymer, Stephen H., 1976. *The International Operations of National Firms: A Study of Direct Foreign Investment*. Cambridge, Mass.: MIT Press.

Vernon, Raymond, 1972. *The Economic and Political Consequences of Multinational Enterprises: An Anthology*. Boston: Graduate School of Business Administration, Harvard University.

Williamson, Oliver, E., 1981. "The Modern Corporation: Origins, Evolution, Attributes." *Journal of Economic Literature* 19, no. 4 (December), pp. 1537–1570.

V Implications for the United States

12 American Multinationals and American Employment

Adhip Chaudhuri

The purpose of this essay is to provide a unifying framework to explain the effects of direct foreign investment by American multinational corporations on American employment. This framework could explain the divergent conclusions reached by several empirical studies on this question,[1] and the controversy that they have generated. I shall try to show that the American multinational corporations have various reasons to locate their production facilities abroad rather than at home, with consequences for American employment. Moreover, I shall argue that whether those consequences are considered to be "gains" or "losses" is simply a matter of interpretation as to whether the location of production facilities abroad was necessary or not.

Multinational corporations have been classified into three groups. Firstly, there are supply-based firms operating mines and plantations abroad which do not involve the question of either gains or losses in US employment. The same is true of the second group, namely service-type multinationals, consisting primarily of banks. However, the third type, the manufacturing multinationals, do involve the employment gains and losses issue, because when they set up production facilities abroad they involve an opportunity cost to the home country.

The behavior of manufacturing multinationals from the United States can be best understood through the product-cycle theory.[2] According to this theory, American manufacturing firms' advantage in world trade lies in innovations and subsequent commercial production of products involving high technology. These products go through a life cycle from the stage of innovation to a mature stage of standardized production. The complete life cycle of a product involves several distinct stages. In what follows I shall describe these stages not as they were originally stated by the proponents,[3] but modified substantially to suit the purpose of bringing out the employment characteristics of each stage.

Stage I consists of innovation of the product and its development through custom-designing for the initial consumers, i.e., making "prototypes" and setting up the production process for large-scale outputs. These functions will be served by the high-technology personnel, also known as R&D personnel. During this stage the marketing of the new product will also be important through experimentations on consumer groups, market research, advertising, etc.

Stage II occurs when large-scale manufacturing is started for domestic (US) sales. This stage, therefore, involves increasing numbers of production workers. With larger outputs there will also be a rise in the staff functions associated with operations, e.g., accountants, auditors, or quality control. There is also a continuing need to keep expanding the market through advertising and marketing.

Stage III comes into being when the product starts being exported. This obviously entails larger domestic production and thus larger blue-collar and white-collar comployment. One might wonder if it is possible to have two distinct stages like this and the previous one, since exports (especially to Europe) could start simultaneously with domestic sales. In the initial studies of the product-cycle theory there was a time lag between the two because Europe and Japan were still significantly below the American standard of living, and therefore income and price elasticity factors put those consumers chronologically behind US consumption. However, the "income gap" has closed; and formulating an export stage only after domestic markets have been covered, can be justified on the grounds that it may be the natural way of doing things by a corporation.

At Stage IV, the corporations start building plants abroad to supply the foreign markets through foreign production replacing exports from home. This export substitution by the multinational firms is where the controversy about the employment effects of foreign investment begins. According to American labor unions the export substitution was "unnecessary," while from the firms' point of view the move was made for "defensive" purposes. I shall discuss the differing perspectives later.

Some products that originated in the United States reach Stage V when foreign subsidiaries are opened in the LDCs by American firms to supply the home country markets. These imports from the subsidiaries displace domestic production, thereby completing a full cycle whereby the product will completely cease to be produced in the United States. These shifts in production locations will come at the nature of the product, when the production processes have become standardized and it is no longer necessary to use skilled labor. The lower wage rates of the LDC workers will, therefore, become decisive in the choice of production locations.

The employment effect of a product during its life can be analyzed by breaking up the labor force into three categories: (a) high-technology personnel consisting primarily of scientists and engineers, (b) production or blue-collar workers, and (c) white-collar workers.

High-technology personnel are the ones who innovate and then develop the product into its commercial stage by custom-designing, building prototypes, and setting up the process for longer production runs. Therefore, there will be increasing usage of this type of personnel up to the end of Stage I. During Stage II their usage will start falling as the product approaches full development, "bugs" are removed, and the production process stabilizes. The decline in their employment will continue throughout Stage II, but will not drop to zero. This is so because their services will be required for maintenance of the production process and also for the sales function if the nature of the product is technically complex. The Stage II level will be carried forth into the export stage, i.e., Stage III, when there might be some increase in the need for maintenance personnel due to expansion of plant capacity and usage. When the export markets are supplied directly by the foreign subsidiaries in Stage IV, this slight gain will be reduced but not completely eliminated, since some home office consultancy will be required for the plants abroad. Finally at Stage V, when all production has shifted abroad, the employment of this group will fall further. However, it will still be positive to provide expertise and advice to the foreign plants. The technical staff will have dwindled down to a skeleton by the last stage of the cycle. These ideas are represented in figure 1.

Consider the history of white-collar employment next. Their employment begins during product development for market research and other sales functions. This would be somewhere in the middle of Stage I. Once mass production and sales begin in Stage II, their employment increases rapidly. With the advent of exports there will be additional employment, but the growth will not be as marked as Stage II because of two reasons. Firstly, exports are typically a small fraction of domestic US sales. Secondly, white-collar workers have some overhead qualities, i.e., they can handle the additional markets without proportional increases in numbers. Once exports are replaced by direct production

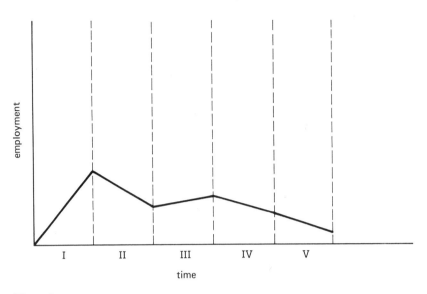

Figure 1
Employment of technical personnel.

abroad it is possible that there might be some decline in the marketing and sales functions for foreign markets in the home office *if* those functions were indeed in the home office to begin with. It is more likely, however, that the export sales and marketing were being conducted through inter-firm relationship with a native firm or an intra-firm trade with a distribution and sales affiliate residing abroad. In any case, there will not be any decrease in the usually centralized functions like finance and accounting, since the home office will continue providing these services to the new subsidiaries. If one adds to that an increase in supporting employment to handle new national laws and environments affecting the multinational firm, one gets a slight increase in Stage IV. The advent of Stage V will hardly be noticeable to the home office white-collar group since only the production plants in the United States will be closing down in favor of new plants in the lower-wage countries. There might be some adverse effects in the staff functions related to production, e.g., payroll, but this will be more than compensated for by more home-office supporting employment for managing the subsidiaries abroad. Not all of these services need be directly supplied by the corporation, but may be obtained from independent "consulting"

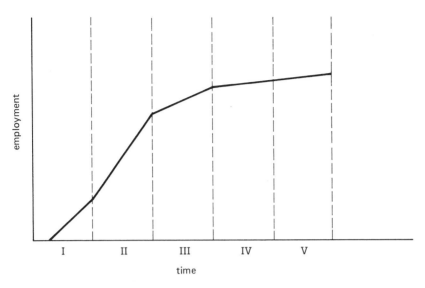

Figure 2
White-collar employment.

firms. The various stages of white-collar employment may be seen in figure 2.

Production and operations workers' employment starts with Stage II and rises impressively throughout this stage as the production increases steadily to supply the expanding domestic markets. When production begins for exports in Stage III, their employment rises, but not at the same rate as Stage II for the same reasons as stated for the white-collar employment above. As foreign subsidiaries are built to substitute for exports, domestic production is displaced and the blue-collar workers start losing their jobs. The fall in the employment of production workers to pre-export levels is compensated for by additional blue-collar employment that will be created to supply the subsidiaries. This is known as the "export stimulus effect" in the literature,[4] and consists of: (1) capital-goods exports to establish foreign production facilities, (2) intermediate goods and spare parts used in the production process and its maintenance in the foreign subsidiaries, and (3) exports of goods complementary to goods produced and sold abroad by the foreign subsidiaries. Not all of the export stimulus jobs will be in the same corporation that manufactures the product, but can be attributed directly

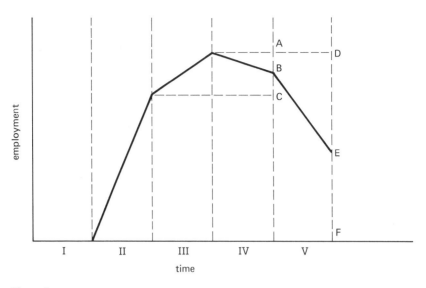

Figure 3
Blue-collar employment.

to it. The story in Stage V, when foreign subsidiaries displace domestic production for domestic sales, is identical to that of the previous stage. In figure 3, it can be seen that employment in Stage IV falls only to *B* rather than *C*, the pre-export level; and in Stage V to *E* instead of *F*, which would be a total loss. So *BC* and *EF* represent the export stimulus effects in Stages IV and V respectively. The other labels on the diagram will be used later.

Before I discuss the total employment effect, it is appropriate to discuss the different motives associated with direct foreign investment, since those are the constituents of the controversies surrounding the blue-collar imployment effect. These motives can be broadly characterized as "defensive" and "aggressive." I define defensive foreign investment as an act which is a *reaction* to: (a) anti-import policies of the host country, (b) entry of host-country firms in the production of the good previously exported by the US firm, or (c) foreign subsidiaries set up by multinationals from other home countries in the LDCs to take advantage of the lower wage rates.

American multinationals have set up subsidiaries in the EEC and in some of the newly emerging developing countries because of anti-import tariffs that have made exports infeasible. The anti-import policies of case (a) above can also be found in restrictive patent laws and the awarding of host-country government contracts for the manufacture of public goods. Case (b) is probably linked with the anti-import policies because the emerging national firms in postwar Europe and the LCDs would seek protection on the basis of the infant-industries argument. But this category can also stand on its own merit. An American firm exporting to a host country would have some genuine disadvantages against a national firm, one of which will be transportation costs. Both these cases (a) and (b) will be dominant in Stage IV of the cycle.

When a product that originated in the United States reaches the mature stage of its life, the knowledge and information about the manufacturing and marketing of the product will be common and firms from other nations will be manufacturing the product as well. It has been stated that Japanese manufacturing firms seek out comparative advantages on a global scale and choose production locations that minimize costs.[5] So, insofar as manufacturing "old" consumer goods are concerned, they typically locate the production facilities in the LDCs and export the goods to the American and European markets. American firms have to follow suit just to protect their home markets, since the prices based on American wages will not otherwise be competitive. That is the basis for case (c).

Within this context I would like to make a slight digression. Those familiar with the antipathy of American labor unions toward foreign investment by American multinationals[6] know that the crux of the problem lies in Stage V rather than in Stage IV, since displacement of production due to export-substitution is not quantitatively or even sentimentally as painful as losing one's domestic production due to imports. Hence we have the outrage against the "exploitation of Third World workers."[7]

The facts about the production process over the life of a product, however, dispel any kind of "blame" held toward the firms. The production process inevitably goes from a labor-intensive to a capital-intensive (automation) method when the levels of output are very high. Thus, if the production source is not moved to the low-wage countries, American workers are likely to be replaced by automated assembly lines. This argument is represented in figure 4.[8] In the diagram, *DD* represents the costs of producing in the United States, *FF* the cost in

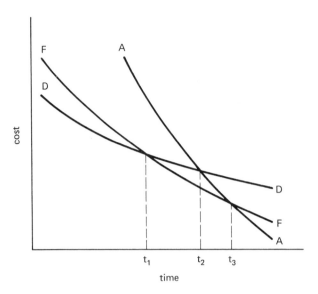

Figure 4
Costs of different production processes.

a low-wage nation, and AA the cost in the United States of production
on a highly automated basis. Assuming a monotonic relationship between "time" and the scale of production, all three processes demonstrate decreasing costs. However, the critical point is the production
in the LCDs becomes less costly than US production at t_1. Here the
production process has become stable and standardized and it is feasible
to use unskilled labor. The automated production process is very costly
at lower levels of production, but by time t_3 the production levels are
high enough to make it least costly. At this point, all production workers
will be replaced by machines. The natural course of events for US firms
has been historically to move from DD to AA at time t_2, but with the
advent of the Japanese-style multinationals, FF has deserved serious
consideration by them to remain competitive during the time period
t_1 to t_2. US labor's displacement has been merely speeded up by the
Third World workers, but the inevitability of the displacement lies
more in automation rather than "sweatshops" in the LDCs.

Aggressive investment decisions are based on motives that are not
dependent on the decisions of economic agents external to the firm
such as the host- or home-country government policies, moves by other

multinationals from the United States or other countries, etc. Essentially it consists of all motives that are exclusive of the four cases presented under defensive investment. Prominent examples of aggressive motives would be Stephen Hymer's explanation of foreign investment,[9] where US oligopolists invest abroad to set up barriers to entry to keep out native firms from entering the industries they dominate. Another example is Stephen Magee's theory of direct foreign investment.[10] According to Magee, multinational firms set up subsidiaries abroad to appropriate monopoly rents from their exclusive "knowledge and information." The "knowledge and information" consists of technical and marketing know-how, and these are traded on an intra-firm basis between the parent and the subsidiaries. In both these explanations, direct foreign investment is not a reaction to a move made by an agent external to the corporation. Similarly, a firm that shifts its production location to a LDC to maximize global profits can be considered to be aggressive if it does so of its own volition. However, if an American firm invests in a low-wage area just to remain competitive with Japanese or other American firms, who are already operating out of such areas, the move can be considered defensive.

This discussion on aggressive and defensive foreign investment helps to explain the differing perspectives and views of the employment gains and losses of the blue-collar workers in the United States. It should become clearer to the reader that even though the two different motives were defined for individual firms they do have some social or national implications. From the national point of view, aggressive foreign investment may be considered "unnecessary" because it displaces American production workers and also hurts the short-term balance-of-payments situation. US labor and possibly the government would frown upon such moves while they may be quite sympathetic to defensive foreign investment, because, even though the losses in employment and the balance of payments are the same, it will be judged to be "necessary."

I will now use figure 3 to explain the consequences of using different assumptions regarding motives for foreign investment. If the foreign production in Stage IV is considered to be defensive, then one can argue that there is a gain of employment amounting to BC, because if the foreign markets were totally lost, i.e., to exports *and* multinational investment, employment would have fallen by AC rather than the

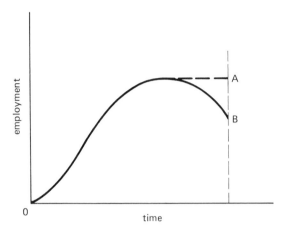

Figure 5
Aggregate employment for one product.

actual decline *AB*. The gain is due to the export stimulus effect. On the other hand, if the foreign investment in Stage IV was taken as aggressive then one would believe that there is a loss of employment amounting to *AB*, since the decline was due to unnecessary export substitution — what has been called the "domestic production displacement effect." The explanation is similar at Stage V. If the foreign investment is considered aggressive then there is a loss of *DE*, and if it is taken as defensive then there is a gain of *EF*.

Looking at the aggregate employment effect, i.e., combining the high-technology, white-collar and blue-collar workers, one can obtain a smooth and continuous time-path, a shown in figure 5. The aggregate employment is represented by the curve *OB*. The employment level depicted by *A* is the peak level occurring during Stage III of the product's life. After this, the sharp fall in the employment of production workers outweighs the gentle increases in white-collar employment and the employment level falls to *B*. After point *B*, the employment path may stabilize if the product lives on in perpetuity; or it may vanish completely if the product "dies" due to technological progress. These possibilities are not dependent on the location of production facilities, but on the wants and needs of consumers. What is more important is that, on the aggregate, *AB* will be the measured loss primarily due to displacement of production workers, if foreign investment is considered to be aggressive. On the other hand, if all foreign investment is considered to be defensive then there is a perceived gain amounting to BC that consists of the export stimulus effect for blue-collar workers and home-office employment effect for white-collar workers.

It is crucial therefore to know what the authors of the empirical studies are assuming about the nature of direct foreign investment of American multinationals to understand their different conclusions about whether American employment is worsened or improved.

In a study sponsored by the AFL-CIO, Stanley Ruttenberg[11] argues that all direct foreign investment by US multinational corporations is unnecessary from a national point of view, and is undertaken at the expense of the domestic economy. He concentrates on the decline in blue-collar employment during Stage V of a product's life and presents it as a pervasive phenomenon in the US economy. Besides the lower LDC wages, he blames the Foreign Tax Credit structure in the United States and also the lenient tariff regulations on imports that have some value added in the United States. Using Bureau of Labor data, he concludes that between 1966 and 1969 the foreign sector of the US economy lost half a million jobs due to export substitution and import orientation by American multinationals.

A study done for the US Senate by Peggy Musgrave[12] was of similar opinion, even though this study was concerned more with domestic capital formation and productivity than with employment. Musgrave asserted that foreign investment is a substitute for domestic investment, and concluded that the widespread foreign investment by US firms after World War II had slowed the growth of domestic employment and productivity.

In response to the critical views put forth concerning the effects of direct foreign investment on the US economy, Robert Stobaugh[13] conducted a case study of US multinational corporations that invested in various locations abroad. The study encompassed a wide variety of corporations, ranging from chemical companies to fruit-canning plants. According to Stobaugh, these multinationals invested abroad largely because high tariffs or stringent tax laws in the host countries effectively prevented US exports. Stobaugh concludes that while these direct foreign investments initially may have resulted in a loss in US employment, they were necessary from a national point of view. While some of the justification and reasoning that Stobaugh uses to support this point of

Table 1

Author	Assumption	Displacement of production workers	Export stimulus	Home office and supporting employment	Net
(1) Ruttenberg, AFL-CIO	100% aggressive	−700	200	. . .	−500
(2) Stobaugh	100% defensive	. . .	250	350	+600
(3) Hawkins	(a) 5% aggressive	−190	260	209	+279
	(b) 10% aggressive	−381	260	209	+ 89
	(c) 25% aggressive	−791	260	209	−322

Source: Neil Hood and Stephen Young, *The Economics of Multinational Enterprise* (New York: Longman, 1979), p. 317.

view is not completely clear, he argues convincingly that overall direct foreign investment by these multinationals had a positive effect on US employment and the US economy.

In a more academic spirit, Hawkins[14] undertook an econometric study of the employment effects of direct foreign investment for 1968. Instead of assuming that foreign investment is either purely aggressive or purely defensive, he showed the quantitative implications of making such assumptions. He took several proportions of the total foreign investment to be aggressive and broke up the impact into various categories which have been described earlier in this essay. Hawkins' results are presented in table 1, juxtaposed with the numerical conclusions of Ruttenberg and Stobaugh. In each case, the quantitative conclusions of the authors are consistent with their assumptions. Ruttenberg and Stobaugh are exactly opposite in their assumptions and therefore in their conclusions. Hawkins gives the net results of various mixes of aggressive and defensive investment assumptions. As explained in the theoretical discussion earlier, the differing assumptions affect only the column under the "displacement of production workers," with the employment loss increasing with a rising proportion of foreign investment interpreted to be based on aggressive motives.

To have a definite view about the sign (positive or negative) of the employment effect, at least for the time period of these studies, i.e., the late 1960s, one would have to establish the plausibility of one of Hawkins' assumptions, since the extreme assumptions of Stobaugh and Ruttenberg are definitely counterintuitive and probably counterfactual.

There has been no attempt to study every single foreign investment decision over a reasonable time period, which could give us the possible proportions of aggressive and defensive motives. There are some case studies, including Stobaugh's own, but the sample size is too small for reliable inference.

There is an indication, however, which might help to form the basis for a tentative conclusion. This is an examination of the applications for insurance from the US-government-backed Overseas Private Investment Corporation (OPIC). This agency is required to evaluate all applications for insurance from US firms investing abroad from the point of view of effects on US employment and balance of payments. It is expected to deny investment insurance to those projects that are considered to be detrimental to the US economy. According to one publication,[15] between 1971 and 1973 OPIC received fifty applications, of which it rejected eleven because they would adversely affect US economic conditions. This would certainly point towards Hawkins' assumption (c) of 25% aggressive investment, leading to a negative employment effect.

To determine a conclusion about gains and losses in American employment due to outward investment we have to have more systematic studies on both the econometric side (Hawkins type) and also on the side of motives and reasons for foreign investment (OPIC type). Though conclusions based on such endeavors will be more reliable, they will still not be general enough to be intertemporal.

That brings me to my last point. If there is no compelling reason to believe that American multinationals adversely affect American employment, why is it that organized labor has made it such a major issue? To put the question in a more interesting way: why is it that labor has become increasingly anti-foreign-investment only in the 1970s, while foreign investment by American firms has been going on for more than a century? The answer lies in the fact that on the aggregate, the employment in the foreign sector in the United States has become a phenomenon much like "technological unemployment."

I have argued that by the time a product plays out is complete life cycle it ceases to be produced in the United States and, even though there are gains for white-collar empoyment, the aggregate employment for this one product will fall. But the scientists and engineers who will be released from this product by Stage II will move on to innovate

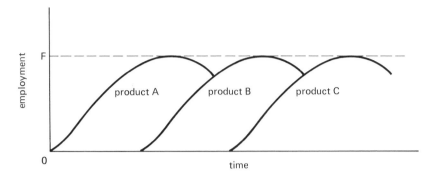

Figure 6
Aggregate employment for several successive products.

new products. The blue-collar workers will also have to make similar transitions by Stage IV, and also white-collar workers after the "death" of the product. The stability of employment due to the foreign sector in the US economy would then depend on two things: (a) steady "waves" of new products and (b) similar market successes for each product to generate stable employment. These ideas are represented in figure 6. As the employment from product A starts declining, product B starts creating new employment opportunities. As long as product B compensates exactly the loss in A (as drawn in the diagram), aggregate employment will remained unchanged. Labor has to make the transition from one industry to another and this burden will be primarily on the blue-collar workers. If the ideal situation continues, i.e., product C picks up for B in the same way, there will be stable employment in the United States in the foreign sector represented by the height OF. If, on the other hand, technological innovations slow down or the new products are less successful in sales (therefore in employment), the foreign sector's contribution to total employment will diminish. It might just be that the source of the adverse employment situation in the last decade is due to those factors rather than foreign investment itself.

Notes

I would like to acknowledge the participants of the Fourth Middlebury College Economics Conference in general, and Richard Newfarmer of the Overseas Development Council in particular, for helpful comments. Valuable research assistance was provided by Kara Boatman.

1. See Ruttenberg, S., *Needed: A Constructive Foreign Trade Policy*, AFL-CIO, 1971; Stobaugh, R. B., "The multinational corporation: measuring the consequences," *Columbia Journal of World Business*, January/February 1971; Musgrave, P., *Direct Investment Abroad and the Multinationals*, US Government Printing Office, August 1975; and Hawkins, R. G., *Job Displacement and the Multinational Firm*, Occasional Paper No. 3, Center for Multinational Studies, Washington, D.C., 1972.

2. Wells, Louis T. (ed.), *Product Cycle Theory in International Trade*, Harvard University Press, Cambridge, Mass., 1972.

3. Ibid. pp. 12–15.

4. Hawkins, op. cit.

5. See Kojima, K., *Direct Foreign Investment*, Croom Helm, London, 1978.

6. See Barnet, R. and R. Muller, *Global Reach*, Simon and Schuster, New York, 1974.

7. Barnet and Muller, op. cit.

8. This idea is borrowed from Arthur Lake, "Technology creation and technology transfer by multinational firms," in R. G. Hawkins (ed.), *The Economic Effects of Multinational Corporations*, vol. I. Jai Press, Greenwich, Conn., 1979.

9. Hymer, S., *the International Operations of National Firms*, Ph.D. thesis, Massachusetts Institute of Technology, 1960; published by The MIT Press, Cambridge, Mass., 1976.

10. Magee, S. P., "Information and the multinational corporation: an appropriability theory of direct foreign investment." in J. N. Bhagwati, (ed.), *The New International Order*, MIT Press, Cambridge, Mass., 1977.

11. Ruttenberg, op. cit.

12. Musgrave, op. cit.

13. Stobaugh, R., et al., *Nine Investments Abroad*, Harvard University Press, Cambridge, Mass., 1976.

14. Hawkins, op. cit.

15. Bergsten, C. F., T. Horst, and T. Moran, *American Multinationals and American Interests*, Brookings, Washington, D.C., 1978, pp. 59–62.

13 Foreign Direct Investment in the United States: Old Currents, "New Waves," and the Theory of Direct Investment

David McClain

We economists have a difficult time verifying our theories. Our discipline shares with others the epistemological problem of the asymmetry between rejecting and accepting (i.e., failing to reject) hypotheses. This results in a collection of not-yet-rejected (or "unpopped balloons," to use Joseph Nye's phrase), the relative prominence of which depends on the sociology of the profession as much as anything else. Worse still, we rarely have the opportunity to perform controlled experiments; we are forced to depend on "nature" to generate a set of data sufficiently powerful to discriminate among competing hypotheses.

Students of foreign direct investment and the multinational corporation have been at a particular disadvantage in this regard. Explanations of the motivation for the establishment of production or sales facilities in one country by a firm with headquarters in another logically center on the theory of the behavior of the firm and on the theory of the international location of production. But attempts to verify or confirm hypotheses in this field have been confounded by poor-to-nonexistent data, and by the special nature of the postwar period, in which firms from the United States performed a great deal of the investment.

"Nature," in the decade of the 1970s, has provided analysts of the multinational enterprise with a rare gift—variation in the meager set of data available on the behavior of the international corporation. European and Japanese multinationals have increased the volume of their foreign direct investment activity dramatically, particularly in the United States. This "grand experiment" should enable us to understand more completely the motivation for foreign direct investment; perhaps it will allow us to winnow out some of the competing hypotheses in the field.

This paper examines the recent foreign direct investment experience in the United States, and analyzes its implications for different theories of direct investment. Section I traces the history of the subject, and outlines the quantitative dimensions of the phenomenon. Information on foreign direct investment in the United States has become much more abundant in the last 5 years, and this part of the paper presents a detailed and up-to-the-present sketch of the phenomenon. Section II is given over to a very brief review "the" theory of direct investment— the industrial organization/market imperfections hypothesis—and a critique of alternative hypotheses, both old and new; some refinements to existing theories also are suggested (in particular, viewing the direct investment process from the vantage point of Tobin's q). In section III, I recapitulate the results of earlier research done on the issue, without the benefit of the data generated from the mid-1970s onward, and conclude that the available data support the market-imperfections paradigm. I also discuss the notion of the "small-country product cycle," a concept which serves to emphasize the unique characteristics of the international economy in the 1950s and 1960s that have colored our view of the direct investment process. Section IV reviews the conclusions of the research discussed in section III, in the light of the experience of the 1970s. Following the dictum to "take no derivative, invert no matrix," I rely only on my own and others' case studies and simple analytic techniques in examining the data. As Niehans (1977, p. 1) has observed, since "the multinational character of firms can emerge from many different sets of circumstances that may have little else in common," approaching an analysis of their behavior by exercises in pure theory or econometrics may not be a promising research strategy. Section V concludes by discussing the consequences of the research findings for the design of public policy toward multinational corporations.

I. The Growth of Foreign Direct Investment in the United States

From the Revolution to World War II

It is by now a cliché to observe that, though foreign direct investment in the United States accelerated dramatically in the 1970s, foreign involvement in the business affairs of this country has been a central ingredient of economic growth since the founding of the Republic.[1] Most of the original investment was of the portfolio variety, particularly in railroads in the nineteenth century. Foreign investment in the US manufacturing industry was extremely limited until around 1900; in part this reflected the rather slow development and refinement of the

Table 1
Stock of foreign direct investment in the United States, 1914–1941 (book values, in billions of current dollars).

Year	Level	% British	% Manufacturing	Level/GNP
1914	1.3	46	15[c]	0.034
1919	0.9	56	10[c]	0.011
1934	1.5[a]	45	37	0.023
1937	1.9	44	39	0.021
1941	2.3[b]	31	31	0.018

Source of direct investment data: See text note 1.
[a]Revised to $1.8 b by 1937 census.
[b]Market value (10–12% below book value); reflects British sale of American Viscose.
[c]My estimate.

general legal concept of a corporation during the nineteenth century. Most investment in manufacturing was also portfolio in nature; 25% of the common stock of U.S. Steel was held abroad on a portfolio basis in 1914 (of course, holdings of this size would be classified as a direct investment in today's statistics).

Direct investments made in the US manufacturing sector near the end of the nineteenth century included those by the British in textiles, primary metals, and food and beverages, and by the Germans in chemicals, beverages, and electrical equipment. Subsidiaries in the United States were established during this time by such familiar multinational corporations as Bayer (in 1865), Merck, Geigy, Bosch, Siemens, Daimler, Lever Brothers, Dunlop, Michelin, and Nestlé.

Many of the subsidiaries established at this time did not survive intact into the post–World War II era. US allies in both world wars were forced to sell off some investments to fund their military efforts; enemies had their property confiscated. On occasion, the US government acted less than honorably toward friend as well as foe. One week before the end of World War I, Congress moved to allow the sale of German patents to a group from the American chemical industry. In 1941, the United States required the British to sell Courtauld's American Viscose subsidiary, the world's largest producer of rayon, at depressed prices to "qualify" for Lend-Lease.

A side effect of the two global conflicts was the creation of fairly reliable benchmark data on the magnitude of foreign direct investments in the United States (table 1).

Table 2
Stock of foreign direct investment in the United States, 1950–1973 (book values, in billions of current dollars).

Year	Level	Compound annual rate of increase	% British	% Manufacturing[a]	Level/GNP
1950	3.4		34	34	0.012
1955	5.1	8.4	34	35	0.013
1960	6.9	6.4	33	38	0.014
1965	8.8	4.9	32	40	0.013
1970	13.3	8.6	31	46	0.013
1973	18.3	11.2	31	47	0.014

Source: *Survey of Current Business*, various issues.
[a]Excluding petroleum.

British holdings during this period were concentrated roughly equally in manufacturing and finance. Among sectors, finance (with 20–25% of the total) and transportation (with 15–20%) ranked second and third during the first half of the century. In 1914 Germany was second to the United Kingdom in the aggregate volume of investment, with nearly 25% of the total. German holdings seized in World War II were less than 5% of the total stock of foreign direct investment at that time.

From Postwar Reconstruction to the 1973 Oil Shock

After World War II, first the task of reconstruction and then the stimulus of rapid domestic and regional growth kept European and Japanese capital at home; often governmental regulation played a role as well. Still, based on the findings of the 1959 benchmark survey, the stock of foreign direct investment grew at an 8.4% compound annual rate during the first half of the 1950s. The rate of increase slowed steadily during the next 10 years (table 2).

The pace of foreign direct investment activity quickened in the latter half of the 1960s, and accelerated still further in the early 1970s, as the growth rates of US inward and outward direct investment became roughly equal. In 1973 alone, the stock of foreign direct investment increased by 23%. Some of this quickening, of course, reflected higher inflation.

During this *Pax Americana* the predominance of the British in the United States was eroded only slightly. The Canadian share, 30% of the total in 1950, was but 22% in 1973. The Dutch fraction of the total rose from 10 to 14% over the period, while the Swiss proportion stayed relatively constant at 10%. Other European countries and non-European countries increased their shares during this time, from 11 to 13 and from 4 to 10%, respectively.

An expanding fraction of investment flowed into the manufacturing and petroleum sectors, at the expense of finance and other sectors. The increase for manufacturing was fairly gradual, though the late 1960s was a period of exceptional activity. The rise in the petroleum share, from 12 to 25%, was also measured, with concentrations near the beginning and end of the period.

Information on the distribution of foreign investment by sub-industry within manufacturing is not published for these years. The 1959 benchmark survey did reveal that, of the $5.1 billion in sales by foreign-controlled subsidiaries and branches in manufacturing, 45% was in the food and beverage category, 17% in chemicals, and 8% in nonelectrical machinery. In 1972, by one estimate,[2] the largest *number* of manufacturing investments had been made in nonelectrical machinery—20% of the sample of 341 subsidiaries of large foreign corporations. Eighteen percent of the investments were in the chemicals industry, 11% were in electrical machinery, and 7% were in instruments.

The last column of table 2 suggests the comparative insignificance of direct foreign investment in the postwar US economy. During this period, the flow of direct investment (which includes claims on current as well as fixed assets) exceeded 1.1% of US private nonresidential fixed investment on only two occasions—in 1970 (1.4%) and in 1973 (2.4%). In the decade ending in 1973, the flow of foreign direct investment in the United States as a fraction of the flow of US direct investment abroad fluctuated in the 10–20% range; only in 1973 did the ratio rise to 30%. And while reinvested earnings were not the principal means for US firms to increase their asset stock abroad until the early 1970s, foreign firms consistently relied primarily on retained funds to build up their asset position in the United States.

The flow of foreign direct investment into the United States during this period was small in relation to the magnitude of investment activity in the source economies as well. As a fraction of UK gross domestic investment, the flow of British direct investment into the United States in 1961–1973 exceeded 2% only in 1970. During this period, a similar ratio for Canada ran above 1.5% only twice—in 1970 (1.6%) and 1973

(1.8%). In the Netherlands, the ratio was customarily 1.5 to 2%; in 1968–1969, it averaged over 3%.

The 1974 Benchmark Survey

The surge of investment in the Unied States during 1973 and the recycling issues raised by the oil shock of 1973–1974 led Congress to mandate a new benchmark study of the phenomenon. This survey[3] has provided the most comprehensive view ever available of the scope and nature of the US operations of foreign multinationals; 7,200 reports were filed covering the activities of 10,200 US enterprises. Its results, however, are not comparable with earlier estimates of direct investment activity in the United States, owing to differences in definition and classification.

In the 1974 survey, a direct investment ownership interest was defined as "the direct or indirect foreign ownership of at least 10% of the voting stock of an incorporated US business enterprise or an equivalent interest in an unincorporated enterprise." In the 1959 survey, a 25% level of ownership was the criterion. Including subsequent revisions to the initially published 1974 survey results, the stock of foreign direct investment at year-end 1974 was estimated at $25.1 billion; based on the 1974 survey, the stock at year-end 1973 was put at $20.6 billion.

Definitional changes also affected the distribution of the foreign direct investment stock by country and industry and reduced the utility of these classifications for analytical purposes. In the 1974 survey, "foreign parent" was defined as the *first* foreign person outside the United States holding an ownership interest in a US affiliate. The "first" foreign parent, of course, could differ from the "ultimate" foreign parent. This definitional change is responsible for the increase in the Latin American share of the 1974 stock, from 2.5% in the 1959 survey-based estimate to over 9%, since many foreign multinationals control their US subsidiaries through holding companies based in Panama or Caribbean countries.

Industry classifications are based on the industry of the primary US affiliate in the 1974 survey, rather than on the industry of secondary US affiliates (owned by the primary affiliates), as in the 1959 survey-based estimates. Since many foreign firms use financial holding companies to control their US manufacturing subsidiaries, this classification change reduced the share of manufacturing in the 1974 stock from 47%

Table 3
Gross product of all US businesses and US affiliates, 1974 ($ billions).

Industry	All US business gross product (1)	Affiliate gross product (2)	(2) as % of (1)	Distribution	
				All	Affiliate
Mining	12.1	0.7	2	1	3
Petroleum	32.2	5.9	5	3	24
Manufacturing	323.1	11.2	3	29	45
Food	31.0	2.2	7	3	9
Printing	16.5	0.5	3	1	2
Chemicals	24.5	2.8	12	2	11
Primary Metals	30.7	1.4	4	3	1
Instruments	8.2	0.3	3	1	a
Other	212.2	4.0	2	19	16
Transport, Comm., Utilities	121.5	0.7	1	11	5
Wholesale Trade	110.6	3.0	3	10	12
Retail Trade	132.8	1.2	1	12	5
Finance, Insurance Real Estate	116.7	1.5	1	10	6
Other Industries	274.6	0.7	a	24	3
Total	1123.6	24.7	2	100	100

Source: *Survey of Current Business*, January 1979.
aLess than 0.5 percent.

to 31%. The share of insurance and other finance rose from 13% to 20%.

The 1974 survey suggested that foreign firms preferred majority control of their affiliates. Sixty percent of the foreign direct investment position was in affiliates wholly owned by foreigners, and foreign firms had a majority stake in affiliates representing over 90% of the investment position.

The relative importance of foreign direct investment to the economy as a whole, and to particular industries, is suggested in table 3, which displays gross product by industry for all firms and for US affiliates of foreign firms.

The 1974 survey concluded that popular concern over massive foreign takeovers of US industry by OPEC nations was unsubstantiated. While

OPEC direct investments were 6.7% of the total, nearly all of it was an investment in a US oil company with producing assets in the OPEC nation making the investment. A year after the survey was published, this transaction was reclassified as a purchase of the US company's foreign branch; thus it was removed from the stock of foreign direct investment in the United States. With this investment removed, OPEC's direct investment position in 1974 was less than 0.5% of the total, and was concentrated in real estate.

The Current Situation

Since year-end 1973, the volume of foreign direct investment in the United States has increased dramatically. At the end of 1980, the stock was $65.4 billion, and preliminary data suggest that the amount at the close of 1981 was about $84 billion—a compound annual growth rate of over 19% since 1973. In the last four years, foreign direct investment in the United States has grown at a 25% compound annual rate, more than twice the rate of increase of US direct investment abroad; the flow of foreign direct investment has been 3–4% of the flow of US nonresidential fixed investment during 1973–1980, and was 5.5% of this aggregate in 1981. Table 4 displays the foreign direct investment position in the United States at the end of 1980.

Trade, finance, and real estate are the sectors which have grown most rapidly; investments in the trade sector now exceed those in petroleum. Among countries, the Netherlands has moved from third to first place, principally because of substantial increases in investments in the petroleum industry. Despite the rapid rate of growth of German and Japanese investments, in no year during 1974–1980 did the Japanese investment exceed 0.5% of gross domestic investment in Japan; only in 1978 was the flow of German investment more than 1% of gross domestic investment in Germany. For smaller economies, of course, this fraction was larger. In Canada and the United Kingdom, the ratio exceeded 2% twice during 1974–1980; indeed, in 1980 Canadian direct investment in the United States was nearly 5% of gross domestic investment in Canada. The flow of Dutch direct investment in the United States averaged about 6.5% of gross domestic investment in the Netherlands in 1974–1980.

Despite its rapid growth, the flow of foreign direct investment into the United States generally has not expanded more rapidly than the

Table 4
Stock of foreign direct investment in the United States, year-end 1980 (figures in parentheses are
compund annual rates of growth from 1973 to 1980, in $ billions).

Country or region	Industry Petroleum	Manufacturing Total	Food	Chemicals	Metals	Machinery	Other
Canada	1.1	5.1	2.2	0.1	0.8	1.3	0.7
United Kingdom	− 0.1	4.3	0.5	1.4	0.9	0.5	1.1
Netherlands	8.3	3.9	0.9	0.9	0.1	0.9	1.2
Germany	a	2.1	a	1.8	0.2	0.4	− 0.2
Switzerland	a	2.3	0.3	1.2	0.3	0.2	0.4
Other Europe	1.6	2.4	0.1	0.5	0.7	0.5	0.6
Japan	0.1	0.8	a	0.2	0.2	0.2	0.2
Latin America	1.1	3.0	0.1	1.7	0.3	0.1	0.7
Middle East	a	a	a	a	a	a	a
Other Africa, Asia, Pacific	a	0.1	a	a	0.1	a	a
Total	12.3 (14.4)	24.1 (16.6)	4.1 (18.1)	7.9 (15.4)	3.6 (20.6)	4.0 (16.6)	4.6 (15.0)

Source: *Survey of Current Business*, August 1981.
[a]Less than $50 million.
Negative entries reflect impact of intercompany accounts on the direct investment position.

Industry					
Trade	Finance	Insurance	Real Estate	Other	Total
1.1	0.4	0.4	0.5	1.0	9.8 (12.9)
3.6	1.0	2.1	0.2	0.3	11.3 (11.2)
1.1	1.1	0.6	0.5	0.6	16.2 (22.0)
1.8	0.2	0.7	0.1	0.4	5.3 (27.5)
0.6	0.2	0.5	[a]	0.1	3.7 (14.6)
1.8	0.6	0.2	0.1	0.3	7.0 (18.5)
2.3	0.8	0.1	0.1	0.1	4.2 (60.8)
0.9	0.4	0.4	0.6	0.2	6.7 (18.3)
0.2	0.3	[a]	0.3	[a]	0.7 (31.1)
0.3	[a]	[a]	0.1	0.1	0.5 (28.7)
13.8	4.8	5.1	2.4	3.0	65.5
(23.6)	(26.9)	(15.0)	(22.1)	(17.0)	(18.0)

combined flow of inward portfolio and direct investment by nonoffficial parties. Excluding valuation adjustments, direct inflows have been 20–30% of total nonofficial inflows since 1974. In 1979, this ratio was 22.6%; in 1980, it was 31.3%, a post-1973 high.

The foreign direct investment position can increase by inflows to both incorporated and unincorporated affiliates, by reinvestment of earnings of incorporated affiliates, and by valuation adjustments. Inflows to incorporated affiliates consist of purchase (net of sales) of capital stock, and changes in intercompany accounts. Purchases of capital stock and reinvestment of earnings of incorporated affiliates have been the major vehicles for the expansion of the position, and have been of roughly equal importance. Excluding valuation adjustments, which usually have been insignificant, all the components of the direct investment position have grown at roughly the same rate from 1974–1980. The rate of growth of intercompany accounts has been most volatile over the period. In 1980, the capital stock and retained earnings of incorporated affiliates accounted for 78% of the foreign direct investment position; intercompany accounts represented 16% of the position, and 6% was due to unincorporated affiliates.

Foreign direct investors in the United States have reinvested between 65 and 80% of their earnings from incorporated affiliates in the years from 1975 onward. By contrast, in the previous decade, the reinvestment ratio never exceeded 0.56; and US multinationals in the aggregate have never reinvested more than 65% of their foreign incorporated affiliate earnings since data on this activity were first collected in 1950.

The rate of return on the foreign direct investment position, defined as the ratio of income (defined as foreign parents equity in the after-US-tax profits of their US affiliates, plus interest on intercompany accounts, less witholding taxes on dividends and interest) to the average of the stock of foreign direct investment at the end of the previous and current year, has varied greatly across industry groups since 1974. The average rate of return in the petroleum sector during the period 1975–1980 was 18.9%; in manufacturing, 8.1%; in insurance 20.0%; in trade, 8.5%; and in other sectors, 11.9%. In manufacturing (including petroleum) it was 11.4%. In the manufacturing sector (including petroleum), the 1975–1980 average rate of return on *equity* of incorporated US affiliates was 12.6% gross of witholding taxes on dividends, and

12.4% net; for manufacturing excluding petroleum, the corresponding rates of return were 8.8 and 8.6%.

The average rate of return on equity for *all* US manufacturing corporations (including those engaged in petroleum refining) during this period was 14.2%. This higher rate in part reflects the fact that yearly additions to the total US stock of equity are a smaller fraction of the stock than additions to the stock of foreign equity in US affiliates compared with the total stock of foreign equity. Thus, a higher proportion of the assets represented by foreign equity were not in place for the full year to which the income figures refer. Further, one expects newer enterprises and recently acquired "bargains" to be less profitable initially than after they reach their steady state. Still, since the petroleum sector (where rates of return have been much higher than average) bulks much larger as a fraction of the total economic activity of US affiliates in manufacturing (including petroleum) than it does in the economic activity of the entire US manufacturing sector, the profitability of US affiliates of foreign parents in nonpetroleum manufacturing industries has been roughly 3 to 4 percentage points lower, on average, than the profitability of all firms in nonpetroleum manufacturing since the mid-1970s.

Further Monitoring Efforts

The dramatic growth of foreign direct investment in the United States in the last decade has prompted Congress to require, via the International Investment Survey Act of 1976, that the Bureau of Economic Analysis (BEA) in the Department of Commerce conduct an annual survey of the operations of certain nonbank US affiliates of foreign companies. Affiliates must file if they have total assets, sales, or net income greater than $5 million, or if they own more than 200 acres of US land; 5,800 affiliates—accounting for 93.5% of total assets in the 1974 benchmark—were represented in the first survey in 1977. In addition, BEA began a survey on US business enterprises newly acquired or established by foreign investors in 1979. Data are now available from the first survey for 1977–1979, and from the second for 1979–1980.

The operations survey yields the following profile of foreign direct investments in the United States at the end of the 1970s:

• Employment in US affiliates in 1979, at 1,642,000, was 2.1% of private-sector employment.

• Total assets of US affiliates in 1979 were $214.2 billion. Fixed assets were $64.8 billion, 1.7% of the gross value of fixed nonresidential private capital.

• 1979 sales were $313.3 billion; sales of affiliates in manufacturing (including petroleum) and wholesale and retail trade were $289.4 billion, 8.2% of total US sales in these industries.

• Affiliate merchandise exports, at $43.0 billion, represented 23% of US merchandise exports in 1979. Half of the affiliate total represented exports to affiliated foreigners. 1979 affiliate merchandise imports, at $59.4 billion, were 28% of US merchandise imports. Seventy-one percent of affiliate imports were from related foreigners.

• New plant and equipment expenditures by US affiliates in 1979 were $10.1 billion — 3.6% of total US nonresidential fixed investment in that year.

• Affiliate R&D expenditures of $1.5 billion in 1979 were 5% of US private-sector expenditures.

• Less than 0.5% of US farmland was owned by foreign direct investors in 1979.

One useful feature of the acquisitions survey is its attempt to distinguish between the "first" foreign parent — the classification used by the 1974 survey and subsequent official statistics — and the "ultimate" beneficial owner (defined as the person in the ownership chain beginning with the foreign parent, that is not more than 50% owned by another person). The survey was able to identify ultimate owners of 90 to 95% of the investments (by value) made in each year. Of these investments, 11% in 1979 had different first foreign parents and ultimate owners; for 1980, the fraction was 18%. Not suprisingly, 1979 and 1980 investment totals were reduced for the tax havens in the Caribbean. The total was also reduced for the Netherlands, the country with the largest stock of foreign direct investment. In the latter situation, Canadian investments in real estate and the Hong Kong and Shanghai Bank's acquisition of Marine Midland had both been accomplished through Dutch holding companies.

OPEC investment outlays, based on a classification by ultimate owner, instead of on the first foreign parent criterion, rose from $61 million to $324 million in 1979 and from $13 million to $239 million in 1980. In each year revised OPEC outlays, which were concentrated in real estate, were 2% of total outlays. Even after revision, however, outlays for the tax haven region noted above remained at 6% of total outlays; undoubtedly some untraceable OPEC investments remain in these aggregates. (Of course, Kuwait's $2.5 billion acquisition of Santa Fe Petroleum in 1981 (discussed in section IV) boosted OPEC's share of the stock of foreign direct investment—even on a first-foreign-parent basis—to 4%.)

Conclusion

During the 1970s, foreign direct investment in the United States became, for the first time since the first part of the century, something more than inconsequential. Though the total remains small relative to the size of the US economy, we have witnessed enough of a "sea change" to justify reexamination of both our beliefs about why such kinds of investment occur, and our public-policy approaches to the phenomenon. Before conducting this reexamination, I will review briefly the theories of direct investment behavior and empirical work relating these theories to the foreign direct investment experience in the United States through the early 1970s.

II. Theories of Direct Investment

"The" Theory

The title of this paper notwithstanding, there is no unique theory of direct investment. Indeed, as one author has recently noted, "The growth of FDI (foreign direct investment) has . . . been excelled by the growth of publications specially on the determinants of these investments" (Agarwal, 1980). I will not attempt to survey the literature on the subject here; several good surveys are available.[4] Rather, I will give a brief statement of what I take to be "the theory of foreign direct investment developed a decade ago" referred to in the call for papers to the Middlebury conference (see foreword to this volume). Following that, I will discuss refinements, modifications, and alternatives to this theory which have been proposed in the 1970s.

"The" theory is, of course, that attributable to Hymer (1960) and Kindleberger (1969), with further refinements by Caves (1971). It rests on the recognition that, in considering the decision to undertake capital formation abroad, a firm finds itself at a disadvantage vis-a-vis a local firm because of the costs of operating at a distance. These costs include the costs of transportation and communication, as well as costs of misunderstanding the characteristics of the local economic environment. In order to make the decision to produce abroad, a firm not only must be able to earn more than by producing at home and exporting, but also it must be able to earn more than local firms, since its costs will be higher. This requires that it possess some countervailing advantage, transferable abroad, but not available to its local competitor. Further, the market for the sale of this advantage must be imperfect, for otherwise the firm would have no incentive to make a direct investment.

Firms possessing such advantages tend to be large and prominent in their home markets; hence this theory, which rests on the existence of market imperfections, is known as the "industrial organization" or "monopolistic competition" theory of direct investment. Within this general framework, one can make a taxonomy of market imperfections that give rise to countervailing advantages. The categorization proposed by Kindleberger (1969, p. 14)—of imperfections in goods markets (product differentiation, marketing skills, administered prices), factor markets (proprietary technology, managerial skills, discriminatory access to capital), economies of scale internal and external to the firm, and government-imposed market disruptions (limitations on output or entry)—makes this approach to the analysis of direct investment behavior most general. In the short term, with capacity to produce for export in place, governmentally imposed imperfections can lead to "defensive" investment (Lamfalussy, 1963), undertaken to avoid a loss on existing investment. Defensive investment also can occur in concentrated industries to prevent competitors from obtaining or enlarging a special advantage which could then be exploited globally (Kindleberger, 1969, p. 15; Knickerbocker, 1973; Graham, 1974).

The acceptance of this theory derived from its predictive power. Direct investment tended not to occur in those industries best approximated by the perfectly competitive model for goods and factors. Multinationals did not tend to license their advantages, or enter into joint ventures with local partners. And cross-investments did take place in the same industry, in part because firms possessed differential advantages, but also because of the dynamics of oligopolistic behavior.

Developments in the Last Decade

Recent refinements of this market-imperfections-based theory of direct investment have focused on the formation of the firm as a response to the existence of significant costs of coordinating the economic relationships of transactors through markets in certain situations. No market is perfect in the sense that it operates costlessly, and firms arise in those situations when the costs of operations outweigh the benefits to individuals from participating in exchange through the market.

These refinements parallel the evolving interest of the profession as a whole in the economic rationales for and consequences of different legal environments, including the legal fiction of a corporation. The works of Knight (1921), Coase (1937), Arrow (1962), and several papers by Alchian and Demsetz were central in this evolution; Furubotn and Pejovich (1972) offer a survey.

In the direct investment literature, McManus (1972) identified these costs of coordination as consisting of the costs of measurement of services from a stock of assets and the costs of enforcement of property rights. He suggested that multinational firms were likely to emerge when these costs were high—that is, as it becomes more difficult to define what services are being exchanged and what actions will fulfill a contract. This led McManus to conclude that multinational firms will arise in industries characterized by substantial interdependence among producers in different countries and significant costs of coordinating their actions through the market mechanism (exports) or a contract (licensing).

Johnson identified "the transference of knowledge . . . (as) the crux of the direct investment process" (1970, p. 35). Because knowledge has the character of a public good, the market for this product is characterized by high coordination costs and is quite imperfect. Hymer (1960) had noted that firms producing the intermediate good of proprietary knowledge have an incentive to expand to bring the transference to this product under the control of the firm, as long as the benefits to the firm of doing so outweigh the costs.

Baumann (1975) suggested that industries with rapidly changing technology were the most likely to satisfy McNamara's criteria of high interdependence of producers and substantial coordination costs. Buckley and Casson (1976, 1978) and Casson (1979) refined and elaborated the notion of direct investment occurring as firms internalized across national boundaries the externalities of imperfect markets in intermediate products such as technical and entrepreneurial expertise. They identified internalization benefits arising from reduction in negotiation and buyer uncertainty, decision-making time lags, and governmental influence via a greater ability to use internal transfer pricing; costs included costs of administration and internal communication. Calvet (1981, p. 56) emphasized the role of "transactional considerations where human and organizational behaviors play a central role" in the determination of whether production is organized via the market or via multinational hierarchies (firms).

Magee (1977a, b) examined in more detail the kinds of information created by a corporation operating in industries in which the demand for new products is high. This led him to advance the hypotheses that (1) multinational corporations specialize in the production of information which is most efficiently transmitted intrafirm; (2) multinationals produce sophisticated, rather than simple, technologies because it is easier for them to appropriate for themselves the social value of these complex ideas; and (3) the appropriability of the returns from, and the complementarities among, different types of information determine optimum firm size. These hypotheses form part of Magee's "appropriability theory" of direct investment. Together with his observation that output growth of new products ultimately leads to an information-saving bias in production, these considerations imply a "technology cycle" at the industry level. Magee notes that the direct investment phase of Vernon's (1966) product cycle can be related to the concern of firms to increase the appropriability of their proprietary technology by reducing its rate of diffusion. This diffusion is attributable to increases in the number and geographical dispersion of plants, which raise both the probability and the costs of preventing a leakage of information.

Paralleling the concentration on firm-specific advantages, several researchers have emphasized the role that location-specific advantages play in an integrated theory of international economic "involvement," defined to include trade, portfolio capital movements, direct investment, and international transfers. Dunning (1973, 1977, 1979) has suggested an "eclectic" theory of production, in which firms possessing specific advantages keep them internal to the firm because of imperfect markets, then decide where to employ these advantages in tandem with other factor inputs on the basis of the standard cost and demand considerations from trade and location theory. In this framework, firms produce abroad when "location specific endowments favour a foreign country, but ownership-endowments favour the home country's firms; these latter being sufficient to overcome the costs of producing in a foreign environment . . ." (Dunning, 1977, p. 399). Hirsch (1976) expressed these notions in a formal model, and specified the conditions under which foreign markets will be "serviced" by alternative routes.

Niehans (1977, p. 8) followed a similar tack when he specified "two general requirements for the emergence of multinational firms:

1. Successive stages of production . . . must be separated by national borders . . . , resulting in international trade in intermediate products.
2. Successive stages of production must be integrated in the same firm across national borders. . . ."

Niehans explained the first requirement—specialization of nations—by reference to international trade theory, and the second by the existence of market imperfections and economies of scale. The interaction of the determinants of these two requirements yields the observed pattern of multinational activity.

Buckley and Casson (1978) observed that a finer disaggregation of this interdependence would require information on factors specific to particular industries, regions, nations (governments), and firms. Given these data, the strategy of a multinational corporation will reflect the combination of locational influences and opportunities for internalizing markets profitably.

How New?

Does the 1970s literature on direct investment provide any distinct alternatives to "the" theory in vogue at the beginning of the decade? It seems to me the answer must be in the negative. Compare the remarks of Dunning quoted above concerning when firms can be expected to produce abroad with the description of "the" theory abstracted from the works of Hymer and Kindleberger at the beginning of this section. The story in both passages is the same: direct investment behavior is a response to market imperfections. The spatial dispersion of economic activity introduces an imperfection into the frictionless, perfectly competitive model, since operating in different locations imposes different costs on a firm; costs of coordination and communication will be higher at a distance. Other frictions are introduced by governmental policies.

A firm must possess "ownership endowments sufficient to overcome the costs of producing in a foreign environment." And the market for the sale of these endowments must be imperfect if it is to the firm's advantage to "internalize" them.

Do the refinements represented by the works of Buckley and Casson, Dunning, Magee, and others add significantly to our understanding of the phenomenon of the multinational corporation? Unquestionably. In the last decade new terms have assumed a greater importance in the language of our profession as we have devoted more attention to imperfect markets, knowledge, information, uncertainty, and the relationship of the legal and economic environments. Students of the multinational corporation are indebted to those who have used the new "lenses" of new paradigms to examine old phenomena.

Whether or not the words "internalization hypothesis," "eclectic theory," and "appropriability theory" will resonate more and longer than explanations of direct investment behavior labeled "market imperfections," "monopolistic competition," and "industrial organization," only time will tell. Dunning views his eclectic theory "as less an alternative theory of ownership advantages of enterprises, than one which pinpoints the essential and common characteristics of each of the traditional explanations" (1977, p. 407). Rugman (1980), on the other hand, views the internalization hypothesis as the unifying concept in the literature on direct investment. Beauty is in the eye of the beholder, and one cannot blame workers in our knowledge-based industry for trying to establish a modicum of product differentiation. However, in my opinion, the recognized essence of the direct investment behavior all these words describe is unchanged from its exposition in Hymer's thesis.

A Digression on Exchange Rates and Capital-Market Imperfections

Since the flexible exchange rate period has coincided with the recent acceleration of foreign direct investment in the United States, it is natural to explore more fully "capital market" and "exchange rate" theories of direct investment, and to establish their relationship to the market-imperfections theory of direct investment as refined in the last decade.

Kindleberger (1969, pp. 24–25) presented "the" theory of direct investment via the formula for the capitalized value C of an asset producing a stream of income I as $C = I/r$, where r is the rate of return on the investment. He distinguished "ordinary" capital movements, defined as those based on differences in r across countries, from direct investment, which is based on differences in I attributable to firm-specific advantages. Kindleberger conceded that differences in r for potential foreign and domestic buyers of an asset could occur, not as a result of a foreign firm's nationality, but because the foreign firm might be larger and have a greater cash flow, and thus be a better credit risk. This "financial" market imperfection really is attributable to the size of the foreign corporation, and hence this situation too is consistent with the industrial-organization view of direct investment.

In considering direct investment from the point of view of modern portfolio theory, several authors (e.g., Agmon and Lessard, 1977) have observed that, while less-than-perfect correlations among asset values in various countries guarantee that individual investors can benefit from international diversification, they do not establish that international diversification at the corporate level is relevant. It is also necessary that there be greater impediments or costs to portfolio-capital movements than to those capital flows associated with direct investment, and that investors perceive that the multinational corporation offers an opportunity for diversification that is not otherwise available. Agmon and Lessard suggested that even if restrictions on portfolio and direct investment capital are nominally the same, the latter will be effectively freer than the former because of the flexibility that multinationals possess in shifting resources among subsidiaries and branches. Adler (1977) observed, however, that restrictions on individuals' portfolio investments need not imply direct investment by corporations, since corporations could simply make portfolio investment decisions on behalf of individual shareholders. Just as corporations always make real investment decisions for their shareholders as a consequence of imperfections in the market for projects, so they will make direct investment decisions only if an *additional* imperfection, beyond the restriction on individual portfolio investments, is present. As an example, foreign securities markets could be poorly organized, so that a multinational, by buying control of foreign firms, could reduce the informational imperfection and profit from it. Agmon and Hirsch (1979) emphasized that, in particular in developing countries, the multinational firm can be viewed as a provider of financial intermediation services.

Kindleberger considered such situations of financial intermediation to be "exceptions to the general theory that direct investment is not so much a capital movement as an effort to take advantage of particular opportunities, open to the investing firm but not local business" (1969, pp. 94–99). He discussed another case in which a capital-market advantage can be *common* to all firms in a given country. If movements of portfolio capital between two countries are controlled by the authorities, and the households in one country have a higher preference for liquidity than those in another, financial intermediation can occur in real assets or direct investment.

Aliber (1970, 1971) emphasized a particular country-specific advantage of firms that he believed was far more central to the direct investment process than firm-specific advantages. He suggested that in international capital market differentials across countries between interest rates and between yields on equities could exceed expected exchange rate changes, with the differences reflecting "a premium for bearing uncertainty about this (exchange rate) change" (1970, p. 29). Firms from countries, the currencies of which command a premium, have an advantage in investing abroad. But since by so investing they acquire a stream of earnings denominated in the currency which is discounted in the market, Aliber postulated that the market capitalizes this host-country stream of earnings differently if it is earned by a source-country firm than by a host-country firm. This could occur, he suggested, because investors are ignorant of the fraction of a firm's income that derives from discounted currency areas; because the source-country firm can provide the investor with a diversified portfolio at a lower cost than he can earn on his own; or because the source-country firm is more efficient in hedging exchange risks. Adler (1977, p. 43) observed that Aliber's "exchange risk" hypothesis thus rests on other capital markets imperfections; and unless those imperfections explicitly constrain portfolio investment by corporations, they need not imply direct investment.

Aliber suggested that the "exchange risk" theory of direct investment explains, and the industrial organization-market imperfections theory does not, the country and industry pattern of foreign direct investment over time, as well as the motivation for takeovers and the decision to license or make a direct investment. The country pattern reflects changing currency premiums over time, while the industry pattern reflects the role of capital (and R&D) in the production process. Takeovers and licensing decisions occur as a result of variations in differences in capitalization ratios applied to source-country and host-country firms' earnings. Any cross-investment within the same industry can be explained by variations in currency premiums over time.

In my opinion, the market-imperfections approach noted in the preceding pages, including the refinements of the last decade, explains all of the above phenomena quite well, save one: the country pattern of investment. Of course, the general fact that there are many host countries and few source countries reflects the specialization of multinational firms in sophisticated knowledge; why some countries have a lot of such firms is bound up with the much larger question of why certain nations are developed and others are developing. However, the timing of "waves" of foreign direct investment by multinationals from developed countries, and the predominance of certain small hard-currency countries (e.g., the Netherlands, Switzerland) as source countries, have a less straightforward explanation; here Aliber's theory, even resting as it does on other capital-market imperfections, has some appeal. Ideally, of course, one wants to know the source of such imperfections; later in the paper, I suggest that they may derive from the special character of the post–World War II period.

A related hypothesis which also addressed the phenomenon of "waves" of direct investment focuses on persistent misalignment of exchange rate *levels*. Makin (1974) observed that an overvalued exchange rate is a tax on export- and import-competing industries, and should motivate goods to flow from the undervalued-currency to the overvalued-currency country, with long-term capital flowing in the opposite direction. A discrete change in an equilibrium exchange rate toward equilibrium would then tend to reduce these flows. Kohlhagen (1977) examined the effect of devaluations on the relative profitability of producing in a source country and a host country. Though the net result depends on the effect of the devaluation on costs and prices in the two locations, his general presumption is that production in a country with a devaluing currency is likely to increase in relative profitability. Production in a devaluing country will be relatively less profitable only when its economy is very open, or when the domestic demand for and supply of tradable goods is relatively inelastic.

These results, of course, obtain in an environment in which purchasing power is not operating. Further, they do not guarantee that, in response to the altered relative profitability of two locations, *direct* investment will take place. An exporter threatened with a "loss of markets" could simply purchase a future stream of income in the newly-more-profitable location via portfolio investment. If such a purchase would not allow the exporter to appropriate most fully the social value of an ownership-specific advantage, then a direct investment would be made, as long as the returns offset the disadvantages of operating in a foreign environment.

Thus in the creation and destruction of a market imperfection such as a disequilibrium exchange rate (or a tariff), governments can alter the relative profitability of production in different locations. But this only leads to direct investment *if* a firm possesses a specific advantage, the full value of which it is unable to realize through licensing. The market-imperfections approach provides only necessary and not sufficient conditions for direct investment, as Agarwal (1980) noted; but in the absence of other imperfections, neither exchange risk or disequilibrium levels of exchange rates are necessary or sufficient for the occurrence of direct investment. They can, however, be "proximate causes" for direct investment.

New Perspectives on Direct Investment

The preceding discussion suggests some dissonance between the theory of direct investment based on the industrial-organization approach, which emphasizes real, technological factors, and those theories based on capital-market imperfections.

Developments in monetary theory and industrial-organization theory in the last decade or so suggest to me a useful new way to frame the direct investment issue. Let me stress that I have no revisions to propose to the essence of the direct investment process—just a new "lens" through which we can view this behavior.

The new perspective I have in mind is Tobin's q—the ratio of the market value of an asset to its replacement cost. Introduced by Brainard and Tobin (1968) and Tobin (1969), q integrates portfolio decisions about the allocation of wealth across existing stocks of assets, including physical capital, with decisions about the accumulation of new capital. For a perfectly durable capital asset which costs p to produce and which yields a perpetual real return R, an investor paying qp for the asset has a return $r = R/q$. In his masterful 1969 article, Tobin showed how, in the short term, with the rate of return on money institutionally fixed, the monetary authority can, by varying the supply of money, force the market return on the existing stock of physical capital to vary from its technological marginal efficiency (i.e., force q to diverge from 1), stimulating or retarding investment in new capital assets. An increase in the money supply increases q and promotes new investment in the short term. In the long term, in the absence of taxes, aggregate competitive equilibrium requires $q = 1$.

Lindenberg and Ross (1981) and Salinger (1981) suggested using q as a measure of or bound for monopoly rents. An inframarginal firm can earn "Ricardian" rents from special factors it possesses that lower its production costs relative to those of marginally competitive firms (i.e., access to very cold river water that provides industrial coolant more efficiently than sources available to a firm's competition). "Monopoly" rents are those attributable to factors which act as barriers to entry (e.g., patents or scale economies). Lindenberg and Ross showed that, in the absence of taxes, $q - 1$ is the capitalized value of the monopoly and Ricardian rents, scaled by the replacement cost of the firm's capital stock.

Lindenberg and Ross employed individual firm data to construct an 18-year time series of measures of q for a cross section of 246 firms. Their results indicated that industries in which firms possess high values of q are, as expected, those with unique products or unique factors of production (e.g., Polaroid's average q for 1960–1977 is 6.4; IBM's is 4.2, as is Coca-Cola's; Searle's is 5.3). Low values of q occur in industries which are either relatively competitive, tightly regulated, or dying (in the sense that firms are not replacing their capital stock) (e.g., Chrysler, 0.90; Duquesne Light Co., 0.90; U.S. Steel, 0.62). Lindenberg and Ross also tested the relationship of q and two frequently used measures of monopoly power—the Lerner index (price less marginal cost, all divided by price) and the four-firm concentration ratio. They concluded that the Lerner index contributes to explaining variations in q, but the concentration ratio does not. Since the aggregate q for US firms declined over this period, they also tested the sensitivity of variations in firm q's to variations in economy-wide q, and found a significant relationship in an overwhelming majority of cases.

Table 5 contains average q values for different industries for 1960–1977 in the United States. In section IV, I explore the relationship of these ratios to the industry distribution of foreign direct investment in the United States. Of course, q's of domestic *firms* in industries populated by foreign firms represent only "lower bounds" on the monopoly and Ricardian advantages foreign firms must possess to compete in the US market. But *industries* with high q's are precisely those in which "the" theory predicts direct investment will occur.

Salinger (1981) addressed the effect of taxation on equilibrium q, concluding that equilibrium q is less than 1 in the absence of monopoly power, and that taxation diminishes the sensitivity of q to the existence of monopoly power. He estimated firm-level investment equations based on this approach to business fixed-investment behavior, and used these equations to distinguish between firms in an industry with temporarily high profits and those with long-term monopoly power.

In principle, the approach of these authors could be extended to a multicountry environment (as did Stevens (1972) in his extension of the neoclassical theory of optimal capital accumulation), and aggregate or firm-level equations for investment could be estimated to assess the effect of the existence of monopoly rents on the level of direct investment. In view of the dependence of firm q's on aggregate economy-wide q's, such regressions also should shed light on the debate over the relative roles of firm-specific and country-specific factors in the direct investment process.[5]

Several other recent developments in finance and industrial organization also seem to be promising for future examination of the direct investment process. These include, in much the same spirit as the internalization and appropriability literature, Jensen and Meckling's discussion (1976) of the role of "agency costs" in the ownership structure of the firm; Nelson and Winter's analyses (1977, 1978, 1982) of the properties regarding innovation and imitation of simulation models of evolutionary Schumpeterian competition in technologically progressive industries; the development of the theory of "contestable" markets— markets in which entry is free and exit is costless—by Baumol, Panzer, and Willig (1982); and the emergence into fashion in corporate suites of the strategic planning paradigm, as presented by Porter (1981, especially chapter 13). Space does not permit me to pursue these de-

Table 5
Average industry values of q, 1960–1977.

Industry	q
Measurement and photographic equipment (SIC 38)	3.08
Oil and gas extractions (SIC 13)	2.94
Chemicals (SIC 28)	2.42
Electric machinery (SIC 36)	1.79
Food products (SIC 20)	1.72
Machinery (nonelectric) (SIC 35)	1.67
Printing industries (SIC 27)	1.66
Leather products (SIC 31)	1.66
Building materials (SIC 52)	1.60
Lumber and wood products (SIC 24)	1.59
Bituminous coal mining (SIC 12)	1.54
General merchandise stores (SIC 53)	1.42
Miscellaneous retail (SIC 59)	1.41
Tobacco manufacture (SIC 21)	1.39
Petroleum refining (SIC 29)	1.39
Nondurable wholesale (SIC 51)	1.35
Miscellaneous manufacture (SIC 39)	1.33
Stone, clay, and glass (SIC 32)	1.29
Metal mining (SIC 10)	1.24
Rubber and plastics (SIC 30)	1.23
Food stores (SIC 54)	1.23
Unclassified (SIC 99)	1.20
Transport equipment (SIC 37)	1.17
Construction (other) (SIC 16)	1.15
Apparel products (SIC 23)	1.13
Paper and allied products (SIC 26)	1.09
Communication (SIC 48)	1.08
Fabricated metals (SIC 34)	1.04
Electric, gas, and sanitation services (SIC 49)	0.94
Furniture and fixtures (SIC 25)	0.93
Textile products (SIC 22)	0.92
Primary metal products (SIC 33)	0.85

Source: Eric B. Lindenberg and Stephen A. Ross, "Tobin's q Ratio and Industrial Organization," *Journal of Business* 54, no. 1, p. 26. See that article for adjustments and other details in the calculation of these ratios.

velopments here, but they suggest to me a useful focus for future research on the theory of direct investment.

III. Research on Foreign Direct Investment in the United States

When I first investigated foreign direct investment in the manufacturing sector several years ago, only a few authors had examined the phenomenon, none in a rigorous empirical fashion. Jenks (1927) and Lewis (1938) are the principal sources for the period prior to World War II, though Wilkins (1970), Faith (1972) and Franko (1971, 1976) provide useful details as well. Elsewhere (McClain, 1974, chapter 1), I have examined the implications of foreign investment in the United States during this period for the theory of direct investment.

Prior to World War I, investments in land, cattle, mining, and finance were made largely on a rate-of-return basis. Edelstein (1974), in examining British portfolio and direct investments in the United States during the period 1870–1913, also found portfolio considerations compelling, with the "push" from growing UK wealth giving way to the "pull" of US railroad-financing needs by the turn of the century. In manufacturing, vertical integration played a role, as British textile manufacturers sought to secure cotton for their factories. Oligopolistic considerations influenced many investment decisions just before World War I; successful cartels obviated the need for direct investment (e.g., the General Electric–A.E.G. market-sharing agreement in 1903), while those that failed often resulted in its occurrence, as in the case of Royal Dutch Shell's initial investment in the United States. Tariffs, in tandem with the American Selling Price system, clearly triggered initial investments in the chemical industry. Some investments came to escape war (e.g., Hoffman-LaRoche prior to World War II), while others were liquidated because of it. Exploiting a technological advantage motivated many investors; Bosch was a classic example.

Journalistic analyses of foreign direct investment in the postwar United States by European companies were conducted by Faith (1971), Hellman (1970), and Tugendhat (1972). Faith and Hellman emphasized the need for firms to secure raw materials, to exploit specialized knowledge, and to learn how to update their knowledge-specific expertise. Tugendhat supported this emphasis on learning, and, in view of the riskiness of the competitive US marketplace, stressed the importance of the renewed availability of financing attained via the dismantling of exchange controls, the development of the Eurodollar market, and the growth in the size of European companies.

Scholarly contributions were made by Vernon (1971), Franko (1971, 1976, 1978), Sametz (1973), and Tsurumi (1973). Vernon suggested that European and Japanese investments in the United States would be based on material-saving or capital-saving innovations, and would be stimulated by the need to service the market, to jump tariff or nontariff barriers, to offset rising transport costs, or to learn about new technology. Franko, drawing on interviews with European managers, emphasized the size of the American market, and the desire to be close to the "innovative stimuli" in the United States; he also stressed the role of streamlined management structures (e.g., the elimination of "mother-daughter" parent-subsidiary relationships) in enabling European corporations to operate effectively at a distance. Sametz suggested that European firms had to be large enough to compete in the United States, and that the formation of the EEC allowed European firms to attain the necessary size. Despite their tradition of material-saving innovations, Sametz believed that European subsidiaries in the United States would focus on learning about labor-saving technology.

Tsurumi applied a variant of the product cycle hypothesis to explain Japanese exports to the United States; when logically concluded, this variant provides a rationale for Japanese direct investment in this country. He observed that Japanese technology is occasionally sufficiently sophisticated to produce for the US market products not yet demanded by the lower-income Japanese consumer—such as color televisions in the late 1960s and early 1970s. Conventional product-cycle considerations, and the need to be in the United States to be abreast of the latest technology, suggested that at some point color TV exports would be replaced by direct investment. Sony's investment is a case in point, though protectionism also played a role.

Daniels (1972) followed the survey approach of Franko and found that, for the majority of approximately 40 firms, tariff and nontariff barriers were the proximate cause for investing in the United States. Arpan and Ricks (1973) surveyed foreign-controlled firms located in the United States, but confined their analysis more to the characteristics of these firms than the motivations of their parents. Their work was an important precursor of the 1974 benchmark survey.

Empirical work on foreign direct investment in the United States was done in the early 1970s by Leftwich (1973), Prachowny (1972), and Hultman and Ramsey (1975). In a time-series regression, Leftwich found that the size of the US market, but not its rate of growth or the average tariff rate, was significant in explaining variations in the flow of foreign direct investment in the United States. Hultman and Ramsey confirmed the importance of market size at a more disaggregated level. Prachowny, in a portfolio framework, found that variations in differential expected rates of return were significant in explaining variations in the ratio of foreign direct investment in the United States to the total value of equities in Canada and the United Kingdom during the period 1953–1964. Blais (1975) obtained similar results.

Recent Empirical Research

These aggregate empirical efforts were susceptible to elaboration in a number of areas. Elsewhere (McClain, 1974, chapters 6 and 7; 1975) I have examined foreign direct investment in the United States from an aggregate perspective and from the vantage point of the firm. The aggregate work placed the foreign-investment decision in the context of an optimal capital-accumulation problem for a firm operating in several countries, following Stevens (1972). My specification allowed a firm's world-wide investment decisions to be interdependent, in the form of competition of projects for scarce funds, and in the form of "portfolio" interdependencies. The latter were represented via a Tobin-Brainard (1968) general disequilibrium framework, while liquidity considerations were captured via variable adjustment speeds of actual to desired stocks, depending on the size of the cash flow relative to the investment task to be accomplished, following Coen (1971).[6]

I estimated investment equations for British firms, at home and in the United States, and similarly for Canadian firms, for 1952–1971. Aggregate investment equations are limited in their ability to test a variety of direct investment theories, particularly those that rest on firm-specific attributes. They can address the role of market size, the user cost of capital (inclusive of effects of taxes and exchange rate expectations), tariffs, hypotheses that emphasize subsidiary independence (e.g., Barlow and Wender, 1955; Penrose, 1956), cash flow, and exchange and capital controls (e.g., the UK investment-currency market). Further, this aggregate specification is ideally suited for analysis of the quasi-historical issue of whether a "demand model" or a "supply model" characterized direct investment in the United States over the sample period. Kindleberger (1969, p. 61), in describing US direct investment abroad, defined these terms in this fashion:

> . . . does it, that is, respond positively or negatively to an upswing in domestic (US) prosperity? In a demand model, a given supply of corporate cash flow . . . is allocated between domestic and overseas use depending on relative profitability. . . . In a supply model . . . there is a fixed profit margin in favor of overseas investment . . . and how much is invested abroad depends on the size of the cash flow. . . .

My results for the United Kingdom suggested that direct investment in the United States by British firms was related significantly to the desired stock of capital in both locations, and to subsidiary cash flow in the United States, but not to cash flow in the United Kingdom. Tariffs and the Interest Equalization Tax had no direct effect, though UK capital controls did. My results indicated that a demand model best characterized the UK experience in the United States, given the caveat that UK capital controls inhibited full expression of supply-model considerations.

In the Canadian case, a supply model obtained as Canadian cash flow proved most important in explaining the flow of direct investment into the United States. This is surprising, since such a model is usually associated with a horizon shift on the part of investors; substantial multicollinearity between US- and Canadian-desired capital stock variables may have prevented full operation of a demand model's effects.

At the level of the firm, I analyzed 2,051 foreign investments in manufacturing industries in existence around the world at the beginning of 1971. These investments were made by 114 non-US multinationals from 11 countries; the Harvard Business School Multinational Enterprise Project collected the data. This data base allowed me to examine, via logistic discrimination analysis, the characteristics of US subsidiaries which distinguish them from subsidiaries located elsewhere—that is, those special factors that characterize foreign direct investment in the United States. I was able to test country- and industry-specific effects, since I augmented the data base on the subsidiaries and their parents with data on the industries in which the subsidiaries produced their principal product and data on the countries of their parents' head-quarters. The large sample allowed me to examine the role of a significant number of characteristics—7 relating to subsidiaries, 6 to parents, 12 to industries, and 10 to countries. Full details are in the works I have referenced; here I will only discuss a few highlights.

My research suggested that parent firms needed to possess exceptional advantages to make a direct investment in the United States. Among the concepts which were statistically significant in distinguishing US subsidiaries from those located elsewhere were the following:

- age of subsidiary (US subsidiaries tended to be younger, implying some direct investment experience on the part of parents);
- degree of parent control (US subsidiaries were more likely to be more than 50% parent controlled);
- degree of subsidiary sales derived from exports (US subsidiaries were less likely to derive 50% of their sales from exports);
- number of 3-digit SICs in which parent produced (US subsidiaries tended to have more diversified parents);
- parent R&D expenditures as a percentage of total sales (US subsidiaries had parents with a large value of this ratio).

Industry variables (US industry measures were used) what were useful in discriminating US subsidiaries from others included, with a positive sign, the 8-firm concentration ratio and industry value-added. US subsidiaries were less likely to be in industries in which US multinationals had made substantial investments abroad, suggesting that "exchange of hostage" behavior did not motivate foreign direct investment in the United States in the sample I examined. Interestingly, US subsidiaries were less likely to be in "high-technology" industries, classified on the basis of the industry ratio of R&D to sales. However, this group included motor vehicles, radios and televisions, and farm machinery, in addition to drugs, industrial chemicals, and instruments. The former group of industries represents mature technologies in which labor costs and process innovations, characteristics which were not the locus of US comparative advantage up to 1970, are more important. After all 12 industry characteristics were examined, categorical (dummy) variables for the instruments, chemicals, and textiles industries retained some discriminatory power, with subsidiaries more likely to be in the United States in the first two cases, and less likely in the last case.

In the sample, I found no evidence that US subsidiaries were more or less likely to be established via acquisition, as opposed to de novo; this was surprising, since the sophisticated nature of the US market has suggested to many that acquisitions are the preferred mode of entry. Industry measures of product differentiation and capital intensity had no independent discriminatory power; collinearity with other industry measures was in part responsible. I was unable to discern any evidence of "follow the leader" behavior (Knickerbocker, 1973), either at the industry or national level. Efforts to discover effects of tariff-jumping motivations or exchange-rate disequilibria were also unsuccessful. Such dynamic effects are difficult to specify and identify in a single cross section, however.

Not surprisingly, in light of the data reported in section I, I found that US subsidiaries were much more likely to belong to parents with headquarters in small, open economies. Since this finding, of course, Agmon and Kindleberger (1977) and the contributing authors of their book have explored this phenomenon in more detail. At the time, I postulated that a "small-country product cycle" might be in operation in the postwar period. This notion is based on an observation of Kindleberger (1970b) in a comment on a paper by Hufbauer (1970):

... small countries can achieve exports in scale-economy goods where standardization is set by large countries; and ... the differentiated products of small countries, such as Dutch electrical equipment, Swedish machinery and telephones, Danish furniture, and Swiss pharmaceuticals (but not Belgian products) get accepted as the international standard.

Consider two corporations in the same industry, producing similar but differentiated products, with one firm in a large country and the other in a small country. As both resume production after World War II, the small-country firm will be forced into exporting before the large-country firm, in order to achieve the economies of scale necessary for efficient production (the polar case here is Tsurmuri's, with all production intended for the export market). If the small-country firm is producing a product which is technologically advanced or which has a high income elasticity of demand, then it is likely to export to the United States. In the technologically sophisticated and competitive US environment, it will be difficult for the small-country firm to maintain profitability by exporting, particularly if, as Carlson (1977) emphasizes, the firm is producing a product with a high "software" content. It will, on the product-cycle logic, make a direct investment in the United States well before its counterpart in the large-country firm. A snapshot of this process taken in 1970 would reveal more firms from small countries with direct investments than firms from large countries.

If one allows for the special relationships of the United Kingdom and Canada to the United States, the small-country product cycle explains the relative ranking of countries responsible for the stock of direct investment in the United States, with the Netherlands and Switzerland ahead of Germany, France, and Japan. Further, the stocks held by firms in Belgium/Luxembourg and Sweden were roughly equal to those of France and Japan, and exceeded those of Italy, in 1970. To be sure, this description has to be tempered with consideration for the German experience of expropriation in both world wars, and with recognition for the substantial role of Shell investments in petroleum in the Dutch total (a country-by-industry classification is not available for 1970). Still, properly qualified, I believe the small-country product cycle has some explanatory power. In particular, it emphasizes the rather special character of the post–World War II international economy.

Graham (1974, 1976), Volpe (1975), and Flowers (1976) also have performed empirical analyses of foreign direct investment in the United States. Graham found that European investment in the United States at an industry level was correlated with lagged values of US investment in Europe, supporting the "exchange of hostage" theory. The strength of this response was sensitive to industry measures of concentration, product differentiation, and R&D. Graham concluded that both exchange of hostage and "exposure to innovative stimuli" behavior were involved, with the former more common in industries producing standardized products and the latter more prevalent in industries producing new, differentiated products.

Flowers tested the notion that follow-the-leader behavior of Canadian and European firms into the United States should be more pronounced in more concentrated industries. He was able to confirm this hypothesis for firms in Canada, the United Kingdom, Germany, France, and the Netherlands. In the United Kingdom, he found that in extremely concentrated industries (concentration indices above 0.7), there was a lessening of such behavior, suggesting implicit collusion by the few firms in such industries. Flowers also confirmed Graham's work in the case of UK investment in the United States.

My own research revealed no evidence of independent oligopolistic reaction or exchange of hostage behavior, when I allowed for the influence of other measures of industrial structure on the direct investment process. In my opinion, the data are insufficiently robust to allow the independent identification of either hypothesis.

Volpe's work focused on the human- and physical-capital intensity of foreign direct investment in the US manufacturing sector. He found that, of the 19 3-digit US industries containing at least 20 foreign subsidiaries in 1972, 14 were both physical-capital intensive (possessing above-average values of non-wage value-added per production worker man-hour) and human-capital intensive (possessing above-average values of wages per production worker man-hour). Sixteen were human-capital intensive, while fifteen were physical-capital intensive. He concluded that foreign subsidiaries in the United States were introducing new technology, embodied in both labor and capital.

Conclusions

The results of the empirical research on foreign direct investment in the United States broadly substantiate the industrial organization/market imperfections approach to the theory of direct investment. Country effects *do* seem to be important, as the small-country product cycle suggests, but these effects relate more to the *proximate* cause for a direct investment, rather than to the fundamental considerations which make a direct investment possible. Basic to research is the emphasis on imperfect markets, particularly in knowledge; however, some analyses highlight the need to *acquire* knowledge, as much as the desire to *exploit* a knowledge-based advantage, as a key reason for investing in the United States. Oligopolistic reaction and imitation also may play a role, though it is hard to uncover with the available data. Nor do the data confirm tariff-jumping or disequilibrium exchange rate motivations; this too may be a simple problem. As argued above, however, these are likely to be proximate, not fundamental, causes.

IV. Interpretation of Recent Foreign Direct Investment Experience in the United States

The research discussed in the preceding section covered foreign direct investment behavior in the United States before the floating-exchange-rate period. In this section I examine recent developments, and suggest some conclusions for the theory of direct investment.

In the popular press, there has been no shortage of "instant analyses" of the forces behind the "new wave" (*Economist*, October 25, 1980) of foreign direct investment in the United States. The British magazine identified the cheap dollar exchange rate, the size of the American market, the stability of the US political environment, fear of rising protectionism, increasingly competitive labor costs, abundant fuel reserves, and the desire to transfer some special American expertise (in marketing, finance, or technology) to a foreign firm's other global operations as motivating factors behind the recent surge of foreign direct investment in the United States.

Official publications contain a similar set of explanations. The Department of Commerce report (1976), drawing on an extensive Arthur D. Little (ADL) study, attributed strong foreign investment growth in the early 1970s to the growth in the size and capabilities of foreign-based corporations. It noted that in 1964 the 200 largest non-US corporations had total sales equal to 45% of those of the 200 largest US companies; in 1974, this ratio stood at 89%. The merger movement in Europe in the late 1960s was important in this regard. The report suggested that European and Japanese firms had made "great progress toward technological equality" (volume 1, p. 99). Managerial structures and techniques had been improved. Non-US firms had gained experience operating in other foreign countries, and this experience had prepared them for investing in the United States. Relaxation of capital controls, notably in Japan after 1969, provided an improved environment for foreign direct investment in the United States. The report targeted the weaker dollar and the depressed stock market as "triggers" for the surge of direct investment into the United States, and it suggested that security of energy supplies and geographic diversification, motivated in part by concerns about political risks, were important considerations for some investors.

The recent report of the Committee on International Investment and Multinational Enterprises (CIME) of the OECD (1981) drew on, and hence echoed, the Commerce Department report in many respects. Its unique observations included the suggestion that a "demand model" had been at work in Europe and Japan, as slower growth there pushed non-US firms into the United States. The slow-growth environment in industrial countries has put more of a premium on process innovation rather than product innovation; non-US firms tend to have advantages in the former, and these advantages have been accentuated by the stagnant state of aggregate demand. The CIME also observed that sluggish demand can explain a broader interest in acquisitions, as opposed to "greenfield" investments, and a renewed interest in geographical diversification, so as to be better able to take advantage of rapidly shifting comparative costs of production in different locations.

More scholarly work on foreign direct investment in the United States in the mid- to late-1970s was done by Little (1978, 1980), by Franko (1978), who explored the growing size and competence of non-US multinationals in depth, and by Stopford (1980), who examined the role of German multinationals in the United States.

Little's work focused on locational decisions of firms planning to produce in the United States. She found that in the 1978–1979 surge of direct investment in the United States, New England was the most attractive region, measured either by the amount of foreign acquisitions and new construction per 1,000 manufacturing employees, or by new construction per 1,000 employees. In 1975–1977, New England was third among eight regions on this basis. Surveys of foreign investors' locational decisions suggest they are extremely complex; Little indicated that perhaps the most important factor is proximity to the target market in the United States. Availability of labor is next on the list, with cost and *quality* both important. The conventional wisdom about the revival of the New England economy is that it has been based on disinvestment in textiles and shoes, and transformation in the direction of knowledge-based comparative advantage. This model is surely too simple, but it is striking that despite its high energy costs (which Little found exert a statistically significant effect on location decisions), New England received a plurality of foreign direct investment in 1978–1979. Little's research provides further circumstantial evidence that the exploitation—and attempted acquisition—of knowledge-based advantages play a central role in explaining direct investment behavior in the United States.

Franko emphasized the importance of the increased size of non-US firms and of a more equal distribution of technological and managerial talents in explaining the increasing competitiveness of these firms, and their interest in exploiting these new advantages in the United States; he suggested that the role of exchange rate changes would have been minimal, had not these other developments occurred simultaneously. In the set of the largest dozen companies worldwide in each of 13 major industries, Franko found that the United States had 71% of these firms in 1959, but only 44% in 1976. He stresed the role of non-US firms' experience in Third-World operations in their maturation. Their ability to offer a "politically differentiated" product—one without connotations of empire or superpower—were important to their success in these areas, as was their experience in operating in a negotiated business-government environment. Also important to Franko was non-US firms' experience in competing in an energy-saving dimension. He cited, as energy-efficient products which have been or stand a good chance of being successful in the US market, French and Japanese locomotives, the Airbus, Michelin's radials, Bosch's fuel-injection equipment, and Pechiney's aluminum-smelting process.

In R&D, Franko noticed that a recent National Science Foundation report stated that German and Swiss privately and publicly funded expenditures, as a fraction of GNP, exceeded those of the United States in 1973. Private-sector R&D as a fraction of GNP is now larger in Germany, Switzerland, the Netherlands, and Japan. Though the long lead times involved in implementing R&D results and the poor quality of the data make it difficult to agree completely with Franko's emphasis of this point, the trend is indicative.

Stopford stressed the role of technological and managerial innovation advantages as fundamental determinants of foreign direct investments in the United States. Following Franko, he observed that European firms have biased their innovation activity towards materials-saving and energy-saving processes (e.g., Solvay's process techniques for soda ash and Bosch's fuel-injection equipment (1980, p. 9)). In the postwar period, German firms preferred to exploit their advantages through exports, in part for historical reasons (memory of asset, and patent confiscations by "Alien Property Custodians"), and in part out of a need to use excess domestic industrial capacity. Concerns about the compatability of managerial structures appropriate to US and German operations kept some German firms out of the American market; more recently, co-determination led workers to resist attempts to build capacity abroad (e.g., the delays in Volkswagen's plans to build a plant in the United States).

Stopford identified four factors which changed German firms' perceptions of the advisability of investing in the United States:

- the dollar's depreciation and labor cost increases in Europe;
- declining US stock market values;
- concerns about the rising social costs of doing business in Germany, coupled with a declining real rate of economic expansion; and
- energy supply concerns.

The impact of the cost changes on the export/foreign production decision was most pronounced for German firms producing products with a high price elasticity of demand, particularly bulk chemical producers and Volkswagen (but not Daimler Benz or BMW). Rising labor costs not only made US production more attractive; they also led European firms to want to learn about labor-saving innovations in the US, perhaps by producing here. Stopford noted that the oil price shocks gave European producers a "windfall" technological advantage in some sectors of the US market, where US producers—faced with artificially low energy prices—had not innovated in an energy-saving direction.

The broad trends identified by Stopford, Franko, and the ADL study represent the distillation of the features of numerous case studies of foreign direct investors in the United States active in the early- to mid-1970s. More recent cases of direct investment in the United States continue to be consistent with the industrial organization paradigm, as firms enter to exploit—and sometimes to acquire—a technological or managerial advantage, or for reasons of vertical integration. Sometimes entry has been prompted by governmental policies at home; the surge of Canadian oil rigs into the United States is one such situation. At other times, protectionist concerns have led to an investment here; Honda's motorcycle and car plants in Ohio are examples from a mature industry, while Hitachi's recent decision to manufacture 64K random access memory units in Texas is an instance in a high-technology sector.

The growing fraction of industrialized countries' output devoted to services no doubt has given further impetus to direct investment flows, since the "software" content of services is higher than that of goods, making it difficult to service markets via exports. The absence of a GATT for services trade may also serve to promote direct investment in these industries.

In several service industries, particularly in retailing, a foreign investor has overestimated his advantage, or underestimated the reason why an acquired firm's stock was so cheap. Tenglemann's soured acquisition of A&P is the classic example, though perhaps the worst debacle was Agache-Willot's experience with Korvette's. Despite these disappointments, and the low margins in the industry, retailers continue to be attracted by the larger US market, less union pressure, and access to the latest technology in inventory and checkout systems.[7]

The disappointments have not been confined to the service sector, however. Renault has been forced to increase its stake in American Motors from 4.7% to 46% to finance AMC's product development program that is essential for its survival.[8] Hiram Walker recently wrote off over 20% of the purchase price of the Davis Oil properties it bought only last year.[9]

Two "Close Cases" Revisited

The difficulties and ambiguities attendant upon the foreign investment decision process are well illustrated by a followup on two case studies I performed several years ago (McClain, 1974, chapter 3). At that time, I examined the investment decision process in two firms in each of two industries, automobiles and computers. In the former, I looked at Volvo's decision, announced in 1973, to build a small-scale production facility in Virginia, and at Volkswagen's reticence to take a similar step. In the minicomputer industry, I examined the acquisition by the German firm Nixdorf of Victor Comptometer in 1972 and subsequent announced expansions, and contrasted this behavior with the reticence of the Dutch multinational Philips to produce in the United States.

Volvo's chairman, Pehr Gyllenhammar, attributed the company's decision to the need to be closer and more responsive to the market which accounted for more than 25% of its sales, and stated that cost considerations were relatively unimportant, as compared with the desire to have improved access to pollution control technology and the concern over rising Swedish sentiment against investment abroad. By contrast, for VW, cost had been at the center of every US production study that had been commissioned since the early 1960s. By mid-1974, the mark's appreciation was so pronounced, and protectionist sentiments in the United States had been rekindled sufficiently by the stagnant economy, caused by the oil shock, that VW's management had tilted toward building a plant in the United States. Considerations of co-determination, noted above, as well as recession-related uncertainties and cash flow problems, delayed the construction of the plant, in Pennsylvania, until 1978. Ironically, while VW was proceeding, in late 1976, Volvo postponed its decision to produce in the United States, only a few months before its plant was to have opened. The company cited the lagged impact of the 1974–1975 recession on Sweden, and the resultant excess capacity there and at other existing plants. Now, of course, Volkswagen is in the process of laying off a significant fraction of its US work force, as it waits for the economy to rebound.

I explained the differing characteristics of the firms' decision processes by reference to the postwar economic environment in which each company matured, and by the type of product which was each company's strength. Volvo was no hothouse flower; it expanded in a small, open economy where wages were high. From the start, it had to be concerned with world-wide sourcing at least cost and with achieving economies of scale by exporting. Because of its small size, Volvo developed a product tailored to the Swedish environment; the durability of a Volvo made it somewhat expensive, and constrained the company to export to countries with similar per-capita incomes and tastes. In such markets, it was able to command high margins. These, its previous international experience, and the diversified product mix it achieved by the early 1970s (trucks, marine engines, and hydraulic equipment), allowed the company to make the US investment decision quickly, and with little attention to costs. However, when demand collapsed, first in the United States, then in Sweden, Volvo was forced to focus on cost and its social responsibilities to the Swedish economy.

Volkswagen, by contrast, was not a diversified firm, and was producing a low-margin, high-volume product, with which consumers were increasingly disenchanted. As incomes had increased in Europe and the United States, its Beetle had become something of an inferior good; efforts to diversify its product line in the late 1960s and early 1970s proved disastrous. Until the company had completed successfully the redesign and retooling process by the mid-1970s, it really had no significant differentiated product, the rents from which it could exploit through direct investment. In this environment, it is not surprising that the company's decision process focused on cost. Even after mid-decade, I believe the company would have preferred to exploit its renewed

advantages via exports, for reasons related to history, managerial structure, and job preservation in Germany. But costs and protectionist
forces would not permit it.

In the computer industry in the early 1970s, Philips had located its
production facilities in Holland for reasons of synergy. Since many
other Philips products required computers in their design, and the largest
market for these products was in Europe, the company naturally chose
to produce there. Further, Philips' own research efforts had begun in
Holland, and its main acquisition in the industry had been the Dutch
firm Electrologica in 1965. At the time (1973–1974), Philips had not
earned a profit on its minicomputer operations in Europe; it had no
need to be closer to suppliers; its subsidiary network in North America
provided sales and marketing support; and it had a substantial research
capability in North America which, despite a general arms-length relationship with the parent, regularly exchanged technical information.
Thus the firm had a variety of reasons for not producing in the United
States; it could stay in Holland and still be close to the "innovative
stimuli" in the United States.

By contrast, Nixdorf, as a small, undiversified firm, had to be in this
country at the nexus of an evolving technology. Some of Nixdorf's
suppliers were expanding downstream into products competitive with
the company's own. The sales and distribution network provided by
Victor was inadequate. The financial risk of expansion was minimized
by the backing of AEG-Telefunken. Perhaps most importantly, Nixdorf
recognized that to get product acceptance of its minicomputer, delivery
of software was as essential as delivery of hardware, and this could
only be done on site.

More recently, Nixdorf established a production plant in Massachusetts and introduced an IBM-compatible line of computers; in 1978,
in the United States, it earned $4 million (25% of world-wide earnings)
on sales of $81 million (15% of world-wide sales). Philips tried, with
little success, to enlarge its market share through the Data Systems
division of its Philips Business System subsidiary; in early 1979, it sold
this division to Pertec Computer, at the time the 31st largest data-
processing concern in the United States. Later that year, Philips tried
to purchase Pertec, but, ironically, it was outbid by Triumph Adler, a
subsidiary of Volkswagen. Nixdorf had rebuffed an earlier VW offer
because VW had wanted majority control.[10]

These two cases illustrate the roles of special advantages and imperfect markets in the direct investment decision process. These considerations are most prominent in industries in which technology is changing rapidly. In more mature industries they are still relevant, but considerations of cost naturally have more prominence.

A Celebrated Case: The Kuwait Petroleum-Santa Fe Deal

Perhaps no direct investment has triggered more concern about the "open door" policy of the United States than the $2.5 billion merger of Santa Fe Petroleum into the Kuwait Petroleum Company (KPC) in the fall of 1981. Besides raising the spectre of OPEC control over a firm in a key sector of the economy, this takeover possessed more direct national security overtones, since C. F. Braun, a Santa Fe subsidiary, was the contractor for the governmental nuclear facility in Hanford, Washington. Further, charges of insider trading were associated with the acquisition, and American and Swiss authorities are still negotiating the release of information about the activities of several Kuwaiti investors in this transaction. The official Committee on Foreign Investment in the United States and the Justice Department had to approve the acquisition because of the national security and antitrust aspects.

The stated purpose of KPC, which paid more than twice the quoted value for Santa Fe's stock, was to obtain the technology embodied in Sante Fe to promote the growth of KPC activities in exploration and production of oil. Santa Fe's oil and gas properties, its supply of drilling rigs and drilling expertise, and the construction experience of C. F. Braun were a good fit for the Kuwaiti strategy of evolving KPC into a company capable of competing with the majors in the oil industry. The acquisition followed an unsuccessful effort by Kuwait to acquire 15% of Getty Oil, the initiation since 1979 of oil exploration activity through and with other firms in the North-Central US, Morocco, the Sudan, Angola, and Australia, and the establishment of a joint venture with Pacific Resources in a Hawaiian refinery. Kuwait also has expressed an interest in buying Gulf Oil's refinery operations in Europe.

Santa Fe has had operations in Kuwait for more than 20 years, and KPC has left the management team at Santa Fe intact. Thus this investment represents, in the near term, more of a *portfolio* reallocation, with longer-term prospects for technology transfer via vertical integration

in the close-at-hand downstream direction. Indeed, the complete acquisition is reported to have been suggested by Santa Fe after KPC
expressed an interest in acquiring 25% of Santa Fe's equity on a portfolio
basis.[11]

Kobrin and Lessard (1976) have noted that "the" theory of direct
investment suggests direct investment by OPEC nations in industrialized
countries would require their possession of a monopoly advantage and/
or circumstances which would motivate a rational OPEC investor to
concentrate assets such that the potential for managerial control exists.
They observed that OPEC's comparative advantages must relate to
capital or petroleum, and interpreted OPEC investments (some by Kuwait) in several privately held European companies as having been
motivated by capital-market imperfections. Clearly, however, the Santa
Fe transaction cannot be explained by reference to such imperfections.

Downstream investments in petroleum by OPEC have the potential
of increasing producer rents. Kobrin and Lessard, however, identified
several factors which would mitigate any advantages. Diminution of
the market role of major oil companies could reduce the global political
influence of the oil industry; further, it could lessen the effectiveness
with which the majors informally police cartel behavior. And such
investments would increase OPEC exposure to risks associated with
the future value of petroleum and petroleum-based products.

KPC clearly perceived that the prospects for additional returns, and
the reduction of risks attendant on downstream integration, outweighed
the increased risks identified by Kobrin and Lessard. These prospects
reflect the advantages of diversifying "close at hand," in a business
that one knows, as well as the imperfections in the market for the
technology embodied in Santa Fe.[12]

"Testing" Theories of Direct Investment

The foregoing descriptions and analyses of the foreign direct investment
process in the United States lend support to the industrial-organization
theory of direct investment, though the timing of investments made
to exploit firm-specific advantages may have been attributable to exchange risk or disequilibrium exchange rate considerations. It is not
feasible to test this conclusion in a robust fashion, but some simple
analytic exercises may be suggested.

The first exercise focuses on the values of Tobin's q for 2-digit SIC's reported in table 5. If q provides an upper bound on monopoly rents, and if the industrial-organization theory is correct, we may observe a greater concentration of direct investment in industries with a higher value of q (strictly speaking, of course, we should examine values of q for individual firms, since the industrial organization theory focuses on firm-specific advantages). Comparison of the industrial distribution of the gross product of US affiliates of foreign firms in table 3 with table 5 suggests that such a relationship may obtain. Recall also that, in my research reported in section III, US subsidiaries were concentrated strongly in instruments (SIC 38) and chemicals, industries with high values of q, and tended not to be in textiles, where q is low.

Correlations of q and gross product of US affiliates of foreign firms, and of q and the number of firms in the 1974 benchmark survey, by 2-digit SIC for manufacturing, mining and petroleum, are $r = 0.12$ and $r = 0.35$, respectively; the latter correlation is significantly different from zero (two-tailed test) at the 15% level of significance, but the former is not significantly different from zero. The correlation of q and the *share* of US gross product accounted for by foreign affiliates also is not significantly different from zero.

However, when the mining and petroleum sectors are excluded from the analysis, the results are striking. The correlations of q and gross product of US affiliates is 0.33, and of q and the share of gross product of US affiliates in total US gross product is 0.45. The correlation of industry values of q and the number of US affiliates in the industry is 0.58. These correlations are significantly different from zero at, respectively, the 20%, 10%, and 5% levels of significance.

Sources of bias in this analysis include the Commerce Department's industry classification practices noted in section I, the omission of the trade and finance sectors (for which a complete set of q estimates is not available), and errors in the measurement of q. Nevertheless, these results provide some degree of confirmation of the industrial-organization approach, at least in the manufacturing sector.

Theories of direct investment that involve the exchange rate can only be examined properly in a fully simultaneous setting where other influences on direct investment are properly weighted. Several primitive tests suggest themselves, however. In the first test, aimed particularly at identifying disequilibrium considerations, I have examined the correlations in a cross section of eight countries (United Kingdom, Netherlands, Sweden, Canada, Switzerland, Germany, Japan, and France) of the percentage difference in real exchange rates against the dollar from 1970 to 1980 and of (a) the cumulative flow of real foreign direct investment into the United States from each country from 1974 to 1980; (b) the compound annual rate of increase of the country's real direct investment position from year-end 1973 to year-end 1980; and (c) the cumulative flows scaled by the cumulative amount of domestic investment in the country.[13] None of these correlations is significantly different from zero at even the 20% level of significance. In the second test, I have calculated time-series correlations for these eight countries of the annual real flow of direct investment into the United States and changes (absolute and percentage) in the real exchange rate (current and lagged) for 1974–1980. I also have calculated the correlations of changes in the real exchange rate and the flow of direct investment into the United States, scaled by the flow of gross fixed capital formation in the home economy.

The results are reported in table 6. In four of eight countries, the available data suggest a significant (and, as expected, negative) correlation at the 10% level, of either absolute or percentage changes in real exchange rates and real foreign direct investment flows. It is noteworthy that in two of these four—the United Kingdom and France—the major factor changing the real exchange rate was changes in relative price levels, not changes in nominal exchange rates. In addition, in several instances (Japan, Sweden, Germany), at least one correlation has an unexpected and significant positive sign.

We observe similar effects for the United Kingdom and France when the direct investment flow is scaled by the flow of gross fixed capital formation in the home economy. Again, there is weaker evidence that this scaled flow is related to changes in real exchange rates for Germany and Switzerland, and for Canada as well.

As noted, many observers have felt that nominal exchange rate changes, in tandem with changes in the relative stock market values of American and foreign firms, have led to a surge of direct investment in the United States. I have tested this hypothesis by examining the correlations of real direct investment flows with current and lagged changes in the ratio of the home country stock market index to the US stock market index; both indices were adjusted for price level changes

Table 6
Correlations of changes in real exchange rates with the flow of foreign direct
investment in the United States for eight countries, 1974–1980.

Country	Lag in real exchange rate change		
	Current	1 Year	2 Year

*1. Correlations of the Real Flow of Foreign Direct Investment in the United States
with the Absolute Change in the Real Exchange Rate*

Country	Current	1 Year	2 Year
Canada	−.549	.362	.278
France	.032	−.877***	−.699**
Germany	−.428	−.552*	.489
Japan	−.554	.247	.631*
Netherlands	.089	−.012	.097
Sweden	−.319	.322	.617*
Switzerland	.096	−.768***	.150
United Kingdom	−.845***	−.366	−.312

*2. Correlations of the Real Flow of Foreign Direct Investment in the United States
with the Percentage Change in the Real Exchange Rate*

Country	Current	1 Year	2 Year
Canada	−.505	.342	.302
France	.176	−.521	−.697**
Germany	−.177	−.669**	.558*
Japan	−.433	.482	.738**
Netherlands	.122	.098	.022
Sweden	−.104	.590*	.686**
Switzerland	.059	−.610*	.286
United Kingdom	−.922***	−.273	−.200

*3. Correlations of the Ratio of the Flow of Foreign Direct Investment in the United
States to the Flow of Gross Fixed Capital Formation in the Home Economy with the
Absolute Change in the Real Exchange Rate*

Country	Current	1 Year	2 Year
Canada	−.493	.352	.319
France	.200	−.539	−.723**
Germany	−.161	−.637*	.561*
Japan	−.441	.537	.795***
Netherlands	.026	.055	.179
Sweden	−.092	.583*	.657*
Switzerland	.079	−.620*	.200
United Kingdom	−.902***	−.262	−.220

*4. Correlations of the Ratio of the Flow of Foreign Direct Investment in the United
States to the Flow of Gross Fixed Capital Formation in the Home Economy with the
Percentage Change in the Real Exchange Rate*

Country	Current	1 Year	2 Year
Canada	−.561*	.352	.261
France	.015	−.862***	−.681**

Table 6 (continued)

Country	Lag in real exchange rate change		
	Current	1 Year	2 Year
Germany	−.458	−.576*	.509
Japan	−.532	.213	.550*
Netherlands	.102	−.034	.015
Sweden	−.333	.325	.661*
Switzerland	.097	−.736**	.230
United Kingdom	−.879***	−.380	−.292

Note: Real exchange rates are defined as units of local currency per dollar, divided by the ratio of the producer price index in the local economy to the producer price index in the United States. These data, and data on home country gross fixed capital formation, are from the IMF, *International Financial Statistics*, various issues. Data on foreign direct investment in the United States are from the *Survey of Current Business*, various issues. The US gross private fixed investment deflator was used to deflate the foreign direct investment series.
* Significant at the 20% level (2-tailed test).
** Significant at the 10% level.
*** Significant at the 5% level.

and expressed in a common currency. I also have examined the correlations of direct investment flows scaled by home country investment with changes in this stock market index ratio.

The results are reported in table 7. They suggest that low-priced US stocks may have been associated with direct investment in this country in the late 1970s by Canadian, British, Japanese, and French investors; with the exception of Canada, the strength of the correlations is generally less than in table 6. Again, some results for Sweden and Japan are of a counterintuitive sign.

This stock market index ratio will, of course, be correlated with aggregate economy-wide measures of Tobin's q. In the absence of good data on q by country, the results in table 7 may suggest a modest role for country-specific q-related considerations in the direct investments made by firms in some countries. Of course, they do not illuminate the relative roles of firm- or industry-specific, as opposed to country-specific, factors in determining a foreign firm's q and hence its advantage or disadvantage vis-à-vis a domestic firm.

These tests are hardly conclusive; certainly, we would want the samples to be larger. They provide mixed evidence on the role of nominal exchange rate changes and changes in stock market valuations in the

Table 7
Correlations of changes in ratios of stock market indices with the flow of foreign
direct investment in the United States for eight countries, 1974–1980.

Country	Lag in stock market index ratio change		
	Current	1 Year	2 Year

1. Correlations of Absolute Changes in Stock Market Index Ratio with Flow of Real Direct Investment into the United States

Country	Current	1 Year	2 Year
Canada	.702**	.581*	.452
France	−.217	.601*	.513
Germany	.385	.508	−.422
Japan	.685**	.077	−.374
Netherlands	.000	.026	−.129
Sweden	.262	−.367	−.869***
Switzerland	.253	.380	−.304
United Kingdom	.659*	.530	.564*

2. Correlations of Percentage Changes in Stock Market Index Ratio with Flow of Real Direct Investment into the United States

Country	Current	1 Year	2 Year
Canada	.653*	.662**	.431
France	−.298	.573*	.473
Germany	.283	.448	−.414
Japan	.572*	.089	−.559*
Netherlands	.048	−.012	−.155
Sweden	.209	−.377	−.850***
Switzerland	−.049	.396	−.302
United Kingdom	.661*	.590*	.578*

3. Correlations of Absolute Changes in Stock Market Index Ratio with Flow of Direct Investment in the United States, Scaled by Gross Fixed Capital Formation in the Home Country

Country	Current	1 Year	2 Year
Canada	.704**	.600*	.402
France	−.308	.094	.671**
Germany	.097	.369	−.172
Japan	.560*	−.419	−.710**
Netherlands	−.050	−.103	−.135
Sweden	.140	−.584*	−.911***
Switzerland	.037	.227	−.538
United Kingdom	.684**	.419	.515

4. Correlations of Percentage Changes in Stock Market Index Ratio with Flow of Direct Investment in the United States Scaled by Gross Fixed Capital Formation in the Home Country

Country	Current	1 Year	2 Year
Canada	.655	.682**	.380
France	−.387	.055	.622*
Germany	.036	.248	−.224

Table 7 (continued)

| Country | Lag in stock market index ratio change | | |
	Current	1 Year	2 Year
Japan	.613*	−.413	−.796***
Netherlands	−.009	−.154	−.176
Sweden	.094	−.576*	−.886***
Switzerland	.023	.236	−.542
United Kingdom	.703**	.486	.510

Note: Stock market indices are from the International Monetary Fund's *International Financial Statistics*, which reports general indices for Italy, Japan, the Netherlands and Sweden, and industrial indices for the other countries. Ratios were constructed with the numerator as the foreign stock index in local currency divided by the foreign consumer price index and converted to dollars at the nominal exchange rate; the denominator was the US stock index divided by the US CPI. Direct investment data were constructed as in table 6.
* Significant at the 20% level (two-tailed test).
** Significant at the 10% level.
*** Significant at the 5% level.

timing of direct investment in the flexible exchange rate regime of the 1970s. In this connection, it is useful to recall the results of Kohlhagen (1977), who found that the discrete parity changes of the late 1960s had a demonstrable effect on US direct investment flows abroad, but that the 1973 transition to floating exchange rates had no discernible effect.

V. Public Policy Conclusions

If, in a broad sense, the foreign direct investment experience in the United States conforms to "the" theory of direct investment developed a decade ago, as refined by Magee, Buckley and Casson, and Dunning, what does this imply about public policy toward these investments? Heretofore, that theory has been associated with a laissez-faire public policy posture, with those investments that raised particular welfare issues addressed on a case-by-case basis. US policy on inward investment has been in this tradition. In view of the "new wave" of foreign direct investment, is there any need for a change?

I think not. Magee (1977b) has suggested viewing the operations of multinationals as international trade in information. Both importers and exporters of information will be attentive to optimal tariff considerations. With foreign firms investing in the United States to exploit, *and* to acquire, knowledge-based advantages, the United States is on both sides of the market. The diffusion of management techniques adopted at several Japanese subsidiaries in the United States may improve our productivity performance. Production in the United States by Japanese and European high-technology firms, or acquisitions of US firms in these industries, may accelerate the diffusion of our innovations in computers or genetic engineering.

In most circumstances surrounding the importation of capital and technology, as Johnson (1970, p. 47) observed, "foreign direct investment cannot harm a country and may confer substantial benefits upon it." As far as the exportation of technology is concerned, the response of US corporations in high-technology sectors will be to develop ever more sophisticated techniques of production, to increase their appropriability, and limit their rate of diffusion. Given equal access to capital by potential domestic and foreign buyers, foreign firms willing to pay for a share of an American firm must be allowed to do so. Of course, antitrust considerations must be satisfied. And as the equal-capital-access clause must apply, the Canadian Nu-West Group's ability to borrow 100% on margin to bid for Cities Service, when any US suitor would have had to abide by a 50% Federal Reserve margin requirement, is inappropriate.[14]

Given the heterogeneity of the information transfers involved in the direct investment process, it makes little sense for the United States to attempt to formulate an optimal tax policy in this area. The most sensible policy remains laissez-faire, supplemented by improved coordination with other countries of patent and other policies relating to information transfer (e.g., exploration of the feasibility of the simpler and shorter duration "utility model" patent which Magee observed has worked so well in Japan and Germany).

Particular noneconomic objectives, such as national defense, can be achieved on a case-by-case basis. The Defense Department offers foreign firms who purchase a US subsidiary involved in classified defense work the following choice: drop the work, or put the operation in a new subsidiary run by a voting trust or related device. Philips' Magnavox subsidiary and Amdahl (25% owned by Fujitsu) have been able to continue their defense-related work within these requirements. The Energy Department has more informal procedures, but they were adequate to identify C. F. Braun's connection to the Hanford nuclear facility.[15]

Foreign direct investment remains a small fraction of the total volume of economic activity in the United States, though the production of foreign firms has become a significant fraction of the output of several industries. However, the magnitude of this phenomenon is still sufficiently small that the United States will maximize the net benefits received from inward investment by adopting an "open door" policy, supplemented by reviews by the appropriate agencies in defense, banking, energy, and related sectors, and by the operation of the Committee on Foreign Investment. In an environment of record and steadily rising federal government deficits (as a fraction of potential output), which must be financed by domestic private-sector saving that otherwise could support capital formation, Alexander Hamilton's contention that "every farthing of foreign capital . . . is a precious acquisition" is as appropriate today as when he drafted his *Report on Manufactures* in 1791.

Notes

My thanks to the Middlebury Conference participants and to Zvi Bodie, Alan Marcus, Bob McDonald, and other participants in the Boston University School of Management Research Seminar for comments on particular issues discussed in this paper, and to Chuck McCallum for able research assistance.

1. A detailed history of foreign direct investment in the United States is in chapter 1 of McClain (1974).

2. US Senate, Committee on Banking, Housing, and Urban Affairs, Subcommittee on International Finance, 93rd Congress, 2nd session, *Foreign Investment in the United States* (Washington, D.C.: US Government Printing Office, 1974).

3. US Department of Commerce, *Foreign Direct Investment in the United States*, Report to the Congress, 9 volumes (Washington, D.C.: US Government Printing Office, 1976).

4. See, for example, Agarwal (1980), Calvet (1981), Dunning (1973), and Ragazzi (1973).

5. One example of the implementation of this general approach is in Coleman S. Kendall's dissertation proposal, "A General q-theoretic Approach to Foreign Direct Investment" (Graduate School of Business, University of Chicago, April 1982). My thanks to Robert Aliber for bringing this to my attention at the conference.

6. Boatwright and Renton (1975) use a neoclassical framework to analyze aggregate UK foreign direct investment abroad, though they do not include in their specification any interdependencies with UK investment at home.

7. Robert Ball, "Europe's US Shopping Spree," *Fortune*, December 1, 1980, pp. 82–88.

8. James Risen, "At (Franco-) American Motors, Paris Takes the Wheel," *New York Times*, February 7, 1982.

9. "Hiram Walker Sets $175 Million Write-Off on Davis Oil Properties Bought Last Year," *Wall Street Journal*, February 4, 1982.

10. "Pertec Signs to Acquire Some Computer Work," *Wall Street Journal*, December 20, 1978.

"N. American Philips and German Firm Settle Pertec Dispute," *Wall Street Journal*, November 21, 1979.

"Nixdorf Computer: Defending Its Home Turf and Expanding in the US," *Business Week*, April 30, 1979, pp. 93–94.

"Fast Growing Nixdorf of Germany Sees Further Gains in Small Computer Sales," *Wall Street Journal*, August 8, 1979.

"Volvo Tables Plan to Produce Cars at Virginia Plant," *Wall Street Journal*, December 10, 1976.

11. Stephen J. Sansweet, "Santa Fe International Agrees to Takeover by Kuwait for $2.5 Billion, A Record for Mideast Oil Investment," *Wall Street Journal*, October 6, 1981.

"Forming Kuwait Oil, Inc.," *Time*, October 19, 1981, p. 78.

"Why Kuwait Wants a US Oil Partner," *Business Week*, October 19, 1981, p. 42.

"Santa Fe International Completes Merger into Kuwaiti Firm after US Clears Bid," *Wall Street Journal*, December 7, 1981.

"Kuwait Petroleum May Be Seeking to Buy Gulf Oil's Refining Facilities in Europe," *Wall Street Journal*, January 28, 1982.

12. Morris Adelman brought the benefits of "close at hand" diversification to my attention.

13. Switzerland was excluded from correlation (c).

14. John Carson-Parker, "Stop Worrying About the Canadian Invasion," *Fortune*, October 19, 1981, pp. 192–200.

15. John J. Falka, "Concern Grows Over Foreign Stake in Companies Doing Defense Work," *Wall Street Journal*, January 8, 1982.

References

Adler, M., 1977. Comments on Niehans's "Benefits of Multinational Firms . . . ," in T. Agmon and C. P. Kindleberger (eds.), *Multinationals from Small Countries*. Cambridge, Mass.: MIT Press.

Agarwal, J. P., 1980. Determinants of Foreign Direct Investment: A Survey. *Weltwirtschaftliches Archiv* 116, no. 4, pp. 739–73.

Agmon, T., and S. Hirsch, 1979. "Multinational Corporations and the Developing Economies: Potential Gains in a World of Imperfect Markets and Uncertainty," *Oxford Bulletin of Economics and Statistics* 41, no. 4 (November), pp. 333–344.

Agmon, T., and C. P. Kindleberger, 1977. *Multinationals from Small Countries*. Cambridge, Mass.: MIT Press.

Agmon, T. B., and D. F. Lessard, 1977. "Investor Recognition of Corporate International Diversification," *Journal of Finance* 33, no. 4, pp. 1049–1055.

Aliber, R. Z., 1970. "A Theory of Direct Foreign Investment," in C. P. Kindleberger (ed.), *The International Corporation*. Cambridge, Mass.: MIT Press.

———, 1971. "The Multinational Enterprise in a Multiple Currency World," in J. H. Dunning (ed.), *The Multinational Enterprise*. London: Allen & Unwin.

Arpan, J., and D. Ricks, 1973. "Foreign Direct Investment in the United States in Manufacturing, Mining, and Petroleum." Paper read at the New York meeting of the Academy of International Business, December 28.

Arrow, K. J., 1962. "Economic Welfare and the Allocation of Resources for Invention," in *The Rate and Direction of Inventive Activity*. Princeton University Press.

Baumann, J. G., 1975. "Merger Theory, Property Rights and the Pattern of U.S. Direct Investment in Canada," *Weltwirtschaftliches Archiv* 7, pp. 676–698.

Baumol, W. J., J. C. Panzer, and R. D. Willig, 1982. *Contestable Markets and the Theory of Industrial Structure*. New York: Harcourt, Brace, Jovanovich.

Barlow, E. R., and I. T. Wender, 1955. *Foreign Investment and Taxation*. Englewood Cliffs, N.J.: Prentice-Hall.

Benchmark Survey of Foreign Direct Investment in the U.S., 1974. *Survey of Current Business*, May 1976.

Blais, J. P., 1975. "A Theoretical and Empirical Investigation of Canadian and British Direct Foreign Investment in Manufacturing in the United States." Ph.D. thesis, University of Pittsburgh.

Boatwright, B. D., and G. A. Renton, 1975. "An Analysis of United Kingdom Inflows and Outflows of Direct Foreign Investment," *REStat*, pp. 478–486.

Brainard, W., and J. Tobin, 1968. "Pitfalls in Financial Model Building," *American Economic Review* 58 (May), pp. 99–122.

Buckley, P. J., and M. C. Casson, 1976. *The Future of the Multinational Enterprise*. London: Macmillan.

————, 1978. "A Theory of International Operations," in M. Ghertman and J. Leontiades (eds.), *European Research in International Business*. Amsterdam: North-Holland.

Calvet, A. L., 1981. "A Synthesis of Foreign Direct Investment Themes and Theories of the Multinational Firm," *Journal of International Business Studies*, Spring/Summer, pp. 43–59.

Carlson, S., 1977. "Company Policies for International Expansion: The Swedish Experience," in Agmon and Kindleberger (eds.), *Multinationals from Small Countries*. Cambridge, Mass.: MIT Press.

Casson, M., 1979. *Alternatives to the Multinational Enterprise*. London: Macmillan.

Caves, R. E., 1971. "International Corporations: The Industrial Economics of Foreign Investment," *Economica*, 38 (February), pp. 1–27.

Coase, R. H., 1937. "The Nature of the Firm," *Economica* (N.S.) 4, pp. 386–405.

Coen, R. M., 1971. "The Effect of Cash Flow on the Speed of Adjustment," in Fromm, (ed.), *Tax Incentives and Capital Spending*. Washington, D.C.: Brookings.

Committee on International Investment and Multinational Enterprise (CIME) of the OECD, 1981. *Recent International Direct Investment Trends*. Paris, OECD.

Cooke, J. E., 1964 (ed.). *The Reports of Alexander Hamilton*. New York: Harper and Row.

Daniels, J. D., 1971. *Recent Foreign Direct Manufacturing Investment in the United States: An Interview Study of the Decision Process*. New York: Praeger.

U.S. Department of Commerce, 1976. *Report of the Secretary of Commerce to Congress in Compliance with the Foreign Investment Study Act of 1974*. Washington, D.C.: US Government Printing Office.

Dunning, J. H., 1973. "The Determinants of International Production," *Oxford Economic Papers*, January.

―――, 1977. "Trade, Location of Economic Activity and the MNE: A Search for an Eclectic Approach," in B. Ohlin, P. O. Hesselborn, and P. M. Wijkman (eds.), *The International Allocation of Economic Activity*. New York: Holmes and Meier.

―――, 1979. "Explaining Changing Patterns of International Production: In Defense of the Eclectic Theory," *Oxford Bulletin of Economics and Statistics* 41, no. 4 (November), pp. 269–296.

Economist, 1980. "New Wave: Foreign Capital Investment in U.S., A Survey." Vol. 277 (October 25), surv. pp. 1–24.

Edelstein, M., 1974. "The Determinants of UK Investments Abroad, 1870–1913: The US Case." *Journal of Economic History* 34, no. 3 (December), pp. 980–1007.

Faith, N., 1971. *The Infiltrators*. London: Hamish Hamilton.

Flowers, E. B., 1976. "Oligopolistic Reactions in European and Canadian Direct Investment in the U.S.," *Journal of International Business Studies* 7, no. 2 (Fall/Winter), pp. 43–55.

Franko, L. G., 1971. *European Business Strategies in the United States*. Geneva: Business International.

―――, 1976. *The European Multinationals: A Renewed Challenge to American and British Big Business*. London: Greylock.

―――, 1978. "Multinationals: The End of US Dominance," *Harvard Business Review* 56, no. 6, pp. 93–101.

Furubotn, E., and S. Pejovich, 1972. "Property Rights and Economic Theory: A Survey of Recent Literature," *Journal of Economic Literature* 10, no. 4, pp. 1137–1162.

Graham, E. M., 1974. "Oligopolistic Imitation and European Direct Investment in the United States." Ph.D. thesis, Harvard Business School.

―――, 1976. "A Defensive Theory of Foreign Direct Investment and European Direct Investment in the United States." Sloan School of Management, Massachusetts Institute of Technology, Working Paper.

Hellman, R., 1970. *The Challenge to U.S. Domination of the International Corporation*. Translated by P. Ruof. New York: Dunellen.

Hirsch, S., 1976. "An International Trade and Investment Theory of the Firm," *Oxford Economic Papers*, July, p. 28.

Hufbauer, G., 1970. "The Impact of National Characteristics and Technology on the Commodity Composition of Trade in Manufactured Goods," in R. Vernon (ed.), *The Technology Factor in International Trade*. New York: National Bureau of Economic Research.

Hultman, C. W., and J. Ramsey, 1975. "Cyclical Behavior of Foreign Investment in the U.S., 1950–71," *Revista Internazionale di Scienze Economiche e Commerciali* 22, no. 11, pp. 1098–1102.

Hymer, S. A., 1960. *The International Operations of National Firms: A Study of Foreign Direct Investment*. Ph.D. thesis, Department of Economics, Massachusetts Institute of Technology, 1960. Published in 1976, MIT Press.

Jenks, L. H., 1927. *The Migration of British Capital to 1875*. New York: Knopf.

Jensen, M. C., and W. H. Meckling, 1976. "Theory of the Firm: Managerial Behavior, Agency Costs and Ownership Structure," *Journal of Financial Economics* 3, pp. 305–360.

Johnson, H. G., 1970. "The Efficiency and Welfare Implications of the International Corporation," in C. P. Kindleberger (ed.), *The International Corporation*. Cambridge, Mass.: MIT Press.

Kindleberger, C. P., 1969. *American Business Abroad: Six Essays on Direct Investment*, New Haven, Conn.: Yale University Press.

Kindleberger, C. P., 1970a (ed.). *The International Corporation*. Cambridge, Mass.: MIT Press.

————, 1970b. Comment on Hufbauer's, "The Impact of National . . . ," in R. Vernon (ed.), *The Technology Factor in International Trade*. New York: National Bureau of Economic Research.

Knickerbocker, F. T., 1973. *Oligopolistic Reaction and Multinational Enterprise*. Cambridge: Harvard Business School Division of Research.

Knight, F. H., 1921. *Risk, Uncertainty and Profit*. Boston: Houghton Mifflin.

Kobrin, S. J., and D. R. Lessard, 1976. "Large Scale Direct OPEC Investment in Industrialized Countries and the Theory of Foreign Direct Investment—a Contradiction?" *Weltwirtschaftliches Archiv* 112, pp. 660–673.

Kohlhagen, S. W., 1977. "Exchange Rate Changes, Profitability, and Direct Foreign Investment," *Southern Economic Journal* 44, pp. 43–52.

Lamfalussy, A., 1963. *Investment and Growth in Mature Economies*. Oxford: Blackwell.

Leftwich, R. B., 1973. "Foreign Direct Investment in the U.S., 1962–1976," *Survey of Current Business*, February, pp. 29–40.

Lewis, C. 1938. *America's Stake in International Investments*. Washington, D.C.: Brookings.

Lindenberg, E. B., and S. A. Ross, 1981. "Tobin's q Ratio and Industrial Organization," *Journal of Business* 54, no. 1, pp. 1–32.

Little, J. S., 1978. "Locational Decisions of Foreign Direct Investors in the U.S.," *New England Economic Review*, July/August, pp. 43–63.

————, 1980. "Foreign Direct Investment in the U.S.: Recent Locational Choices of Foreign Manufacturers," *New England Economic Review*, November/December, pp. 5–22.

Magee, S. P., 1977a. "Multinational Corporations, The Industry Technology Cycle, and Development," *Journal of World Trade Law*, July/August, pp. 297–321.

————, 1977b. "Information and the Multinational Corporation: An Appropriability Theory of Direct Foreign Investment," in Jagdish Bhagwati (ed.), *The New International Economic Order*. Cambridge, Mass.: MIT Press.

Makin, J. H., 1974. "Capital Flows and Exchange Rate Flexibility in the Post-Bretton Woods Era," *Essays in International Finance* 103. Princeton University Press.

McClain, D., 1974. "Foreign Investment in United States Manufacturing and the Theory of Direct Investment." Ph.D. thesis, Department of Economics, Massachusetts Institute of Technology.

McClain, D., 1975. Foreign Direct Investment in the United States: A Microeconometric Analysis. Presented to the Third World Congress of the Econometric Society, Toronto.

McManus, J. C., 1972. "The Theory of the International Firm," in G. Paquet (ed.), *The Multinational Firm and the Nation State*. Toronto: Collier-Macmillan.

Nelson, R., and S. Winter, 1977. "Dynamic Competition and Technical Progress," in B. Balassa and R. Nelson (eds.), *Economic Progress, Private Values and Public Policy: Essays in Honor of William Fellner*. Amsterdam: North-Holland.

————, 1978. "Forces Generating and Limiting Concentration Under Schumpeterian Competition," *Bell Journal of Economics* 9, pp. 524–548.

————, 1982. *An Evolutionary Theory of Economic Change.* Cambridge, Mass.: Harvard University Press.

Niehans, J., 1977. "Benefits of Multinational Firms for a Small Parent Economy: The Case of Switzerland," in Agmon and Kindleberger (eds.), *Multinationals from Small Countries.* Cambridge, Mass.: MIT Press.

Penrose, E. T., 1956. "Foreign Investment and the Growth of the Firm," *Economic Journal* (London) 66, pp. 220–235.

Porter, M., 1981. *Competitive Strategy.* Glencoe, Ill.: Free Press.

Prachowny, M. F. J., 1972. "Direct Investment and the Balance of Payments of the United States: A Portfolio Approach," in F. Machlup et al. (eds.), *The International Mobility and Movement of Capital.* New York: Columbia University Press.

Ragazzi, G., 1973. "Theories of the Determinants of Direct Foreign Investment," *IMF Staff Papers,* July, pp. 471–498.

Rugman, A. M., 1980. "Internalization as a General Theory of Foreign Direct Investment: A Reappraisal of the Literature," *Weltwirtschaftliches Archiv* 116, pp. 365–379.

Salinger, M., 1981. Tobin's *q*, Investment, and Monopoly Power. Cambridge, mimeo.

Sametz, A. W., 1973. *The Foreign Multinational Company in the U.S.* Working Paper No. 9, Salomon Brothers Center for the Study of Financial Institutions, New York University, October.

Stevens, G. V. G., 1972. "Capital Mobility and International Firms," in F. Machlup et al. (eds.), *The International Mobility and Movement of Capital.* New York: Columbia University Press.

Stopford, J. M., 1980. "German Multinationals and Foreign Direct Investment in the United States," *Management International Review* 20, no. 1, pp. 7–15.

Survey of Current Business, various issues.

Tobin, J., 1969. "A General Equilibrium Approach to Monetary Theory," *Journal of Money, Credit and Banking,* February.

Tsurumi, Y., 1973. "Japanese Multinational Firms," *Journal of World Trade Law,* January/ February, pp. 74–90.

Tugendhat, C., 1972. *The Multinationals.* New York: Random House.

Vernon, R., 1966. "International Investment and International Trade in the Product Cycle," *Quarterly Journal of Economics* 80 (May), pp. 190–207.

————, 1971. *Sovereignty at Bay: The Multinational Spread of US Enterprises.* New York: Basic Books.

Volpe, J. M., 1975. "Some Preliminary Findings on the Factor Intensity of Foreign Direct Investment in US Manufacturing," *American Economist* 19, no. 1 (Spring), pp. 67–73.

Wilkins, M., 1970. *The Emergence of Multinational Enterprise: American Business Abroad from the Colonial Era to 1914.* Cambridge, Mass.: Harvard University Press.

14 Linking Negotiations on Trade and Foreign Direct Investment

Rachel McCulloch and Robert F. Owen

I. Introduction

National policies toward foreign direct investment constitute an important class of nontariff trade distortions. Surprisingly, although the Tokyo Round of multilateral trade negotiations focused its efforts on nontariff barriers, the trade-distorting effects of policies toward foreign direct investment were largely ignored. Now, however, the relationship between trade and investment issues has been formally brought into the GATT framework, as US and Canadian negotiators attempt to resolve conflicts over restrictions imposed on US-based firms by the Canadian Foreign Investment Review Agency.

This paper explores the relationship between trade and investment policy, and discusses theoretical and policy questions raised by a linkage of international negotiations on trade and investment. Section II of the paper deals with host-country policies toward foreign direct investment and their impact on trade. The section presents data on the incidence of host-country policies affecting US subsidiaries world-wide as well as detailed information on foreign subsidiary performance and regulatory policies in Canada, the most important host country for US direct investments abroad. Section III draws on various strands of the theoretical and empirical literature on trade and foreign direct investment to analyze avenues of interaction between trade and investment policies as co-determinants of the location of production. Section IV evaluates the potential benefits and pitfalls from a linkage of trade and investment issues in the GATT or in bilateral negotiations between the United States and its major trading partners. Some conclusions and suggestions for further research are presented in section V.

II. National Investment Policies and Their Impact on Trade

The phenomenal growth of foreign direct investment by multinational corporations has stimulated an equally phenomenal growth of research intended to sort out the complicated benefits and costs for home and host countries and the implications for global efficiency. Although no consensus has emerged from that research, most national governments have drawn their own conclusions and have proceeded to encourage, limit, or otherwise regulate the activities of multinational corporations (MNCs). In this section we analyze the motives, forms, and consequences of host-country regulation of foreign investment, focusing on the relationship to trade flows. A central conclusion is that policies toward foreign investment do exercise a potentially important influence on trade flows through both direct and indirect channels. Moreover, a comparison of the economic performance of foreign subsidiaries with that of their domestic counterparts strongly suggests that the trading behavior of MNCs is itself an important reason underlying the perceived need for host-country regulation of MNC activities.

Why and How Host Countries Regulate Foreign Direct Investment

Host countries appear to view direct foreign investment as a necessary evil of national economic life. The literature abounds with anecdotal evidence of MNC excesses (especially but by no means exclusively in developing host countries), and virtually no host country is willing to allow MNCs completely free reign within its borders. Yet even fewer nations have gone to the opposite extreme of excluding foreign investment. Rather, various national policies are applied in an effort to extract maximum benefits from foreign direct investments.

Although schemes for maximizing national benefits are as varied as the economic systems and philosophies that give rise to them, an increasing number of host countries now follow a "carrot-and-stick" approach toward foreign direct investment. The carrot consists of foreign investment incentives such as favorable tax treatment, below-market loans, and protection via tariffs or nontariff barriers from potential competitors for the domestic market. The stick consists of a variety of "performance requirements"—restrictions on the established subsidiary with regard to export or import levels, techniques of production, levels of employment, or such diverse matters as local research and development, repatriation of profits, and financial arrangements. The carrot-and-stick combination allows host governments to promote national objectives without eliminating incentives for investment. With performance requirements alone, a significant cost is imposed on investors, so that some portion of the potential flow of new investment would be deflected to other locations. However, when incentives are provided as well, the overall profitability of investing in a given country may be unaffected or even increased.[1]

Nationalism and xenophobia no doubt provide much of the necessary political support for host-country regulation of foreign direct investment. However, serious economic arguments in favor of regulatory policies almost always center on market imperfections. Experts agree that the existence of foreign direct investment virtually requires a significant departure from conditions approximating perfect competition. Accordingly, standard neoclassical analyses favoring nonintervention on economic efficiency grounds do not apply. Host-country measures to regulate foreign direct investment fall into two somewhat overlapping categories intended to correct two distinct types of market imperfections: market power and externalities in production.

The first category consists of measures to offset "restrictive business practices" that are part of the monopolistic or oligopolistic parent firm's global profit-maximization strategy. While long lists of such practices have been compiled, the most important relate to restrictions on exporting (particularly when a subsidiary has been created to serve a protected local market), required imports of components or complementary products, and limitations on the subsidiary's further use of the parent firm's unique technology. Typical performance requirements can thus be viewed as placing limits on the parent firm's ability to maximize global profits by controlling the operation of its subsidiaries.

Performance requirements are also designed to take account of positive externalities from MNC operations within a given country. Many host countries, especially LDCs, seek foreign investment precisely for its anticipated positive externalities, particularly technology transfer through on-the-job training of the local workforce. Measures that mandate verticaly integrated production operations, set levels for various categories of local employment, or require local research and development activities all seek to increase the nation's social payoff from direct investment through enhanced production externalities.

National regulation of foreign direct investment has been widely analyzed from the perspective of global economic efficiency as well as that of costs and benefits to home and host country, yet surprisingly little has been done except at the most abstract level to integrate the analysis of foreign investment with that of tariffs and other barriers to trade. This is a significant gap, since some of the most frequently employed performance requirements are obviously intended to affect trade of multinationals directly through explicitly specified minimum export and maximum import levels (local content requirements).[2] In addition, both investment incentives and performance requirements are likely to have a pervasive indirect effect on trade through their influence on decisions regarding the location and operation of MNC subsidiaries. These interrelationships of direct investment, trade, and policies to regulate them are highlighted in this paper.

Economic Performance of Foreign Subsidiaries: The Canadian Case

Host-country concerns that motivate regulation of foreign direct investment are based on observed or anticipated differences in the unconstrained behavior of foreign subsidiaries and domestically controlled firms. Although there is considerable evidence in the literature of large differences in the performance of subsidiaries and domestic firms,[3] we focus here on evidence from recent data for Canada. These findings are particularly interesting in light of Canada's importance as a host country, its high level of industrialization, and its recent policies toward foreign (overwhelmingly US) direct investment.

Canada is unique among industrialized nations in the extent of MNC involvement in its economy, with foreign subsidiaries accounting for about 60% of total sales and total assets in manufacturing. In several extractive industries, foreign control is equally high. Indeed, until recently Canada was the world's most important host country (it has now been surpassed in absolute although not relative terms by the United States). Accordingly, the benefits and costs of foreign direct investment have been a traditional focus of controversy in Canadian politics, and activities of MNCs are frequent targets of nationalistic critics.

Recent Canadian policy toward foreign investors raises concerns in the United States for several reasons.[4] First, the United States-Canadian trade and investment relationship is large enough to be important for its own sake. Canada is the largest US trading partner and the most important host country for US foreign investment. (From the Canadian viewpoint, the importance is even greater. Approximately 70% of Canadian trade is with the United States, and US-based firms account for 90% of all foreign investment in Canada.) Second, the recent emphasis on nontariff trade distortions in the Tokyo Round of multilateral trade negotiations makes the Canadian policies conspicuous as yet another variety of policy with important direct and indirect effects for trade. Third, because Canada is the largest host country for US investment, and also a country in a highly favorable situation to use national regulation to increase its share of the gains from MNC activities, Canadian policies and their results may provide advance notice of what is to be expected in other host countries.

Yet Canada is far from being a typical host country. Canada's potential ability to dictate terms to multinational firms operating within its borders far exceeds that of any developing host country. The more attractive the host country, the more conditions it is able to impose in dealings with multinationals without much loss in the volume of inward investment. The greatest leverage can be exercised by a host country "with a large, dynamic, resource-rich economy, a stable and capable government with high-quality infrastructure and low transactions costs."[5] This profile puts Canada at the top of the list of host countries capable of wielding considerable influence on the activities of foreign investors through national regulation. And, unlike the United States, Canada is small enough as a *home* country relative to any other host country that retaliation (at least in kind) by other nations is a minor consideration.

A statistical analysis reveals striking disparities with regard to import propensities and R&D performance between foreign subsidiaries and domestic firms in Canada. Recently released data on Canadian imports by domestic- and foreign-controlled enterprises indicate that, overall, foreign-controlled firms are responsible for over 80% of Canadian imports and that these firms have an average import propensity (as measured by the ratio of imports to sales) nearly four times greater than that of domestic firms.[6] Moreover, foreign subsidiaries' imports are overwhelming sourced from the home country (87% in the case of the United States, 74% for other countries). In several industries the relative import propensities of foreign subsidiaries are dramatically higher. In the service sector, for example, the import propensity of foreign subsidiaries is nearly twenty times that of domestic firms. Moreover, the US-Canadian Auto Pact has been associated with a significant increase in the import propensities of US firms in Canada. At the manufacturing and wholesale stages, the import propensities of US auto firms are now respectively 7.0 and 8.6 times as great as those of domestic firms.

Paralleling these disparities are differences in the ratios of R&D expenditures to sales for Canadian domestic firms and foreign subsidiaries. On average, Canadian firms undertake more than twice as much R&D activity relative to sales as their foreign counterparts; in 87 out of 115 manufacturing industries, the ratio of R&D expenditures to sales is higher for Canadian domestic firms.[7] This is consistent with the standard prediction that most R&D activities of multinational corporations will be concentrated in the home country.

These statistics provide a clear empirical basis for Canada's concerns regarding the economic performance of susidiaries. Nonetheless, these disparities in mean import and R&D propensities, while impressive, are not conclusive proof of differences in performance between subsidiaries and domestic firms. Rigorous econometric analysis would control for firm size, diversification, and other pertinent characteristics of these firms.

Canadian Policy toward Foreign Investment

After decades of successful wooing of foreign investors and perennial consternation over the extent of foreign ownership, Canada developed during the 1970s an explicit mechanism for screening new inward direct investments. Established by the Foreign Investment Review Act of 1972, Canada's Foreign Investment Review Agency (FIRA) began in 1974 to oversee new MNC activities in Canada[8] and to ensure that these investments provide benefits to Canada as well as to their foreign owners. Although virtually all nations impose some restrictions to entry by MNCs, the Canadian policy represents the most explicit example of entry control.[9] All proposed investments must gain FIRA approval. Evaluation by FIRA is supposed to be on the basis of ten criteria, including impact on Canadian employment and productivity, contribution to technology, use of Canadian resources, and expanded exports.

Since the vast majority of projects submitted to FIRA are eventually approved, it appears that whatever benefits (apart from noneconomic ones, e.g., psychological or political) derived are not from screening out undesirable investments but rather through the effect on the actual terms of specific investments. Evaluation of the results is inevitably subjective, since it is impossible to know how foreign investors would have acted in the absence of the new policies. On the basis of its early activities, some observers dismissed the FIRA as a relatively innocuous and ineffective measure intended primarily to defuse criticism from Canadian nationalists.[10] But recent events suggest that at least to some American firms, the effects are both real and potentially very important.

The activities of the Foreign Investment Review Agency have been a source of US-Canadian frictions since the agency began screening foreign takeovers of Canadian companies in 1974.[11] Since 1981, US officials have been concerned by FIRA-imposed terms for takeovers and new investments as distortions of US trade in goods and services. Contribution to Canadian trade performance is a part of the "significant benefit" potential investors must demonstrate in order to win FIRA approval. Specific examples of recent FIRA deliberations involving US-based firms seem to support the contention that FIRA is using its authority to influence trade.

In the case of Gannett, a New York publisher, acquisition of a Canadian billboard company was approved only after Gannett agreed to purchase Canadian newsprint for its US operations.[12] Gannett also agreed to "sell" laser printing technology to a Canadian firm for a token $1.[13] In another publicized case, Apple Computer was allowed to enter the Canadian market after agreeing to buy Canadian-made parts, where competitive, and to recommend Canadian-made computer peripheral equipment to its dealers world-wide.[14]

From the perspective of Canadian officials, its screening procedures merely assure that new investments will be advantageous to the nation. The Foreign Investment Review Act does not set specific minimum levels for exports or for utilization of Canadian inputs. Rather, potential investors themselves set such targets for their proposed activities, presumably in order to gain prompt FIRA approval. Nonetheless, the United States claims that recent Canadian practice conflicts with that nation's obligations under the GATT; a formal complaint was made by the United States within the GATT framework on February 17, 1982.[15] What ultimately happens in the US-Canadian dispute will presumably set a legal precedent for other cases, at least where GATT members are involved. However, many developing nations, whose use of investment incentives and performance requirements is more extensive than that of industrialized nations, are not GATT members. For the United States, the most important of these in terms of trade and investment ties is Mexico.

Department of Commerce data on US subsidiaries in Canada indicate that the systematic influence on FIRA activities has been relatively minor, at least through 1977.[16] Commerce compared the percentage of investment incentives and performance requirements reported for Canadian subsidiaries organized or acquired before 1970 with those organized or acquired between 1970 and 1977 (the latter period includes the first three years of FIRA operation). The data showed a decrease in the number of reported incentives (16% in the later period compared with 19% for the earlier period) and an increase in the percentage of reported performance requirements (6% in the later period in comparison to 4% for the earlier period). However, the Commerce Department report suggests that these figures understate the present extent of FIRA influence and that a larger percentage of subsidiaries affected by performance requirements would be found for later years, as "the 1977 benchmark data does not cover the period in which we believe the incidence of performance requirements in Canada to have increased significantly."

A report on other nations' investment incentives and performance requirements prepared for a private committee of US companies and labor unions goes further, contending that "Canadians have ... succeeded in forcing foreign investors to conform with their national trade policy without regard for the interests of other states or the efficient international allocation of production."[17] The report emphasizes that FIRA's criterion of "significant benefits" to Canada explicitly includes the effects on utilization of "Canadian parts, components and services and on Canadian exports." It notes that about a third of all proposals approved by FIRA specified some export-related benefits, while nearly two-thirds included some commitment to resource processing or procurement in Canada. However, it is not possible to infer from these statistics the extent to which FIRA distorts trade. Even without the screening process, in the course of pursuing their own interests many foreign-controlled enterprises would export, while most would make use of Canadian parts or processing. However, the report

stresses that approved investments *are* monitored for compliance with
the terms and conditions of the proposal and that the Act provides for
enforcement of these terms.

Other Foreign Government Policies Affecting US Direct Investment

While no other host country is as important to US-based multinationals
as Canada, recent data on the experience of US affiliates world-wide
indicate that Canada's active regulation of foreign direct investment is
paralleled by policies in other nations. Data collected by the US Department of Commerce from US parent companies (with mandatory
reporting)[18] show that as of 1977 about 14% of US affiliates world-
wide were subject to performance requirements of some kind, while
about twice as many—26%—were subject to investment incentives.

Among the most significant investment incentives are tax concessions,
tariff concessions and subsidies—respectively 2, 8, and 9% of US affiliates
were subject to these. Not surprisingly, tariff incentives are used more
frequently by developing countries, whereas tax incentives are used
extensively by both groups. Minimum local labor requirements accounted for over half of all performance requirements; there were also
significant numbers of minimum export requirements, maximum import
levels, and minimum local input requirements (of US affiliates, respectively 2, 3, and 3% were subject to these latter).

Across industries, there are important differences in the extent to
which investment policies affect subsidiaries. In manufacturing transportation equipment the level of both investment incentives and performance requirements (respectively 41 and 27%) is substantially higher
than for most other industries. Other industries with particularly high
levels of investment incentives include food products and electrical
machinery, while more than one-quarter of US affiliates in mining are
subject to some form of performance requirements.

These data also show significant differences across countries in the
extent of host-government measures. Although the overall level of reported investment incentives was approximately equal between developed and developing countries, the latter use performance
requirements far more frequently (25 vs. 6%). Differences are even
greater from country to country. For example, in South Korea and
Taiwan over one-half of all foreign subsidiaries benefit from some form
of investment incentive, whereas more than half of all subsidiaries in

Libya, Peru, Venezuela, and Chile are subject to performance requirements. The high reported incidence of these measures for some individual countries, the substantial cross-country variation in their specific forms, and the much higher average use of performance requirements by developing countries all suggest that regulation of this kind may be central to some nations' strategy for industrial development. Accordingly, international negotiations to limit these trade-distorting measures are likely to encounter major obstacles.

III. The Interaction Between Trade and Investment Policies

Any case for linking trade and investment negotiations must rest on the strength of the relationship between commercial policy and investment policy as co-determinants of the location of economic activity. Mutual gains from trade reflect an appropriate international division of labor, with production processes located according to comparative advantage. In recent decades, however, multinational corporations have become a primary vehicle for the "internationalization of production." Responding to differentials in cost and profitability world-wide, MNCs break down into many separate steps production processes that begin with extraction of raw materials and end with distribution and service of final products; each step in the complex operation is moved to the location most advantageous to the firm. The significance of multinational activities for international trade flows is obvious from available data. In the case of the United States, for example, approximately half of total exports involve multinational corporations, while a quarter consist of intra-corporate transactions and are thus potentially affected by MNC transfer-pricing policies.[19]

Trade Barriers and Foreign Direct Investment

In a world without trade barriers or other distortions, the process of internationalization would imply not only that each good is produced at the location offering lowest cost, but that each step in its production is located so as to minimize overall cost of serving a particular market. Of course, under real-world conditions, production cost differentials reflecting comparative advantage are just one of several important factors determining the location of economic activity. Location decisions are also influenced by tariffs, quantitative trade restrictions, taxes, and subsidies, as well as by national policies toward foreign investment. Thus, changes in trade barriers may have important implications for direct investment decisions. Conversely, the efficiency and distributive effects of trade barriers depend crucially upon the extent of induced capital flows, so that policies toward foreign investment may have an important although indirect influence on the consequences of protection and the gains from trade liberalization.

Ultimately, the impact of tariffs and nontariff barriers, including restrictions on foreign direct investment, depends crucially on the degree to which foreign investment and trade are substitutes or complements. Initial evidence from research on the role of tariff levels in explaining the distribution of foreign investment across manufacturing industries in Australia, Canada, and Europe established the role of high tariffs or other barriers to trade as investment incentives for MNCs seeking to sell in the protected market.[20] Likewise, the role of protection in attracting foreign investments to developing nations has been well documented in the literature evaluating import-substituting industrialization policies. However, several recent studies for Canada have found little support for the substitutability hypothesis, so that the overall evidence on this issue appears to be inconclusive.[21]

Although the relationship between trade barriers and foreign investment has been used mainly as a way to explain differences in the extent of MNC activity across industries within a country, the same logic suggests that *discriminatory* trade barriers may promote investment flows between particular countries. Selective trade restrictions used by the United States to slow down the growth of its imports from Japan and certain other nations have undoubtedly contributed to the rapid growth of Japanese foreign investment in the United States, especially by firms that have already incurred substantial costs in developing a US market for their products. For similar reasons, Japanese firms may have accelerated their foreign investments in Asian developing countries not affected by voluntary export restraints and orderly marketing agreements on trade with the United States, resulting in faster relocation of production than would have occurred on the basis of changing relative costs alone.

Direct Investment in the Product Cycle

A large part of MNC production and trade is linked to innovation and the international dissemination of new technology, as described in the now-familiar international product cycle. The product cycle implies links between trade and investment policy through its associated "foreign investment cycle" for the innovating firm, and also has implications for the complementarity/substitutability issue.

According to the product-cycle scenario, a new product is developed first for an important home market. Products that succeed at home then become candidates for exporting. At this stage, foreign direct investments by the firm are typically complementary to its export performance, e.g., distribution and service facilities abroad. Indeed, some foreign investment in these forms is virtually essential to export success.[22] Later on, as the world market for the new product grows, the successful product becomes standardized and imitations begin to appear. At this point, the innovating firm is likely to shift production to foreign subsidiaries on the basis of relative cost advantage. Although production by foreign subsidiaries is often seen as a substitute for exports, establishment of foreign subsidiaries may be "defensive," simply allowing the innovating firm to retain its share in a market that would otherwise be lost to competitors with production facilities more advantageously located. Finally, if the relative cost advantage of foreign production is important, the home market may eventually be served through foreign production. But even at this stage, the internationalization of production still implies the possibility of continuing exports of components and services or of complementary products by the parent firm.[23]

Each step in the product cycle and associated foreign investment cycle represents a managerial decision based on comparative costs along with trade and investment policies. In particular, trade barriers *or* investment incentives abroad should accelerate the transition from exporting to establishment of foreign production subsidiaries. Likewise, investment incentives abroad, especially paired with implicit or explicit export performance requirements, encourage the innovating firm to serve its own home market through imports, while import-limiting performance requirements tend to cut down on complementary flows of components or related products in the latter stages of the cycle.

Trade Barriers and the Competitiveness of MNCs

Because a key difference between MNCs and domestic firms is the degree of internationalization of production, changes in trade barriers will have important effects on their relative competitiveness.[24] General reductions in trade barriers, such as those negotiated in the Kennedy and Tokyo Rounds, may increase incentives for foreign investment *globally* by allowing MNCs greater latitude for internationalization of production according to comparative advantage. Trade liberalization tends to increase the advantage of international firms over domestic ones, as MNCs are better able to capture the potential efficiency gains from reduced barriers, especially in the short term. If effective protection rates fall, domestic firms encounter increased foreign competition, whereas MNCs have the ability to serve an established domestic market by imports. Moreover, in light of their substantially higher import propensities (see section II), foreign subsidiaries are likely to enjoy greater cost reductions than domestic firms as a result of across-the-board tariff reductions. Thus, for a country like Canada, with a large existing *stock* of foreign investment, participation in the multilateral trade negotiations may have actually improved the competitive position of foreign subsidiaries and exacerbated the foreign domination of industry, notwithstanding the role played by protection in attracting the foreign capital in the first place.

A further consequence of the MNCs' "international·technology" is that scale economies in any particular stage of production can have important implications for the effects of trade policy on investment patterns and of investment policy on trade patterns. Multilateral trade liberalization should promote investments to centralize production activities subject to important scale economies.[25] Moreover, in the presence of scale economies, trade barriers, investment inventives, and/or export performance requirements can lead to a reversal of the pattern of trade that would be implied by comparative advantage alone.[26] In the case of export performance requirements, the subsidiary once established may exceed the minimum level set by the host country—so that the requirement appears, misleadingly, to be redundant. In fact, the requirement in this instance may have played an important role in determining the size of the production subsidiary established in the host country; once the fixed costs have been committed, the higher export level is determined by the firm's own profit calculations.

Implications of Imperfect Competition

As our discussion of innovation and scale economies has already acknowledged, multinationals thrive where markets deviate in important ways from the standard competitive assumptions. This suggests an additional and important source of complications in analyzing the interaction between policies toward trade and investment. For example, to the extent that MNC strategy is based on price discrimination across separated national markets, tariffs and import or export restrictions may have effects quite different from those predicted under perfect competition.[27] More generally, policy prescriptions based on the purely competitive case have doubtful relevance where trade flows are dominated by multinational firm transactions. More theoretical analysis explicitly incorporating an economic motive for direct investment is required.[28]

IV. Implications for Negotiating Strategies

Section II of this paper argues that host-country regulation of foreign direct investment, while an established prerogative of sovereign nations, also constitutes a potentially important class of nontariff trade distortion. Section III indicates a number of ways in which trade and investment policies interact, with implications for the volume, direction, and terms of trade. Taken together, this material suggests that there is a logical link between negotiations on trade and negotiations on investment. The 1982 US decision to bring its investment dispute with Canada to the GATT makes this link a matter of current practical interest as well. In this section we explore some questions raised by bringing trade and investment issues together in the GATT or in other bilateral or regional negotiations. While the previous sections draw on available data and widely accepted theory, here our approach is speculative, intended primarily to provoke debate and stimulate further research, rather than to provide a final answer to a difficult question.

Nontariff Barriers and the Tokyo Round

The Tokyo Round signaled a belated recognition that trade policy trends in the 1960s and 1970s have been increasingly in conflict with a fundamental principle of the GATT—that trade intervention for legitimate national objectives should take exclusively the form of tariffs, "which constitute a known and constant barrier that it is possible for a foreign producer to overcome if he is competitive enough. . . ."[29] Despite the success of the Kennedy Round in negotiating important across-the-board reductions in tariff rates, the lasting gains achieved in terms of freer international trade have been called into question by the subsequent proliferation of nontariff distortions.[30] In part, this trend undoubtedly reflects substitution of other policy tools to achieve largely unchanged domestic objectives once met by tariff protection. The Kennedy Round succeeded in reducing tariff protection but had no significant effect on the motives for protection or the power of domestic interest groups, whose appeals now elicit trade-distorting policies of unprecedented variety and sophistication. However, the increased prominence of nontariff distortions is also a natural consequence of a major change in the role of governments. Trade flows have inevitably been affected along with domestic economic activity as governments exercise a greatly expanded mandate for intervention and regulation in areas once left primarily to private action. As a result, rather than the known, constant, and ever-decreasing barriers envisioned by framers of the GATT, contemporary trade policy is characterized by "its very complexity, subtlety and potential to inflict damage. . . ." In comparison with the straightforward protectionism of the 1930s, "we have moved in the trade sphere, as in the military, from a conventional to a thermo-nuclear world."[31]

The Tokyo Round negotiations, which produced "codes of conduct" governing certain nontariff trade barriers, implied a major redefinition of GATT's role and domain. The codes of conduct represent the first formal multilateral effort to regulate the broad range of government policies that directly or indirectly (even at times inadvertently) favor domestic producers over their competitors abroad. By focusing attention on the panoply of government actions that can influence the volume, direction, and terms of trade, the Tokyo Round in effect made a matter for multilateral negotiation and GATT surveillance of policies previously regarded as sovereign nations' unilateral prerogatives.

Investment Issues and the GATT

The logic of the Tokyo Round seems to apply in the case of policies toward foreign direct investment. However, host countries have increasingly assumed the right to regulate new foreign investment. Although somewhat more controversial, many nations have also sought to alter the terms of established foreign investment, i.e., to change the rules of the game once appreciable sunk costs are involved. Thus, unlike international negotiations on trade liberalization, where there is considerable agreement regarding relatively neutral rules and disagreement is focused more on the specific applications of these rules, the underlying principles of international negotiations on investment are themselves likely to be controversial, with host and home countries pursuing antithetical objectives. Furthermore, the potential division between host and home countries corresponds roughly to the division between developing and developed countries.[32] This suggests both that the United States, by far the world's most important home country in absolute terms, plays an asymmetrical role in international negotiations relating to investment and that the most important potential gains may involve countries which are simultaneously important home and host countries of multinationals, in particular, the United States and certain other industrial nations.[33] Accordingly, whether investment issues should be brought into the GATT process or linked to trade issues in bilateral or regional negotiations is perhaps better viewed in practical terms: specifically, is a linking of investment and trade negotiations likely to produce more desirable outcomes than the status quo (in which there is virtually no international framework governing policies toward foreign investment), or alternatively, a hypothetical situation in which a separate international agency or GATT-like agreement deals with all issues related to investment?[34]

Obviously, this question has no ready answer. To begin with, current knowledge of the importance of investment policies as trade distortions is at best sketchy. Although the data summarized in section II suggest that the influence of such policies is pervasive, there is at present no evidence that the economic costs are large, either in absolute terms or relative to that of other nontariff barriers—including many important ones yet to be addressed successfully by the GATT, e.g., safeguards.[35] Any practical argument for bringing investment issues under the GATT umbrella would have to be bolstered by quantitative documentation of their trade-distorting impact.

A more basic issue is that as with other governmental policies affecting trade, GATT success in limiting trade-distorting practices in the investment area ultimately depends upon the willingness of its members to surrender national sovereignty in a politically sensitive area. Despite the successful efforts of the Tokyo Round in negotiating the new codes on nontariff barriers, the degree to which members are willing *in practice* to accept limits on their domestic options in order to promote collective goals remains in doubt. To extend the GATT's fragile achievements in this difficult area to a set of issues as sensitive and politically explosive as host-country regulation of foreign direct investment could be premature and counterproductive.

A related consideration is that any GATT-sponsored effort to limit host-country prerogatives on efficiency grounds might well be interpreted as further evidence that the GATT remains primarily a rich man's club dedicated to preservation of the status quo in the world economy. Given present North-South differences on foreign investment issues and the role of the United States in the dispute currently before the GATT, initiatives to extend the GATT mandate to include host-country investment regulation (or even just trade-related investment performance requirements) have the potential of reversing the modest progress made in the Tokyo Round toward bringing less-developed countries into fuller participation in the GATT.[36] For this reason, a GATT code on investment may well have to incorporate an explicit double standard for developed and developing nations, as has already been instituted in the Tokyo Round for a number of other areas. Yet, even this will not necessarily diffuse opposition from developing nations in the GATT, since the major developing host countries are "middle income" nations near the point of "graduation" from special and preferential status.[37]

Finally, bringing together trade and investment issues, whether within the GATT or outside, carries all the well-known advantages and disadvantages of issue linkage. Issue linkage has the important virtue of enlarging the potential for mutual gains. In practice, however, this means that technical economic issues tend to be submerged by other, "larger" considerations such as military and strategic objectives. In fact, to a certain degree the successes of the GATT may be attributed to the Agreement's rather narrow scope. The more ambitious International Trade Organization (ITO), whose intended role in the trade area was eventually assumed by the GATT, would have had jurisdiction as well over investment issues (and, among others, international commodity agreements). The US Senate's dissatisfaction with the investment provision played an important role in the Senate's failure to ratify the ITO Charter.

Negotiating Outside the GATT

Does a linkage of trade and investment policy issues in the case of bilateral negotiations between the United States and other individual nations or regional groups provide greater potential benefits and fewer pitfalls? In the instance of the United States and Canada, the extent of the trade and investment relationships between the two nations implies a rich agenda of bilateral economic issues for negotiation,[38] while the relatively similar economic and political attitudes of the two reduce the likelihood that negotiations will move quickly from the economic sphere into unrelated foreign policy concerns.

Even here, however, serious obstacles remain. Since the offending trade targets in the US-Canadian case are set by the investing firms themselves rather than by the FIRA or by Canadian statute, it is not obvious what concessions short of abolition of FIRA and elimination of its screening function would be acceptable to the United States. Given the present domestic political climate in Canada and the fact that foreign investment there is overwhelmingly by US-based firms, such an offer is unlikely to be forthcoming from Canadian negotiators. The US decision in early 1982 to take the issue to the GATT suggests that at least from the official US point of view, a trade-investment linkage within the GATT framework offers greater promise than the bilateral approach.

In comparison, US-Japanese bilateral negotiations on economic issues may offer considerable potential for a mutually beneficial linkage of trade and investment issues without the same difficulties. In its current quest for bilateral trade balance (so-called trade reciprocity) with Japan, the United States has stressed a variety of nontariff barriers to trade. In view of the recognized complementarity between foreign direct investment and exporting and Japan's highly restrictive policies toward inward foreign investment, a logical step for US negotiators would be to emphasize liberalization of Japan's barriers to foreign investment.

In North-South and especially US-South relations, the domestic political acceptability of direct negotiations to reduce LDC screening and regulation of foreign direct investment is even more problematic than in the Canadian case. However, there continue to be important potential gains from North-South negotiations on trade issues, and success in this area would also tend to reduce the perceived need on the part of Southern nations for trade-distorting investment regulation. Because past rounds of multilateral trade negotiations focused primarily on trade among the industrial nations, they have left unexplored a major source of mutual gains from trade liberalization along lines of comparative advantage.

On average, developing nations have much higher import barriers than the United States or other industrial nations. These are in part a legacy of import-substitution policies and in part a reflection of the sideline role that developing nations have played in the reciprocal bargaining process of the GATT. On the other hand, the United States, along with most industrialized nations, affords much higher than average protection to manufacturing industries that compete directly with rapidly growing LDC exports—notably textiles and apparel, but also a growing number of other products. This pattern of protection has had two important effects on North-South economic relations. On the trade side, it has slowed down the adjustment of North-South trade flows *in both directions* to changing patterns of international competitiveness. On the investment side, it may have dampened the rate of direct investment in areas of current and future LDC comparative advantage, while maintaining incentives for inefficient import-substituting investments. The latter are often assembly or packaging operations that merely substitute imports of parts or bulk products for imports of final products, at high cost to consumers in the protected local market. Such a misdirection of investment contributes to the observed high import propensities and poor export performance that are a key source of Southern dissatisfaction with MNC practices.

Given the current pattern of protection, *reciprocal* North-South trade liberalization offers the potential for important mutual gains. Unlike most other proposals to increase the access of Southern exporters to Northern markets, e.g., the Generalized System of Preferences, reciprocal liberalization offers tangible gains to *Northern* nations in the form of increased export opportunities for their own products, so that the domestic political appeal is far greater.[39] An additional consideration is that reciprocal trade liberalization by itself would tend to improve the export performance of subsidiaries in developing countries and to increase the amount of foreign investment in areas of comparative advantage. This in turn could reduce the perceived need on the part of developing nations for investment incentives and trade-distorting performance requirements.

V. Conclusions

The trade-distorting effects of national policies toward foreign investment are a new and potentially important concern for policymakers. Our work here has been primarily exploratory, intended to present information, provoke debate, and suggest avenues for future research on this subject. The major focus of the paper is the relationship between trade policy and foreign investment policy. We have examined this relationship from several perspectives: the extent to which investment policies influence trade, the role of MNC trade performance as a motivation for national regulation of investment, the ways in which trade and investment policies interact as co-determinants of the location of production and pattern of trade, the implications of trade liberalization for the relative competitiveness of MNCs and domestic firms, and considerations affecting the prospects for a future link between trade and investment negotiations in the GATT or outside.

Some specific conclusions of the analysis are summarized by the following points:

(1) Host-country regulation, while an established prerogative of sovereign nations, also constitutes a potentially important class of nontariff distortion, at least when measured in terms of frequency. However, little information is yet available about the quantitative impact of investment regulation on trade flows. Detailed studies, both across industries and across countries, are needed.

(2) US subsidiaries in virtually every host country are affected to some degree by investment incentives and performance requirements, although their incidence and form varies significantly across countries and by industry. The importance of performance requirements is much greater on average for developing countries than for industrialized countries. This suggests that performance requirements of various kinds may be central to some nations' preferred strategy for industrial development. Accordingly, these nations may be reluctant to negotiate reductions in their sovereignty in this area.

(3) In the specific case of Canada, the most important host country for US investment and probably the nation best able to alter the terms of foreign investment within its borders, striking differences with respect to importing and R&D performance of subsidiaries and domestic firms provide a clear empirical basis for Canada's perceived need for active

regulation of foreign direct investment. However, the trade-distorting impact of Canadian regulation is difficult to document. The screening procedure gives potential investors an incentive to stress the export and domestic-content requirements of their proposals. Trade targets are set by the firms themselves, although in light of the impact of promised trade performance on the prospects for speedy approval.

(4) Because a key difference between MNCs and domestic firms is the degree of internationalization of production (as documented in this paper for the Canadian case), general reductions in trade barriers tend to increase the advantage of multinational firms over domestic ones, especially in the short term. For a country like Canada with a large existing stock of foreign investment, multilateral trade liberalization probably exacerbated the foreign domination of industry by improving the competitive position of foreign subsidiaries relative to their domestic counterparts.

(5) The timing of the international product cycle and its associated direct investment cycle has important implications for the United States, whose comparative advantage is in production of new goods. Managerial decisions that determine timing are crucially affected by trade barriers and by host countries' policies toward foreign direct investment, both incentives and performance requirements.

(6) Because the typical environment for MNC activity deviates in important ways from the standard competitive assumptions, the interaction between trade and investment policies may include effects quite different from those predicted under perfect competition. Policy prescriptions based on the purely competitive case thus have doubtful relevance where trade flows are dominated by multinational firm transactions. Theoretical analysis explicitly taking account of the economic motive for direct investment is required.

(7) Negotiations on trade issues are facilitated by the dual role of every nation as importer and exporter. As a consequence, there is considerable agreement regarding rules, and disagreement is focused on the specific applications of these rules. In contrast, the underlying principles of international negotiations on investment are themselves likely to be controversial, with home and host country pursuing antithetical objectives. This suggests that the greatest potential gains from negotiations are for the group of countries with important interests as

both home and host countries, in particular, the United States and some other industrial nations.

Notes

Comments on this paper by the Middlebury Conference participants are gratefully acknowledged. Dr. Asim Erdilek also provided helpful comments. The work was supported in part by National Science Foundation Grant No. PRA-8116448.

1. We do not attempt to evaluate the effectiveness of host-country regulation in achieving national objectives. It is worth emphasizing, however, that regulatory intent and actual outcome do not necessarily coincide.

2. Allocative consequences of such performance requirements have been analyzed by Munk (1969) and Grossman (1981).

3. For example, Brash (1966) and Safarian (1966).

4. The recent controversy centers on Canadian policies restricting the activities of US-controlled subsidiaries. A decade earlier, US-Canadian conflict resulted from the effects on US trade of incentives offered to other foreign investors. In response to grants, subsidized loans, and preferential tax treatment, the French-owned Michelin tire company established two production plants in Nova Scotia to produce steel-belted radial tires for the North American (primarily US) market. The United States treated the estimated value of the Canadian incentive package as an export subsidy and applied a countervailing duty on imports of Michelin tires from the two plants. See Volpe (1976).

5. Hawkins and Walter (1980).

6. Statistics Canada (1981).

7. Based on data used in Owen (1982).

8. Including foreign takeovers of Canadian firms and expansion into new activities by foreign firms already established in the Canadian market.

9. Hawkins and Walter (1980).

10. For example, see Spero (1981).

11. *Wall Street Journal*, May 7, 1975.

12. *Wall Street Journal*, February 16, 1982.

13. *Business Week*, November 23, 1981, p. 43.

14. *Wall Street Journal*, February 16, 1982.

15. *New York Times*, February 18, 1982.

16. Department of Commerce (1981b).

17. Labor-Industry Coalition for International Trade (1981).

18. US Department of Commerce (1981a). The responses relating to investment incentives and performance requirements are summarized in US Department of Commerce (1981b).

19. Data cited by Corden (1974).

20. For example, Brash (1966), Safarian (1966), Horst (1972a, 1972b), Scaperlanda and Mauer (1969), and Schmitz and Bieri (1972).

21. Including Hewitt (1975), Orr (1973, 1975), and Owen (1982). One possible explanation of the apparently conflicting evidence is that, given substantial fixed costs of entry,

subsidiaries established in a protected market may remain profitable to operate even after protection is reduced.

22. Bergsten, Horst, and Moran (1978).

23. Ibid.

24. Obviously, the strength of this argument depends on the "true" source of MNC advantage and thus ventures into an area of unresolved conflict among the experts. See, e.g., Kindleberger (1969), Magee (1977), and Aliber (1970).

25. Where scale economies are relatively unimportant, reduced trade barriers may have an opposite effect. To reduce risk from a variety of country-specific sources, MNCs may follow a diversification approach, establishing production facilities in a number of countries.

26. Horst (1971).

27. Ibid.

28. One such analysis is Markusen (1980).

29. Johnson (1965).

30. The classic reference is Baldwin (1970), who notes the potential trade-distorting effects of investment policies only in passing.

31. Curzon (1981).

32. Notable exceptions to this division are Canada, Australia, and South Africa.

33. Not entirely coincidentally, the OECD has succeeded in formulating a voluntary code governing many aspects of foreign investment.

34. Goldberg and Kindleberger (1970) are credited with this proposal. Dunning (1974) has argued for what he terms an issue- or problem-oriented approach that would treat trade and investment policies together as part of a "General Agreement on International Production." Also see Vernon (1974).

35. On what the Tokyo Round left undone, see Corbet (1979).

36. Indeed, developing countries have been working through the United Nations Center on Transnational Corporations on their own investment code, which reaffirms the right of host countries to regulate foreign direct investment.

37. On preferential treatment and graduation of LDCs, see Frank (1977).

38. See Grey (1981) for a comprehensive discussion.

39. See the discussion of targeted most-favored-nation liberalization of trade in McCulloch (1981).

References

Aliber, Robert Z., 1970. "The Theory of the International Corporation: A Theory of Direct Foreign Investment," in C. P. Kindleberger (ed.), *The International Corporation*. Cambridge, Mass.: MIT Press.

Baldwin, Robert E., 1970. *Non-tariff Distortions of International Trade*. Washington, D.C.: Brookings.

Bergsten, C. Fred, Thomas Horst, and Theodore Moran, 1978. *American Multinationals and American Interests*. Washington, D.C.: Brookings.

Brash, D. T., 1966. *American Investment in Australian Industry*. Canberra: Australian National University Press.

Corden, W. M., 1974. *Trade Policy and Economic Welfare*. London: Oxford University Press.

Corbet, Hugh, 1979. "The Importance of Being Earnest about Further GATT Negotiations," *The World Economy*, September, pp. 319–341.

Curzon, Gerard, 1981. "Neo-protectionism, the MFA and the European Community," *The World Economy*, September, pp. 251–262.

Dunning, John H., 1978. "The Future of the Multinational Enterprise," *Lloyds Bank Review*, July 1974. Reprinted in Bela Balassa (ed.), *Changing Patterns in Foreign Trade and Payments*. New York: Norton.

Frank, Isaiah, 1979. "The Graduation Issue for LDCs," *Journal of World Trade Law*, May/June, pp. 289–302.

Goldberg, Paul M., and Charles P. Kindleberger, 1979. "Toward a GATT for Investment: A Proposal for Supervision of the International Corporation," *Law and Policy in International Business*, Summer, 295–325.

Grey, Rodney de C., 1981. *Trade Policy in the 1980s: An Agenda for Canadian-U.S. Relations*. Montreal: C. D. Howe Institute, September.

Grossman, Gene, 1981. "The Theory of Domestic Content Protection and Content Preference," *Quarterly Journal of Economics*, November, pp. 583–603.

Hawkins, Robert G., and Ingo Walter, 1980. "Multinational Corporations: Current Trends and Future Prospects," in *The International Economy: US Role in a World Market*. Washington, D.C.: Joint Economic Committee of the Congress of the United States, December 17.

Hewitt, Gary K., 1975. "U.S. Penetration of Canadian Manufacturing Industries." Ph.D. thesis, Yale University.

Horst, T., 1972. "Firm and Industry Determinants of the Decision to Invest Abroad: An Empirical Study," *REStat*, August, pp. 258–266.

————, 1972. "The Industrial Composition of US Exports and Subsidiary Sales to the Canadian Market," *American Economic Review*, March, pp. 37–45.

————, 1971. "The Theory of the Multinational Firm: Optimal Behavior Under Different Tariff and Tax Rates," *Journal of Political Economy*, September/October.

Johnson, Harry G., 1965. *The World Economy at the Crossroads*. Montreal: Canadian Trade Committee, Private Planning Association of Canada, April.

Kindleberger, Charles, *American Business Abroad: Six Lectures on Direct Investment*. New Haven, Conn.: Yale University Press.

Labor-Industry Coalition for International Trade, 1981. *Performance Requirements*. Washington, D.C.: Labor-Industry Coalition for International Trade, March.

Magee, Stephen P., 1977. "Information and the Multinational Corporation: An Appropriability Theory of Direct Foreign Investment," in J. N. Bhagwati (ed.), *The New International Economic Order: The North-South Debate*. Cambridge, Mass.: MIT Press.

Markusen, James R., 1980. "Multinationals and the Gains from Trade: A Theoretical Analysis Based on Economies of Multi-plant Operation." Institute for International Economic Studies, University of Stockholm, Seminar Paper No. 160, October.

McCulloch, Rachel, 1981. "Gains to Latin America from Trade Liberalization in Developed and Developing Countries," *Quarterly Review of Economics and Business*, Summer, pp. 231–258.

Munk, B., 1969. "The Welfare Costs of Content Protection: The Automotive Industry in Latin America," *Journal of Political Economy*, January/February.

Orr, Dale, 1973. "Foreign Control and Foreign Penetration in the Canadian Manufacturing Industries." Unpublished paper, July.

————, 1975. "The Industrial Composition of US Exports and Subsidiary Sales to the Canadian Market: Comment," *American Economic Review*, March, pp. 230–234.

Owen, R. F., 1982. "Inter-Industry Determinants of Foreign Direct Investments: A Canadian Perspective," forthcoming in A. Rugman (ed.), *New Theories of the Multinational Enterprise*. New York: St. Martin's.

Scaperlanda, A. E., and L. J. Mauer, 1969. "Determinants of US Direct Investment in the EEC," *American Economic Review*, September, pp. 558–568.

Spero, Joan Edelman, 1981. *The Politics of International Economic Relations*. New York: St. Martin's, pp. 102–134.

Statistics Canada, 1981. *Canadian Imports by Domestic and Foreign Controlled Enterprises*. Ottawa: Ministry of Supply and Services.

US Department of Commerce, 1981. *U.S. Direct Investment Abroad*. Washington, D.C.: US Department of Commerce, April.

US Department of Commerce, Office of International Investment, 1981. *The Use of Investment Incentives and Performance Requirements by Foreign Governments*. Washington, D.C.: US Department of Commerce, October.

Vernon, Raymond, 1974. "Competition Policy Toward Multinational Corporations," *American Economic Review*, May, pp. 276–282.

Volpe, John, 1976. *Industrial Incentive Policies and Programs in the Canadian-American Context*. Montreal: Canadian-American Committee, January.

Author Index

Subject Index

Achnacarry Agreement, 125
Advertising
  as barrier to competitive role, 80, 81
  biasing factor intensity, 182
  and differentiated consumer goods industries, 175
  effect on domestic profitability, 96
  and ideology of consumption, 175
  and income distribution, 182
  increases in, in multinationals, 173, 174
  industrial concentration of, in developing countries, 174, 182
  and profitability, 175
  and shifting consumption patterns in third world, 175, 182
Advertising agencies, multinational, 173
Agency costs, 302
Andean Pact, 185
Appropriability as motive for FDI, 236, 294, 302
Appropriability mechanism and MNC procapitalist support, 22
Arbitrage and foreign direct investment, 222
Aristotelian political model, 198, 199, 200

Bain-Sylos model, 104
Bargaining power, 183
Barriers to entry
  as barriers to exit, 116
  capital and labor as trade incentives, 64
  capital cost, 104–120
  concentration, 108
  and domestic profitability, 78, 96
  and economies of scale, 104, 120, 168
  as explanation of domestic profitability, 96
  and foreign market operations, 77
  in host market, 103–120
  interindustry determinants of, 107
  and tariffs, 116
Barriers to exit
  and economies of scale, 117
  in host country, 103–120
Box-Cox technique estimates and transformation analysis, 100
Bretton Woods Conference, 241

Canada
  drug industry tax advantages in foreign production, 155
  economic dependence on US, 212, 338
  employment structure of drug industry relative to US, 149
  foreign direct investment in, 337
  foreign control in, 211, 338
  import propensity of, 338, 339
  labor costs in drug industry relative to US, 147–48
  material costs in drug industry relative to US, 146
  performance compared with US, 141
  performance requirements, 341, 342
  policy toward foreign direct investment, 337, 338, 339, 342
  R&D expenditures, 148, 339
  tariff policy, 119
  trade barriers lowering productivity, 141
  transfer prices on drug imports, 152
  US-Canadian conflict, 340
Capital
  capital/labor ratio and equilibrium policy, 32
  capital/output ratio, 30
  cost barriers, 104–120
  cross flows at endowment levels, 29
  emigration of and effect on wages, 23
  geographic concentrations of, 23, 33
  increasing returns of, 23, 31, 32
  intensity of, in MNCs, 176
  international cross flows of, 23, 34
  lobbying effort and contribution of, 29
  migration policy, 21
  mobility as determinant of FDI, 219
  mobility and tariffs, 121
  net capital formation as consumer cost, 212
  polarization of, 32
  product-specific, 105, 109
  unstable endowments of, 23
  unstable equilibrium and capital stock, 29
Cartel
  and backward-sloping supply function, 126